CLINICAL SOCIOLOGY

BARRY GLASSNER
Syracuse University

JONATHAN A. FREEDMAN
Hutchings Psychiatric Center

Original photographs by Simpson Kalisher

LONGMAN
New York and London

CLINICAL SOCIOLOGY

Longman Inc., New York
Associated companies, branches, and representatives
throughout the world.

Developmental Editor: Edward Artinian
Editorial and Design Supervisor: Linda Salmonson
Interior Design: Pencils Portfolio, Inc.
Cover Design: Jahnus Vizon
Manufacturing and Production Supervisor: Louis Gaber
Composition: Book Composition Services
Printing and Binding: The Maple Press

Library of Congress Cataloging in Publication Data

Glassner, Barry.
    Clinical sociology.

    Includes index.
    1.   Social psychiatry.   2.   Psychotherapy.
3.   Small groups.   I.   Freedman, Jonathan A., joint
author.   II.   Title.
RC455.G53   616.8'9   77-18307
ISBN 0-582-28049-4

Manufactured in the United States of America

Preface

This book proposes that groups and group members who have sociological ailments need and deserve the care of sociological therapists. It is designed to introduce prospective therapists and clients to the types of diagnoses and therapies currently available and those awaiting development.

In part 1, we attempt to describe the place of clinical sociology and some ways in which work in related practices can assist the clinical sociologist. Similarly, the ideas and practices of clinical sociologists can be useful to other types of practitioners. This book is directed not only to clinical sociologists but also to nurses, social engineers, social workers, academic sociologists, crisis interventionists, clinical psychologists and psychiatrists, peer and professional counselors, community physicians, and others in the "helping professions."

The presence of clinical sociologists, and the practices of clinical sociology, offer alternatives to the psychological and psychiatric assumptions which underlie most all of contemporary therapy. Many human needs are in reality social and thereby seldom amenable to the psychological help traditionally offered. As a consequence, criticisms of psychologically based therapies have increased both in number and potency during recent decades, as different groups' experiences with these therapies have increased. Chapter 2 discusses some major difficulties with methods of traditional therapy, and ways in which clinical sociological practices can avoid such pitfalls.

Part 2 begins our description of the structures and techniques involved in clinical sociological practice. Here we suggest ways in which the major theories and methodological techniques of academic sociology may be employed for achieving clinical diagnosis.

Diagnoses are analyses of the constructive or destructive processes of major sociological features within the group, group member, and community. Part 3 describes these *vital features,* namely, age, ethnicity, stratification, change, family, and everyday metaphysics.

In part 4, we move from diagnosis to therapy. Therapy consists of learning which alternative choices are more beneficial than a current state and acting to bring one or more of these choices to reality. The two major varieties of clinical sociological work are (1) therapy for groups and (2) therapy for members of groups. In the first, the clinician works with social groups to develop more adequate structural or interactional patterns. In the second, the clinician works with individuals to develop effective strategies for group living. Several specific techniques are offered for sociological therapy for both types of clients, and illustrative case histories are included.

In short, the book as a whole advocates a model for clinical sociology which is built around diagnosis and therapy of sociological problems. Diagnosis begins with rigorous listening to and observing the apparent difficulties (chapter 6). The results of these observations and inquiries are then considered with reference to the social location of the person. Determination of this location is achieved by ascertaining the relationship of the group or group member to the various vital features presented in part 3. Thus, an American clinician who hears the same set of complaints from a 16-year-old, poor Indian woman, and a 45-year-old, upper-class white male will suspect different problems in each. Both may say that their problems are work-related, but the problems can begin to be interpreted by the clinician only when he or she understands the role of work in these specific locations. Questions such as the following might be asked initially: Who works in poor Indian communities and in upper-class white communities? For what reasons? What are the norms and expectations for the unemployed in both communities? Which processes in the larger social systems brought about these work problems for each party? In what ways and to what degree are work roles (and the material outcomes of working) entrenched in other aspects of the clients' worlds? How do their ethnic backgrounds affect their work patterns?

Such questions are asked not only of the client, but through research into the sociological literature on the relevant vital features. After reaching a thorough understanding of the vital features relative to the client, the clinician begins to consider the possible sources of difficulties. On the basis of suspected sources of the difficulty, the clinician then chooses one or more therapeutic techniques. These may range in the example above from sociodramas (chapter 14) directly designed for the single client, to community organization (chapter 17) for large numbers of persons, including the single client.

Despite obvious similarities, our proposal for clinical sociology departs frequently from the usual practices employed in clinical medicine. For instance, we suggest that the clinician should work for preventive therapy and become part of the group she or he is assisting.

We try to leave our prescriptions for a clinical sociology descriptive and explanatory, but sufficiently open-ended so that this book may initiate a clinical sociology rather than fully systematize it. We fear, like Shakespeare's Brutus, that "nothing new is quite perfect" (or even fully formed), and like John Locke that "new opinions are always suspected, and usually opposed, without any other reason but because they are not already common."

We intend each chapter to accomplish two feats: first, to be comprehensible and interesting to both practitioners and students who have never read a sociology book; and second, to contribute significant new perspectives for academic sociologists and others who are well versed in the sociological literature but novices to clinical practice. We achieve these concurrent ends by means of a *canonical* approach; that is, by both describing and prescribing clinical sociology.

The book is intended, then, for persons preparing for, or active in, the human services professions. Only some readers will engage in clinical sociological practice per se. Nurses, social workers, psychologists, psychiatrists, physicians, educators, and others will find that clinical sociological practices complement their own concerns.

We have many persons to thank for helping to create this book. Many of the insights in chapter 1, and in several locations throughout the book, are from discussions with philosopher Jonathan Moreno. Talks with Gary Spencer, Ephraim Mizruchi, Louis Kriesberg, Manfred Stanley, James Prevost, John Sheets, Howard S. Becker, Shirley Rubert, Joseph Eaton, Donna LeFlore, Maury Stein, Morrie Schwartz, Sol Ice, and Robert Bogdan all contributed to the book. Many of the staff at Hutchings Psychiatric Center shared insights. Hutchings' librarian, Thelma Fitch, deserves a special accolade, as does sociologist Margret Ksander, who substantially assisted in the library research.

In addition, each author received considerable support during this project from Jo, Lorin, Michael, Noah and Florence Freedman, Sharon Lehman, the staff of the Education and Training Department of Hutch-

ings Psychiatric Center, members of the Sociology Department at Syracuse University, and members of the Reevaluation Counseling Community of Syracuse.

The sociological photography is by Simpson Kalisher, a noted professional photographer who was kind to permit us to select photographs
from his impressive collection. Some appear in *Propaganda and Other
Photographs* (Danbury, N.H.: Addison House, 1976).

This book has no senior author. Each chapter combines the insights
of both authors and has benefited from each author's critique and re-
working the other's ideas. The book is a beginning. We hope that the
insights from our work will help you in your work.

Contents

Part 1
Delineating Clinical Sociology

Chapter 1

What Is Clinical Sociology?

We still hold these truths to be self-evident:

> One of the most striking facts with regard to the conscious life of
> any human being is that it is interwoven with the lives of
> others. It is in each man's social relations that his mental
> history is mainly written, and it is in his social relations likewise
> that the causes of the disorders that threaten his happiness
> and his effectiveness and the means for securing his recovery are
> to be mainly sought.
>
> James Jackson Putnam

> No matter how mean or hideous a man's life is, the first thing
> is to understand him; to make out just how it is that our com-
> mon human nature has come to work out in this way. This
> method calls for patience, insight, firmness, and confidence in
> men, leaving little room for the denunciatory egotism of a certain
> kind of reformer. It is more and more coming to be used in dealing
> with intemperance, crime, greed, and in fact all those matters in
> which we try to make ourselves and our neighbors better.
>
> Charles Horton Cooley

> Only the sham knows everything; the trained man understands
> how little the mind of any individual may grasp, and how many
> must co-operate in order to explain the very simplest things.
>
> Hans Gross

These mottos grace the frontispiece of Mary Richmond's *Social Diagnosis,* a long influential bible in the field of social work first published in 1917. These mottos, respectively of a neurologist, a sociologist, and a criminologist of that era, are as true today.

Mary Richmond delineated ways to emphasize the "social" in social work practice. The task of this book is somewhat different. We explore a particular use of sociology—as a basis for clinical practice with groups, group members, communities, and organizations. We believe that the discipline of sociology provides a comprehensive approach for understanding people. As Dr. Putnam suggests, "It is in each man's social relations that his mental history is mainly written." Sociology as a discipline centers on social relations at a number of different levels. Through the information presented in this book, we plan to demonstrate that the systematic use of sociological knowledge is crucial in clinical practice, regardless of the disciplinary background of the practitioner.

If you ask most contemporary clinicians (physicians, nurses, psychiatrists, etc.) whether they consider social factors in their diagnoses and treatments, a majority would probably respond affirmatively. But understanding the subtleties of sociology requires a great deal more information and skill than merely asking questions of a social nature. It is usually possible for persons and groups to change their social conditions and, at times, clinicians who are sensitive to sociology can be instrumental in this change. Too often, however, the clinicians working with these persons or groups completely overlook sociological factors which could make the difference between successful and unsuccessful changes during therapy.

Consider Mrs. A, a 74-year-old black woman participating in a day program for geriatric patients. Her case was presented to a staff with outside experts (including a clinical sociologist) because she had resisted parts of the therapeutic day program and spent time sitting in a corner, repeating words over and over again. After a variety of questions were considered, the sociologist asked what turned out to be a key question: "What is her religion?" "Pentecostal. She was a Pentecostal missionary when she was younger and she is still deeply religious—too religious for the local churches." The sociologist discovered that she objected to the part of the day program that used audio-visual aids, which she considered sinful devices because they were not mentioned in the Bible. The mumbling turned out to be "speaking in tongues," a key part of the woman's religion. With this knowledge, treatment became more productive. This is a simple example of clinical sociology. The sociologist raised a sociological question and related it to the lifestyle of the woman, thereby leading to a therapy plan.

The clinical sociologist can work on levels other than those with individuals. For example, a sociologist was consulted on a functioning library for the poor. Superficially, the library appeared to be a success. As soon as the school day ended, neighborhood youths crowded into the converted house and frequently remained there until the library closed at night. Usage figures were astounding.

At one point in his observation, the sociologist deliberately stopped looking at the library as a library and concentrated upon the actual social activities going on in the place. He discovered that while young people were having a great time in the facility, they were interested in the books only when a paid monitor checked on them. Just before she would arrive, most of the youths grabbed the nearest book and looked at it until she departed. After asking a few questions, the sociologist discovered that one had to have a book in hand in order to be in the building. He also uncovered that the local community had little say about the library's programs. After further checking, the sociologist recommended that both the community center function of the library and the reading level of most of its users needed bolstering. This led to programs that emphasized materials other than print and to the strengthening of a community board that initially advised, and later determined, the direction of the library.

Clinical sociology is the application of a variety of critically applied practices which attempt sociological diagnosis and treatment of groups and group members in communities.

THE HISTORY OF CLINICAL SOCIOLOGY

The term "clinical sociology" is not new. Louis Wirth of the University of Chicago titled his 1931 paper in the *American Journal of Sociology*, "Clinical Sociology." [1] Wirth had observed the creation of several clinics throughout the United States "in which, in addition to the usual psychiatrists, psychologists and social workers, the staff includes sociologists as well." Some of these clinics even identified themselves as "sociological clinics." For the most part the clinics worked with child behavior problems, and Wirth's vision of clinical sociology is largely limited to one aspect of a full clinical practice, namely, therapy for group members. But Wirth recognized several of the major internal and external issues confronting clinical sociology.

The value of the sociological perspective as a corrective for traditional modes of therapy, a topic to which we devote the next chapter, was a central concern of Wirth's:

> Perhaps the greatest contribution of the sociologists thus far has been the attempt to correct the shortcomings and especially the particularistic fallacies of those who have traditionally been concerned with these problems. The positive contributions of the sociologist, the results of which in practical terms have thus far been only partially realized, seem to consist in what may broadly be characterized as the cultural approach to behavior problems. . . . It is not desirable that the sociologist should displace the physician, the psychiatrist, the psychologist, or the social worker, but he should bring to them the insights which his approach furnishes not merely in order to modify their viewpoint but to understand the child's behavior more completely as a social phenomenon. . . .
>
> Nothing indicates more clearly that the sociological approach has been largely neglected by psychiatrists and psychiatric social workers in the past than the outlines for history-taking that are still in use in most clinics. These outlines are oriented largely with reference to the psychiatric and psychological factors and the physical resources for the treatment of the patient. In most of them, for instance, there is a great deal of attention paid to biological inheritance, and almost none to family traditions; much to the physical surroundings, and little to the social world; a great deal to the delinquencies and failures to adjust to school, to the home, to companions, and occupation, and relatively little to the interplay of attitudes between the child and those with whom he comes in contact and the cultural conflicts under which he labors.[2]

Wirth's major point in this paper is that the "behavior problems" of persons are not objectively real in the same sense that, for example, bacterial problems are objectively real. The presence of bacteria can be concretely and materially demonstrated with the aid of a microscope. "Behavior problems" are present mainly because a community regards certain behaviors as problems. Specific actions of individuals are problems (or at least noticed) when they are defined in specific ways by the community. "Even stealing," Wirth notes, "is not a problem in a child that lives in a family of thieves, although the community may regard it as such."

Wirth viewed the clinical sociologist as a member of a therapeutic *team*, responsible for any of three possible activities: research; teaching the "cultural approach" to psychiatrists and social workers; or assisting such professionals with the social histories or community-related problems of their patients.

The eminent sociologist Karl Mannheim delineated the differences between psychology and sociology during a lecture at the Institute of Sociology and World University Service in London.[3] Mannheim argued with the usual distinction between psychology and sociology, that psychology deals with individuals and sociology deals with masses. To understand the individual one must view that individual not in isolation, but in social settings; and to understand masses of people one must understand the behavioral and attitudinal possibilities which exist within individuals. All too often, psychology assumes that the ultimate origin of individual behavior is the individual psyche, and sociology assumes that the ultimate determinants of individual behavior are the institutions to which the individual belongs.

Mannheim's position is that both sides are partially correct and partially incorrect. Sociologists often view institutions and other societal structures as "superhuman," as objective entities beyond human control. On the contrary, the established social forms are the result of specific human needs and reactions to scarcity:

> The unceasing interplay between our primary impulses which seek for satisfaction and their repudiation or remoulding by the counter-action of the already established relationships makes the theme of the history of mankind. If in the observation of this interplay one is more interested in the subjective origin of these psychic driving forces and in their concatenation in the life-history of the individual, one becomes a psychologist. If one is more interested in the power of these "established relationships," and primarily wishes to know how they react upon the

newborn individual from the very first day of socialization; and if one follows up the existing configuration of these institutionalized activities viewed from their objective function in a given society, one becomes a sociologist.[4]

By and large, the beginning of anything resembling clinical sociology goes back only to the 1930s and was limited primarily to distinguishing a place for sociologists in the diagnosis and treatment of individuals. Sociologists since that time have been employed as advisors, administrators, or assistants in a variety of largely psychological settings and projects, ranging from public school administration to corporate management to psychiatric hospitals. Some have written extensively about their experiences in these settings.[5] Others have undertaken research studies in clinical settings, but only a few have considered their activities or findings as a basis for a clinical discipline.

Then, during the 1960s, another dimension of clinical sociology was discussed, albeit vaguely. Alfred McClung Lee argued that a popular methodology within sociology is clinical in nature. Lee characterized participant observation techniques as "the clinical study of social interaction." He considered this type of work in sociology parallel to psychoanalytic interviewing.[6] We will develop in chapter 6 the diagnostic uses of participant observation and other traditional research techniques from academic sociology.

THE PLACE OF CLINICAL WORK WITHIN SOCIOLOGY

This book describes that special usage of sociology we call clinical sociology. To understand any specialization one needs not only descriptions of the specialty itself, but also how other fields handle such a specialization, and some idea of its relation to other areas in the same field. When we consider physical sciences such as biology, chemistry, or physics, we recognize their activities as two-dimensional. On the one hand, the scientist aims at understanding through classification of phenomena and formulation of general laws concerning these phenomena. On the other hand, an inseparable activity of science has been the intervention of the scientist into the *processes* at issue. Such *exodisciplinary* interventions have included disease control, space travel, and weather-proofing. In sociology, exodisciplinary intervention has seldom occurred. We can note some cases—such as crisis intervention and corporate consulting—but these have been infrequent, and *clinical* interventions have been almost nonexistent. Yet, clinical exodisciplinary interventions have taken place regularly in closely aligned disciplines such as psychology, economics, and political science.

Clinicians—whether in medicine, psychology, or sociology—are professionals who interpret information obtained through research in their discipline for the purposes of diagnosis and therapy. They depend upon the work of academic theorists and researchers, but usually the clinician's work is not academic. Academic practitioners are concerned with theoretical and research problems in vogue in the discipline itself; clinicians are concerned with theoretical and research questions as these improve their ability to aid their clients and the clients' community.

To draw an indelible line between clinical and academic sociology would be a mistake, however. The research and theories of clinicians arise out of client-related work, but may inform discussions within academic sociology. "Today," Ralf Dahrendorf reminds us, "questions and problems are so closely intermeshed that neither the theorist nor the practitioner can avoid reasoning about them in a single context and with equal intensity." [7]

The divisions within academic sociology greatly affect the clinicians. First, because they are often affiliated with academic institutions or with members of these institutions, and, second, because they use the work of academic sociologists. It is therefore useful for us to describe clinical sociology in terms of the divisions which have existed within academic sociology.

Robert Boguslaw and George Vickers [8] argue that the many subdivisions within sociology fall under three major divisions: the pure science orientation, the applied science orientation, and the critical science orientation. We will argue in chapter 6 that sociology is not only a science, but in many ways an art. For now the three distinctions will help us to describe the place of clinical sociology within the broader sociological discipline.

The *pure science* orientation seeks to discover and develop general laws which govern human behavior. Value judgments are to be avoided, as they may bias the research. A major goal of persons working from the pure science orientation is to be able to predict accurately how things occur in social worlds. The central activity of this kind of sociologist is research.

The *applied science* orientation seeks practical knowledge that will help solve those social problems which are of concern to social scientists or their clients. Rather than seek out general laws for human behavior, the applied sociologist seeks whatever type of sociological knowledge will help to solve pressing social problems (e.g., alcoholism, poverty, sexism).

The *critical science* orientation holds that developing natural laws for human behavior is not the appropriate major interest of sociology, but neither is the solution of immediate problems. Critical sociologists emphasize the importance of understanding social relations in terms of historical processes, and in terms of the future goals that motivate the current actions of persons and groups. The focus is upon large-scale (macro) social structures, usually with special attention upon the means of production of material goods and ideas. For instance, many contemporary critical sociologists study the history and current operation of international capitalism.

How does clinical sociology fit into these divisions? Clinical sociology clearly is *not* pure science sociology. The clinician regularly uses the findings of pure science sociologists, but neither seeks nor expects laws of social relations. The unit for analysis and therapy in clinical work can be either the group or members of a group, and a group can range from two persons to the entire world population. Hence, clinical sociology does not fit neatly into the critical perspective. Clinicians may well be concerned primarily with history, macro social structures, or means of production, but not in every case.

Perhaps the most descriptive way to compare clinical sociology to the divisions within academic sociology is to place it within a type of *critical-applied sociology.* Clinicians are unlikely to become fully critical sociologists owing to a desire to begin therapy whether or not a complete treatment plan is available (e.g., to assist a single community despite the involvement of other communities in the difficulties). They do not necessarily pay special attention to history, either. Nor are clinicians applied sociologists in the traditional sense, because of their concentration on the general health of specific groups or group members rather than upon the social problems of these groups. Applied sociologists have tended to concentrate on single social problems as these are distributed throughout a society. For example, large numbers of applied sociologists have attempted to reduce the alcoholism rate in the United States. Applied sociologists attend to a single problem (or series of problems) at a time, while the clinician attends to webs of difficulties.

A medical surgeon must attend not only to the few inches of the human body which will be touched by the surgical instruments, but also to the operation of the rest of the body during surgery. Thus, in heart surgery the surgeon must pay attention to the operation of the circulatory, respiratory, and other systems (or cooperate with others who attend to these systems); and after the surgery to the eating habits, secondary illnesses, and exercise patterns of the patient. Without attention to these various dimensions of the apparent illness, the surgery is likely to be ineffective. Similarly, the clinical sociologist recognizes the limited effectiveness of attending to a group's alcoholism without attending to the family, age, stratification, sex, and other aspects of the group's social web.

SOME CRITICAL-APPLIED PRACTITIONERS

At least five types of social practitioners—crisis interventionists, engineers, activists, social pathologists, and social workers—perform exodisciplinary services of a critical-applied nature. There are probably cases in which these sociologists have accomplished their work with the same sorts of procedures a clinical sociologist would employ. In general, however, they exhibit important differences from clinical practitioners.

Crisis Interventionists

A fundamental distinction between crisis intervention and clinical practice is obvious: crisis interventionists deal only with crises. Clinicians may be called upon to assist individuals or groups during crises, but clinical work as we are defining it is an *ongoing* interaction between clinicians and clients, neither beginning nor ending with emergency.

"Crisis intervention practice can be operationally defined," according to Edwin Schneidman, a prominent practitioner, "in terms of the specific goal of restoring an individual to his pretraumatic level of overt functioning. Obviously, the occurrence of some external traumatic event is implied." [9] In this definition we find a couple of distinctions between crisis intervention and clinical practices. First, the crisis interventionist works primarily with individuals, and, second, this work is based largely upon needs arising from a single event. In short, the relationship between the crisis interventionist and the clinical sociologist is similar to that between the emergency room physician and the family practitioner.

The focus on individuals has led crisis interventionists to psychology

and counseling more than to sociological practice. Indeed, a major debate among crisis interventionists concerns how closely to follow the
usual approaches of psychology and psychiatry. One group of crisis
interventionists has argued that the best way to help during crises is not
with specialized techniques, but with "the human qualities of warmth
and empathy which ordinarily enable one person to provide support for
another." [10]

The work of crisis interventionists can be quite instructive for some
aspects of clinical sociological practice, however. Most notably, the
clinician needs awareness of which events in the life cycle tend to produce crises for group members. Caplan has attempted to isolate these
major "hazardous circumstances": birth, puberty, climacteric, illness or
death, entry into kindergarten, transfer to grade school, transfer to high
school, leaving school, getting the first job, moving to a new community, getting a new job, undertaking new social or occupational responsibilities, or relinquishing job responsibilities through retirement. [11]

Engineers

An applied use of sociology which is sometimes mistakenly considered clinical is the engineering approach. In such practice, a
sociologist is hired to provide solutions to problems which the client
has defined. Whereas clinicians assess their clients' situations and devise their own definitions of the relevant problems, engineers work
primarily with the problem and interpretation presented by their
employer.

Alvin Gouldner notes this distinction in the case of an industrial firm
which hires a consulting organization to survey employee attitudes
about working conditions. The consultants typically will devise a questionnaire or interview schedule which asks all the questions requested
by the company's management. A report will be filed, indicating which
sorts of employees hold which sorts of attitudes about the firm. This
may be supplemented with recommendations for ways to change
employee attitudes. The sociologist sells management a series of technical solutions to the problem as it has been defined.

Gouldner suggests that in such a firm the communication between
management and employees may have broken down and this breakdown may actually have been the reason the survey was requested in
the first place. But the survey would do nothing to alleviate the communication problems, and might even increase the distance between

the groups, for example, if management had been battling a union and used the survey to support its own vested interests.[12]

Clinicians concern themselves with diagnosing and treating groups in as complete a way as possible. Rather than serving the immediate needs of one faction, the clinician attempts to understand and treat the problems of the group as a whole. From a clinical viewpoint, the engineering procedure described above is analogous to a physician limiting his or her treatment of a broken limb to writing a prescription for pain killers.

Activists

Another distinction is between the clinical sociologist and the sociological activist. In general, the activist can be characterized as a person whose treatment of social situations is based upon advocacy of specific political or moral beliefs. The clinician's context for diagnosis and treatment is not a set of predetermined beliefs but a set of situations in which the client or clients are coparticipants. The activist Charles Fourier in nineteenth-century France applied his sociological notions concerning the best forms of social life in the design of utopian communities or "phalansteries." Other activists have put their skills on the line for radical causes, governments, industries, jury selections, and elsewhere. In contrast, the clinician J. L. Moreno during the first part of this century used sociometric questionnaires to analyze problematic social relations in a variety of groups.

The distinction is similar to that between activists and clinicians in other realms. Surgeons who performed heart transplants, either on the grounds that such techniques should be encouraged or that such techniques are likely to become a common treatment in the near future, are activists in our sense. This is quite different from the heart surgeon who considers transplant the only practicable treatment in a particular instance.

Social Pathologists

Clinical sociology may remind some sociologists of a group of practitioners from the early part of the 1900s called the "social pathologists." This group concerned itself with analyses of social problems and provided something of a turning point in the history of sociology. Prior to the social pathologists, academic sociology had been primarily concerned with describing general laws of human behavior ("pure science"). The social pathologists encouraged sociologists to investigate not only how social worlds operate, but what is *wrong* with these operations ("applied science").

The social pathologists differ from clinical sociologists, as we conceive clinicians, in several ways. First, the pathologists did not practice actual therapeutic intervention techniques. Rather, as C. Wright Mills noted, the social pathologists were primarily concerned with promoting the "normality" of the traditional norms of rural America, thereby misconstruing the appropriately "normal" community:

> In this literature the operating criteria of the pathological are typically *rural* in orientation and extraction. Most of the "problems" considered arise because of the urban deterioration of certain values which can live genuinely only in a relatively homogeneous and primary rural milieu. The "problems" discussed typically concern urban behavior. When "rural problems" are discussed, they are considered as due to encroaching urbanization. . . .
>
>   The ideally adjusted man of the social pathologists is "socialized." . . . He does not brood and mope about but is somewhat extrovert, eagerly participating in his community's institutions. His mother and father were not divorced, nor was his home ever broken. He is "successful"—at least in a modest way—since he is ambitious; but he does not speculate about matters too far above his means lest he become "a fantasy thinker," and the little men don't scramble after the big money. The less abstract the traits and fulfilled "needs" of "the adjusted man" are, the more they gravitate toward the norms of independent middle-class persons verbally living out Protestant ideals in the small towns of America.[13]

The social pathologists were academic activists, albeit conservative activists, and this led them to another practice which clinicians try to avoid. Social problems such as those of poverty, family disruption, and mental illness are almost always viewed as in need of correction, rather than as parts of larger social worlds. Groups and group members are called upon to adjust to problems and changes in social worlds, whereas in clinical practice the clients are called upon to preserve their own well-being while changing these social worlds.

Social Workers

Social workers are trained to relate human behavior to the social environment. Because social work has barely developed theories of its own, training usually borrows from developmental psychology (normal and pathological) and psychiatry. Training in other social science concepts is something of a rarity.[14]

Social workers become adept at one or more of the following methods: casework (one to one), group work, family therapy, and community organization. Social workers, once they receive their diploma, usually end up working for social agencies and frequently submerge their own judgment into the tasks and policies of the agency. The agency, whether public or private, is usually a preserver of the status quo, chartered to stamp out pathology in the areas of mental health, social welfare, child and family services, or corrections. If new services are created, they tend to be in the image of the old. Extensive paperwork, especially in the public sector, limits the use of their social welfare methods.

A smaller number of social workers become advocates for clients, representing them or consulting with them on how to make the agency system meet the clients' needs. Such advocates frequently get caught between representing the needs of their clients and their own need to maintain a job.

Social workers differ from clinical sociologists in that they stick primarily to the psychological tradition, usually defer their own critical judgment to that of the agency or client, and tend to be unable to vary the methods in which they are trained in order to meet the needs of the person, group, or situation.

CONCERNING NORMALITY

To talk of sociological diagnosis and therapy is to suggest that something is different about some people or groups that requires change or repair. And to speak of something being in need of repair suggests a difference from a normal state. An everyday notion of illness is that of deviation from the normal state; a physician is expected to change our physiological condition so that we can "return to normal."

What do we mean by normality? A commonsense notion of normality is that provided by dictionaries: "Conforming to usual standards, average." This is also the position argued by one of the founders of sociology, Émile Durkheim:

> If we designate as "average type" that hypothetical being that is constructed by assembling in the same individual the most frequent forms, one may say that the normal type merges with the average type, and that every deviation from this standard of health is a morbid phenomenon.[15]

Durkheim bases his argument on the assumption that the most widespread forms must be the most advantageous to the organism or social group, that otherwise evolutionary processes would have caused them to disappear. Anything that occurs regularly must be contributing to the adaptation of the entity which contains it, and is therefore normal.

But such a notion will not cover every case which is considered normal or abnormal. The average child (i.e., a majority of children) contracts mumps at some time during childhood. If we maintain that normality is what usually happens, or the average occurrence, then mumps is not an abnormality, since it is what would be expected in a majority of cases. Nor is there reason to assume the Durkheimian implication that the widespread occurrence of mumps suggests that the illness contributes to survival.

Equating normality with the usual also suggests logical extensions which we would not want to maintain. For instance, certain illnesses in parents are usually acquired or inherited by their children. But we would not want to maintain that children are abnormal or ill because they do not contract from their parents an illness they are expected to contract.

An idea that comes closer to covering most cases views normality in terms of conventions. Although the average child contracts mumps, and we know our child probably will, we do not expect to wake up and discover that the child has contracted mumps. Normality is then viewed as a departure from everyday conventions. Mumps is an abnormality and disease when our child contracts it because it changes the child from his or her conventional state.

If we consider normality in terms of conventions we are committing ourselves in turn to a variety of additional understandings. First, conventions do not occur as entities unto themselves or as majority votes. Conventions always occur in *social communities*. To stick to physiological examples, consider the case of a six-foot-five-inch-tall basketball player. In the community of other basketball players and coaches, such a person is not abnormal, but to communities constructing tables of average heights he is certainly abnormal.

The importance of social community can be seen especially clearly in cross-cultural studies. The average pigmy is far shorter than the average American but is certainly not abnormal. Similarly, normal *behavior* differs cross-culturally as a result of differing conventions. The average Alorese would be considered anxious by Western standards; the normal Mundugumor would be very hostile; and the Zuni noncompetitive.[16] All of this suggests that to determine normality or abnormality we need to understand the social communities of the person, group or symptom, and the conventions that exist in these communities.

The importance of community in turn suggests that normality is pluralistic. Given that there are many different social communities, each with many conventions, there are necessarily many normalities. This pluralism should not be construed as an "everything-is-normal" argument, however. The emphasis on social communities and conventions does not require that we abandon the benefits of the normality and abnormality distinction, only that we situate each case in its appropriate location.

The usual/average and the convention/community definitions of normality can perhaps best be delineated by considering a hypothetical contemporary American gang of murderers. Any member of such a gang would probably be considered abnormal (and mentally ill) by most people, but not by the other members of the gang. The authors of this book believe that members of the gang are abnormal. Let us demonstrate that this conclusion can be reached with either definition of normality, but that the convention/community definition is preferable.

The gang members can be considered abnormal because they are not like the usual/average contemporary American, who is not a murderer. But this does not distinguish the murderers from a long list of others who also are not like the usual/average American. Americans of certain ethnic groups, education levels, belief systems, body builds, places of residence, and so on, are unlike the average American. Indeed, there are very few persons and groups that meet all of the criteria of being average. Perhaps more important, though, are two other deficiencies in this perspective: first, human differences are not only "the spice of life," but the possibility for human creativity and are to be cherished in many circumstances; and second, the average American may not be such a wonderful type that others' normality should be judged in its terms.

The gang members can be considered abnormal because they are a danger to members of their community. This is not the case (except under special circumstances) with the other groups listed above. Of course, the counterargument is that the gang member's community is the gang, and the member is not a threat to other members of the gang. But this is not accurate. Gang members have interactions with persons outside the gang. In addition to killing some of them, gang members probably rely upon their agriculture, modes of production, and so forth. The gang members are clearly part of the larger community, whether they accept that reality or not.

This is not to say that gangs of murderers are always abnormal, however. Armies and revolutionaries, when they are serving their communities, are not abnormal (though they may be undesirable). The major determining factor is the place of persons or groups in the communities to which they belong.

A more extreme example is that of Nazi Germany. Nazi theory and tactics were clearly abnormal and constitute sociological illness. But within Germany at the time they were usual and average. What makes them abnormal is that Germany interacted with the rest of the world and damaged such everyday conventions as life and safety throughout much of the world community.

In some cases the matter of normality is more confusing, as illustrated by recent debates concerning homosexuals. Opponents of gay rights bills contend not only that homosexuals are not usual or average people, but that they are destructive to conventions within mainstream society. One group, called Save Our Children, contends that homosexuals attempt to influence children to become homosexuals and may molest children.[17] Other opponents argue that homosexuality violates "moral normality," that important moral conventions are endangered by homosexuals.[18] Let us attempt as clinicians to determine the normality or abnormality of homosexuality according to convention/community criteria.

The American Psychiatric Association recently removed homosexuality from its *Diagnostic and Statistical Manual of Mental Disorders*. Some of the reasoning behind this action is pertinent to our own considerations and was expressed by Robert Spitzer in his proposal to the APA:

> For a mental or psychiatric condition to be considered a psychiatric disorder, it must either cause subjective distress, or regularly be associated with some generalized impairment in social effectiveness or functioning. . . . Clearly, homosexuality, per se, does not meet the requirements for psychiatric disorder since . . . many homosexuals are quite satisfied with their sexual

orientation and demonstrate no generalized impairment in social effectiveness or functioning. . . .

The only way that homosexuality could therefore be considered a psychiatric disorder would be the criteria of failure to function heterosexually, which is considered optimal in our society and by many members of our profession. But if failure to function optimally in some important area of life as judged by either society or the profession is sufficient to indicate the presence of a psychiatric disorder, then we will have to add to our nomenclature the following conditions: celibacy (failure to function optimally sexually), revolutionary behavior (irrational defiance of social norms), religious fanaticism (dogmatic and rigid adherence to religious doctrine), racism (irrational hatred of certain groups), vegetarianism (unnatural avoidance of carnivorous behavior), and male chauvinism (irrational belief in the inferiority of women).[19]

The conventions examined by the psychiatrist are subjective distress and social effectiveness, neither of which are necessarily violated by homosexuals. The relevant community here is the broad and generally heterosexual community in which homosexuals often interact.

We can employ Spitzer's sort of analysis to consider the "moral normality" question emphasized by those who want to consider homosexuality as abnormal. Again the relevant community is the broad community in which homosexuals interact (*not* simply the gay community, as some gay activists want to contend). In this community there is no single morality which is dominant, nor even a set of generally accepted moral conventions regarding heterosexual practices. As studies such as those by Kinsey and Hite have repeatedly shown, little agreement exists within the United States and Europe regarding conventions concerning sex outside of marriage, frequency of intercourse, oral sex, masturbation, and many others. Conventions vary among age groups, ethnicities, regions, social classes, and other divisions. A recent example is research indicating that by the age of 19, over 80 percent of black Americans have engaged in premarital intercourse, a rate much higher than that for young whites. However, those whites who do engage in premarital sex do so much more frequently than do black nonvirgins.[20] Obviously the white and black sexual conventions are both normal, although different.

Similarly, the "danger-to-children" argument does not hold up in light of the varying conventions present in the relevant community. This argument holds that homosexuals may influence children, who have yet to form a sexual identity, to choose homosexuality, which in turn destroys the fundamentally necessary convention of reproduction of the human species. A most obvious conflicting convention is found, however, among the many heterosexual couples who decide not to have children. Should there also be a movement to prevent these people from having interactions with children? An argument could be given in quite the opposite direction, that in a world which is overpopulated and running out of energy and food, survival demands that persons engage less in heterosexual intercourse, or that persons who desire such intercourse be encouraged not to reproduce.

The topic of normality-abnormality will be considered in terms of constructive and destructive processes in part 3. For now it suffices to have delineated our convention/community distinction.

NOTES

1. Louis Wirth, "Clinical Sociology," *American Journal of Sociology* 371(1931):49–66.

2. Ibid., pp. 58–59, 64.

3. Karl Mannheim, "A Few Concrete Examples Concerning the Sociological Nature of Human Valuations," *Essays on Sociology and Social Psychology by Karl Mannheim* (London: Routledge, 1953), pp. 231–42.

4. Ibid., pp. 240–41.

5. The literature search undertaken for this book pointed out one book and one article which used the term clinical sociology. The book, *Patterns in Human Interaction,* by Henry L. Lennard and Arnold Bernstein is subtitled *An Introduction to Clinical Sociology.* The authors of this volume regard it as quite a complex introduction. The article by Lucien LaForest, "The Concept of Positive Mental Health: Foundations of Socio-Clinical Intervention (Clinical Sociology) in Alcoholism and Addiction," *Toxicomanies* 4(October 1971):381–90, suggests that sociologists have not played an active role in clinical intervention and makes suggestions about how that role could be played.

6. Alfred McClung Lee, "On Context and Relevance," in John Glass and John Staude, eds., *Humanistic Society* (Pacific Palisades, Cal.: Goodyear, 1972), p. 251.

7. Ralf Dahrendorf, "Sociology and the Sociologist: On the Problem of Theory and Practice," *Essays in the Theory of Society* (Stanford, Cal.: Stanford University Press, 1968).

8. Robert Boguslaw and G. Vickers, *Prologue to Sociology* (Santa Monica, Cal.: Goodyear, 1977).

9. Edwin Schneidman, "Crisis Intervention: Some Thoughts and Perspectives," in Gerald Specter and William Claiborn, eds., *Crisis Intervention* (New York: Behavioral Publications, 1973), p. 9.

10. Ibid., p. 2.

11. G. Caplan, *Theory and Practice of Mental Health Consultation* (New York: Basic Books, 1970).

12. Alvin Gouldner, "Exploration in Applied Social Science," in Alvin Gouldner and S. M. Miller, eds., *Applied Sociology* (New York: Free Press, 1965).

13. C. Wright Mills, "The Professional Ideology of Social Pathologists," in Irving Louis Horowitz, ed., *Power, Politics and People* (New York: Oxford University Press, 1963), pp. 541–42, 551–52.

14. One of the authors taught social science concepts in a school of social work for four years. The content of the course was an anomaly in the curriculum.

15. Émile Durkheim, *Rules of the Sociological Method* (New York: Free Press, 1938), p. 56.

16. S. Kirson Weinberg, *Society and Personality Disorders* (Englewood Cliffs, N.J.: Prentice-Hall, 1952).

17. "Battle Over Gay Rights," *Newsweek*, 6 June 1977, p. 20.

18. George Will, "How Far Out of the Closet?" *Newsweek*, 30 May 1977.

19. "A Proposal about Homosexuality and the APA Nomenclature," reprinted in *Advocate*, 16 January 1974.

20. Melvin Zelnik and John Kantner, "Sexuality, Contraception, and Pregnancy among Young Unwed Females in the United States," paper prepared for the Commission on Population Growth and the American Future, May 1972.

THE CLINICIAN'S LIBRARY

At the end of each chapter we will present several books or articles especially relevant to the issues being discussed in the chapter. Since this is the first book (to our knowledge) concerning clinical sociology, no specific works deal with the issues per se. A couple of informative overviews of sociology discuss several of the topics in this chapter, however:

Berger, Peter. *Invitation to Sociology.* New York: Doubleday Anchor, 1963.
Boguslaw, Robert, and George Vickers. *Prologue to Sociology.* Santa Monica, Cal.: Goodyear, 1977.

Chapter 2

The Sociological Perspective in Therapy

The Friday night theatergoers in New York finish their curtain call applause and begin to make their way to the buses, taxis, and subways out of the area. Some head west. Eighth Avenue in the forties is a mixture of exotic movie houses, bars catering to various sexual tastes, streetwalkers, and people cruising for excitement.

As the Eighth Avenue bus arrives, a bear-like hulk of a man with outstretched dirty hand approaches the well-dressed people boarding the bus. He does not talk but makes guttural sounds, moving his hand to his mouth. He is old, but there is no way of telling how old. A month's growth of hair covers the sores on his face. He drools over the faded denim shirt and ill-fitting, torn pants. The crowd, like magnets repelled by a negative force, try to enter the bus at the greatest distance from his presence, but he stands near the door making guttural sounds, but no one gives. He touches a man's back and the man shies away as if his touch were contaminating.

In fairy tales, the man might be the beast who would turn into a handsome prince when kissed by a beautiful woman, and they would live happily ever after. In the crowd boarding the bus, there are no volunteers. In the reality of Eighth Avenue, he is alive. He is a human being. He has no prospects, no work, no resources. . . . No one is willing to risk the magic kiss. And does the combined wisdom of our human service providers provide an answer? . . . A pickup by the police, perhaps a trip for psychiatric observation, then release. Those with whom he comes in contact will throw up their clean hands in resignation and recognition of their failure.

This incident would be tragic enough if it happened to only a few men and women in New York City. Those who process them or try to ignore them often dehumanize them by seeing them as "bums," non-persons. Such a view is symptomatic of the poverty of a human services orientation which places individuals within category groups in order to remove them from the rest of society. Yet we all have much in common with this man. Fairy tales remind us that everyone has a potential for princely qualities; so too do we have aspects of this man in our diverse selves. We may share ethnicity, gender, social class, similar childhood experiences, the ability to love and hate, the same neighborhood, the same street corner, or any number of other commonalities. In short, the bear-like man is a member of some of the same human groups as are we. This chapter argues that only by placing a person within such social locations—understanding how and why those locations arose and are important—can we hope to develop adequate human services diagnosis and therapies.

THE NEED

Who needs clinical sociology? Don't we already have an established body of knowledge for dealing with problems in living? Aren't clinical psychology, social work, and psychiatry more than adequate? The idea of concentrating on groups, even when using psychological tools, has been sharply criticized. Reuven Bar-Levav has claimed that all therapy, including group psychotherapy, is therapy of individuals. According to this view, only individuals suffer pain and can be considered ill.

> Individuals seek therapy and engage themselves in it as individual patients. Group psychotherapy is, therefore, somewhat of a misnomer, since the group does not have a psyche, or internalized object representations. Groups may need to be changed structurally, economically, or politically, but they cannot and need not be therapized or healed. . . . But therapy is related to an agonizing individual, and all theories of group psychotherapy that make any sense must, therefore, be derived from theories of individual therapy, and must be extensions of such theories. The many failures of group psychotherapy and group treat-

ment in its various forms may well stem basically from a failure to understand this simple but all-important truth.[1]

We would dispute nearly all these assertions, but they underlie the problems of the psychology-dominated therapies we critique in this chapter. The most basic difficulty is one pointed out in the early 1900s by William James: just because we have called someone an individual does not mean he or she is nothing but that, any more than having once called someone an equestrian means that the person is no longer able to walk. It is not so easy to say that "it is not the group that is sick," as illustrated by our examples of the gang of killers and Hitler's Germany.

Thus, while it is true, by definition, that the group has no psyche, it does, by definition, have a *socius*.[2] Although groups per se may not be "agonized," group members are frequently agonized simply by virtue of being group members, not as individuals. Consider the ethnic group member who is persecuted as a member of that ethnic group. Or as R. D. Laing put it:

> All in all
> Each man in all men
> all men in each man
>
> All being in each being
> Each being in all being
> All in each
> Each in all
>
> All distinctions are mind, by mind, in mind, of mind
> No distinctions no mind to distinguish.[3]

We argue in this chapter that diagnoses and therapies derived exclusively from psychology are logically incorrect, have historically been inadequate, and ignore the sociological nature of persons' problems. Persons' experiences as individuals are formed and structured by groups. Language and communication (including that of psychotherapy) are group processes. Schools, the workplace, and the market are social settings. Our neighborhoods, communities, cities, and societies are not individual creations, but depend on the interrelations of many persons and, in turn, affect the social health of these persons. Our growth, illness, morality, crime, conformity, and deviance are socially grounded. As sociologist John Clausen states:

Man is at the same time an organism, a member of society, the bearer of a culture, and a person or personality. Human potentialities become manifest only in society, and the bent they take in any particular society can be fully understood only in the context of the culture and social organization of that society. The self arises in the process of social interaction, and the structuring of goals and motives in the person is likewise a product of interaction within a framework of norms and values basic to a culture. This being so, sociology—the systematic study of social organization and of group life—can hardly fail to have relevance for psychiatry.[4]

When these social worlds are examined today, what stands out?

DEHUMANIZATION

The psychology and sociology of personality and interpersonal relations have been in the past, and still are, vitiated by three sets of assumptions and tendencies. The first is a rigid ideal of scientific exactness which produces in the minds of many social scientists a bias towards selecting, or emphasizing, those facts and aspects of reality which lend themselves best to a precise, and if possible, quantitative investigation. This results in the neglect of those facts and aspects which resist or elude precise or exact analysis. The second is the set of silent assumptions rooted in the ideological or cultural background of the society to which the particular psychologist or sociologist himself belongs. These silent assumptions often induce the social scientist to ask only those questions and to select only those problems suggested by the accepted ideology (cultural pattern). The third is the tendency to neglect, or even to ignore, certain very important facts and problems because those facts and problems appear to be quite obvious.[5]

In order to gain an overview of the problematic social worlds of today, the tendencies Gustav Ichheiser noted above must be overcome. It is difficult to know when one has done this, but let's venture some observations which are (1) difficult to verify scientifically, (2) somewhat outside the ideological and cultural backgrounds of the authors, and (3) in some cases, obvious facts and problems.

We are born into a world clearly functioning at a far from optimal level. There is poverty, illness, violence, unequal opportunities, and addictions. Decisions are made not on the basis of human needs but on the basis of bureaucratic needs of organizations or systems. Humanitarian sentiment is often ruled out as unscientific or unfeasible, and civil rights are sometimes ignored. Persons are placed in prison situations where "the interaction between functionary and inmate is carried on without effective governance of societal norms." [6] Examine Watergate from this perspective, or the conditions of poor persons, the elderly, prisoners, the mentally retarded, the mentally ill, Attica, or skid rows.

But not only our defined social problems can be viewed in terms of bureaucratic needs. Schools teach young persons to memorize and follow orders rather than to be creative or achieve technical expertise. The family is under pressure from numerous sources, leading to an increasing divorce rate. For many, work is a boring, repetitive endeavor, yet so is leisure. Growing older does not change things; each year appears a repetition of the earlier years. As an effect (and partial cause) of all this, community life has come to be characterized by apathy. Decisions that affect many are made by a few, and until the decision strikes close to home, most people don't care. Many organizations have become vestigial, with a few members hanging on and creating an illusion of power.

We are told again and again that our actions can make the world a better place. Parents hope that the world of their children will be better than their own world. Yet, American society as it exists today hardly uses the talents or meets the needs of many of its members. As Harvey Jackins suggests: "We estimate that the successful adult in our present culture, the man or woman whom everyone would agree is doing just fine, is operating on about ten percent of his original resources of intelligence, ability to enjoy life, and ability to enjoy other people." [7]

The quality that characterizes these conditions is dehumanization, a reduction of persons' uniquely human potential. What do we do about this state of affairs? Mainly, we talk. Mass media has turned society's problems—from violence to capitalism to sex addiction to loneliness—into the educational and entertainment filler between advertisements which promise an improved life if only we will buy the product. Governmental programs are designed to combat the conditions, but most do not alleviate the problems they were designed to change, and some create new problems. They are usually designed to appease more than to assist.

Within sociology and other academic disciplines, we have persons who employ scientific procedures to better understand these problems, and they bring us information and their own analyses. Frequently, the analysts leave us with a clearer understanding of the overwhelming problem, but no practical remedies. There are many books and courses on social problems, few on social solutions. Basically, the research social scientists and media commentators clarify but do not relieve the suffering of persons, either because they feel it's not up to them to alleviate such suffering, or because they have been professionally socialized to believe that they don't know how to help.

Social scientists who do assist others tend to treat specific persons who are suffering from dehumanization by offering them ways to cope with the situations, frequently calling these ways "therapy." Traditional therapies follow a social pathology model of deviance. This model maintains that there is something wrong with the individual who does not conform to societal norms or succumbs to dehumanization. The person must be caseworked or group worked, reeducated or rehabilitated to accept the prevailing norms. If the person does not conform after such efforts, the person becomes a victim and is blamed for his or her sorry state. Frequently placed in a situation which provides a control over freedom and opportunity—a prison, mental hospital, ghetto, or reservation—the victim is both devalued and feared. "None of those people in my neighborhood," or "No, I won't shop downtown. There are people who scare me there," or "No, I won't live in the city. It's unsafe."

Comedian Dick Gregory put it in personal terms:

> About a year ago in Chicago I was walking down the street, downtown in the Loop, about ten o'clock in the evening. A white cat walking down the sidewalk, he see me coming, he jump all the way off the sidewalk and get in the gutter. Scared to death. He say, "Mister, you're not going to bother me, are you?" I said, "No, my man, I'm Dick Gregory. I'm dedicated and committed to non-violence." "You mean you are *the* Dick Gregory? You don't carry no gun or no knife?" I said, "No." He said, "Well stick 'em up, nigger." [8]

DEHUMANIZATION AND THERAPY

To the rescue comes the therapist. A victim has been defined as someone needing help. The therapist is defined as the helper. The

therapist usually has been trained in techniques that emphasize changing the psyche of the victim; aiding in understanding, coping, delaying
gratification, and acting with power to change one's own life—middle-
class themes that frequently contradict the experiences of the victim.

> Most therapists see the poor and the severely disturbed as untreat-
> able, except by the manipulative techniques of the grosser
> forms of behavior therapy, and most community mental
> health proponents seem to see them as objects of social manipula-
> tion to be planned for, not with.[9]

The person in relationship to the social environment becomes the
problem. The therapist proceeds to minimize or disregard the roots of
the client—class, ethnicity, age cohort, religion—and frequently makes
a fatal assumption: the client's aspirations must be similar to the
therapist's. Even when roots are acknowledged, there is an attempt to
minimize the effects of those roots on the course of therapy:

> Generally, mental health professionals are not aware of, and sensi-
> tive to, the differences in values, life styles, emotional expres-
> siveness, family structures and nonverbal communication
> patterns of America's working-class ethnic groups.[10]

People are not easily manipulated robots, however. Traditional
therapy frequently fails to bring improvement, and fails most often
with persons from the lower socioeconomic groups where the prevalence of mental illness is the greatest.[11] The usual apology for this failure is that people will not respond to treatment. Even when other sorts
of programs are designed, an education-rehabilitation model is often
used, providing information and some supporting resources to allow
those in need to "pull themselves up by their bootstraps." Once this
self-uplifting process has begun, they must overcome the additional
dehumanizing conditions experienced by the successful persons of society.

Is this the best that can be done? Or is there another perspective that
can explain what goes wrong and provide a different focus? Perhaps we
have been using the wrong lenses to examine the situations we desire to
affect. Let's focus on how persons come to be clients in a therapist-client
relationship, and what this relationship looks like. In this way we may
be able to develop an alternative set of lenses which might prove more
beneficial.

Sociologist Thomas Scheff (in line with Erving Goffman, Howard S. Becker, Edwin Lemert, and others) has noted that in order for a person to become a patient he or she must be labeled as such. Simply emitting a certain type of behavior does not permit one to become a mental patient. The behavior must be labeled mental illness by others before one can become a patient. Specifically:

> The diverse kinds of rule breaking for which our society provides no explicit label, and which, therefore, sometimes lead to the labeling of the violator as mentally ill, will be considered to be technically *residual rule-breaking*. . . . psychiatric symptoms such as withdrawal, hallucinations, continual muttering, posturing, etc. may be categorized as violations of certain social norms—those norms which are so taken for granted that they are not explicitly verbalized, which we have called residual rules. . . . If it proves to be correct that most symptoms of mental illness can be systematically classified as violations of culturally particular normative networks, then these symptoms may be removed from the realm of universal physical events where they now tend to be placed by psychiatric theory, along with other culture-free symptoms such as fever, and be investigated sociologically and anthropologically, like any other item of social behavior.[12]

Scheff notes several ways in which such "residual rule breaking" occurs.[13] Other authors have attempted to communicate what happens in the actual therapeutic relationship. Lennard and Bernstein, using a functionalist perspective, discuss therapy as a system of action:

> In our view, a therapist's task as a socializer is analogous to that of a parent socializing a child into the family or of a teacher socializing a student into the school situation.
> It is clear that the socialization of the patient into the "patient role" is one of the crucial and necessary tasks in the construction and maintenance of therapeutic systems.[14]

As persons learn other social roles, so they learn the social role of being a patient. Strupp and Bergin in an extensive review of research in psychotherapy concur:

The basic values transmitted by therapist (or teacher) are those of the culture. In our culture, prominent values include independence, self-direction, self-discipline, careful channeling of aggressive and competitive impulses, and the like. Psychotherapy to an important degree is training in socialization and it may be considered an elaborate and sophisticated educational or teaching process.[15]

These statements suggest that there are sociological components in therapy. Unfortunately, most commentators forget this. Perhaps, as Ichheiser's quote above suggests, it is belaboring the obvious, but if these components are obvious, there is little indication that the fields involved in therapy act on the basis of the obvious.

The existing lenses of therapy come from the medical model, as made specific for psychiatry by Freud and his followers. The pervasive influence of this genius casts a shadow on the allied human service professions of psychology, nursing, and social work, so that now all are pervaded by a medical model. The medical model assumes that the patient is ill and needs treatment and that mental illness is a physical disease best treated by physicians as leaders in the hierarchy of services centered in hospitals.

Criticism of the medical model has come from a number of sources. Thomas Szasz, a psychiatrist, believes psychiatry distorts the medical model:

It is customary to define psychiatry as a medical specialty concerned with the study, diagnosis and treatment of mental illnesses. This is a worthless and misleading definition. Mental illness is a myth. Psychiatrists are not concerned with mental illnesses and their treatments. In actual practice they deal with personal, social, and ethical problems in living.[16]

Psychiatry is the sewer into which societies in the second half of the twentieth century discharge all their unsolved moral and social problems. As sewers emptying into rivers or oceans pollute the waters into which they discharge, so psychiatry emptying into medicine pollutes the care and cure of the sick. . . .

Nearly everyone who speaks of the "medical model" in psychiatry uses this term incorrectly. Those who support the "medical model" evidently believe that if they could convince the politicians that "mental patients" are sick, they could treat them for their illness, regardless of whether or not the patients want to be treated. Hence, they act not like internists but like pediatricians, who must convince the parents that their child is sick and, having convinced them, can treat the child, regardless of whether or not he wants to be treated. . . .

All this illustrates that both institutional psychiatry and antipsychiatry rest on the "pediatric model" characterized by domination and coercion—rather than on a truly "medical model" characterized by cooperation and contract.[17]

A less controversial psychiatrist, George Engel, attacks the medical model of psychiatry per se:

But the existing biomedical model does not suffice. To provide a basis for understanding the determinants of disease and arriving at rational treatment of health care, a medical model must also take into account the patient, the social context in which he lives, and the complementary system devised by society to deal with the disruptive effects of illness, that is, the physician role and the health care system. This requires a biopsychosocial model. . . .

The boundaries between health and disease, between well and sick, are far from clear and never will be clear, for they are diffused by cultural, social and psychological considerations. The traditional biomedical view, that biological indices are the ultimate criteria defining disease, leads to the present paradox that some people with positive laboratory findings are told that they are in need of treatment when in fact they are feeling quite well, while others feeling sick are assured that they are well, that is, they have no "disease." . . .

The psychobiological unity of man requires that the physician accept the responsibility to evaluate whatever problems the patient presents and recommend a course of action, including referral to other helping professions. Hence the physician's basic professional knowledge and skills must span the social, psychological, and biological, for his decisions and actions on the patients' behalf involve all three.[18]

"Biopsychosocial" implies a much greater range than is usually considered in the human services. Biological factors do play a role in social and psychological situations, as the expanding field of sociobiology and as discovery of apparent biological connections with mental illness have made clear. Psychiatry is viewed by many as using a psychosocial model. The authors believe that this model is actually *psycho*social, as the social elements come from examining the individual. In this book, we place great emphasis on the social, explaining and examining the sociological considerations necessary in understanding group members, groups, and communities.

Regardless of causation, it is in the social realm that a person's difficulties frequently first appear and it is in the social realm that services are delivered, therapy is given, and success noticed. Let's first examine the social realm of psychotherapy as it now is usually practiced.

THE WORLD OF ORGANIZED PSYCHOTHERAPY

Keeping in mind the socializing nature of therapy and the inherent difficulties in the usual medical model applied to psychiatry, let us examine organized psychotherapy. From a distance, organized psychotherapy appears quite benevolent and well organized. Move in closer.

In the United States there are two major systems of mental health care, a private system mostly for people who can afford to pay for services and for others who appeal to therapists as "interesting cases," and a public system for those who cannot afford the private system. There is increasing government regulation of the private system now that public funds are frequently used (Medicaid and Medicare), and private practitioners complain about government interference. During periods of economic hardship, middle-class and even a few upper-class persons enter the public system where they are exposed to the working class and the poor.

The locales where the private system operates are private offices, general hospitals, and private psychiatric hospitals. "Some are good and some are terrible. Some are run to make money, others are non-profit. Some are cheaper than anything but the state hospital; many are so expensive that a year's stay will wipe out a well-to-do family's reserves and send them into debt." [19]

The locales for the public system are state maintained psychiatric hospitals, day treatment centers, and community mental health centers. For many persons, getting help for emotional problems is viewed as a sign of inferiority. Many more persons are willing to state on a health questionnaire that they have felt on the verge of a nervous breakdown than are willing to state that they have received professional services to treat the disturbance.[20]

Negative images of the mental hospital are reinforced by the mass media. Horror movies use creaky sanitariums as settings. "Cuckoos' nest" designates a collection of strange "birds." Weird behaviors are reported as human interest stories. Many persons view mental illness as a permanent affliction, and the public mental illness system of services comes under increasing pressure to be the mental health police, keeping harmless people who act strangely off the streets.

Mental illness also becomes entangled with government. Large hierarchical bureaucracies exist, with psychiatrists usually at the top of the pyramid. Sometimes the production of written accounts of diagnosis, treatment plans, and behavior narratives for later evaluation by numerous accrediting bodies routinizes the treatment. Directives come down from levels of the bureaucracy quite remote from patients and day-to-day local management. Frequently the direct patient contact is handled by paraprofessionals with less clinical training than the professionals who get promoted to handle administration, paperwork, meetings, and regulated appointments with patients.

The public mental health system is comparable to a factory. The patients are the products; the paraprofessionals are the assembly-line workers; the professionals are the foremen; the administrators are the plant managers; the central administrators are the absentee owners; the citizens of the state are the uninterested stockholders; and, all too often, decisions are made by computers.

This approach to the delivery of mental health services is another example of dehumanization. Here, in a situation where people are supposed to be caring for other people, the increasing dehumanization (combined in many states with budget cuts) makes effective therapeutic treatment improbable. Open and loving interactions, which frequently have been denied to persons who end up in mental institutions, are not fostered in these settings. This was dramatized by D. L. Rosenhan, Professor of Psychology and Law at Stanford University, and seven other sane persons who gained admission to twelve mental hospitals. Each received a psychiatric diagnosis and was admitted to the hospitals. These pseudopatients initiated contact with staff no more than once a day to get information about some element of their treatment. The following table adapted from Rosenhan's study [21] delineates the responses:

TYPE OF RESPONSE	PSYCHIA-TRISTS	NURSES AND ATTENDANTS
Moves on, head averted	71%	88%
Makes eye contact	23	10
Pauses and chats	2	2
Stops and talks	4	0.5

In contrast, when strangers were approached on a university campus and in a university medical center, the vast majority of persons stopped to talk (78 percent).

Nor can it be argued that lack of contact represents good therapy. Psychologists Charles Truax and Robert Carkhuff have distinguished several qualities of therapists that increase effectiveness:

> The major implication of the present tentative analysis is that the therapists or counselors who are high in empathy, warmth, and genuineness are more effective in psychotherapy because they themselves are more potent positive reinforcers; *and* also because they elicit through reciprocal affect a high degree of positive affect in the patient, which increases the level of the patient's positive self-reinforcement, decreases anxiety, and increases the level of positive affect and positive reinforcement received from others. By contrast, counselors or therapists who are low in communicated accurate empathy, nonpossessive warmth and genuineness are ineffective and produce negative or deteriorative change in the patient because they are noxious stimuli who serve primarily as aversive reinforcers *and* also because they elicit negative affect in the patient. . . .[22]

The absence of contact as reported by Rosenhan, when examined in the light of Truax and Carkhuff, points up the extent of dehumanization in mental health institutions.

HOW PEOPLE BECOME PATIENTS

Let's examine four important determinants of how persons end up in mental hospitals:

1. *Unemployment sends people to mental hospitals.* M. Harvey Brenner has traced this relationship over many decades and finds that one of the effects of a rise in unemployment is a rise in state mental hospital admissions (suicides, state prison admissions, homicides, deaths from cirrhosis of the liver, cardiovascular and renal disease also rise).[23] The 1.4 percent rise in unemployment which began in 1970 had an economic cost of over six billion dollars between 1970 and 1975 with the rise in state hospital usage costing $82 million.

It is somewhat ironic that an increasingly employed behavioral therapy approach in mental hospitals, the token economy, mimics the capitalist system by providing pay in tokens for acceptable ward performance. Indeed, many social rehabilitation programs have work-for-pay as the ultimate goal, with many steps along the way, including vocational work samples, sheltered workshops, job training, and subsidized employment. In line with the factory analogy, the goal of the mental health factory is "products that work." [24]

The ability to get paid for work is one of the outward signs of a basic level of mental functioning. Often it is assumed by therapists that to reach this goal, personal therapy must take place. There must be something in people's heads, not general socioeconomic conditions, that make millions of people jobless. For those who don't make it, the society provides subsidies through welfare programs.

2. *Membership in a social class sends some persons to mental hospitals.* Within any society, there are general standards for acceptable behavior and permissible deviations from that standard. Enforcement of standards is related to social class. Behavior that is eccentric, but accepted, among the affluent may be treatable or punishable among the poor. The choice of locale for treatment or punishment frequently is made in terms of whether the violators appear to be responsible for their acts and how extensive are their systems of interpersonal and monetary support. High responsibility and high support frequently lead to little restriction. High responsibility and low support frequently lead into the criminal justice system. Low responsibility and high support frequently lead to outpatient psychiatric services. Low responsibility and low support frequently lead to inpatient psychiatric services. Only certain explanations of the rationale for one's actions are permitted by the standards and acceptable ranges of deviation of one's group. When these explanations become extreme, and the existing support systems become exhausted, and the behaviors become recognized as bizarre and inappropriate, a person enters the world of the psychiatric hospital.

3. *Previous labeling as a psychiatric patient leads persons to the mental hospital.* Once a person has had psychiatric difficulty, an assumption is made that future problems also have psychiatric origins.

4. *Acting differently from other persons in one's age group can lead to the mental hospital.* Taking alternative sex roles, ingesting mind-changing drugs, acting too young or too old, being hyperactive in school, being "the different one" in the family, all can be viewed as psychiatric difficulties.

How can such nonpsychological and nonmedical processes result in psychiatric disorders? Much of the answer was given by Lothar Kalinowsky:

> Psychiatry differs from other fields of medicine in a deplorable lack of facts on which all psychiatrists can agree. There is no generally accepted etiology of most mental diseases, and the entire foundation of the specialty of psychiatry is based on theories believed by some and opposed by others.[25]

The American Psychiatric Association's Task Force on Nomenclature and Statistics has just finished a revision of the *Diagnostic and Statistical Manual* (DSM III). This manual has to be used by psychiatrists and other mental health staff, whether or not they believe in labeling, in order to comply with state and insurance practices. There are over two hundred separate diagnoses divided into the following broad classes of disorders: organic brain, drug use, schizophrenic, paranoid, schizoaffective, affective, anxiety, factitious, somatoform, dissociative, personality, psychosexual, sleep, disorders usually arising in childhood or adolescence, and various miscellaneous categories. For each category, when known, essential features, associated features, course of illness, and operational criteria are presented. It is beyond the scope of this book to go into the details of these categories.

For the first time, the DSM III now suggests a classification that has two socially oriented axes: "severity of psychosocial stressors" and "highest level of adaptive functioning during the past year." Each has a seven-point scale that provides a simple range from no stress through catastrophic and from superior functioning through grossly impaired functioning. While it is encouraging to note this important move toward acknowledging social elements as factors within diagnosis, the result is quite simplistic and does not take into account the detailed sociological factors as discussed in this book. Until now, most social factors were minimized in coming to a diagnosis. Within these diagnostic categories, there is wide latitude of definition.[26]

Kramer's observations on discordant admission rates for depressive disorders and schizophrenia into mental hospitals in En-

gland and Wales and the United States led to a major study,
known as the United States–United Kingdom Diagnostic Project,
in which a research team, composed of American and British
trained psychiatrists, explored the reasons for these differences.

The study has demonstrated that the higher incidence of
schizophrenia in the United States is mainly due to different
diagnostic rules and conclusions in the two countries. In filmed
and videotaped interviews of patients, for example, American psychiatrists found flatness of affect present and diagnosed
schizophrenia, but their British colleagues rated this symptom as
absent and diagnosed neurosis or personality disorder. In
another patient, American doctors diagnosed schizophrenia on
the basis of delusions, passivity feelings and thought disorder,
but British psychiatrists diagnosed personality disorder.[27]

A "MODEL" MENTAL HEALTH FACILITY

One of the authors has worked since 1971 at Hutchings Psychiatric
Center in central New York State. This state hospital is considered one
of the model facilities in New York and receives high marks during its
biennial national accreditation. Yet, even with all this success, its services do not fully rehabilitate some clients. A description of the facility
will illustrate some additional difficulties that arise when the medical
and psychological model is institutionalized. The activities described
below are delivered, on the whole, by competent persons who desire to
help others feel and perform better. The facility is new, well designed,
and well furnished, and has competent, concerned leadership.

Moderately to severely disturbed persons who feel, or are felt to be, in
need of center services come voluntarily, or against their will with the
certification of two physicians, the county mental health director or his
designate (any physician). The potential patient is evaluated by one or
more members of the evaluation team (either professional or para-
professional). This is followed by a second interview with a physician
(usually a psychiatric resident in training), and a decision on whether to
admit or refer is made. A geriatric evaluation team provides similar
services to the elderly. If the decision to admit is made, the person is
transported to one of the treatment teams, is welcomed, and assigned a
room and a therapist (usually a master's-level psychologist or a social
worker). The team psychiatrist conducts a separate interview and files
his or her findings and follow-up as a legal requisite.

After further interviewing and observation, a case conference is held and a treatment plan developed. A number of options for the treatment plan are available, and considerable effort is made to individualize the treatment plan for the patient. Individual, group, family and chemotherapy, activity programs, extensive social and vocational rehabilitation programs, basic social skills instruction, courses, and help in locating a new place to live—all of these services are available to the patient.

Staff-patient ratios are quite good, and considerable training is available to the staff. The activities of the center are extensively researched. Central administration tries to keep on top of problems and has changed organizational structures steadily to increase effectiveness. There is even a clubhouse for patients' own recreational activities. The overall environment is a therapeutic one.

The average length of stay in any inpatient treatment team is about three weeks. Planning for the discharge of the patient begins with the treatment plan. Frequently, part of the discharge plan involves other center services. Numerous neighborhood-based day treatment centers, halfway houses, and supervised apartments have been set up for patient referral. Many more persons are involved in outpatient and community services at any given time than are using the inpatient services.

Some persons go through the service system once and never return. Either they no longer need help or get help elsewhere. However, some persons continue to use services for several years, as the following table points out:

PATIENTS ACTIVE ON JANUARY 1, 1977, BY YEAR THEY FIRST
RECEIVED SERVICES [28]

YEAR	PERCENT ACTIVE
1966	2.2
1967	3.3
1968	2.2
1969	3.3
1970	3.4
1971 *	3.8
1972	10.5
1973	11.5
1974	11.4
1975	15.3
1976	33.1

* The figures from 1966–71 are from a smaller predecessor institution that served a portion of Onondaga County and might not be comparable with the later percentages.

Projections are that 488 out of every 100,000 persons who receive services will become chronic, needing some form of service throughout their lifetimes.[29] An estimate by John Cumming places those who will continue to need mental hospital services at 15 percent of those who enter.

Even with its less than optimum success rate, Hutchings Psychiatric Center is considered an outstanding mental hospital. Short lengths of stay combined with highly rated community-based programs contribute to this success. The work is not easy. Some staff members feel "burned out" after a few years of work, in part because some patients come back again and again, improving for a while and then seemingly getting worse.

WHAT'S WRONG HERE?

Where could the difficulties lie? The usual place to look is at the way services are delivered. Some difficulties are easy to identify: There could be better coordination within the center and between the different levels of government involved in the mental health service delivery system. The center is not fully staffed due to the state's fiscal crisis, and as a result the existing staff is asked to work even harder. The central campus design of the center has become an anachronism in the prevailing community-centered treatment philosophy that has emerged recently. These are only the most obvious problems, however.

One very helpful way to examine the strengths and weaknesses of an organization—a way that proved useful in the development of Hutchings Psychiatric Center—is an institution-building model of Milton Esman's that is derived from comparative analysis of new organizations of developing countries. "This conceptual framework provides a means for identifying operational methods and action strategies that could be helpful to practitioners and to persons actively engaged as change agents, particularly in cross-cultural situations."[30]

The framework delineates five clusters of variables that are essential to comprehend in any emerging institution. These are (1) Leadership, the groups of persons who formulate the goals and develop the program of the institution; (2) Doctrine, the formulated goals, values, and modes of operation that underlie the activities; (3) Program, the translation of doctrine into patterns of action; (4) Resources, "the financial, physical, human, technological and informational inputs of the institution"; and (5) Internal structure, staff roles, patterns of authority and communication, commitment of personnel to the organizational doctrine which form the basis for how the organization is structured, maintained, and changes.

There is a second set of variables termed linkages—"the interdependencies which exist between an institution and other relevant parts of the society." Institutions must relate to appropriate networks in their environment in order to survive. Specific linkages relate to each of the five institutional variables. Institutional leadership has to develop tactics to manipulate or accommodate these linkage relationships.

For any emerging institution, each of these components could be examined in detail and a statement of strengths and weaknesses prepared. It is likely, however, that such a statement would not reveal anything specifically keeping the Hutchings Center from doing a substantially better job. Improvements could be made organizationally, but even if the style of operation were shifted from staff-centered (most services are delivered weekdays during daylight hours) to client-centered (services available at all times), the range of success with current clientele would not increase substantially. A weakness of this conceptual framework is that it emphasizes the organization at the expense of the members of the organization.

It further assumes that the model of organizational structure that has developed is the best one to provide the services to be delivered. Yet there is great debate on whether this organizational model is the most useful one for the delivery of mental health services. Lawrence Kolb, an internationally respected psychiatrist and past Commissioner of the New York State Department of Mental Hygiene, noted the essence of the difficulty:

> Modern methods of rehabilitation, effective as they are, continue to be prescribed without a cohesive theoretical base. While the powerful psychopharmaceuticals modulate intensive pathologic emotional states, those who espouse this therapeutic measure as the major approach to social rehabilitation overlook the inability of this prescription to effect the often necessary new social learning for the individual or the often necessary relearning. Those who advocate the dynamic psychotherapies base their treatment largely on correction or expansion of psychological defenses developed to protect against pathological affect. The sociotherapists have given us a more comprehensive view of the way the social group therapeutic processes bring about change in the personality system. They

indicate the imperatives of any social system including: (1) accommodation of the individual to the unalterable; (2) dedication to consummation of the attainments of the social system; (3) integration of the facts of the social system; and (4) establishment of motivation to commitment to actions required by the social system.[31]

We believe that the time has come to view the organizational structure of psychotherapy as yet another symptom of an inadequate therapeutic philosophy. If this is the case, most organizational analyses would be equally symptomatic. We need to move from organization-based analysis to models which examine more closely the interplay of key relationships within a human service setting.

AN ALTERNATIVE MODEL

Our alternative model attempts to be more comprehensive, trying to better grasp the interplay of service delivery. Begin with the worker in the human services setting.

Worker

The worker cannot operate alone. He or she is linked to two significant foci: the social agency and the client. Each is linked to each other in

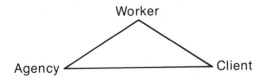

specific ways. The worker is linked to the agency by the roles he or she plays within the agency. The agency is linked to the worker through a job description and some form of contractual agreement. The worker is linked to the client by the tools and techniques of the practice. The client is linked to the worker by how he or she responds to the worker. The agency is linked to the client by how it delivers services, and the client is linked to the agency through how she or he uses the services offered.

This relationship does not take place in a vacuum. It takes place in both community and societal contexts. The values and structure of the

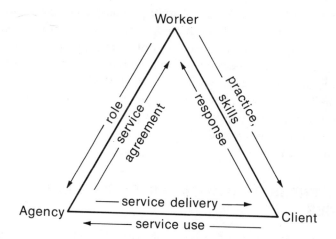

community and society determine the social context of the human service activity.

The client can be a person, a group of persons, an organization, or a community, yet this interplay remains important. When the head of a family has a nervous breakdown, the entire family suffers and needs help. When community leadership breaks down, major segments of the community may need help. Within each part of this model, it is useful to apply the Esman model, since each segment—group member, group, organization, community, society—is involved in the variables of leadership, doctrine, program, resources and internal structure, and the linkages to other elements.

EFFECTIVENESS OF MEDICAL PSYCHOLOGICAL THERAPIES

But does it matter that comprehensive models such as ours have not been employed? A counterargument might be that psychotherapy has been successful enough that alternate views are unnecessary.

Many studies have examined the effectiveness of medical-psychological therapies.[32] A recent work, *Basic Psychological Therapies: Comparative Effectiveness,* appears to be a comprehensive review of the issue. This book evaluates psychotherapy, behavior modification, and modeling and comes to the following conclusions regarding psychotherapy:

> Research on the outcome of psychotherapy has failed to show that any given technique or system is superior to any other technique or system. On average, psychotherapy has not been shown to produce benefits above the improvements found when no therapy is given. Psychotherapy, therefore, has not been shown to "cure" or "heal." Recent research, however, has indicated that certain therapists help patients, while others produce a negative effect: The patients are worse off than if they had never been treated by these practitioners at all.[33]

The authors suggest that a variety of studies show that facilitative communication is the effective component of various forms of psychotherapy. Specifically, confrontation may be the critical factor for communication skills, because such confrontation gives the patient guidance.[34]

A paper by Lester Luborsky et al. supports these findings.[35] Using a series of box scores between different regimens of treatment, they point

out approaches that appear to be more effective. The scores are revealing in their comparisons of psychotherapy and "control" groups,
including no psychotherapy, wait-for-psychotherapy, minimal psychotherapy, or hospital care:

Psychotherapy was better	20
Tie	13
Control group was better	0

Psychotherapy proved superior to the controls only 60 percent of the
time. *No therapy proved equal to psychotherapy 40 percent of the time.*
Does this box score and level of ineffectiveness indicate efficient use of
resources, workers, agencies, and clients?

Obviously, the absence of more comprehensive models cannot be
excused by the effectiveness of existing methods of therapy. Nor is it
that more comprehensive notions have been unavailable (the previous
chapter noted that they have been available during most of this century). Why, then, do nearly all mental health therapists (and even their
critics) concentrate largely upon the therapist-client relationship without placing it in the community or societal context that our alternative
model suggests?

One clue is that patients who have the greatest chance of success
through psychotherapy are those who have characteristics most similar
to most therapists. This would overshadow the influence of community
and society. As Barbara Lerner points out:

> Regardless of whether researchers investigate who is most likely to
> be considered a desirable client, who is most likely to receive
> psychotherapy, who is most likely to remain in therapy or
> who is most likely to have profitted from therapy, the results are
> essentially the same: mildly or moderately disturbed middle
> or upper class people are good clients; severely disturbed and/or
> lower class people are poor ones rejected by and rejecting of
> professional therapy and therapists.[36]

Another clue can be found in examining everyday counseling situations:

> Each of the necessary and sufficient conditions of therapeutic per-
> sonality change formulated by Rogers (1957) can be seen in less
> obvious fashion, in everyday behavior—in the person re-

garded as a good listener who understands the other person's
feelings; in the person regarded as spontaneous, open,
"straight," self-disclosing; or in the person described as having an
accepting nature. A few unusual people possess these traits in
combination.[37]

A third clue might be found in how psychotherapy is frequently
used. Psychiatrist Nathan Hurwitz states:

> The persistence of psychotherapy that does not succeed in fulfil-
> ling its manifest purpose suggests that it may have a more latent
> purpose. This latent purpose is to serve as a means of social
> control. This purpose is achieved in two ways—by the ideology of
> psychotherapy and its practice. Each aspect of the ideology
> and the practice reinforces the other aspects: and ideology and
> practice reinforce each other. In this way, psychotherapy creates
> powerful support for the established order—it challenges,
> labels, manipulates, rejects, or co-opts those who attempt to
> change the society. It may be suggested that every society
> uses the means of control available to it—the mass media, edu-
> cational institutions, police, courts, etc., including theories and
> practices of psychotherapy which are in accord with the pre-
> vailing value system of the society.[38]

A final clue comes from the recent review of the comparative effectiveness of psychological therapies by A. James Fix and E. A. Haffke:

> In our opinion, the modeling techniques have clearly demon-
> strated their usefulness as effective therapeutic techniques.
> They have been shown to be more effective in inducing be-
> havioral change than the simple classical conditioning methods.
> Given the lack of documentation of specific behavioral
> changes that result from traditional psychotherapeutic activities,
> the behavioral results attained by means of modeling procedures
> show that they are probably superior to the traditional ap-
> proaches as well.[39]

Herbert Strean, a supervising psychoanalyst, suggests that for the
chronic schizophrenic the best therapist might be the inexperienced
social work student who might not even have mastered the terminology
of the field.

Unperturbed by previous therapeutic failures, unimpressed by the cautionary admonitions of their mentors, unencumbered by a bevy of therapeutic procedures swimming in their heads, the social work student unconditionally regards his patient positively and truly accepts him where the patient is. . . . The patient seems to respond after some testing with, "Wow, no one has ever had faith in me before. That makes me love you. Let's work together." The student's benign and humane attitude seems to alter the vicious cycle and self-fulfilling prophecy that have been perpetuated by experienced professionals, who have often unwittingly communicated to the patient the message, "You are crazy, pathological, and even a bit inhuman. I shall move cautiously with you because your prognosis is so guarded." [40]

Let's consider what these clues tell us.

Psychotherapy improves the quality of life of a relatively small percentage of clients, and these tend to be middle- and upper-class persons who perhaps could have done as well with a friend who is a good listener. Many or most psychotherapists sincerely want to help their patients, but psychotherapy has come to play a social control function in society, and psychotherapists have generally come to accept their roles as social controllers. This is illustrated by the spread of behavioristic therapies. Thus, modeling is considered "therapy" although it consists solely of the clinician showing the patient what is considered acceptable social behavior. All of these are good reasons why psychotherapy is not placed in a community/societal context. To do so would undermine the social uses to which psychotherapy is regularly put.

THE NEED FOR CLINICAL SOCIOLOGY

The ineffectiveness and social control usage of psychotherapy, and the social nature of mental illness, suggest that adequate care needs to include sociological diagnosis and therapy. A sociologist and a psychiatrist put it well:

Perhaps, at last, psychiatrist and sociologist can help each other. And perhaps we can work out new relations to the whole society that will serve to put theoretic and practical problems in a different perspective. I believe the problem to be urgent in my own field, sociology, and it seems, only more evidently, urgent in psychiatry.[41]

Human beings, society and man and his total environment are functioning wholes in nature with unique attributes that cannot be understood by analysis of the parts alone. New approaches are needed to emphasize the holistic nature of man and of the systems—biological, psychological, and social—of which he is an integral part.[42]

The promise of clinical sociology is that one can gain a powerful perspective on the relationship between persons, groups, communities, and societies; how they interrelate, and how to work for change via manipulation of these interrelations. The conditions described at the beginning of the chapter are social facts that affect large segments of the population. It appears that a therapeutic approach which attempts to comprehend and devise actions based on social facts is a necessity in contemporary culture. Sociology has great promise in providing the necessary theories, methods, analysis of vital social features, and action applications. By thinking about and carefully applying the points of view presented in this book, the authors believe that progress can be made in solving complex personal and societal problems. This means a movement from the areas of medicine, psychiatry, and psychology into the realm of the social sciences:

Any situation which cripples or enervates the human organism, however unusual or vague its roots, is a pathological condition. The task of medicine conceived as a social science (which is not exclusive of medicine as a natural science) is to build into its diagnostic procedures a sensitivity to this dimension of the contemporary human experience.[43]

The conditions and practices that have been described in this chapter need to be examined in a new way if positive changes are to be made.

New light, if it is to be had, will come out of new relations and new enterprises, and the relation and the enterprise, as in psychoanalytic theory itself, is the beginning both of the new theory and the new act. I therefore look to an encounter, more profound than any before it, between the best representatives of the two great perspectival systems, who are the possessors of great, rich chunks of profound acquaintance with how we do, personally and severally, behave: the psychologically sensitive social scientists and the socially and sociologically sensitized psychological theoretician-therapists.[44]

NOTES

1. Reuven Bar-Levav, "Group Psychotherapy—a Technique in Search of a Theory," in L. Wolberg and M. Aronson, eds., *Group Therapy 1976* (New York: Stratton Intercontinental Medical Book Corp.), p. 134.

2. J. L. Moreno, *Who Shall Survive?* (Beacon, N.Y.: Beacon House, 1953).

3. R. D. Laing, *Knots* (New York: Vintage Books, 1970), p. 82.

4. John A. Clausen, "Sociology and Psychiatry," in A. M. Freedman, H. I. Kaplan, and B. J. Sadock, eds., *Comprehensive Textbook of Psychiatry/II*, vol. 1 (Baltimore: Williams & Wilkins, 1975), p. 373.

5. Gustav Ichheiser, *Appearances and Realities* (San Francisco: Jossey-Bass, 1970), pp. 7–8.

6. Bernard Rosenberg, Israel Gerver, and F. William Howton, *Mass Society in Crisis* (New York: Macmillan, 1964), p. 161.

7. Harvey Jackins, *The Human Side of Human Beings* (Seattle: Rational Island Press, 1965), p. 59.

8. Dick Gregory, "Dick Gregory Is Alive and Well," in Paul Jacobs and S. Landau, eds., *To Serve the Devil*, vol. 1 (New York: Vintage Books, 1971), p. 218.

9. Barbara Lerner, *Therapy in the Ghetto* (Baltimore: Johns Hopkins University Press, 1972), p. 11. Dr. Lerner goes on to show that it is possible to do individual psychotherapy with the poor.

10. Joseph Giordano and Marian Levine, "Troubled Americans," *New York Times*, 14 April 1976.

11. See pp. 37–40.

12. Thomas Scheff, *Being Mentally Ill* (Chicago: Aldine, 1966), pp. 34–39.

13. Ibid., chapters 2 and 3.

14. Henry L. Lennard and Arnold Bernstein, *The Anatomy of Psychotherapy* (New York: Columbia University Press, 1960), p. 25.

15. Hans H. Strupp and Allen E. Bergin, "Some Empirical and Conceptual Bases for Coordinated Research in Psychotherapy," *International Journal of Psychiatry* 7(February 1969):27.

16. Thomas Szasz, *The Myth of Mental Illness* (New York: Harper & Row, 1961), p. 296.

17. Thomas Szasz, *Heresies* (Garden City, N.Y.: Anchor Books, 1976), pp. 119–20.

18. George Engel, "The Need for a New Medical Model: A Challenge for Biomedicine," *Science* 196(8 April 1977):132–33.

19. Clara C. Park with Leon N. Shapiro, *You Are Not Alone* (Boston: Little, Brown, 1976), p. 228.

20. Gerald Gurin, *Americans View Their Mental Health* (New York: Basic Books, 1960), esp. chapter 11. Also Leo Srole, *Mental Health in the Metropolis II* (New York: Harper & Row, 1977); and Scheff, *Being Mentally Ill*, pp. 47–50.

21. D. L. Rosenhan, "On Being Sane in Insane Places," *Science* 179 (19 January 1973):255.

22. Charles B. Truax and Robert R. Carkhuff, *Toward Effective Counseling and Psychotherapy* (Chicago and New York: Aldine-Atherton, 1967), p. 161. They believe these positive qualities can be increased through training and they and others have developed programs to increase these skills. See Robert Carkhuff, *The Art of Helping* (Amherst, Mass.: Human Resources Development Press, 1973); Steven Danish and Allen Hauer, *Basic Helping Skills* (New York: Behavioral Publications, 1973); and Norman Kagan, *Interpersonal Process Recall* (East Lansing: Michigan State University, 1975).

23. M. Harvey Brenner, "Personal Stability and Economic Insecurity," *Social Policy* 8, no. 1 (May/June 1977):2–4.

24. For a critical discussion of the broader implications of a rather extreme token economy, read Kenneth J. Neubeck, "Capitalism as Therapy?" *Social Policy* 8, no. 1 (May–June 1977):41–45.

25. Lothar Kalinowsky and Hanns Hippius, *Pharmacological, Convulsive, and Other Somatic Treatments in Psychiatry* (New York: Grune & Stratton, 1969), p. 367. For informative research studies on the relationship between one's place in the social structure and entry into the mental health system, see the following: Allan Horwitz, "Social Networks and Pathways to Psychiatric Treatment," *Social Forces* 56, no. 1 (1977):86–105; Jerome K. Myers, L. Bean, and M. Pepper, "Class and Psychiatric Disorders: A Ten Year Follow-Up," *Journal of Health and Social Behavior* 6(Summer 1965):74–79; and Walter Gove and Michael

Geerken, "The Effect of Children and Employment on the Mental Health of Married Men and Women," *Social Forces* 56, no. 1 (1977): 66–76.

26. American Psychiatric Association, *Diagnostic and Statistical Manual III* (New York: American Psychiatric Association, 1977), forthcoming.

27. Heinz E. Lehman, "Schizophrenia: Clinical Features," in A. M. Freedman, H. I. Kaplan, and B. J. Sadock, eds., *Comprehensive Textbook of Psychiatry/II*, vol. 1 (Baltimore: Williams & Wilkins, 1975), p. 911.

28. J. Tannenbaum, J. Holland, and S. Crawford, "Demographic Characteristics of Patients Active on January 1, 1977," Research Department, Hutchings Psychiatric Center, 1977.

29. Morton Kramer, "Population Changes and Schizophrenia 1970–85," paper presented at the Second Rochester International Conference on Schizophrenia, May 1976. For a comprehensive discussion of the needs of the population which do not appear to benefit from usual services and of what services need to be developed for this group, see John L. Sheets, *The Fourth Revolution in Psychiatry* (Kalamazoo, Mich.: Behaviordelia), forthcoming.

30. Milton Esman, "The Elements of Institution Building," in Joseph Eaton, ed., *Institution Building and Development* (Beverly Hills: Sage, 1971), pp. 22–23.

31. Lawrence Kolb, "Personality Assets and Social Rehabilitation: Overlooked Aspects of Personality Functioning," paper prepared for Statewide Rehabilitation Conference, 11 May 1977, Albany, N.Y., p. 2.

32. The following reviews would prove helpful to readers interested in delving into this fascinating topic: Hans H. Strupp and Allen E. Bergin, "Some Empirical and Conceptual Bases for Coordinated Research in Psychotherapy: A Critical Review of Issues, Trends and Evidence," *International Journal of Psychiatry* 7, no. 2 (February 1969); Lester Luborsky et al., "Factors Influencing the Outcome of Psychotherapy," *Psychological Bulletin* 75, no. 3 (March 1971); Thomas Oden, "A Populist's View of Psychotherapeutic Deprofessionalization," *Journal of Humanistic Psychology* 14, no. 2 (Spring 1974); William G. Herron, "Further Thoughts on Psychotherapeutic Deprofessionalization," and Thomas Oden, "Consumer Interests in Therapeutic Outcome Studies: A Reply to Herron," *Journal of Humanistic Psychology* 15, no. 3 (Summer 1975); A. James Fix and E. A. Haffke, *Basic Psychological Therapies: Comparative Effectiveness* (New York: Human Sciences Press, 1976); Robert L. Spitzer and Donald F. Klein, *Evaluation of Psychological*

Therapies, Proceedings of the Sixty-fourth Annual Meeting of the
American Psychopathological Association (Baltimore: Johns Hopkins
University Press, 1976).

33. Fix and Haffke, *Basic Psychological Therapies,* pp. 44–45.

34. Ibid., p. 101.

35. Lester Luborsky, Barton Singer, and Lise Luborsky, "Comparative Studies of Psychotherapies: Is It True That 'Everybody Has Won
and All Must Have Prizes'?" in Spitzer and Klein, *Evaluation,* p. 12.

36. Lerner, *Therapy in the Ghetto,* pp. 3–4.

37. Gerald Goodman, *Companionship Therapy* (San Francisco:
Jossey-Bass, 1972), p. 28.

38. Nathan Hurwitz, "Psychotherapy as Social Control," *Journal of
Consulting and Clinical Psychology* 40, no. 2 (1973):237.

39. Fix and Haffke, *Basic Psychological Therapies,* p. 220.

40. Herbert S. Strean, "A Note on the Treatment of the Schizophrenic Patient," *Psychoanalytic Review* 64, no. 2 (Summer 1977):209.

41. John Seeley, "Psychiatry: Revolution, Reform and Reaction," in
Seeley, *The Americanization of the Unconscious* (New York: International
Science Press, 1967), p. 35.

42. Lewis Robbins, "Traditional Reductionism Is Unsatisfactory,"
International Journal of Psychiatry 7, no. 2 (1969):154.

43. John McDermott, *The Culture of Experience* (New York: New
York University Press, 1976), p. 170.

44. John Seeley, "The Beneficial Encounter," in Seeley, *The
Americanization of the Unconscious,* p. 453.

THE CLINICIAN'S LIBRARY

ON DEHUMANIZING SITUATIONS

Bernard, Viola W., Perry Ottenberg, and Fritz Redl. "Dehumanization:
    A Composite Psychological Defense in Relation to Modern War."
    In Robert Perrucci and Marc Pilisuk, eds., *The Triple Revolution.*
    Boston: Little, Brown, 1968.
Ryan, William. *Blaming the Victim.* New York: Random House-Vintage,
    1972.

ON THE PRACTICE OF THERAPY

Danish, Steven, and Allen Hauer. *Basic Helping Skills.* New York: Be-
    havioral Publications, 1973.

Freedman, Alfred M., H. I. Kaplan, and B. J. Sadock. *Comprehensive Textbook of Psychiatry II*. Baltimore: Williams & Wilkins, 1975.

Lennard, Henry L., and Arnold Bernstein. *The Anatomy of Psychotherapy*. New York: Columbia University Press, 1960; and *Patterns in Human Interaction: An Introduction to Clinical Sociology*. San Francisco: Jossey-Bass, 1969.

Truax, Charles B., and Robert R. Carkhuff. *Toward Effective Counseling and Psychotherapy*. Chicago and New York: Aldine-Atherton, 1967.

ON SOCIAL FACTORS IN THERAPY

Clausen, John A. "Sociology and Psychiatry." In Alfred M. Freedman, H. I. Kaplan, and B. J. Sadock, *Comprehensive Textbook of Psychiatry II*, pp. 373–82. Baltimore: Williams & Wilkins, 1975.

Giordano, Joseph. *Ethnicity and Mental Health: Research and Recommendations*. New York: Institute on Pluralism and Group Identity, 165 E. 56th Street, n.d.

ON THE EFFECTIVENESS OF THERAPY

Fix, A. James, and E. A. Haffke. *Basic Psychological Therapies: Comparative Effectiveness*. New York: Human Sciences Press, 1976.

Herron, William G. "Further Thoughts on Psychotherapeutic Deprofessionalization." *Journal of Humanistic Psychology* 15, no. 3 (Summer 1975); and Oden, Thomas. "Consumer Interests in Therapeutic Outcome Studies: A Reply to Herron." *Journal of Humanistic Psychology* 15, no. 3 (Summer 1975).

Oden, Thomas. "A Populist's View of Psychotherapeutic Deprofessionalization." *Journal of Humanistic Psychology* 14, no. 2 (Spring 1974).

Spitzer, Robert L., and Donald F. Klein. *Evaluation of Psychological Therapies*. Proceedings of the Sixty-fourth Annual Meeting of the American Psychopathological Association. Baltimore: Johns Hopkins University Press, 1976.

Strupp, Hans H., and Allen E. Bergin. "Some Empirical and Conceptual Bases for Coordinated Research in Psychotherapy: A Critical Review of Issues, Trends and Evidence." *International Journal of Psychiatry* 7, no. 2 (February 1969).

SOCIOLOGICAL PERSPECTIVES ON THE MENTAL HOSPITAL

Goffman, Erving. *Asylums*. New York: Doubleday, 1961.
Stanton, Alfred H., and Morris S. Schwartz. *The Mental Hospital*. New York: Basic Books, 1954.
Strauss, Anselm, et al. *Psychiatric Ideologies and Institutions*. Glencoe, Ill.: Free Press, 1964.

SOCIOLOGICAL PERSPECTIVES ON MENTAL ILLNESS

Roman, Paul, and Harrison Trice, eds. *The Sociology of Psychotherapy*. New York: Aronson, 1973.
Rosenhan, D. L. "On Being Sane in Insane Places." *Science* 179 (19 January 1973).
Scheff, Thomas. *Labelling Madness*. Englewood Cliffs, N.J.: Prentice-Hall, 1975.
Weinberg, S. Kirson, ed. *Sociology of Mental Disorders*. Chicago: Aldine, 1967.

ON THE DELIVERY OF MENTAL HEALTH SERVICES

Chu, Franklin D., and Sharland Trotter. *The Madness Establishment*. New York: Grossman, 1974.
Dean, Alfred, A. Kraft, and B. Pepper, eds. *The Social Setting of Mental Health*. New York: Basic Books, 1976.
Enos, Darryl, and Paul Sultan. *The Sociology of Health Care*. New York: Praeger, 1977, especially chapter 9.
Hansell, Norris. *The Person in Distress*. New York: Behavioral Publications, 1975.
Park, Clara C. *You Are Not Alone*. Boston: Little, Brown, 1976.

PROVOCATIVE THINKERS ABOUT THE MEANINGS OF MENTAL ILLNESS IN CULTURAL CONTEXT

The following writers have produced numerous works. We suggest that the reader go to a local library or bookstore and choose titles that are of interest.

N. O. Brown	John Seeley
R. D. Laing	Philip Slater
Herbert Marcuse	Thomas Szasz

NOVELS AND FILMS

Green, Hannah. *I Never Promised You a Rose Garden.* New York: Holt, Rinehart and Winston, 1964; also film.

Kesey, Ken. *One Flew Over the Cuckoo's Nest.* New York: Signet, 1975; orig. 1962; also film

Wiseman, Frederick. *Titticut Follies.* Film.

Part 2

Theories
and
Methods

We are always looking at the world through sets of lenses. Just as it would be impossible to make sense of visual objects without the lenses of our eyes, so it would be difficult to make sense of social situations without sociological lenses to put the myriad events into perspective. As Kant reminded us, the objective world outside of our minds is always mediated by our thoughts, never directly apprehended by us. The quality of a social lens can be evaluated with criteria similar to those we apply to the lens of an eye. It should consistently provide useful, coherent, and complete representations. If it fails to do so, we try to repair it or supplement it with other lenses.

The sociological lenses come from the application of sociological theory to concrete situations. The comprehension of theory broadens our perspective, allowing us to move beyond what we already sense about our worlds and the world of significant others (including clients). The following three chapters present potentially useful perspectives from the major theoretical positions within sociology since its birth in the early nineteenth century. Much as physical lenses always distort, so do theoretical lenses. The sociological distortions are largely of three types.

Chapter 3 discusses those perspectives which rely upon analogies, or the type of lens that brings two discrete entities into focus simultaneously. Theorists use analogies as short-cuts which permit the comparison of something already understood with something one wishes to understand. The three analogies to be considered are organic, systems, and dramaturgical.

In chapter 4 we consider perspectives that deal with conflict, or lenses which bring into focus the moving and changing dimensions of social worlds. These perspectives include that of general conflict, exchange, and Marxist perspectives.

Chapter 5 looks "behind the scenes" to those perspectives that emphasize the subjective or interpretive nature of social life as it exists within human interactions. The theories of Weber and those of symbolic interaction and ethnomethodology are discussed.

Our discussion of theories is intended to be instructive and practical for the clinician, rather than comprehensive as might be expected in a volume devoted principally to sociological theory. Thus, exchange theory might also be considered an analogy (i.e., one which models all human relations upon economic relations); or the dramaturgical might be grouped as an interpretive theory.

A variety of activities are possible with lenses, including theoretical ones, and readers might wish to experiment with some of these even as they first read our descriptions and proposed uses for the lenses. Persons can switch lenses, add filters to lenses, interpret what comes through the lenses, discard lenses, hold a lens at various distances or angles to alter the image in size or shape, compare lenses, and so forth. Your own biography, creativity, and current clinical needs will make some of these perspectives more appealing than others. One activity which is *not* useful, however, is to pile the lenses one upon the other, until all that remains is a blur. Sometimes you may wish to use several theoretical perspectives to look at the same phenomena, but many are incompatible, and even those which are compatible lose their effectiveness when piled too high. We will offer suggestions for the appropriate uses of these theories by pointing out positive and negative aspects of each position presented, and through a discussion at the end of chapter 5 concerning how to choose theoretical lenses for specific clinical uses.

In chapter 6 we consider techniques traditionally employed by sociologists to explore concrete social situations. The formal methods—participant-observation, historical and documentary analysis, interviewing, surveys and statistics, and coordinated subsets—are rigorous forms of looking, listening, questioning, reporting, and critical thinking.

The major clinical use of these various theories and methods is *diagnosis*. In order to ascertain the problems of communities, groups, and group members, the clinician chooses some appropriate theoretical perspectives and methods for investigating the social situation and proceeds to conduct an analysis.

Chapter 3

Three Analogies

ORGANIC ANALOGIES—SOCIETY AS ANIMAL

Philosophers for many centuries compared societies with living organisms, but sociologists Herbert Spencer (1820–1903) and Charles Cooley (1864–1929) are credited with building systematic analyses of social life upon such analogies. Spencer noted that biological organisms and social units are distinguished from inorganic matter by growth throughout their lives. A tiny puppy grows up to be a full-sized dog; a tiny community becomes a major city. In both cases, the unit tends to continue enlarging until it either divides, gives birth to new entities, or is overwhelmed by outside forces and dies. Both also increase in structure as they increase in size. An embryo has few distinguishable parts, and in small communities most people engage in all activities. But after the embryo becomes a mature and independent organism, its parts are differentiated, and as a community develops so do its divisions of labor. Different organs perform different duties in animals, as do different occupations in societies, and in both cases these various parts come to rely upon one another for the survival of the larger unit. Destroying the lungs of an animal quickly stops the beating of the heart; a strike by seed producers quickly curtails farming activities.

When the larger organic or social unit is destroyed its individual parts may continue to live, at least for a while. We see this in the continuing contractions of muscles after the death of an animal, and in the continuing activities of certain agencies after a government has collapsed. However, a much more frequent situation is the continuation of a larger unit amid the death of some of its individual parts. Cells are constantly dying and being replaced within our bodies. Similarly, the personnel of an institution will change over time, and a healthy institution will not suffer as a result of this turnover. Indeed, successful organizations develop formal mechanisms for placing people in roles vacated by others who retire, die, or quit.

The distinction between the individual and society was of special interest to Charles Cooley in his organic analogies. Cooley did not construct elaborate comparisons with organic systems as did Spencer, but rather attempted to understand social units through analyses of the interactions of individuals within them. His major contribution was to specify that groups and individuals live and grow through interaction with one another, and hence changes affecting any part of a social unit affect the entire unit:

> A separate individual is an abstraction unknown to experience
> . . . . Society and individuals do not denote separable
> phenomena, but are simply the collective and distributive
> aspects of the same thing.[1]

Likewise, he saw debates about the relative importance of various units to be false issues. Controversies such as heredity vs. environment, mind vs. matter, and the individual vs. society disappear in Cooley's work. His organic view denies that any factor or factors are ultimately more important than any others.

Cooley analyzed the interactions within two types of social groups—the primary and the secondary. Primary groups are characterized by intimate, face-to-face interactions of individuals whose feelings and personality differences determine much of what transpires. The family, friendship groups, and tightly knit groups of workers or friends are examples. In contrast, secondary groups are characterized by more formality and less affective interactions. Only primary groups are capable of developing and maintaining social ideals such as faith, service, kindness, freedom, and separating right and wrong. These ideals can be learned only through direct and participatory experiences in a unified group.

Clinical sociologists will frequently encounter attempts to infuse such primary ideals into secondary groups and have to deal with the subsequent confusions among leaders of the groups when the attempts fail. An example many people experience occurs during childhood within formal schools. Teachers sometimes instruct students to care about one another, to value freedom, and on other ideals from primary groups. But these concepts frequently have no more personal impact upon the students than do algebraic equations, because in the school environment interactions with other people are largely restricted to formal exchanges between teacher and student or formal games between students on the playgound or informal exchanges in halls or bathrooms which are frequently limited and monitored.

In mental hospitals, sometimes the attempt is made to improve the primary values of the clientele through therapy. Staff members are formed into a team whose actions are supposed to demonstrate a therapeutic community. In most settings this is difficult to achieve because the staff also have to relate to each other in a hierarchical manner and have to produce so many records that the primary group emphasis is destroyed.

Functionalism

A major theoretical position which employs the organic analogy is *functionalism*. Its basic assumption is that any social unit (e.g., a group, an organization, or a society) transcends its constituent parts. Consequently, to understand any of the parts we must explain how they serve the larger unit as a whole. Every social practice is seen to serve a useful purpose for the whole, and those which cease to do so are expected to disappear. The organic image here is Social Darwinism; only the parts that are fittest survive.

Parsons   The leading contemporary functionalist is Talcott Parsons, who has defined four "functional imperatives" for all social units. These must be present for the social unit to survive.

Adaptation simply refers to the need for any group to produce the general materials necessary for its survival. The primary requisites are economic—the production of goods and services. Often the requisites are more complicated, however, as in the case of a medical clinic which requires licensed physicians, without which it cannot operate.

Goal attainment involves the use of resources. Most resources can be used in more than one way, and any group will be forced to decide how to expend its resources according to what it wishes to accomplish. City governments decide whether to put resources into cleaning up parks or increasing the salaries of teachers; families decide whether to buy a new stove or send a child to the eye doctor. Once the decision is made, the resources are goal-directed.

Pattern maintenance and tension management are the mechanisms which keep a social system running smoothly. Ongoing groups and organizations develop a variety of activities designed to keep at a minimum such processes as hostility and apathy. Most groups arrange ways for their members to release tensions so that the tensions will not harm the group. Among the most common are "coffee breaks" in work settings and the prejudices that ethnic groups display against one another.

Integration is accomplished through referees who try to resolve disputes between members of social units. At the societal level these are usually the legal systems, while in small groups they may be a single charismatic leader.

Parsons's "imperatives" can be found operating in most all clinical settings, and a good way for clinicians to evaluate the degree to which a setting is reproducing itself (i.e., remaining unchanged) is to check its success in accomplishing these four processes. An organization which is not accomplishing any of these processes is proabably undergoing a period of change, although its members may not be aware of the impending change. If the organization cannot reestablish these "imperatives," it will either become vestigial or extinct.

Durkheim   A most influential early functionalist was Émile Durkheim (1858–1917), whose ideas of *collective conscience* and *social facts* are indispensable in clinical settings. Often the clinical sociologist hears comments such as the following: "The direction of any community organization depends upon the personal whims of its leaders," or "Her father caused her suicide." These comments may appear quite different, but Durkheim would have found the same fallacy in each. Actions by the community leader, the father, and the daughter cannot be adequately understood on the basis of psychic processes alone, because their actions are influenced by the social worlds which surround them. Each of these persons acts not only on the basis of an individual conscience but also from a *collective conscience,* which consists of the interpenetration of many individual mentalities within groups and societies but results in a distinctive psychic unit. This collective conscience is not reducible to any individual within the society.

Most of our ways of thinking and acting are repeated by ourselves and by others. They become patterns which are distinguishable from the particular events within which they occur. As such they are *social facts* in themselves, quite apart from their particular manifestations within individuals. We can recognize a social fact by two of its properties: its power of coercion over individuals and its general diffusion within the group or society. We feel the effects of social facts and of the collective conscience almost daily. When we speak of "the system," "the Man," or even "they," we are often talking about such forces. When we act in a manner that upholds the status quo, our rationale is usually tied up with the collective conscience.

Even the most dynamic leader is constantly employing the general ways of thinking and acting within his or her society. Where else could a leader obtain basic material for developing a course of action except by comprehending the collective conscience. In the case of the suicide noted above, Durkheim's own study of suicides in the mid-1800s demonstrates the importance of social facts in understanding this phenomenon.

Durkheim observed that various events precede suicide. In one case a soldier committed suicide after being punished for a crime he did not commit; another person committed suicide after not being punished for a crime he did commit. Poor people and rich people both commit suicide, as do members of all ethnic groups. Amid the variations, Durkheim found three types of suicide:

Egoistic suicide occurs among people who have loose group attachments. Durkheim found that Protestants have a higher suicide rate than do Catholics or Jews, which, he explains, results from Protestantism being a less integrated or formal religion than Catholicism or Judaism. Durkheim argued that Jews had the lowest rate of all groups as a result of Jewish persecution and the resulting tight integration of the Jews in nineteenth-century Europe. He also found statistical evidence of higher rates for married people without children than for those with children, and higher rates for single, divorced, and widowed people.

Altruistic suicide is the other side of the coin. When individuals are too strongly integrated into a group they often commit suicide to avoid a loss of honor. Examples include elderly persons in nomadic tribes who end their lives to avoid being a burden on the rest of the tribe, and

Danish warriors who killed themselves to avoid the disgrace of growing old.

Anomic suicide results from extreme irregularity in social life. Durkheim found that suicide rates rise not only during times of economic depression but also during sudden periods of prosperity. In both cases the social equilibrium is shaken and stress results.[2]

Durkheim acknowledges that social facts are often difficult to distinguish from individual cases, but he notes:

> Statistics furnish us with the means of isolating them. They are, in fact, represented with considerable exactness by the rates of births, marriages, and suicides, that is, by the number obtained by dividing the average annual total of marriages, births, suicides, by the number of persons whose ages lie within the range in which marriages, births, and suicides occur. Since each of these figures contains all the individual cases indiscriminately, the individual circumstances which may have had a share in the production of the phenomenon are neutralized and, consequently, do not contribute to its determination. The average, then, expresses a certain state of the group mind.[3]

Whether via statistical or other analyses, it is only with careful scrutiny that the sociologist locates the influences of social facts and collective conscience. One difficulty is that individual and social facts are interrelated, as Durkheim noted in an organic analogy with a living cell. The cell consists of chemical elements, but the life of the cell is distinct from and external to these elements. Likewise, individuals make social facts and collective conscience, but these forces are external to individuals.

Another problem in investigating such forces is their apparent invisibility. Persons in everyday life seldom question the social location, history, or function of their decisions and usually prefer to attribute the decisions to their own immediate needs or psychological states. A clinical sociologist who pays particular attention to the functions of social processes operating in a given community can thereby provide a kind of "behind the scenes" description which may inform (and sometimes anger) actual participants in the situation.

For example, the sociologist may point out that persons of different classes, ethnicities, and religions are scattered throughout a city. Sociologists frequently note enclaves of persons of similar classes, races, and cultures clustering together. If individuals are asked why they live where they do, the reasons given are frequently personal, not collective. One must turn to quantitative data to see the patterns of distribution. Locate an orthodox synagogue and you will find Jews living in close proximity. And look to the fringes of the central city to find your skid rows and public housing.

Merton   Among the most informative functionalist concepts for clinicians are those of *latent functions* and *functional alternatives,* as proposed by Robert Merton. Latent functions are those which were unintended by the participants but nevertheless affect the social system of which they are parts. Recent events at a midwestern senior citizens' center exemplify the concept. Leaders at the center were faced with two interrelated problems: first, financial resources were running low, necessitating cutbacks in operating hours and maintenance of the facilities; and second, the reputation that the center was "going broke" made it difficult to recruit new dues-paying members. The leaders countered these problems with newsletters announcing that "our lean days are about to end," and that substantial contributions would be forthcoming from undisclosed sources. In their daily interactions around the center the leaders presented themselves as feeling optimistic and secure. The intended functions of these actions were to bolster morale of current members and encourage potential members to join the center. As the weeks passed without real financial improvement, the latent function of the propaganda was to create a credibility gap which eventually contributed to the demise of the center. The members no longer trusted the leaders, even when they actually acquired new funds.

Often the decision makers within a social system recognize that certain functional needs must be met, but unnecessarily limit the tactics available to meet these needs. The idea of *functional alternatives* sensitizes us to other possible ways to accomplish the same intended end. For instance, a clinical sociologist might have suggested to leaders at the senior citizens' center that they organize a fund-raising "local arts" weekend, or a protest demonstration at city hall—either of which might have functioned to improve morale through collective participation and the possibility of financial improvement.

An example of the functional alternative approach can also be seen in the proposal for an alternative to war by William James. His goal was for mankind to find a truly human enemy such as disease or poverty to replace warfare between nations. Anyone who has worked seriously in a community poverty program or in a committed medical research laboratory has experienced the feelings of being battleworn and in need of better armament.

On the other hand, it is equally important to be able to recognize when persons are employing functional alternatives—which may seem poor choices to an outsider—that are actually the only ones available that do not force the group to change other practices they value. Thus, in Zulu society women physically and verbally attack men during periodic "rituals of rebellion." These events may seem unusual until we recognize that (1) in Zulu society women are dominated by men, (2) Zulu women are prohibited from expressing aggression in everyday life, and (3) dominated groups tend to need some outlet for their aggression.[4] Other alternatives would require major changes in many aspects of Zulu culture, changes which the Zulu may not desire or of which they may be incapable.

Merton also theorized that not every member of the society might be conforming to the same goals or agreeing to the accepted means. He delimited in addition to conformists, "innovators," who accept goals, but not existing means for reaching the goals; "ritualists," who accept means, but lose sight of the goals; "retreatists," who accept neither means nor goals; and "rebels," who wish to substitute new means and goals for those that exist. This paradigm is useful for the clinical sociologist in determining the foci of individual clients or groups.

Warning: Analogies May Be Dangerous

Physical and social scientists frequently construct analogies, and to much the same end as literary people employ metaphors. Analogies and metaphors offer tremendous potential for understanding phenomena. Their power probably stems from the fact that many apparently discrete entities share features in common. Physical scientists used analogies between the heart and its vascular system and pumps and systems of pipes, with resulting discoveries of relationships between the mass of the heart, heartbeat frequency, and total mass of the animal. The relative usefulness of various analogies depends upon the degree of isomorphism between the items being compared, that is, the degree to which the items are similar along relevant dimensions.[5] An analogy between the heart and an egg beater would not have been adequate, for example, because similarities between the items are not significant. The analogy with pumps and pipes was obviously constructed with extreme care and on the basis of confirming or disputing empirical evidence. Clinicians need to be aware of the limitations within sociological analogies as well.

Spencer himself noted a couple of important differences between organic and social entities: first, an organic unit either lacks consciousness or concentrates it in a small and distinct location, while each member within social units has consciousness; and second, the parts of an organic unit exist for the continuance of the whole, while social units exist to ensure the continuance of the individual members. Both of these limitations are crucial concerns to symbolic interactionism. (See chapter 5.)

Others have pointed out that social units consisting of the same parts may constitute fundamentally different types,[6] as when a group of factory workers becomes an organized union. Such changes in type are difficult to imagine among organic units, except perhaps during metamorphoses.

Clinicians must also recognize that functionalist thought is found in a variety of sciences, and is often termed *teleological*. Teleological thought contends that each item or process is designed to fulfill a purpose. So fundamental are teleological assumptions in fields such as biology and anatomy that it is difficult to imagine such disciplines without this underlying view of the world. It seems "just natural" that "the function of the bladder is to excrete urine," for example, and much of the way we understand such processes rests upon these initial assumptions.

If we are to use teleological reasoning in clinical sociological practice, however, we need to be clear about what we mean by such usage, and under which conditions the usages are appropriate. Immediately a distinction needs to be made between *purposive* and *functional* activities. Group members get hungry, which is functional for the group, but it is automatic rather than purposive. The process is functional but not purposive. On the other hand, a group can decide to run around a city block with no function in mind other than accomplishing the running. Here is a case of purposive process which is not functional. If this distinction is ignored we are likely to attribute some "function" or "purpose" to every process, and often inappropriately.

The assignment of functions in organic sciences is based upon indications that the item contributes to one or both of the fundamental processes of reproduction and maintenance of life of the larger organic unit.[7] We would argue (as would the conflict theorists and Marxists described below) that maintenance of the life and reproduction of existing social systems is not the fundamental process of social units. Spencer's assertion that social units exist for the continuance of their individual members is the crucial distinction here. The fundamental processes of such systems are necessarily those of adapting to the needs of their internal parts, rather than to contingencies in their external environment. Hence, when we speak of the function of parts of a social unit we must limit ourselves to those which contribute to the larger unit's ensuring the future of the individual parts. This may even mean that a process which contributes to the death of an existing social unit is functional, if this death contributes to the betterment of the individual members. This is not to suggest that survival is seldom important for social units, only that it is not the fundamental process, and that we cannot determine functionality on the basis of contributions to survival.

This revised view of functions in social life also suggests, however, that integration of the parts within a social unit is to be accomplished for ends different than those of organic units. Integration of an organic unit is successful if it assists the unit in dealing with the outside world. Consequently, the best arrangement of parts in an organic system is one best suited to preparing the unit for encounters with external forces. Social units are of little value if they are so arranged that they deal effectively with external contingencies to the detriment of the needs of their members.

An additional limitation on the appropriate use of teleology is applicable not only to sociological uses, but to uses in any field of inquiry. Teleological views can blind us to the possibilities for choice and creativity if we attribute determinism to them. Finding that something is functional does not imply that it is *necessary*. The presence of a heart in vertebrates may be functional, but is not necessary for the vertebrate; for example, properly designed artificial pumps can perform the heart's function. Similarly, in-group unity may be functional for threatened groups, but so would be immediate removal of the threat by some especially capable members.[8] It is often as beneficial for a clinical sociologist to recognize or develop alternative ways of accomplishing functions within a social unit as it is to recognize the functions played by existing units.

GENERAL SYSTEMS THEORY—SOCIETY AS COMPUTER

A type of analogy which in recent years has replaced organic analogies among some sociologists has been that of complex machinery, most notably those which are self-regulating. In recent decades some sociologists have become fascinated with computers, as have persons in many other fields of inquiry.[9] In chapter 6 we will see some ways in which computer technological development and reasoning have affected the method of inquiry in sociology. They also affect the theoretical perspective which some sociologists employ to understand social phenomena.

Any set of elements which are related to one another in a nonrandom manner may be called a *system*. The planets and moon make up the solar system; related persons make up a family system; a series of persons and agencies make up a city government system. A system is not simply the sum of its constituent parts, however. Any system must be understood in terms of the relative positions of the elements to one another in space, and their movements over time.

A major goal of systems theorists is to construct *models*, or blueprints, which describe the ways in which systems look and operate over time. Once the theorist derives an accurate and complete model, he or she expects to be able to predict how the system will run in the future. Usually, the goal is to develop mathematical models which describe the movement of the elements of the system relative to one another (much as astronomers have provided for the movements of planets in solar systems).

The relationship of systems to one another is also very important. A systems theorist who attempts to understand the health care delivery system will research all of the systems involved—the biology of individuals, physicians' offices, international health agencies, and so forth. At each point the researcher is concerned to determine the echelons of the various systems and their organization in a hierarchy of systems (e.g., the relationships between community health systems and national health systems).

At each level of analysis systems theorists tend to explain the structures and operations of social systems by analogizing to complex machines. Perhaps the most frequently used aspect of these analogies is the input, output, and feedback processes found in many modern machines. Systems theorists have illustrated these processes with the example of thermostatic heating units. Temperatures produced by other systems in the environment are the input. When the temperature reaches a specified minimum level, the thermostat turns on the heating unit, which produces an output (heat). This heat is then influential in the later input temperatures of the system and thereby constitutes a feedback loop. Feedback can be either positive or negative. Positive feedback occurs when the relative change in the level of output results in a similar relative change in subsequent input: when an increase in output results in a subsequent increase in input, or when a decrease in output results in a decrease in input. Conversely, negative feedback occurs when the relative changes are just the opposite: when an increase in output results in a decrease in input, or when a decrease in output results in an increase in input.

Negative feedback systems are not difficult to find in clinical settings, and all result in imbalances in the systems. Examples include the business which increases the number of commodities it produces but profits per item decrease substantially enough that overall profits for the business go down, or the training center in which dropout and flunkout rates are rising, and in an attempt to offset this decrease in output of graduates the center becomes overcrowded by "creaming," that is, letting in additional new students of higher caliber.

Examples of the dangers of positive feedback are noted by medical sociologists Leon Robertson and Margaret Heagarty:

> A system may cease to operate when decreased output results in a later decrease in input. The physician who discovers a nonserious heart murmur in a child but does not explain that the child's activity need not be curtailed may initiate such a process. The parents, operating under the assumption that heart patients should not participate in vigorous exercise, decrease the child's activities. As a result of sedentary living, the child may gain weight and use oxygen less efficiently, thereby increasing the amount of work his heart must do. The resulting shortness of breath and lethargy may reinforce the parents' perception that the child is ill, causing them to limit his activities even further. If this cycle continues without interruption on the part of an environmental element, such as new information from the physician or other source, the heart or some other essential subsystem could conceivably be affected to the point that essential processes cease. The system is then static; that is, the person dies prematurely.[10]

Dangers of Systems Analogies

Most of the above critique of functionalist analogies applies to systems analogies, but some additional notes are in order. Most fundamentally, even sophisticated "artificially intelligent" machines are incapable of human action and must depend for their creation and continued existence upon human actions and social *interactions*. Human creativity invented the very machines which systems theorists are using to understand human social life.

In one regard such usage of machine analogies is very appropriate, however. As archeologists and some media researchers have emphasized repeatedly, our material creations reflect our social selves— our values, biographies, societal structures, and so on. Marshall McLuhan has noted:

> All media are extensions of some human faculty—psychic or physical. . . . The wheel is an extension of the foot. . . . Electric circuitry is an extension of the central nervous system. . . .[11]

Similarly, our machines are creations based upon observations of the ways our bodies are structured and operate and the ways other processes around us operate, including societies and social groups. Indeed, systems analogies are just barely removed from organic analogies. Key concepts in systems theory are often noted to occur in such organic systems as cells, ecosystems, or solar systems. Specific descriptions rely upon comparisons to the operation of similar processes in man-made material systems. The uses of systems analogies are therefore grounded, albeit circuitously, in human nature.

Nevertheless, systems analogies are inappropriate in several regards. A major difficulty emerges directly from the positive aspect noted above. To understand social phenomena via analogies to man-made systems is logically to eliminate any understanding beyond that which has already occurred in the creation of the existing material systems. Thus, sociological analogies based on processes operating in thermostatic heating systems will generally be limited to describing how the same creations used by persons in constructing thermostatic heating are used by persons in constructing social phenomena. This limits sociological discovery primarily to application of existing discoveries in other fields of inquiry. Evidence is readily available that people create processes and structures in social worlds which are not to be found in other man-made systems. Religious and ideological dimensions of social worlds are obvious cases. Systems theory may be applicable in describing various interacting units concerned with religion or ideology, but the insights derived from systems analogies concerning such phenomena are not likely to offer very complete understandings.

In many cases, systems theory is not even applicable. Consider Robert Boguslaw's distinction between established and emergent situations:

> An established situation is one in which all action-relevant environmental conditions are specifiable and predictable; all action-relevant states of the system are specifiable and predictable; available research technology or records are adequate to provide statements about the probable consequences of alternative actions. In contrast, an emergent situation is one in which some of these conditions do not prevail.[12]

Established social situations occur only in the most formal social environments, such as assembly-line work or in certain army barracks. Yet systems theory assumes established situations, or at least situations in which almost all conditions are understood and predictable.

Certainly many people and groups act predictably and as if they had no choices. In some cases, such as extreme poverty or under totalitarianism, many people in fact do not have choices. But to view social life as naturally or normally uncreative and devoid of choices is inappropriate. In clinical usage such an approach can encourage the sociologist to exclude important aspects of social situations simply because they are unpredictable (or uncorrelated with other aspects). These include historical processes, all of which are emergent.

The very language of systems theory can be destructive to clinical practice. Few people want to be considered "environmental elements" or "personnel requisitions." To think of them as such may be unethical, and is always incomplete. Although persons may be such things from the point of view of the system as a whole or major persons within the system, to themselves and their friends they are conceived quite differently.

DRAMATURGICAL ANALOGY—SOCIETY AS THEATER

Shakespeare reminded us in *As You Like It* that

> All the world's a stage,
> And all the men and women merely players:
> They have their exits and their entrances;
> And one man in his time plays many parts,
> His act being seven ages.

Elaborate and systematic use of the life-as-drama analogy characterizes the influential work of Erving Goffman and other *dramaturgical* analysts. Among their most basic concepts is that of *role*, a phenomenon so widely recognized that one hears people in everyday life talk about their "role in society," "playing the role of teacher," and so forth.

Goffman's analyses provide clinicians with a variety of techniques for understanding social situations, especially those at the micro (i.e., small group) level. Thus, a clinical sociologist working at a hospital would have a ready understanding of this incident reported to one of the authors by a medical student:

> They brought a guy into the operating room today who had greased-back hair and a tattoo on his chest. The surgeon and anesthesiologist explained to him about the operation and the procedures in a very formal way, calling him Mr. B., while they were putting him to sleep. But the second he was unconscious they started making fun of him and laughing to one another and telling dirty jokes. It was amazing and a little upsetting to see such a change in the doctors.

The change is an example of *frontstage and backstage* behavior. Everyday actors, like actors on the stage, provide different behavior when they are performing their "stage" roles than when they are not. The doctors noted above were playing their roles as proper professionals in front of their audience, the patient. When the patient was asleep the doctors began their backstage behavior, or the way they act with one another. Of course, in most settings there are more front- and backstages present than those which are immediately apparent. What is frontstage for one audience is backstage for another. The physicians' behavior after the patient was asleep probably represented another of their roles, that of colleague, which includes joking and irreverence; at home they may have had another frontstage behavior in the role of parent or spouse.

Most people play a variety of roles. Almost inevitably performance in some roles hinders performance in others, and may result in role conflicts. An example frequently seen in clinical practice with families is the conflict between occupational and leisure roles. Some occupations demand long periods away from the home, for instance, which can provoke difficulties with duties stemming from family roles. In other cases the difficulty comes from employing aspects of one role when performing in another role, such as the "bossy husband."

One might expect that persons with many roles would be more likely to encounter role conflicts than those with relatively few. To the contrary, research indicates that the more organizations an individual joins, the more likely she or he is to be active in all of them.[13] Role conflicts seem more often to result from the need to play two dissimilar roles at once, such as lover and therapist, or foreman and "one of the gang."

Clinicians can assist their clients by pointing out ways to effectively handle role conflicts or the impossibility of handling such conflicts. The simplest (though not necessarily most spontaneous) way is often to keep the roles separated. A therapist may choose to confine all romantic or sexual feelings to persons who are not patients; and a foreman may decide to be "one of the gang" only with other foremen, or with persons outside the workplace.

A less extreme remedy is to construct roles so that they adapt to one's needs, rather than consistently the other way around.[14] A therapist may choose to discuss with patients the reality that attractions may occur, and the costs and benefits of the various changes in the therapist role which could result; and a supervisor may decide to redefine his role with his superiors as one which permits him to be loyal to some of the workers' values when these are in conflict with those of management.

Another possibility is what Goffman calls *role distance*. This procedure permits a person to view the role being played *as* a role, thereby not taking it so seriously and discouraging others from taking it too seriously. The therapist may treat his or her role lightly by making jokes about the formality of other therapists; the foreman may encourage a bit of rule violation among "the gang," or gossip with them about what goes on in the executive offices.

In addition to analyzing roles, it is also instructive to view social situations according to the *types of plays* which occur. Consider the following factory situations:

In factory A the workers sit beside the conveyor belt from 9 A.M. to 5 P.M. daily, and each does his or her own piece of the work as the materials pass by. The workers seldom talk to one another. At 10:30 A.M. and 3 P.M. they go for ten-minute coffee breaks, and at noon they have a half-hour lunch break. They are supervised by a foreman, who paces up and down the line and disciplines the other workers, except when she or he is called into the plant manager's office to be disciplined or instructed concerning the changes on the assembly line. The plant manager sits in an office and receives communications from the district executives and dictates production reports for the secretary to send to those executives. One thousand items (plus or minus eight) are produced daily at factory A.

In factory B the workers sit beside the conveyor belt in groups of four. The members of each group work on a single aspect of the product's construction, while engaging in friendly conversation. Several of these foursomes make up a team, which holds meetings once a week to determine lighting conditions, union activities, starting and break times, and so forth, all of which change periodically. The teams in turn elect leaders who meet with the plant manager and occasionally with district executives concerning the operational strategies at the factory and the selection of new foremen and managers. One thousand items (plus or minus 50) are produced weekly at factory B, but some days' schedules are heavier than others, depending upon the kinds of meetings scheduled.

Factory C produces the same sorts of items as A and B, but in a variety of different colors, sizes, shapes, and prices; some are mass-produced and some handmade. Seldom will any particular batch of the items be closely duplicated. There are no workers, foremen, or managers on an ongoing basis, though at any particular moment persons may be serving those functions. The conveyor belt runs frequently, and persons sit around it working, but the ways they work and the speed of their work changes, along with the designs for the products. Often the belt is turned off and the people work in larger circles throughout the plant, putting things together or exchanging design suggestions. Some weeks 300 elaborate and creative "collectors" versions of the item are produced at factory C, other weeks 1200 which look like those at factories A and B.

The differences between the factories should be apparent. A and B are formal, scripted factories. Factory A's script is written by bosses distant from the factory itself. The actors themselves write the script for B. C is an avant-garde factory, in which there is no script and the activity is improvised by the actors throughout the production. Of course, in actual settings each type of play would take on many forms, depending upon the details; for example, in the avant-garde situation there might be improvisations with a director, specified length of performances, ascribed roles, flexible scripts, and so on.

The different types of plays offer various possibilities and limitations for the everyday actors. The goal in formal, scripted plays is to present the existing script in a way which is appealing to the audience. This is quite unlike the major goal in unscripted, avant-garde plays, which is to produce a unified series of creative improvisations which awaken new understandings or skills in both the audience and the actors. Formal plays have predictable outcomes but may lead to boredom, alienation, or decreasing creativity for the actors, while avant-garde plays provide possibilities for high involvement and creativity by the actors, but offer very little security, since the outcome cannot be accurately predicted in advance. The choice of which type of play is best for a given group can be made by evaluating the needs of the actors and their audiences.

The valuable skill which a practiced clinical sociologist can offer is to inform the everyday actors of the possibilities within various forms of production. In most cases the everyday actors are not even aware that they have chosen one among many types of plays.

Dangers

Dramaturgical analogies have their limitations as well, stemming from differences between everyday life and the theater. The most basic difference is that persons in everyday life usually believe themselves to be the roles they are playing, while stage actors do not. A stage actor will be Hamlet only on stage, and only for the run of the play. Indeed, most acting techniques recognize that one indication of acting talent is the ability to distance oneself from the part one is playing; any actor who thought himself to be Hamlet while offstage might be hospitalized for his delusions. On the other hand, the actor *is* expected to completely accept and display the everyday role of "professional actor" (and "lover," "friend," "parent," etc.). Goffman calls this distinction between playing a fictional role and playing an everyday life role *playing a role* vs. *playing at a role.*[15]

Another criticism is that dramaturgical analogy removes our attention from social processes which are not created by everyday social actors, but result from factors beyond their control, such as biological limitations and talents, class structures, or the functions people serve within the larger social system without being aware that they are doing so.[16] The implications of this criticism are two-fold. First, the dramaturgical analogy suffers from a kind of philosophical idealism in which inadequate attention is paid to the material forces affecting, and distinct from, the acts we perform for one another. Second, many of the aspects of social life neglected by dramaturgical analogies are carefully attended by other perspectives (e.g., the functions of roles). These suggest the need for testing a variety of sociological perspectives ("lenses") in clinical analyses, until one finds the combination which consistently gives useful understandings of the given situation.

NOTES

1. Charles Horton Cooley, *Human Nature and Social Order* (New York: Scribner, 1902), pp. 36–37.
2. Émile Durkheim, *Suicide* (New York: Free Press, 1951).
3. Émile Durkheim, *The Rules of Sociological Method* (New York: Free Press, 1964).
4. Max Gluckman, *Custom and Conflict in Africa* (New York: Barnes & Noble, 1964).
5. N. Rashevsky, "Is the Concept of an Organism as a Machine a Useful One?" in P. Frank, ed., *Validation of Scientific Theories* (New York: Collier, 1961).
6. A. R. Radcliffe-Brown, "On the Concept of Function in Social Science," *American Anthropologist* 37, no. 3 (1935):394–402.
7. Morton Beckner, "Teleology," *Encyclopedia of Philosophy* (New York: Macmillan, 1967):88–90.
8. Carl Hempel, *Aspects of Scientific Explanation* (New York: Free Press, 1965).
9. Walter Buckley, *Sociology and Modern Systems Theory* (Englewood Cliffs, N.J.: Prentice-Hall, 1967); and Leon Robertson and Margaret Heagarty, *Medical Sociology: A General Systems Approach* (Chicago: Nelson-Hall, 1975).
10. Robertson and Heagarty, *Medical Sociology: A General Systems Approach*, pp. 6–7.
11. Marshall McLuhan and Quentin Fiore, *The Medium Is the Massage* (New York: Bantam, 1967).
12. Robert Boguslaw, *The New Utopians* (Englewood Cliffs, N.J.: Prentice-Hall, 1965), pp. 7–8.
13. Erik Allardt et al., "On the Cumulative Nature of Leisure Activities," *Acta Sociologica* 3(1958):165–72.
14. Ralph Turner, "Role-taking: Process versus Conformity," in Arnold Rose, ed., *Human Behavior and Social Process* (London: Routledge, 1962).
15. Erving Goffman, *Encounters* (Indianapolis: Bobbs-Merrill, 1961), pp. 99–100.

16.   Alvin W. Gouldner, *The Coming Crisis of Western Sociology* (New York: Avon Books, 1970), p. 380.

THE CLINICIAN'S LIBRARY

Several informative overviews describe the spectrum of sociological theories which we consider in the present chapter and in chapters 4 and 5. These include the following:

Coser, Lewis, and Bernard Rosenberg, eds. *Sociological Theory.* New York: Random House, 1967. A collection of major writings by major theorists.

Hawthorn, Geoffrey. *Enlightenment and Despair.* New York: Cambridge University Press, 1976. A pithy history of sociological theories placed in philosophical contexts.

Martindale, Don. *The Nature and Types of Sociological Theory.* Boston: Houghton Mifflin, 1960. Comprehensive, comparative, and critical, though somewhat dated.

Timasheff, Nicholas. *Sociological Theory: Its Nature and Growth.* New York: Random House, 1967. Inventory of important aspects of most theoretical perspectives.

Truzzi, Marcello. *Sociology: The Classic Statements.* New York: Random House, 1971. Contains excerpts from many of the most influential theoretical writings in sociology.

Turner, Jonathan. *The Structure of Sociological Theory.* Homewood, Ill.: Dorsey Press, 1978. A careful and critical overview.

ORGANIC AND FUNCTIONAL THEORIES

Among the most significant statements by the creators of organic analogies and functionalism are the following:

Demerath, Nicolas, and R. Peterson, eds. *System, Change and Conflict.* New York: Free Press, 1967.

Durkheim, Émile. *The Rules of Sociological Method.* Chicago: University of Chicago Press, 1938; and Spaulding, J., and G. Simpson, trans. *Suicide.* New York: Free Press, 1951.

Malinowski, B. *A Scientific Theory of Culture and Other Essays.* Chapel Hill: University of North Carolina Press, 1944.

Merton, Robert K. *Social Theory and Social Structure*. New York: Free
    Press, 1968.
Parsons, Talcott. *The Social System*. New York: Free Press, 1951.
Radcliffe-Brown, A. R. *Structure and Function in Primitive Society*. Lon-
    don: Cohen and West, 1952.
Spencer, Herbert. *The Principles of Sociology*. New York: Appleton,
    1898.

Critical works concerning organic analogies and functionalism
include Martindale (noted above), plus the following:

Gouldner, Alvin. *The Coming Crisis of Western Sociology*. New York:
    Basic Books, 1970.
Zeitlin, Maurice. *Rethinking Sociology*. New York: Appleton, 1973.

SYSTEMS THEORIES

The work of Parsons (noted above) is often a type of systems theory
and analogy. General systems theory per se is described in the following volumes:

Buckley, Walter. *Sociology and Modern Systems Theory*. Englewood
    Cliffs, N.J.: Prentice-Hall, 1967.
Robertson, Leon, and M. Heagarty. *Medical Sociology: A General Systems
    Approach*. Chicago: Nelson-Hall, 1975.

Two of the best critiques are:

Boguslaw, Robert. *The New Utopians*. Englewood Cliffs, N.J.: Pren-
    tice-Hall, 1965.
Hoos, Ida. *Systems Analysis in Public Policy: A Critique*. Berkeley, Cal.:
    University of California Press, 1972.

DRAMATURGICAL THEORIES

Most of the highly influential books concerning dramaturgical
theories are by a single author:

Goffman, Erving. *Asylums*. Garden City, N.Y.: Doubleday Anchor,
    1961; *Encounters*. Indianapolis: Bobbs-Merrill, 1961; *Frame*

Analysis. New York: Harper Colophon Books, 1974; and *Presentation of Self in Everyday Life.* Garden City, N.Y.: Doubleday Anchor, 1959.

Huizinga, Johan. *Homo ludens.* Boston: Beacon Press, 1955.

A critique of the dramaturgical analogy appears in Gouldner's *Crisis* (noted above).

Chapter 4

Conflict Theories

Perspectives which pay special attention to the material forces in social life are often called conflict theories, because they examine the struggles between persons and groups for goods and privileges. We consider below two specific theories of conflict—Marxist and exchange theory—but first a discussion is appropriate concerning the more general conflict perspectives.

One of the oldest and most persistent debates throughout the history of the world involves the question, "Is human existence characterized by stability or by change?" Han Confucianism in Japan long held that the universe and its parts are stable and orderly, but the beliefs of the Confucians were challenged by Madhyamika Buddhism in the sixth century A.D., which emphasized universal change.[1] In the West, Heraclitus posited change as omnipresent. Another thoughtful warrior against "natural" stability was Niccolò Machiavelli, who wrote at the beginning of the sixteenth century. In his *Discourses* he describes the inevitability of jealousy within power relationships, which leads to conspiracies against leaders and overthrows of existing orders.

A major conflict theorist in the seventeenth century was Thomas Hobbes, who emphasized the incompatible desires of men and groups. He stressed that when people band together in groups, conflicts are inevitable as the various factions attempt to satisfy their desires at the expense of others. Hobbes's solution to this constant strife was the State, ruled by a sovereign who would settle all disputes.

Ludwig Gumplowicz was probably the first major sociological conflict theorist. Writing in the late nineteenth century, he argued the importance of social groups in provoking conflicts and determining what shape they took. The group is viewed as the source of desires and morals; individuals are simply the products of their social groups. Groups inevitably fight with one another, and Gumplowicz offered two hypotheses for why this is so: either polygenetic theories are correct and the human species developed from different original groups which had no blood bonds; or hatred between groups has simply built up over the years and become insurmountable.[2]

The important conflict notion of *interest* emerged in the work of Albion Small, who brought conflict theory to prominence in American sociology during the early part of this century. Small contended that interests were the sociological equivalents of atoms in the physical sciences. They are the basic units of which social life is built.

The fundamental interest is said to be health, and humans share this with other animals. But humans organize groups and societies because they have a wide variety of additional interests as well, which can be satisfied only (or more easily) through such agencies. The major social interests noted by Small are wealth, sociability, knowledge, beauty, and rightness. Group interests exist as well:

> The practical politician looks over the lobby at Washington, and
> he classifies the elements that compose it. He says: "Here is the
> railroad interest, the sugar interest, the labor interest, the
> army interest, the canal interest, the Cuban interest, etc." He uses
> the term "interest" essentially in the sociological sense but in
> a relatively concrete form, and he has in mind little more than
> variations of the wealth interest. He would explain the legislation
> of a given session as the final balance between these conflicting
> pecuniary interests. He is right, in the main: and every social
> action is, in the same way, an accommodation of the various
> interests which are represented in the society concerned.[3]

Small's conflict theories describe persons and groups competing to achieve their various interests. Whenever some interests are realized, the overall social structure is changed. Usually the change is a shift in which of the individuals and groups possess goods and privileges.

Small translated into English the conflict theories of Georg Simmel, a nineteenth-century German sociologist, who emphasizes the positive uses of conflict. The most famous of these is that conflict can be the basis for formation of groups or for increasing cohesion within a group. Thus, persons may form an army to fight a common enemy and will tend to become a more unified army when the enemy is most threatening.

Another positive use of conflict frequently seen in clinical practice is the release of tensions and, concurrently, the unspoken sources of these tensions. Some clinicians go so far as to recommend that married couples engage in periodic conflict in order that tensions be released and emotional interactions initiated. The couples are encouraged to learn how to fight fairly. Simmel warns that within close primary groups such as families there is the tendency to deal with conflict by avoiding it, often because the individuals fear that the group cannot endure a major battle. In fact, a battle is an occasion of high levels of interactions, and groups or relationships which are worth keeping should be able to live through such periods and actually derive important learning from the conflict.[4]

Conflict is seen as a social *process* by Simmel, rather than a one-time disruption of an ongoing order, as would be suggested by some forms of the organic analogy or certain interpretations of functionalism. Some functionalists have also recognized the utility of conflict, however. Lewis Coser listed several "functions of social conflict" in addition to the uses noted by Simmel and the earlier conflict theorists:

1.   Conflict may be a means of last resort to a desired end. Once the less traumatic means have been exhausted, conflict is sometimes a reasonable alternative.
2.   In addition to increasing group unity, conflict with other groups can increase acceptance of deviants within a group. This results from group members coming to view their similarities as more significant (in the face of an enemy) than their differences.
3.   Conflict can result in more accurate assessments of groups concerning each other, and the establishment of a balance of power.
4.   Factions may arise during conflicts and view one another as having the same interests, with the result that new alliances develop.[5]

Recognizing the utility of conflict in given situations can help clinicians to see through the mere appearances presented by clients, and to accomplish what Nietzsche called "the art of mistrust." For instance, vicious and continuous anger is not necessarily as deadly as it seems. Any feeling has limits, and ongoing conflicts are usually carried out according to a set of mutually understood rules which restrain the opponents from conquering one another. These rules exist for a couple of reasons: both parties want to retain some ability to predict what will occur in future days and weeks, even during a state of warfare; and both parties expect to have to live with one another after the battle.

The need to understand the uses and boundaries of particular conflicts is illustrated by a study of fights on an elementary school playground. Many fights occurred whenever the children were playing together, but the fights were of two distinct varieties. During "play fights" (1) no one was going to consider himself or herself badly hurt, (2) the fighting partners were either ambivalent toward one another or were friends, and (3) the outcome (i.e., who would win) was considered very important, but this outcome settled nothing more than who was the best fighter. "Real fights" were just the opposite. It was expected that someone might be seriously injured, the fight partners defined themselves as enemies, and the outcome determined something besides fighting ability (e.g., "you're going to stop bothering me").

The point to be emphasized, however, is that to a casual observer the play fights would appear more violent and dangerous than the real fights. A child was likely to be more tired after a play fight than after a real fight, and often greater strength was used during the play fights. The amount of objective injury (bruises, blood shed, etc.) seemed about the same in both fights, but much more crying was exhibited after real fights.[6]

One of the functions of sports in our society is to provide controlled conflict allowing for tension release. Different sports take different forms, and one's preference might have something to do with how one wants conflict served up.

EXCHANGE THEORY

A perspective influenced heavily by the work of Simmel is Peter Blau's *Exchange and Power in Social Life*, published in 1964 and already a major influence on many sociologists. Blau maintains that social exchange is the fundamental activity which occurs in and between social groups and institutions. Reciprocity is viewed as an essential condition for the accomplishment of social life, with persons constantly in give-

and-take relationships with one another. In general, the giving occurs in order to get something back, or to avoid the punishment which is expected if one refuses to give.

Blau's own major application of exchange theory was a study of relationships between supervisors and workers in formal organizations, such as offices, factories, and hospitals. He found that supervisors seek favorable evaluations from workers and exchange "favors" in order to get such evaluations. The favors are services which the supervisor voluntarily provides in addition to the expected services (such as regular pay and coffee breaks). Effective favors include nonenforcement of some of management's rules, or joining the workers in making nasty comments about the factory or about management. In these ways the supervisor exchanges gifts for personal loyalty and respect.

Exchange theory has also been applied in a quite different manner in a study of prejudice by Swiss workers against foreign workers. The Swiss workers are in an exchange relationship with their employers (as in Blau's studies), and one of the favors which the employers can offer their Swiss workers is antagonism against foreign workers. This antagonism is beneficial to the Swiss workers because they are in competition with the foreigners for jobs and raises. The foreigners work for less pay than do the Swiss. When employers discriminate against foreign workers and support anti-immigration laws, they receive loyalty and better bargaining positions with the Swiss workers.[7]

What happens when exchange relations break down is illustrated by a study of a British boarding school. A charismatic and respected headmaster permitted the students much more freedom than in traditional schools, and things ran smoothly until the headmaster retired. The new leadership was less charismatic, and unaware of the exchange arrangements of privileges for good behavior. In the face of impending anarchy throughout the school, the new headmaster began strict enforcement of rules, which resulted in angry reactions from the students.[8]

The Swiss and British studies illustrate that social exchange has two faces. Not only do we exchange privileges and compliments, we also exchange restrictions and antagonisms.

MARXISM

By far the most elaborate and influential conflict theories are those of Karl Marx and persons who have built upon his analyses. They focus especially upon the modes of production, techniques for coordination, and persons involved in transforming nature into human products. Marx analyzed in detail the dominant modern mode of production—capitalism—and described how it affects social relations. The material relations of production are shown by Marx to direct the general drift of politics, the arts, ethics, and people's everyday lives.

Marx can be viewed as an economic therapist. He analyzes the ill effects of capitalism and proposes as a more healthy state a system of voluntarily and democratically organized communist collectives. We are not concerned here with presenting a general introduction to Marxism or the works of Karl Marx. The details of his economic theory, analyses of the rise and fall of capitalism, his political program, and the debates with other philosophies are not central to the daily work of clinical sociologists. But at least four notions within Marx's work are generally applicable in clinical practice: class, alienation, power, and dialectic.

Social Classes

Most of us get up each morning and go either to a job, to school to prepare for a job, or to the marketplace to apply for a job. Most of our time is spent laboring, thinking about laboring, or preparing to labor. The centrality in Marxist thought of man as a laborer distinguishes most all of its analyses from those developed on other basic sociological views of man, such as man as an actor, man as a trader, or man as an organic part. For Marx, the conditions of a person's or group's labor determine most everything else about that person or group:

> As individuals express their lives, so they are. What they are . . . coincides with their production, both with what they produce and *how* they produce. The nature of the individuals thus depends on the material conditions determining their production.[9]

The fundamental distinction between persons is that some own the means of production and others do not. The owners Marx called "bourgeoisie," and the others, who must sell their labor to the bourgeoisie, he called the "proletariat." Marx recognized that within these two basic groups are many subunits, and that few persons are fully members of the bourgeoisie or proletariat throughout their entire lives. Nevertheless, our position within the system of production does give us a distinct set of common interests and experiences with others in similar positions. Thus, the development of a central city convention center serves the interests of people who own businesses in the central city, as well as people who will be employed in jobs created by the center. On the other hand, it is detrimental to the interests of people who are displaced from their homes by construction of the center. Central cities tend to be populated by lower-class and unemployed persons, while convention centers tend to support the labor and entertainment of middle- and upper-class persons.

The various experiences and interests within social classes result in another difference as well, different values. Middle-class values include achievement and ambition, independence, and manners, while working-class values include collectivism, staying home, and "not putting on airs." One clinician, born in the middle class, quickly lost respect and effectiveness in working with a lower-class organization when he stressed development of projects which would "get you out of this run down neighborhood and dependency upon neighbors who are as poor as you are."

Although lower-class persons do appear more collectivist in their neighborhoods and their public opinions than do the middle and upper classes, Marx pointed out that they are not as unified as they first appear, nor as they should be for their own good. Lower-class persons come together more often in large groups and live more collectively than do upper- and middle-class persons residing in anonymous suburban dwellings. But so far the most massive collective social activity in the world is that of monopoly capitalism. The small neighborhood business has been replaced throughout the Western world by large "chain" stores. Mergers and internationalization of business operations have turned most smaller businesses into cogs within huge conglomerates. Lower-class persons may see their neighbors more often, but they neither own nor control their neighborhoods.

Monopoly capitalism affects the social lives of individuals and groups daily, and in ways important for the clinician to recognize. Capital expansion is the central concern of corporations, and to accomplish such expansion they must raise prices, decrease production costs, or sell more items to produce higher profits (i.e., new capital). What is actually produced are increasing amounts of what Marx called "surplus value"—the value that is in addition to that needed to provide for the subsistence of the workers and is turned into expansion capital in one way or another. Some common ways to produce such surplus value are assembly-line speed ups, built-in obsolescence, style changes, fads, automation, extended credit, poorer quality goods, and creating new "must haves" (e.g., self-cleaning ovens and television computerized games). We are in many ways *capital created people*, and the source of frequently occurring clinical problems can sometimes be explained in terms of the needs of monopoly capitalism. The alcohol abuse or drug use of bored or harried factory workers, the frustration or introversion of teenagers whose parents cannot afford to buy them the newest styles, the husbands who abandon their families after extending credit beyond their means, and the depression of talented persons forced to accept uncreative jobs or go on welfare are just a few of the problems. Indeed, conditions such as inflation, job insecurities, and the confusion of spiritual happiness with material acquisition affect most of us daily. They damage many of our social situations. Yet each of these conditions generally benefits monopoly capitalism and members of the upper class.

As described in chapter 2, many clinicians do their part to maintain the system. Psychiatrist Ron Leifer critically describes the "community psychiatry" approach:

> Described in nonmedical terms, community psychiatry is a quasi-political collectivist movement that, by means of social interventions supported by state sanctioned social power, attempts to palliate personal troubles, to foster the orderly and productive functioning of individuals in their communities and organizations, to alleviate certain disturbances of domestic tranquility, to organize and integrate community action programs, to implement the dominant social ideology. . . .[10]

The influence of capitalism's needs is not limited to the material dimensions of our lives, however. "The ideas of the ruling class are in every epoch the ruling ideas: i.e., the class which is the ruling material force of society, is at the same time the ruling intellectual force. The class which has the means of material production at its disposal, has control at the same time over the means of mental production," Marx contends. This is apparent not only in obvious cases such as selection by members of the upper classes of "great" art for museums and "proper" English for classroom usage, but more importantly, in the everyday thoughts of members of other social classes. The ideology of individual success and competing with others of one's social class in order to move up slightly on the income and prestige ladder is another example, as were the radical "law and order" demands of a few years ago by the working class, the reaction of middle-aged whites against the social protests of working-class blacks, and that of middle-class youths in the United States.

Most contemporary Westerners live rather isolated lives. The lower classes seldom directly encounter the upper classes, who live and work elsewhere. Many middle-class persons have lately created suburbs which remove them from any extensive contact with either the lower or the upper classes. Production facilities are divided into sections, each containing persons from only one social class (e.g., production lines and management offices).

In a study of middle-class, white-collar workers, C. Wright Mills concludes:

> Newly created in a harsh time of creation, white collar man has no culture to lean upon except the contents of a mass society that has shaped him and seeks to manipulate him to alien ends. . . . This isolated position makes him excellent material for synthetic molding at the hands of popular culture—print, film, radio, and television.[11]

This popular culture is full of advertising images and messages from the monopoly capitalist corporations who determine what will be distributed and what will not.

Alienation

This Marxist concept is so descriptive of much of modern everyday life it has found its way into daily usage, albeit in distorted ways. Marx described three specific aspects of alienation, all of which derive from the objective conditions of capitalism: workers are alienated from the products they produce; their work activities are alien to them and thereby cause them to see even themselves as alien beings; and they are alienated from their "species being," or from their human capacity for conscious and creative activity. All of these aspects result from the nature of capitalism, which exploits labor to create capital, which in turn is used to further exploit labor.[12]

Labor itself is not alienating in Marx's view. Indeed, labor can be a major source of happiness, but only when it is productive of the development of persons, of our spiritual well-being. Under capitalism labor is seldom productive of our selves, but rather is productive solely of material items and of additional capital to produce other material items.

Any person who has struggled to create a hand-crafted gift for someone else, or to deliver a child, or to cook an elegant meal, or to really understand an intellectual idea, can appreciate this positive side of laboring. As Hannah Arendt put it:

> There is no lasting happiness outside the prescribed cycle of painful exhaustion and pleasurable regeneration, and whatever throws this cycle out of balance—poverty and misery where exhaustion is followed by wretchedness instead of regeneration, or great riches and an entirely effortless life where boredom takes the place of exhaustion and where the mills of necessity, of consumption and digestion, grind an impotent human body mercilessly and barrenly to death—ruins the elemental happiness that comes from being alive.[13]

For most of us today the intrinsic value of labor is seldom experienced, since our labor is exchanged primarily for material goods. This is true not only for the poor and the rich, or for the bored assembly-line worker and the tired retailer, but also for persons in potentially more interesting work. Many nurses soon after their training become clockwatchers and paper-shufflers rather than people-helpers, and many professors come to campus only to recite lectures which bore even themselves. A frequent syndrome among students is the nonintellectualism of studying "for the grade," which is exchangeable for jobs or graduate training (in turn exchangeable for jobs). And who can blame any of these people in a society which places everything in monetary and consumptive terms?

Economist Thorstein Veblen noted at the turn of the century that a major pastime of the upper classes, and increasingly of the other classes, was what he called "conspicuous consumption."[14] For the upper classes, consumption of expensive items serves to distinguish a person's status. Driving a larger car, drinking an older wine, and redecorating or enlarging the family's house all constitute status symbols which are major sources of pride for many persons. In middle-class families this is no less prevalent, although "keeping up with the Joneses" may require fewer dollars.

Clinicians involved in therapy with group members frequently encounter clients who temporarily relieve their depressive or bored states through consumption. A client once told an author of this book,

> The only reason our family needs therapy is because we over ex-
> tend our credit to the verge of bankruptcy. My salary is $20,000
> a year, but we're always broke. Whenever I get depressed I
> go shopping in order to get up enough energy to go back to work
> the next week. And whenever my wife gets bored she buys a
> whole new wardrobe. The kids feel cheated because we refuse to
> give them as much spending money as their friends have, and so
> they are left out of the Saturday afternoon trips to the shopping
> center.

Our alienation has become so generalized that we even judge qualita-tive items in quantitative terms. Food and drink are often evaluated not only on the basis of their taste, but by comparing the reputation and price of chefs or brands. Even more alarming in this regard is the gen-eral application of cost-benefit reasoning in human policy decisions. When a "developer" wishes to destroy family farms the discussion is typically put in monetary or consumptive terms, both by governmental decision makers *and* the farmer. The value of the farm to the farmer is compared to the value of the new businesses or housing to the larger community. Usually the farm is purchased at a price prescribed as ap-propriate to the market value of the property, considering the income the farm would provide in the next few years plus the hardship the sale will cause the farmer. But is hardship something which can or should be defined monetarily? How does one measure in dollars the change in lifestyle for the farmer and his family (including members who will be born after the sale)?

Alienation, then, is not only a malady which hits persons who seem "out of it." Our modes of production have created nations consisting for the most part of alienated persons. We are alienated from our labor, from our land, from our neighbors, even from our machines—how many of us feel free to unplug our telephones when we do not wish to be disturbed, much less know how to repair them when they break?

The Dialectic

Plato introduced the process of logical discussion called "dialectic" in his *Republic*. It is a method for eliciting from persons information that they possess, but of which they are not immediately aware. Plato illustrates the technique by Socrates' questioning of Meno, a slave child who had never studied geometry. Some theories of Euclid are elicited from the boy through a line of questioning which proceeds as follows: Socrates proposes a thesis, then requests a contrary (but equally reasonable) *antithesis*. This process is repeated several times with theses and antitheses about the phenomenon being studied. Eventually a true account emerges which encompasses and reconciles the major thesis and antithesis into *synthesis*.

Hegel, probably the most influential German philosopher of the nineteenth century, extended Plato's notion beyond the realm of discourse or teaching. For Hegel, dialectical processes were the actual way events occur in the world, quite apart from our discussion of these processes. All change—and Hegel paid special attention to historical change—takes place in the form of dialectic: a thesis is produced, an opposition (antithesis) develops, a conflict ensues, and the conflict is resolved into a synthesis which includes both thesis and antithesis.

Hegel found the dialectic operating both in physical nature and in societies. An acorn has its own form and substance quite distinct from an oak tree, and yet acorns become oak trees. Nations have their form and substance as well, and during a nation's development it produces its opposition. Eventually there is a conflict between the nations and from the struggle emerges a new nation which synthesizes aspects of the previous nations but is distinct. This new nation in turn produces its own antithesis, and so the process continues ad infinitum.[15]

The analysis of history as a dialectic was revised by Marx, who as a young German intellectual had been greatly influenced by Hegel's writings. Marx stressed that the significant social opposites in the world are not nations but social classes, and that the unity of opposites is not as immediate as Hegel claimed (e.g., some acorns never get planted, some social classes are separated from one another).[16]

The primacy of the dialectic of class conflict has emerged historically, according to Marx. First the king-states broke down into opposites of kings and slaves. From this conflict emerged the new synthesis, feudalism, which dissolved into conflict between lords and serfs, then synthesized into capitalism. Now capitalism is breaking down, Marx claimed, into employer and employee (bourgeoisie and proletariat), and the new synthesis is predicted to be Marxian democratic socialism.[17]

Few clinical sociologists have occasion to develop dialectical analyses of history, though in many cases they may wish to place their client groups within such analyses in order to better understand their problems and social relations. On the other hand, dialectical reasoning can be quite useful to clinicians for understanding changes within and between groups. One can diagram the battles between two opposing factions, take into account the likely effects of mediating contingencies, and often develop some general idea of the synthesis which is likely to develop. Thus, in a battle between two community organizations, one can often determine the mediating factors (e.g., physical distance or local government intervention), the deeply entrenched values and goals of each group, and upcoming interaction situations. From an understanding of these may be predicted the type and chronology of syntheses which are possible, such as a new organization absorbing both of the older ones or an agreement for mutual cooperation in some endeavors.

Appreciation of dialectical processes can also prevent the prevalent confusion of *qualitative* and *quantitative* dimensions of social phenomena. In physical worlds we easily recognize that when water is properly heated it becomes steam, and that water and steam are different physical qualities. The difference cannot be adequately understood simply in terms of the difference in quantities of temperatures. But some social analysts regularly confuse qualitative and quantitative changes. For instance, the difference between a hospital ward which is serving the real needs of its patient and employee populations and one which is not doing so cannot be reduced to the number of patients per nurse, cost per patient, types of protocol between patients and staff, allocation of space, or the like. The wards do not simply contain quantitative differences, they contain social processes and structures which are qualitatively different as well. The differences between such adequate and inadequate wards are historical differences which have developed through the conflicts of opposing groups in meeting the changing conditions in which they find themselves. To understand the wards one must understand these processes. Friedrich Engels noted:

> The great basic thought that the world is not to be comprehended
> as a complex of ready-made *things,* but as a complex of *pro*
> *cesses,* in which things apparently stable no less than their
> mind-images in our heads, the concepts, go through an uninter
> rupted change of coming into being and passing away, in
> which, in spite of all seeming accidents and of all temporary re
> trogression, a progressive development asserts itself in the

end—this great fundamental thought has, especially since the time of Hegel, so thoroughly permeated ordinary consciousness that in this generality it is scarcely ever contradicted.[18]

Reification

Social situations are not usually viewed by persons in everyday life in the ways we have been discussing. The tendency is rather to view social worlds, which are products of human processes, as external and objective reality. Social worlds are taken-for-granted reality, and therefore conceived as outside human control.[19] This process of *reification* occurs constantly, with the educator who stresses "the school's needs" to the politician describing "what this country really wants." Relationships between people are given the appearance of things rather than processes.

Peter Berger and Thomas Luckman note a type of reification which clinicians working with married couples find regularly:

> Marriage . . . may be reified as an imitation of divine acts of creativity, as a universal mandate of natural law, as the necessary consequence of biological or psychological forces, or, for that matter, as a functional imperative of the social system. What all of these reifications have in common is their obfuscation of marriage as an ongoing human production.[20]

The forms which reifications take are usually of the variety, "I can't help it, the system makes me do this," or "That's just the way things are, and you must adjust to them or suffer the consequences." Reification is the cover story for feelings of powerlessness.

Clinical Marxism?

Throughout this discussion of Marx and Marxism we have used the perspective for diagnosis of sources of certain difficulties. Some readers may wonder what purpose is served by diagnoses claiming that "the needs of monopoly capitalism are producing your family fights." On the surface, such an analysis may seem of as little value to a sociological client as would the medical diagnosis that "streptococci in your environment caused your sore throat." The client's question becomes, "So what can I *do* about it?"

Most community physicians realize that sufficient answer to such a question is seldom a simple, "Take this medication." Among the possible responses to the patient's question are the following recommendations: reorganizing the environment in which one lives (or removing oneself from that environment) to avoid reinfection at a later date; protecting one's friends and acquaintances from the disease; accompanying the medication with other methods of treatment (e.g., rest); and avoiding secondary infections.

So it is with Marx-influenced diagnosis and therapy. Marx did offer prescriptions for the ills of society, most notably in his *Manifesto* with Engels. He recommended a proletarian revolution and democratic socialism.

Some clinicians prefer weaker and more readily available prescriptions. In fact, some sociologists who consider themselves Marxists have proposed remedies, even long-term ones, which do not include revolution. Regardless of the sort of restructuring of the modes of production one feels is most appropriate, that cannot be the total therapy program.

Therapists working with problems created by capital can be of immediate use to their clients through a three-stage program. First, a good deal of suffering can usually be relieved by bringing the clients to the understanding that theirs is not an isolated, individual feeling or difficulty but rather a societal difficulty that manifests itself in a variety of ways in different classes and groups. The pain of some forms of alienation can be relieved almost completely by the realization that other persons who seem so alien are experiencing life situations much like one's own. This accounts for the expansion of self-help groups, as described in part 4.

Similar sorts of pain relief often result from the application of a historical perspective to group members' problems. C. Wright Mills, a scholar of Marx's work, specified the dangers of confounding the notions of biography and history. *Biography* refers to those conditions which an individual experiences as uniquely his or her own. *History* refers to the widespread changes within social structures and interaction patterns over time which affect the life situations of societies, groups, and individuals. Sorting problems according to this distinction can provide the appropriate context for dealing with the problems. Persons often experience history as a series of personal difficulties, when these problems are actually shared throughout communities.[21]

The therapist can also assist in locating or constructing environmental and labor possibilities which do not require blind submission to such needs of capitalism as conspicuous consumption and alienated work. This kind of assistance may vary from recommending and helping to locate a different job for the 50-year-old adult, to showing a 15-year-old that skepticism about schooling was discussed by the Greek Skeptics prior to the birth of Christ.

Finally, the clinician can help groups consider their plans for the future by instructing them in the dialectical thinking process of thesis, antithesis, and synthesis. The clinician can also be helpful in pointing out reifications that emerge or when the dialectical logic is faulty. A "how-to" for using dialectics in thinking about immediate problems was recently suggested by Howard Sherman:

1.   Specify the problems in question into relations, interconnections, and conflicts of opposing social forces;
2.   Go beyond seeing any of the problems as statics (always insist upon locating ways in which they are processes);
3.   Question how social relations relative to the problem are changing and evolving;
4.   If a social process shows a discontinuity, ask which continuous changes led to it (and vice versa—if continuous, ask what discontinuity may occur in the future); and
5.   Ask what new social forces may be in conflict with, or negating, old established social structures, and what may be the new set of relations after discontinuity.[22]

Through the use of such concrete procedures clinical Marxism is possible, and without an immediate revolution.

AN EXAMPLE: THE BEAR-LIKE MAN REVISITED

Chapter 2 began with an example of a derelict. How can this situation be approached from the conflict perspectives? Begin with the incident itself. The bear-like man approaches the people waiting for the bus and a conflict situation is thereby created. He takes on an occupation well known in some corners of capitalistic societies (including his own arena of activity), that of beggar or panhandler. However, the usual exchange inherent in the practice of this occupation—the exchange of a few coins from an upper- or middle-class person to a lower-class person—cannot take place because of the appearance of the man. He looks *too* unfortunate. Therefore, instead of being viewed as human by those with whom he comes into contact, he is reified into "someone else's problem."

He certainly does not appear to be a capitalistic success story. He does not have gainful employment, nor does he produce a product, nor hold a job, nor appear capable of conscious and creative activity. He might be considered alienated. However, we must see his current position as part of an ongoing process. It is difficult to grow up in Western society and not be under considerable pressure to become a success in the work world. If we knew his biography, it is likely to be filled with conflict between the needs of the capitalist society and his inability to conform to those needs. The society's efforts at social control are met in part by his resistance. The observed incident is one five-minute segment in his ongoing conflict and quite unimportant for him perhaps. We cannot tell how his situation will evolve. We can assume that if he continues to engage in the same activity in the same condition with similar "audiences," his social relations will be marked by fear, embarrassment, and avoidance, except by those persons whose occupation within the capitalist society is to "handle" such persons: the police, social welfare personnel, and so forth.

The bear-like man is only one example of surplus labor walking the streets of the cities. At the time of the observation, about nine percent of those persons actively looking for work could not find it. How long and in what manner can a capitalistic society continue to support this man and others not able to work? At what level of unemployment does an ideological change occur that places a new value on those who cannot work? Is there a dialectic at work? What technological inventions might we anticipate that will still further reduce the need for workers? At what point might we anticipate a proletarian revolution brought on by increasing alienation and awareness of the failures of capitalism? Is it inevitable?

NOTES

1.   William de Bary, *The Buddhist Tradition* (New York: Modern Library, 1969), p. 262.

2.   F. Moore, trans., *Outlines of Sociology* (Philadelphia: American Academy of Political and Social Science, 1899).

3.   Albion Small, *General Sociology* (Chicago: University of Chicago

Press, 1905), pp. 425–36. David Riesman's concept of "veto groups" is similar.

4.   Albion Small, trans., "Sociology of Conflict," *American Journal of Sociology* 9(1904):518.

5.   Lewis Coser, *Functions of Social Conflict* (New York: Free Press, 1956).

6.   Barry Glassner, "Kid Society," *Urban Education* 11, no. 1 (April 1976):5–22.

7.   Isidor Wallimann, "Toward a Theoretical Understanding of Ethnic Antagonism: The Case of the Foreign Workers in Switzerland," *Zeitschrift fur Soziologie* 3(February 1974):84–94.

8.   Maurice Punch, "Sociology of the Anti-Institution," *British Journal of Sociology* 25(1974):312–25.

9.   Karl Marx and Friedrich Engels, *German Ideology* (New York: International Publishers, 1947), p. 7.

10.   Ronald Leifer, *In the Name of Mental Health* (New York: Science House, 1969), p. 240.

11.   C. Wright Mills, *White Collar* (New York: Oxford University Press, 1951), p. xvi.

12.   Karl Marx, *Economic and Philosophical Manuscripts of 1844* (London: Lawrence and Wishart, 1970), pp. 108–13.

13.   Hannah Arendt, *The Human Condition* (Chicago: University of Chicago Press, 1958), p. 108.

14.   Thorstein Veblen, *The Theory of the Leisure Class* (New York: Macmillan, 1902), pp. 68–101.

15.   George Hegel, *The Science of Logic* (New York: Macmillan, 1929).

16.   Karl Marx, *Grundrisse* (Middlesex, England: Penguin Books, 1973).

17.   Marx and Engels, *German Ideology*.

18.   Friedrich Engels, *Ludwig Feurback and the Outcome of German Classical Philosophy* (New York: International Publishers, 1941), p. 44.

19.   Karl Marx, *Capital: A Critique of Political Economy*, edited by Friedrich Engels (New York: International Publishers, 1974).

20.   Peter Berger and T. Luckman, *Social Construction of Reality* (Garden City, N.Y.: Doubleday Anchor, 1967), p. 90.

21.   C. Wright Mills, *The Sociological Imagination* (New York: Oxford, 1959).

22.   Howard Sherman, "Dialectics as a Method," *The Insurgent Sociologist* 6, no. 4 (1976):57–64.

THE CLINICIAN'S LIBRARY

Two works stand out as useful summaries concerning the variety of conflict theories:

Collins, Randall. *Conflict Sociology*. New York: Academic Press, 1975.
Turner, Jonathan. "A Strategy for Reformulating the Dialectical and Functional Theories of Conflict." *Social Forces* 53(March 1975): 433–43.

EXCHANGE THEORY

The seminal work which created exchange theory is:

Blau, Peter M. *Exchange and Power in Social Life*. New York: Wiley, 1964.

MARXISM

A couple of good introductions to Marxist thought are the following:

Anderson, Charles. *Toward a New Sociology*. Homewood, Ill.: Dorsey Press, 1974.
Lewis, John. *The Marxism of Marx*. New York: Beekman, 1972.

Perhaps the most central works for students of Marx are the following by Marx and Engels:

Caute, David, ed. *Essential Writings of Karl Marx*. New York: Collier, 1967.
Marx, Karl. *The Communist Manifesto* (appears in many collections).
———. *Capital*, S. Moore and E. Aveling, trans. New York: International Publishers, 1967.
———. *Wage, Labor and Capital*. New York: International Publishers, 1948.
———, and F. Engels, *The German Ideology*, R. Pascal, trans. New York: International Publishers, 1947.

Critiques of Marx abound. Find them throughout much of Weber's work, and a couple especially relevant to clinical concerns are the following:

Albert, Michael. *What Is to Be Undone?* Boston: Sargent Publishers, 1974.
Stojanovic, Svetozar. *Between Ideals and Reality: A Critique of Socialism and Its Future.* New York: Oxford University Press, 1973.

Chapter 5

Human Action and Interaction

A man who admired, criticized, and expanded the thought of Marx was Max Weber. Consideration of Weber's work will lead us into discussions of two additional perspectives—symbolic interactionism and ethnomethodology.

MAX WEBER

The work of Max Weber provides clinical sociologists with valuable discussions of *ideal types, rationality,* and *meaning and action.* The work of this turn-of-the-century German thinker can only be presented as a perspective unto itself. As Geoffrey Hawthorn notes, Weber's work never falls neatly into a theoretical "school":

> He is quite alone in the history of social theorizing in western Europe and North America in having set himself against the classical sociological project of furnishing comprehensive typologies and complete causal accounts yet in having managed at the same time to produce an interpretation of the singularity of western capitalism which carries more weight than any but Marx's, and in its historical sensitivity, more weight than any.[1]

Weber was as fascinated with the intermingling of capitalism and human culture as was Marx, but Weber concentrated on the social *feeling* of capitalism, what he termed "the spirit of capitalism." Mature capitalism is based not only on acquisitive or exploitative desires, but on a set of attitudes which maintain that it is a good thing to spend one's energies making more money than needed to provide for necessities. This spirit includes the desire to maximize wealth through most any efficient means.

This spirit of capitalism is so well engrained today that most of us confuse it with human nature. In his *Protestant Ethic and the Spirit of Capitalism*,[2] Weber locates the roots. He begins by noting that flexibility, innovation, and usury were absent from social worlds in Europe for much of its history, having been traditionally forbidden by the Church. How did these processes, which are essential to capitalism, arise? Or to ask the question another way, Why did capitalism emerge as the major economic system at particular times and locations?

Weber found his answer in the rise of Protestantism. He compared various regions of Europe and found that the more predominantly Protestant areas also housed the more fully developed capitalist economic systems. Protestantism supported traditional Christian values of selflessness and charity, but for the first time in the history of Christianity also stressed the importance of doing well on earth. Protestant teachings emphasize salvation through ascetic industry during one's lifetime, as well as the ethic of individuality. These religious values are a perfect precondition for capitalism's conceptions of work and investment as ends in themselves.

What Weber uncovered were the distinctive and essential characteristics of Protestantism and capitalism which made them so compatible. He described what he called the *ideal types* of both phenomena. An ideal type is a hypothetical individual which entails the significant and distinctive characteristics of the social phenomenon under discussion. Ideal types are *not* the morally desirable nor the statistically average version of the social phenomenon, but rather the precise and unambiguous description of a prototypic case.

The usefulness of ideal types can be seen in one of Weber's own applications of this conceptual tool to a prominent dimension of many clinical problems, authority. Weber defines authority as "the probability that a specific command will be obeyed" and distinguishes three ideal types:

Legal authority is based upon the idea that laws enacted and enforced through formally correct procedures must be obeyed. Obedience is directed not at individuals per se but at the formal rules which they are enforcing. A man who stops beating his wife when the police arrive typically does so assuming that there are local laws which make beating punishable.

Traditional authority depends upon belief in the continuity of the social order and those values which maintain the social order. Formal and written rules need not be part of traditional authority. Respect for traditional authority comes from beliefs of the variety, "Groups X and Y have always been authorities, so they must *rightfully* be in command." A man who stops beating his wife when the priest arrives is likely doing so in light of the traditional authority of the Church.

Charismatic authority rests on the unique leadership talents which some individuals possess:

> They comprise especially magical abilities, revelations of heroism, power of the mind and of speech. The eternally new, the non-routine, the unheard of and the emotional rapture from its sources of personal devotion. The purest types are the rule of the prophet, the warrior hero, the great demagogue. . . . Obedience is given exclusively to the leader as a person, for the sake of his nonroutine qualities, not because of enacted position or traditional dignity.[3]

A man may stop beating his wife after hearing an emotionally stirring argument from a charismatic neighbor.

Weber contended that in modern times all types of authority have one thing in common: to command obedience they must appear *rational*. Indeed, rationality is about the most widespread social phenomenon in the Western world, according to Weber. This can be seen in contrast to non-Western societies. In the arts, one finds polyphonic music throughout the world, but rational tone intervals in Western music result in unique harmonies not found in the music of the East. The development of "perspective" for representational painting developed in the West but is missing from traditional Eastern art. The Western form of government, since the Romans, is uniquely dependent upon rationally ordered and published laws.

The systematizing and ordering found in Western science, architecture, art, and compartmentalized studies in universities are all processes of the increasing rationalization of the world in Western thought.

Rationality becomes a kind of social environmental demand upon persons and groups which leads them to choose compartmentalized and hierarchical ordering both in their material creations and in their human groups. It has nearly become a norm, for instance, that random or nonstructured activities within and between groups be prevented as much as possible. (Later in this chapter, in our discussion of ethnomethodology, we will discuss in greater detail several dimensions of rationality in everyday life.)

It should be apparent that Weber's perspectives stressed the spiritual and other mental dimensions of social life far more than do many of the other major theoretical perspectives we have examined thus far—including the varieties of conflict theories, functionalism, and systems and organic analogies. Weber brought to sociology a concern which has been central to the field ever since, the importance of understanding social phenomena via *meaning and human action.*

Weber argued that the forms of social phenomena, such as societal structures and interaction patterns, are the results of concrete human actions. To understand social phenomena one must first understand the actions which produce these phenomena. These actions, in turn, can be understood only by understanding the meaning they have for the persons who are acting. The subjective intentions of the persons who create social situations become the key to understanding these situations. For action to be social it must be oriented toward others. So the goal of sociology must be to understand the ways in which persons interpret situations and how these interpretations direct their behaviors toward others.

"Understanding at the level of meaning" occurs in two ways in Weber's work. First, there is the possibility that simply by watching others we can understand what their intentions must be. When someone takes out a calculator and several bills, we conclude that he or she is somehow involved in computation. When a hunter aims a gun at an animal, we are also fairly certain what the act means. Second, we can understand the motive behind an act by learning the manner of reasoning of the other person and the emotional context, and then reconstructing the situation in our own minds according to such patterns of reasoning and emotionality.

Weber called the basic process of understanding social action "the operation *verstehen.*" It consists of being able to imagine the emotions and thought patterns of others as these are produced within specific social situations. Out of this appreciation we can then imagine the types of action which will follow. By observing and talking with persons in their various social situations for a long enough period we can eventually come to an empathetic understanding of the ways in which they see and act upon their social worlds. Techniques for listening and observing in clinical settings are presented in the next chapter in greater detail.

The process of *verstehen* has brought a great deal of criticism to Weber's work, mostly because he did not specify a systematic procedure for accomplishing *verstehen* or verifying that the resulting understandings were correct. These difficulties do not mitigate the tremendous importance of *verstehen* for sociological understanding, however. Anyone who has cared deeply and sympathetically about another person knows that *verstehen* is possible and valuable.

Biographies, both written and unwritten, frequently contain passages such as the following (from a confidential diary of a female college sophomore):

I never understood dad or even cared to until last week when I was home for Christmas. I guess people only see their parents as parents, never as people, until they are grown up (almost!) and away from home, and then it must be too late for a lot of them.

It wasn't too late for me. Dad came home from the plant looking exhausted and dirty, like he always does. He went straight to the fridge and guzzled three beers and yelled at mom, cutting up her housekeeping and telling her she was getting fat. When she started crying he beat on her. I couldn't stand it, because I'd seen it too many times. I was ready to go back to college and spend Christmas vacation alone in the dorm. Every couple of days when I was in high school he'd come home and get drunk and nasty. Probably once or twice every single week he would beat on mom.

I don't know why, maybe because I don't have to live there anymore (or maybe because I'm older) I decided to figure it all out this time. For the first time instead of getting mad and screaming at him I just sat there listening to the things he was saying. First he was telling mom that someone had been hurt at the plant, just one team over from dad's team, and that it had been caused by faulty wiring that had been reported to the foreman a couple of weeks ago. Then dad remembered that the foreman—Mr. C.—was the one who had been promoted four years

ago, when dad was up to be promoted. When dad remembered, that was when he really started getting angry and swear-
ing about all he'd been through at the plant and calling everybody there dirty names. He just went on and on about his
twenty years there and how everybody else his age was "off the
line by now.". . .

Pretty soon dad was stomping around the kitchen and mom
was asking him to calm down, which only made him mad-
der. He yelled at mom something about how she gets to watch
television all day while his cough gets worse down at the plant
and that all she does is tell him to calm down when he gets home.
Then she started to cry, and first he walked into the living room
and got really quiet. Then he walked back to the fridge for
another beer and she was still crying when he walked past her. He
couldn't stand *any* of it anymore and started beating up on
her until he was exhausted and whimpering like a little kid. It
was pathetic.

Dad fell asleep on the couch in the living room, with the
news blaring twice as loud as it needed to be. . . .

I don't like my dad for what he does, but I think I understand it
better now. He's trapped by the whole world. Poor mom can't
change the things that happen to him at the plant, and she's
terrified of him now so she just doesn't give him anything at all, or
the wrong kind. He can't fight back anywhere else in the
world, so he does it here. . . . The more he fights the more tired
he gets, and he must know that soon enough he will fall asleep
and be away from being trapped. . . .

Examine this selection in the following manner. Note how the social
structure in the factory situation impinges upon the interaction in the
home. This *verstehen* which comes to the college sophomore daughter
allows her to comprehend the actions of her father for the first time. She
is able to interpret the underlying meanings of family interaction by
sympathetically placing herself in the position of her father and assuming how he must feel.

Verstehen can be important to clinical practice in at least three ways.
First, clinicians may teach group members to accomplish some insight
into others' subjectivities so that they can better understand the social
situations in which they participate. Second, clinicians may encourage
the sharing and communication of *verstehen* among group members
through several of the techniques discussed in part 4. Third, the clini-

cian's own diagnosis and other understandings of social worlds may come in part from a Weberian perspective which sees social structures and interactions as the result of human actions based on interpreted meanings. The specific perspectives of symbolic interactionism and ethnomethodology build upon concerns we have noted in Weber's work.

GEORGE HERBERT MEAD

Faithful to many of Weber's teachings is *symbolic interactionism,* a major form of sociological interactionism. To understand this perspective requires at least a summary appreciation for the work of its major pioneer, George Herbert Mead. At the University of Chicago in the early 1900s Mead lectured on his philosophy for social psychology, and these lectures formed the basis of three volumes put together by some of his students. The volume *Mind, Self and Society* [4] contains the discussions which underlie much of symbolic interactionism.

Mind

According to Mead, we regularly engage in the process of "imaginative rehearsal" of the ways we will act upon the material and social worlds. Such mental rehearsal is possible as a result of our minds' capacities (1) to employ symbols to designate objects which are outside of ourselves, (2) to imagine various courses of action toward the objects, and (3) to censor possible actions which are inappropriate.

Mead, along with Weber and John Dewey, considered life an ongoing *interpretive process,* in which persons and groups select courses of action for manipulating their environments. This position contrasts with several forms of organic and mechanistic interpretations which see persons' actions as predetermined reactions to stimuli. For Mead, responses emerge only after delaying, organizing, and mentally experimenting with both the stimulus and the response.

The use of symbols demonstrates the inherent social nature of individual minds. Persons come to share the uses and interpretations of certain symbols. When someone utters the sound "cat," we imagine an animal which is zoologically a carnivorous quadruped. Each person may choose to imagine a different color or size of animal, but the symbolic utterance "cat" provokes in all of us a common notion of the object being discussed.

Our ability to share in symbolic discourse also permits us to "take the role of the other," to imagine not only our own possible lines of action, but also those of others. We continually indicate to ourselves the roles of other persons and thereby are continually making choices about our own actions on the basis of social considerations.

Self

Mead's conception of the self provides clinicians with a valuable corrective to the asocial conception of the self held by some psychologists and psychiatrists. Building upon his notions of mind, Mead reveals that the self is a social process consisting of two phases, the "I" and the "me." The "I" is the impulsive, spontaneous response of the individual to the attitudes and actions of others. In adults the "I" process emerges only when our "guards are down," such as when we are alone with close friends or when we are intoxicated. The "me" consists of reflections of others' attitudes about ourselves, which we obtain through taking the perspective of the other. In deciding what to make of ourselves (or our groups) we cannot limit the inquiry to self-reflection because we are continually aware that there are other competent perspectives for considering our selves; namely, the perspectives of other persons who watch us:

> It is through taking this role of the other that he is able to come
> back on himself and so direct his own process of communica-
> tion. This taking the role of the other . . . is not simply of
> passing importance. It is not something that just happens as an
> incidental result of the gesture, but it is of importance in the
> development of co-imperative activity. The immediate effect of
> such role-taking lies in the control which the individual is able to
> exercise over his own response.[5]

The "me" involves two types of others. First, we consider specific others who are important to us, "significant others." A husband, for example, is likely to derive much of his sense of self from the ways in which his wife thinks of him. Mead's colleague Charles Horton Cooley called this sort of self-perception "the looking-glass self," a quite descriptive phrase for those occasions in which we form a definite impression of how we appear to a particular person. Much as we evaluate our figure or attire in a mirror and are pleased, displeased, or unsure according to how we like what we see, so do we imagine the evaluations of another person and choose ways to handle such evaluations.[6]

Alternatively, we can view ourselves not from the position of a specific other person, but from the perspective of a *type* of person, or "generalized others." A husband is also likely, then, to consider his self from the perspective of wives in general, in terms of the ways in which wives tend to think of husbands such as himself.

The "I" and the "me" work together; they are not competitors as are Freud's superego and id. The "me" takes account of others' feelings about the self, and the "I" creatively projects the self for others to consider.

Society

Mead's views on society follow from his philosophy of the mind and self. The structures of society are not objective realities which determine the actions of groups and group members (as stressed by forms of functionalism and Marxism, for instance). Rather, society is the patterned interactions which result from persons interpreting others' actions and choosing their own actions relative to those of others.

Social institutions are constantly fluid and changing if people choose to make them so. Mead emphasizes that persons *construct* social worlds and can *re*construct them in different ways. Although societies and institutions are considered by many people to be concrete, fully developed structures, they are in fact nothing other than patterns of human interactions. Some of our patterns of interaction (mostly those resulting from the needs of the "me") create stability, while others (notably the spontaneous actions of the "I") produce changes or conflicts in social structures.

SYMBOLIC INTERACTIONISM

The symbolic interactionists, primarily under the leadership of Mead's student Herbert Blumer, have developed Mead's philosophy into a sociological perspective that emphasizes the production and interpretation of symbols.[7] People interpret each other's actions, and on the basis of these interpretations decide which course of action to employ in response. The self is crucially important in determining the interpretation and resulting actions which occur. Persons are able to act toward themselves—we get angry with ourselves, argue with ourselves, make plans with ourselves, and so forth. Similarly, we make indications to ourselves about events in our social environments, and our later actions are the result of the types of indications we make.

Social life is viewed by the symbolic interactionist as occurring in the following manner: (1) acting units (individuals, families, businesses, etc.) find themselves in situations (markets, conflicts, love, etc.); (2) the acting units interpret the situation (tasks, means, dangers, demands, etc.); (3) the acting units assess the situation and decide courses of action (fight, flee, endure, etc.); (4) the acting units act according to the decisions.

Sometimes persons will use habitual patterns of interpreting and acting, based upon the ways they operated in similar situations in the past. Symbolic interactionists emphasize, however, that sociologists cannot *assume* that antecedent conditions explain current social actions or social structures, because the antecedent conditions are simply some of the many items interpreted in deciding upon present courses of action.

Blumer points out how the symbolic interactionist perspective contrasts with some others (which we noted earlier in the chapter):

> Human society is to be seen as consisting of acting people, and the life of the society is to be seen as consisting of their actions. The acting units may be separate individuals, collectivities whose members are acting together on a common guest, or organizations acting on behalf of a constituency. Respective examples are individual purchasers in a market, a play group or missionary band, and a business corporation or a national professional association. There is no empirically observable activity in a human society that does not spring from some acting unit. This banal statement needs to be stressed in light of the common practice of sociologists of reducing human society to social units that do not act—for example, social classes in modern society. Obviously there are ways of viewing human society other than in terms of the acting units that compose it. I merely wish to point out that in respect to concrete or empirical activity human society must necessarily be seen in terms of the acting units that form it.[8]

Structural features such as "institutions," "social systems," even "social roles" are settings for human actions, not determinations of these actions. Symbolic interactionists claim that people do not act toward such structures, but only toward other persons, and in light of the particular situations in which they find themselves. Social organization and social structure are viewed as processes rather than established entities.

A symbolic interactionist understanding of a clinical question would likely emerge from a series of discussions and observations designed to ascertain the ways in which persons are viewing and interpreting the situations in which they find themselves, the actions they are choosing, and how these actions collectively form patterns of interaction over time. In short, the clinician would seek the relationship between the "I" and "me," and the extent and nature of significant others in persons' lives.

Sometimes determining the ways a client views the world, or a segment of the world, is critical to determining the best ways to work with the client. Consider the actual case of Lynn, who was involuntarily committed to a state mental hospital as a manic depressive. The story in Lynn's clinical file (and in a local newspaper report) was that she had operated her automobile at 110 miles per hour in a chase with a police officer and had then wrecked her car and begun talking "nonsense" with great rapidity when arrested.

Not until a clinical sociologist spent several hours talking with her about various dimensions of her world did anyone in the hospital derive an understanding of this incident. The clinician found that for Lynn the events occurred as follows. Throughout her life she had been pursued by men, some seeking to rape her, others to seduce her, others chasing her with marriage proposals, and so forth. Lynn is a strikingly attractive woman and a professional model. She noticed that a man in a car a short distance behind her on the freeway was approaching her car and signaling with his hand out the window that she should pull to the side of the road. She had long ago learned not to pull to the sides of roads (or sidewalks or hallways) when requested to do so by men chasing her, so she sped up her car to avoid the man. He in turn increased his speed and began to force her off the side of the road, which terrified her and caused her to speed up even more, and finally to crash.

We might add, in Mead's terms, that her "I" took charge, leading her to conduct herself according to her "primitive" social instincts, rather than to pay attention to "me" demands which might have permitted her to check the man more closely and recognize that although his automobile was unmarked, he was wearing a uniform and police cap.

ETHNOMETHODOLOGY

The several perspectives presented thus far offer a variety of insights, but really only two basic viewpoints of social life. The functionalist and organic analogies, and the conflict perspectives, while very different in many respects, all focus on the material and structural determinants of social life. In contrast, the dramaturgical analogy, Max Weber, and symbolic interactionism focus on people interacting and interpreting in order to produce social life. In philosophical terms, the former are more nearly *realistic,* holding that material events exist independent of our minds and determine what we think and do. The latter are closer to philosophical *idealism,* maintaining that the most important element of reality is the mind. (Some of the perspectives transcend the dichotomy, however; critical Marxism, for example, concentrates on interests, which are properties of the mind developed from material concerns.)

Both sides have been criticized for ignoring the other dimension. Symbolic interactionists, for instance, have been accused of conceiving social worlds in immaterialist terms, or as existing without matter.[9] Indeed, Blumer goes so far as to claim that "the nature of an object—of any and every object—consists of the meaning that it has for the person for whom it is an object." [10] Surely the nature of objects depends also upon their material properties. It may be true that we cannot know the material properties except as these are processed by our minds, but our "meanings" are also in perpetual states of interpretation.

The difference between these types of perspectives is also comparable to that between environmental and organic studies of disease. A major branch of cancer research concentrates upon environmental causes of cancer in food, cigarettes, the air, and so forth. Another branch concentrates upon the processes which occur within animals and organs of animals which have already contracted cancer. Both types of research are crucial.

Ethnomethodology attempts to study the interpretations of material worlds both in terms of their macrosocietal structures and from the perspective of individuals and groups. The starting point for ethnomethodology is W. I. Thomas's dictum, "If men define situations as real, they are real in their consequences." This suggests that to understand any social situation or social structure requires an understanding of how it looks to those persons who are the constituent parts of the situation or structure, because the persons will act according to how it looks to them.

This central point is emphasized by a study conducted by Peter McHugh.[11] College students were told by the experimenter that psychotherapy is a time-consuming and complicated method for giving advice about personal problems, and that the experimenter was looking for a simpler method. Each student was to think over a personal problem and come up with questions about that problem which could be answered with "yes" or "no." Each student was then put in a room and left alone with an intercom. The student was permitted to ask a psychotherapist ten questions through the intercom. After receiving answers to these questions the student was to summarize what had been learned during the therapy session.

Students asked questions about a variety of matters ranging from love to money to education, and most of them made sense out of what they learned from the therapist's yes and no answers. A couple of examples from their summary statements:

Talking things over makes you learn something about your situations. It's not that fathers don't want to help out, that's not why you ask anyway. You ask them anyway because they may not be listening closely, even when they do want to help. . . .

My family may come around anyway, after we're married; you can never be absolutely sure ahead of time about these things. It's always a possibility. Very interesting. Even a poor psychiatrist can be helpful if you just talk about yourself.

The students defined the situations despite the fact that *they had actually been given random responses to their questions.* The "therapist" had used a random numbers table to determine which questions would be answered "yes," and which would be answered "no."

McHugh's study points to the tendency for persons to make sense out of situations, in ways useful to them, whether or not the situations "objectively" make sense in those ways. More specifically, McHugh found two general elements which persons use to define situations. *Emergence* refers to the assumption that the future will resemble the past. People expect themes and patterns which have occurred regularly in the past to repeat themselves in new situations, and they fit events to expectations of such repeating patterns. Thus, some students searched for patterns of dialogue with the therapist which resembled dialogue protocols they had encountered in other settings. *Relativity* refers to the expectation that there are a variety of ways in which people handle situations, and that we can make sense out of what is happening in a situation by understanding how the various parties are acting. A major part of this procedure is to typify another person's behaviors according to the way "that sort of person" would do things. Some students made sense of unusual or contradictory answers by the therapist on the basis that therapists "are like that."

Most ethnomethodological research has not occurred in laboratories, but in everyday life situations, and has often involved very unconventional techniques. A leading ethnomethodologist, Harold Garfinkel, asked students during the 1960s to behave in their own homes as if they were boarders. The students used formal speech and dress and acted quite distant and polite to their families. In most of the cases the other family members became disturbed. The students' reports were filled with accounts of astonishment, anxiety, and anger. Some students were accused by their families of being insane, stupid, or going through periods of crisis.

In other studies Garfinkel sent researchers to supermarkets with instructions to question the price of standard items, for example, to argue that a 28¢ can of beans *should* cost 27¢. Another experiment involved the researcher thrusting his or her face to within a few inches of a person with whom he was engaged in ordinary conversation.[12]

The extreme reactions produced by these slight variations in behavior are used by ethnomethodologists to determine which rules and processes are being employed by persons in given situations to "construct social reality." In other words, which aspects of social worlds are people considering as real and taken for granted, and how do these aspects structure their social situations? Why does the checkout clerk in an American grocery store not even *consider* negotiating prices, while a merchant in Florence, Italy, expects to negotiate prices in almost every transaction? Answers to such questions can provide clinicians with an understanding of the fundamental rules and processes by which individuals in specific social situations produce an ongoing social reality, and what they expect that reality to look like.

Garfinkel's own analysis of the uses of "rationality" under various social conditions helps to clarify the place of this taken-for-granted property in various clinical settings. Rationality is like many social phenomena, it seems to be a singular process but really has "multiple realities" in its many uses. Garfinkel notes fourteen prevalent meanings of "rationality." Among the most common:

Categorizing and comparing is often sufficient for persons to conclude that rationality has occurred. "Sometimes rationality refers to the *fact* that he searches the two situations with regard to their comparability, and sometimes to his *concern* for making matters comparable."

Search for "means" refers to the rationality consisting of reviewing rules of procedure which worked effectively in the past, in light of ends desired at present.

Strategy is a general plan which will be followed whenever similar sets of conditions are met.

Predictability consists of determining some empirical constants which one can normally expect under whatever course of action is chosen, so that one will not be surprised at the results of the action.

Grounds of choice for an action, when made explicit and defensible, may indicate that a rational decision has been reached. Often people indicate the logic of their choice to demonstrate their rationality.

Compatibility with scientific knowledge is a rationality whereby the person makes her or his choice of action in accordance with what is considered "most scientific," on the basis of current scientific research and theories in the relevant areas.[13]

ON "GOING NATIVE"

Major ethnomethodologists, as well as some symbolic interactionists, argue that in order to understand a social situation one must live through that situation. They call upon researchers to become full-fledged members of the social groups and settings which they are attempting to understand or assist. The claim is that any researcher "by having to perform in [another's] world, must develop and adopt the perspective that goes with that world." [14]

Ethnomethodologists have proposed, for instance, that to understand a mental illness one must learn how to experience the world in the same ways that persons living through mental illness experience the world. Analyses of paranoia or schizophrenia are to be abandoned in favor of describing the actual experience of being paranoid or schizophrenic. The recommendation is that any researcher should first *become* whatever social phenomenon he or she is investigating, then provide others with understanding of it by exemplifying it. Explanation and even description are to be avoided.[15] These recommendations, though worthwhile and useful for clinicians in some instances, are troublesome in others. (Consider the viability of becoming Lynn, for instance, who was described earlier.)

Pro

Perhaps the major source of tension in and between social groups results from various parties not understanding one another's realities. As we have seen in our discussion of ethnomethodology, people take their own social world to be social *reality*. When others operate in ways different from that reality, they may be threatening, "difficult to live with," or forced to fit into the presumed reality.

These situations were beautifully illustrated by a study in which eight researchers presented themselves for diagnosis and treatment at mental health facilities, each claiming that they heard voices but otherwise acting normal. All eight were admitted for treatment. They immediately stopped faking their symptom of hearing voices and continued to act normal. Staff reports treated their behaviors as pathological, and nurses and psychiatrists treated them impersonally and with brevity. They were hospitalized for up to ten weeks, although they were in no sense mentally ill. [16]

A clinician who really learns to think and behave in a particular way can sometimes reduce tensions by exemplifying this mode to those who are confused or threatened by it, and thereby bring them to a sense of the subjective reality of persons they do not understand. We can imagine cases in which a clinician might actually want to experience and exemplify a mental illness. In a hospital in which the success rate of treatment is low and the tension between staff and patients is high, communication between the two groups might be improved by a clinician exemplifying to staff members what the hospital and staff look like to patients. It might also be improved by the clinician exemplifying to patients what the hospital and patients look like to the staff. This might be done over the course of several weeks, during which the clinician becomes a member of the group she or he will exemplify, complete with all rights, risks, and restrictions.

Through such *ethnomethods* a clinician is able to present theoretical positions that are crucial but often missing in social settings, the everyday social theories of actual participants in social situations. Persons construct theories to explain why and how social life occurs, and they do so on the basis of their own experiences and needs. It is usually upsetting when other people's behaviors do not coincide with the predictions we construct from our everyday social theories, and we tend to disapprove of behavior which is inconsistent with our theories. If we understand how others' behavior is predictable from their own alternate theories of social life, the behavior is often less upsetting, and communication becomes more feasible.

Quite a different use of ethnomethods in clinical practice is in the development of the clinician's own attempts to understand a setting. Perspectives such as functionalism and Marxism have usually stressed the features of social situations which are *not* readily available within everyday theories (e.g., macro structures). As we have noted, ethnomethods stress that regardless of the reality outside people's perceptions, we can understand why and how people act only if we understand their theories of reality:

> The distinction between natural science and social science . . . is based on the fact that men are not only objects existing in the natural world to be observed by the scientist, but they are creators of a world, a cultural world, of their own. In creating this world, they interpret their own activities. Their overt behavior is only a fragment of their total behavior.[17]

A use of ethnomethods for clinicians, then, is in understanding various everyday theories in order to construct their own interpretations. Rather than relying strictly upon observed behaviors and verbal reports, the clinician might want to attempt to experience the various perspectives present in a social situation in order to "see them" as they look from the inside.

Con

Cultural anthropologists have been debating for many years the possibility and desirability of "going native," which is their term for taking on the culture of those persons being researched. From their experiences and debates, at least three negative points about the process seem significant for clinicians. First, becoming one of the participants may necessitate that the clinician act in ways in which he or she does not wish to act. One sociologist working among adolescents was put in the position of having to steal if he became "part of the gang."[18] Others have been forced in their participant role to make negative statements about other persons in a setting, and such statements are not necessarily forgotten once the researcher adopts a new position within the group.

Second, persons never choose exactly which places they will have in a social situation; this is always in part influenced by the desires of others in the group. The exact position in which a researcher is placed will depend upon the desires and power relations within the group, as well as the age, sex, attractiveness, and so on, of the researcher, and how these are perceived by the group. The point here is that by "going native" we do not learn the *general* perspective of a type of person in a social situation, but rather those *specific* perspectives that depend upon our placement. We do not learn what the world looks like to persons who are depressed, but rather what it looks like to that very special person ("me") in a specific social situation.

Third, there are fundamental questions about the basic assertion that performance in another person's world leads to adopting the ways of thinking of that other person. We can convince ourselves (and others) that we are performing from a specific perspective without actually doing so. It is difficult to imagine any method whereby one could determine whether he or she is actually thinking and acting the way the other person would. A good actor can learn the appropriate gestures, postures, and lines necessary to convince an audience that she or he is *really* the part being played. We frequently perform roles in a detached manner, without adopting them or even accepting that "I" am the role.[19]

All three of these problems indicate the lack of historical perspective inherent in such ethnomethods. Groups and social situations have histories, which in important ways determine the ways in which people act in the present. A person who tries to enter a specific position within a group cannot fully do so, not having experienced the components of that position which have already occurred.

This lack of historical perspective among ethnomethodologists is part of the broader problem that critics note concerning most all of the interactionist sociologies. Predictably, perhaps, the interactionists are dismissed for ignoring macro, or large-scale structural questions.[20] How does one explain, ask the critics, that societies seem to have a "life of their own" quite distinct from the interactions within and between groups which comprise the societies? How can major shifts in demographic characteristics of a nation be explained through interactionist analyses? Why do millions of people go to work each morning at the same time if the essence of being human is the interpreting which people do? The interactionist reply to such questions is that such processes are actually the *gestalt* (fully formed pattern) of many smaller interactions, each of which contains series of interpretations and symbolic meanings for the persons who are acting.

The fundamental question which remains within these debates, however, is derived from the ancient idealist-materialist battle we have noted previously. Do the established patterns of social organization determine the actions and interpretations of individuals and groups, or vice versa? One's answer to this question depends upon the degree to which one views power relations, material forces, group and societal structures, and so forth, *as established*. An interactionist argues that we have been fooled into misperceiving these forms as established when they are really emergent or even random. Our suggestion for clinicians is to investigate each situation under consideration to determine the objective and subjective possibilities for therapeutic change.

CHOOSING PERSPECTIVES

In the last three chapters we have introduced major theoretical perspectives in sociology and suggested their utility for understanding and diagnosing clinical situations. In actual practice, of course, clinicians must familiarize themselves with the fuller discussions of persons who have developed these theories. But how does a clinician choose perspectives for use in specific situations?

In actual practice this question has been answered in a variety of ways, ranging from "grab bag" approaches which pick and choose almost at random, to the activist approach noted in chapter 1, in which a single perspective is considered so insightful that it is used in every instance. Both of these approaches, even in their less extreme forms, are more likely to be fashionable than useful:

> Particular theorists are subject to alternating periods of attention and neglect, as are particular parts of their work. The early writings of Marx on alienation have in recent years received more attention and praise amongst social theorists than the later writings on the political economy of capitalism. Simmel's essays on methodology and social philosophy now receive more attention than his empirically oriented theorizing about group dynamics.[21]

Within particular organizations, and among particular colleague or friendship groups of clinicians, certain perspectives are likely to become habitually employed, even when they are not the most useful.

Our own alternative strategy for selection of theoretical perspectives in specific clinical instances entails consideration of three items: the kinds of problems being diagnosed, the kinds of issues addressed by the theorists under consideration, and the support (or lack thereof) which the theories have received in sociological research. All three concerns are usually of equal weight and should be considered as simultaneously as possible.

Definition of *problems* is determined by techniques described in the next section. Once a theoretical perspective has been ascertained the problems may be revised or expanded. In order to determine which theoretical insights will be useful, however, the problems must be mapped out. What size unit is involved? Does it involve a small group, several affiliated groups, a city, the world? What is the essential nature of the problem? Is this problem sexual, economic, institutional, educational, political, communicative? What is the metaphysic of the problem? For example, is it material or spiritual? What are the moral dimensions of the problem? Are there value conflicts, issues of leadership ethics, norm conflicts?

It is often helpful for the clinician to actually draw a map of the problem, in which the various concerns are diagrammed. The dimensions which appear primary may be drawn in larger letters, or higher on the map. The connections between dimensions can be indicated with one- or two-way arrows. Some clinicians may even prefer to shape the map according to the dominant dimensions and place the other dimensions within the dominant ones, as supporting parts. On page 129 is an example of a problem map.

The issues addressed by theorists have been discussed in quite general terms throughout the preceding chapters. The practicing clinician should maintain a library of theoretical books and papers which are organized according to issues. Some clinicians accomplish such organization through continual familiarity, so that they have memorized the major issues addressed by the various theorists and can relocate discussions of such issues as needed. Others prefer to keep a card catalogue or other type of listing, with issue headings such as *micro, macro, capitalism, verstehen, structure,* and so forth, with author and page references listed.

Some issues within theories go deeper than the topics discussed, however. Each theory contains assumptions about the nature of social

JOE'S   MARY'S

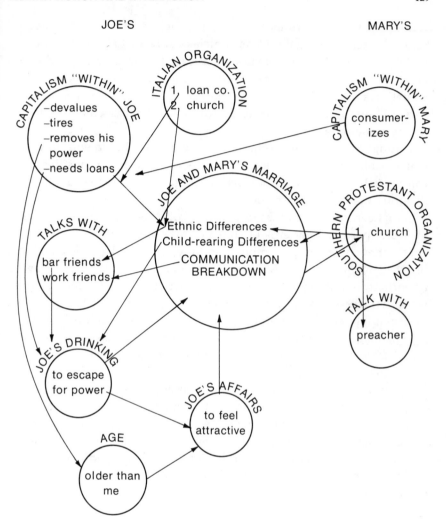

life and its actors, and about the possibilities for change. Thus, most forms of functionalism assume a society which is moving toward integration and order, and the implied moral stance is that clinical intervention is appropriate insofar as it assists in bringing about this order. In contrast, most conflict theories assume that social worlds consist of battles, and the implied moral stance is that clinical intervention should reduce or change these battles for the betterment of specific interested parties or principles. Obviously, attention to such underlying assumptions will inform a clinician's choice of perspectives.

Support for the various theories is to be found in the sociological research literature. Again, some clinicians are able to keep up with this material simply by regular reading of research journals and papers, and good memories. Others prefer notekeeping and organized systems. Sometimes research notes are maintained in a card catalogue or on long lists. Other clinicians prefer to file the research notes along with the theory issue notes.

Through comparisons of these three items one should end up with a manageable and appropriate body of theoretical work to consider when confronted with specific problems. A couple of simplified examples will illustrate the initial phases of the process.

Let us consider two types of marital problems. Couple A is battling over one partner's patterns of conspicuous consumption. The partner goes out every few days and buys clothing, gifts, and gadgets, and as a result the family is deeply in debt. Several theoretical issues may be important, but immediately the clinician would do well to look at those works which deal with market economies. Others which discuss escapism might also be important, or perhaps some which consider status or self-image. The available research related to such issues would further describe which theoretical insights have been related to similar situations in the past.

On the other hand, quite different theoretical perspectives might be of special significance for working with couple B, in which one member is acting in a very authoritarian manner not only at work but within the spouse relationship as well. Again, several theoretical issues would be considered, but certainly the couple would be likely candidates for role analyses emerging from dramaturgical and symbolic interactionist perspectives.

NOTES

1.   Geoffrey Hawthorn, *Enlightenment and Despair* (London: Cambridge University Press, 1976), p. 163.

2.   Max Weber, *The Protestant Ethic and the Spirit of Capitalism* (New York: Scribner, 1958).

3.   Hans Gerth, trans., "Three Types of Legitimate Rule," *Berkeley Journal of Sociology* 4(1958):1–11.

4. George Herbe1. Mead, *Mind, Self and Society*, Charles Morris, ed. (Chicago: University of Chicago Press, 1934).

5. Ibid., p. 254.

6. Charles Horton Cooley, *Human Nature and the Social Order* (New York: Scribner, 1902.)

7. Herbert Blumer, "Society as Symbolic Interaction," in Arnold Rose, ed., *American Behavior and Social Process* (Boston: Houghton Mifflin, 1962), pp. 179–92.

8. Ibid., p. 186.

9. Barry Glassner, *Essential Interactionism* (chap. 2), in process.

10. Herbert Blumer, *Symbolic Interaction* (Englewood Cliffs, N.J.: Prentice-Hall, 1969), p. 11.

11. Peter McHugh, *Defining the Situation* (Indianapolis: Bobbs-Merrill, 1968).

12. Harold Garfinkel, *Studies in Ethnomethodology* (Englewood Cliffs, N.J.: Prentice-Hall, 1967).

13. Ibid., chap. 8.

14. George Psathas, "Ethnomethods and Phenomenology," *Social Research* 35(September 1968):519.

15. Hugh Mehan and Houston Wood, *Reality of Ethnomethodology* (New York: Wiley, 1975).

16. D. L. Rosenhan, "On Being Sane in Insane Places," *Science* 179(1973):250–58.

17. Psathas, "Ethnomethods and Phenomethodology," p. 510.

18. Gary Fine and Barry Glassner, "The Promise and Problems of Participant Observation with Children," *Urban Life* (forthcoming, 1978).

19. Glassner, *Essential Interactionism*, chap. 9.

20. See, for example, Denis Gleeson and Michael Erben, "Meaning in Context: Notes toward a Critique of Ethnomethodology," *British Journal of Sociology* 24, no. 4 (1973):474–83.

21. Bryan S. R. Green, "On the Evaluation of Sociological Theory," *Philosophy of Social Sciences* 8(1977):33.

THE CLINICIAN'S LIBRARY

An excellent argument for the primacy of human action for understanding in both social scienc˜ and physical science is a volume by Von Wright:

Von Wright, G. H. *Explanation and Understanding*. Ithaca, N.Y.: Cornell University Press, 1971.

WEBER

Clinicians may find most helpful the following works:

Hans, Gerth, and C. W. Mills, eds. *From Max Weber: Essays in Sociology*. New York: Oxford University Press, 1946.

Weber, Max. *The Protestant Ethic and the Spirit of Capitalism*. New York: Scribner, 1958.

――――. *Ancient Judaism*, Hans Gerth and D. Martindale, trans. Glencoe, Ill.: Free Press, 1952.

SYMBOLIC INTERACTIONISM

Mead never wrote a book, but his students put together three volumes from the lecture notes:

Morris, Charles, ed. *Mind, Self and Society*. Chicago: University of Chicago Press, 1934.

――――. *Movements of Thought in the Nineteenth Century*. Chicago: University of Chicago Press, 1936.

――――. *The Philosophy of the Act*. Chicago: University of Chicago Press, 1938.

Blumer wrote a central book on symbolic interactionism:

Blumer, Herbert. *Symbolic Interaction*. Englewood Cliffs, N.J.: Prentice-Hall, 1969.

Ethnomethodology is introduced in depth in a variety of works which use its inquiry strategies. Systematic descriptions of the assumptions of ethnomethodology appear in two volumes:

Garfinkel, Harold. *Studies in Ethnomethodology*. Englewood Cliffs, N.J.: Prentice-Hall, 1967.

Mehan, Hugh, and H. Wood. *The Reality of Ethnomethodology*. New York: Wiley, 1975.

Turner's *Structure of Sociological Theory* (noted in the library list for chapter 3) offers critiques of Weber, Mead, and symbolic interaction. A critique of ethnomethodology is the following:

Piccone, Paul, "Review of Mehan and Wood: The Reality of Ethnomethodology." *Telos*, no. 26 (Winter 1975–76): 195–205.

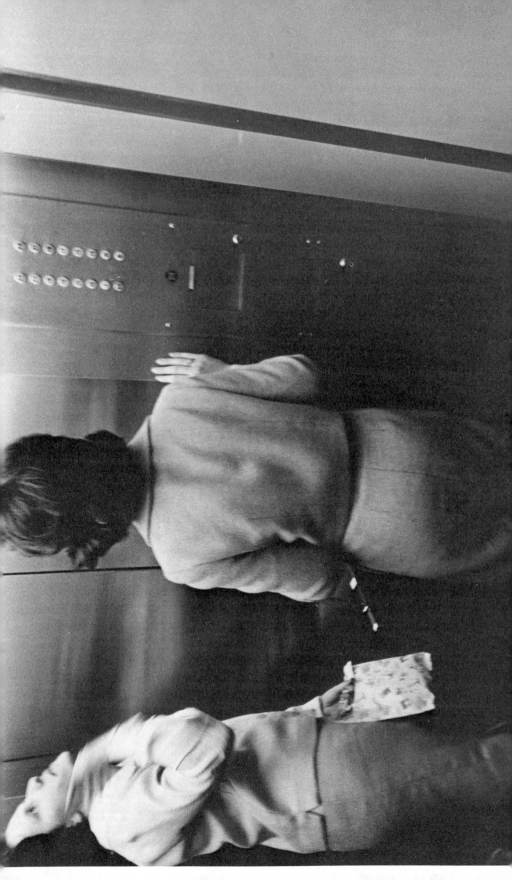

Chapter 6

Methodology

In the last three chapters, we have shown how some of the major theoretical perspectives in sociology may be used by clinicians. A major determinant of which theoretical perspective would be used in a particular situation was said to be a thorough description of the problem. In this chapter, we discuss some traditional and not-so-traditional sociological methods for analyzing social situations. These methods have been developed throughout the history of sociology most extensively by academic sociologists of the "pure science" orientation described in chapter 1. Their goal has been to accomplish reliable and insightful research into the nature of social life.

Sociological methods also can be used by clinicians for *diagnosis*. Such application can provide the information for the first of the three-part diagnostic procedure we mentioned earlier: (1) describing the problem, (2) addressing the problem with theoretical insights, and (3) locating research support for these theories.

This chapter contains a general introduction to the major methodological techniques in sociology. Each reader already is equipped with the necessary tools of the trade. Each of us relates to the people, places, and things of the world we inhabit. It is now time to turn that relationship into a sociological one.

In this chapter we will start from scratch. The first half presents the tools, and ways for readers to sharpen their sociological skills. Development of these skills is an ongoing, time-consuming task, and we can only begin the process here. Only after such development is achieved can the clinician use these tools in the formal techniques described in the second half of the chapter. Yet, familiarity with formal methodology is necessary in order to comprehend the strengths and weaknesses of methods when one locates research support for theories as part of sociological diagnosis.

STOP: LOOK AND LISTEN

For a minute, stop reading this book. Look at and listen to the situation you inhabit at this moment. What do you see? What do you hear? What do all your senses tell you about where you are? Take a minute and write down what you discover.

You have made a statement about what you perceive about the world of the moment just past. Some of what you perceive is likely to be a description of your immediate surroundings and perhaps how you feel toward them. Let us raise some sociological questions about your perceptions.

What belongs to you in what you've described? What meanings do your belongings have for you and for others?

Who arranged the setting you are in? Why do you think it is arranged the way it is? What single word best describes the purpose of the setting? What part of the setting do you control? Who controls the rest of the setting? If you were to change part of the setting you do not control, what would likely happen?

Did you observe other people during your description? Why were they present or absent? What can you tell about who they are? Can you discover who they are without asking them their income, religion, ethnicity, age? How do you think you know these factors?

What groups do you belong to? What would the majority of the members of each of these groups think about what you are doing in this setting? Are there any persons important to you who influence what you are doing right now?

How much money do you have with you right now? How much in the bank? Who are all the people connected to this money? How are they connected?

What do you hope to accomplish through reading this book? Will there be changes in your status, income, skills, attitudes, or knowledge on the basis of this activity? What will such changes (if any) mean to you, your friends, family, people who live near you, people in your state, nation, universe? If it seems that there will be little effect, why?

Underpinning most sociology are looking, listening, questioning, and reporting skills. All sociological methods have these skills at their roots. Elaborate statistics, detailed participant-observation studies, survey research all rely on someone's looking, listening, questioning, and then writing down the results of what they've seen or heard. These skills are taken for granted by many who teach sociology in an attempt to rush the student to sophisticated methods. In clinical sociology, these basic skills are very important; frequently it is the insights based on these skills that provide the necessary understanding of groups, group members, or communities. Each of us interacts with the people, places, and things of the world we inhabit. Each of us can enhance our sociological understanding of that world by increasing our basic sociological skills.

LEARNING TO SEE SOCIOLOGICALLY

Most people see the world as it impinges upon them, but we each view it somewhat differently because of our interests, projects, and other types of social experiences. The teacher views a classroom from a different perspective than a student and their perspectives are probably quite different from that of a custodian. As each of us moves about in our everyday life, we develop pathways to deal with the expected— what routes to take, what obstacles to avoid, what timetables to follow to get done what we think we have to do. We also have ways of handling the unexpected. Think about some of the regularities of your own life, what you do over and over again, what side of the bed you get up from, what you eat regularly, what routes you take to get where you must go. Do patterns emerge? Think also about patterns in how you handle unexpected situations.

Other people also have regularities and ways of handling the unexpected. When enough people agree about a necessary pathway, these regular routes take social forms. For example, when people believe that young persons should be educated but that this task is too difficult and time consuming for the individual to accomplish, an educational system is set up governed with laws, rules, mores, and personnel undertaking specialized tasks with shared perspectives on what they are doing. Likewise, when people need to accomplish complex manufacturing tasks that are beyond the capability of a few people to complete, factories develop using assembly lines where workers do only a small part of the total job, where money gets exchanged for labor, and the activities are governed by laws, rules, mores, with personnel undertaking specialized tasks with shared perspectives on what they are doing.

Each of us ends up knowing some people, some places, some pathways, some social forms quite well and some not at all. We discover that some people have developed similar pathways to our own, coping with situations similar to the ones with which we cope and that some people seem to be running again and again in the ruts of the same circles. To think sociologically, we have to consider people as they move from place to place via pathways, the social forms that are set up to facilitate the movement, and the persons' own perspectives of why they do what they do when they do it.

We increase our capability to observe this sociological world by actively observing in it. A good way to begin developing observational skills is with yourself. Watch yourself move through your everyday life. Which pathways do you take? Which social forms do you encounter? What is your perspective of what you go through every day? Which rules, regulations, and mores do you accept? Which do you challenge? We tend to have more insight into ourselves and why we believe we do what we do than we have insight about other people and their actions. These insights, our perceptions and perspectives, are quite important, but we must recognize that all our beliefs and rationales are not necessarily shared by anyone else, even those closest to us. We must recognize that just because we believe our way is correct does not give us a right to believe others are wrong. Each of us is unique, on the one hand, and a member of a society with shared meanings and shared experiences, on the other. Each of us has had particular experiences that have aided in the development of what we believe, but we also have had many shared experiences, with parents and siblings, with persons of our own age who grow up at a certain place at a certain time, with persons of a common ethnic or religious background, with the entire global village facing shortages of energy or advancement of weapon technology. We must take all this into account when we observe sociologically, recognizing that sometimes our own perspective may be less valuable than others, and is surely incomplete.

Recently one of the authors went to a bachelor party to celebrate the impending marriage of a former student. Ten men ranging in age from 20 to 55 were present. The evening consisted of drinking, gambling, eating, pornographic films, sextalk, and shoptalk. The author's initial perception of the situation was that sexism was rampant, and he was appalled. He missed much of the meaning the party might have had for the other participants. The celebration could be viewed as a *rite of passage* for the guest of honor and an opportunity for the men to verbalize without censorship both their negative feelings about women and their continuing desires for the perfect sexual relationship. While both perspectives are related, the latter is based on more general observations and would have greater utility in understanding the situation.

Each of us, every minute, moves through situations, sometimes conscious of the experience, sometimes oblivious to the movement. To improve looking skills, it is necessary to heighten our awareness of experience so that it becomes possible to report what is taking place from our perception at any given moment.

OBSERVING OTHERS

We can also observe others as we go about our regular activities. What can we tell about them? Begin without interacting.

Sociologists are quite interested in what are called demographic factors: age, income, race, social class, religion, ethnicity, sex, and so on. Some of these demographic factors can be ascertained rather accurately through observation, while for others we can only get clues. These variables become useful in placing persons in the situation being observed into relevant categories. Objects can also have demographic characteristics. A building has an age, and its condition can indicate income. Its usages can relate to other demographic variables.

In contemporary society, some of our traditional ways of using observation to get at this information have broken down. Clothing used to be a major indicator of social class—blue-collar and white-collar working status used to be based quite literally on the color of the collar a man wore to work, but not anymore. Workclothes, especially denim, have invaded the white-collar world, and shirts of all colors are acceptable in many work settings. We used to be able to tell the age and sex of people by looking at them. With the development of unisex styles, face lifts, hair coloring, and youthful clothing produced for persons of all ages, this is increasingly difficult. And one's speech—slang, grammar, or regional dialect—used to be good indicators of place of residence, but with the development of the mass media, job relocations, and easy, inexpensive transportation, some of these distinctions become homogenized.

Such factors suggest the need for caution in drawing conclusions from what you see. Be prepared to be surprised. We have a tendency to assume that a new environment will be like similar settings already experienced. Making such assumptions can keep the clinician from discovering the most important aspect of a new situation—that which makes it different from others.

When observing places and things, it is important to recognize that these can be significant indicators of the social situation that takes place. Places can be physically organized so as to influence the social meanings people have when they move through them: public spaces can be built on a scale to dwarf the people who move through them; and offices can be set up to enhance or diminish the status of the occupant while putting visitors in their place.

It is important also to observe the placement of objects in a setting, their textures and condition. Many people place objects of importance to them in shrine-like locations in settings they control. Attention to texture can indicate usage. Some spaces are designed to be seen by strangers; others are private spaces for the eyes of very few. Learn to recognize what Erving Goffman calls front-stage and back-stage settings. Photography can be an aid. With its aid one can reexamine a place or an event and perhaps pickup elements missed on first viewing.

One instance in which place and object observations are important is in home visits. Important observations include how the home is organized, what social meanings can be drawn from the placement and texture of the furnishings, which objects are placed in shrines:

A particular vertical arrangement is evident in altarlike assemblies of objects. The dictionary defines an altar as "a raised structure, or any structure or place, on which sacrifices are offered or incense is burned in worship of a deity, ancestor, etc." In many homes, there are areas of central focus of interest framed by candles or other tall objects that suggest such a definition. Pictures of deities are usually replaced in contemporary houses by framed oil paintings or reproductions of a secular nature, but the presence of lamps and candles attests to the perhaps unconscious wishes of their owners to suggest an altar. Sometimes oil paintings are substituted by a mirror in which the self is given an opportunity to become the object of worship. Further bric-a-brac furnishes additional ornamentation of the kind found in holy places.[1]

Place and object observation is useful also in getting to know a neighborhood. Much can be learned about an area by the condition, placement, and signs indicating social meanings. Can one note ethnicity by the names on the shops or the special food in the market? Can you discover whether homeowners or renters live there from the condition of property or the number of cars on the street? Can you discover neighborhoods with populations in flux from the number of "for sale" or "for rent" signs?

LEARNING TO LISTEN

We tend to find it difficult to listen, really listen to other people. Frequently, when we try to listen, we are only preparing what we are going to say in response to what the other person is saying. At times, the response we prepare is merely one that will enhance the other person's perception of us; how wise, witty, competent, and powerful we are.

Another obstacle to real listening is noise. Many of us try to listen in settings in which many things are going on loudly and simultaneously. Sometimes this cannot be avoided, but at other times we can control the noise level. At other times we cannot listen because the content of what the person is saying either does not interest us (we've heard it all before) or pains us. Or we translate the words and thoughts of others into our own words and thoughts.

People can learn to give their undivided attention to other people. What others say and how they say it is obviously important to them, but it is also important to the clinical sociologist. We must be trained to pick up many nuances of what the other is saying. Each person can become a significant informant for us. Some clinicians only half-listen to the salient facts of a problem because they assume they've heard it all before and that their usual all-purpose prescription for what the person should do will be right on target. Such a general approach does not allow for the specific conditions that the person is facing to be drawn into a plan. This lack of specificity brings difficulty (e.g., Is the therapist really paying attention to me?) and can lead to the termination of the therapeutic relationship. The special attention that can be communicated by a deeply involved therapist who is really listening makes a critical difference.

There are a number of approaches to improving listening skills. As with observation skills, begin with short periods of trying to remember verbatim what someone else has said, keeping in mind that tone of voice, facial expression, and gestures (nonverbal communication) are all part of what the person is saying. Increase the remembering time until 15 to 30 minutes can be handled with ease. Sometimes remembering a key phrase can be a device to bring back an entire conversation. Cassette recordings can be a useful tool in developing listening facility.

In learning to look and to listen we are trying to grasp the subjectivities of others. How can we really know other people's subjectivities? After all, we cannot get inside their heads and look through their eyes or comprehend their consciousness. Yet social structures and social interactions do not exist simply as objective entities, but as entities which depend upon the interpretations human beings have of them. As the symbolic interactionists remind us, a group of people standing together in a public square become a riot only when they or others watching them decide that they have become a riot. Under other interpretations their same actions might be considered playful, festive, or those of the mentally ill.

The phenomenologist Herbert Spiegelberg has suggested a five-step strategy to achieve access to others' subjectivities:

1. The investigator imagines him or herself as occupying the actual place of the other and tries to see the world as it would present itself from this other perspective.
2. This transposal is not merely a type of "if I were you" seeing. Rather, one's original and historical self is left behind during the transposal. This may mean learning new abilities or abandoning existing ones.
3. The investigator must not attempt to "go native." Rather, he or she must move back and forth between his or her own place and understanding and that of the other. "If we lost ourselves head over heels in his place we should no longer be expanding our . . . grasp."
4. Clues are sought from the situation into which we have put ourselves imaginatively, in order to build the other's world and self as he or she is likely to do.
5. Throughout the process we must revise and reconsider our imaginative constructions in light of new clues from the other's behavior or our own constructions while trying to assume his or her perspective.[2]

LEARNING TO QUESTION

The methodological skills we have described are skills that involve minimal interaction with others. Questioning can also be noninteractive, or it may involve interactive questioning of participants, clients, or community acquaintances.

It is important for the clinical sociologist to be able to analyze the situations or experiences in which he or she is involved—to move back from the immediate experience and analyze what it might mean. There is a particular resonance one is looking for—the reverberations of sociological theory and practice that the experience brings to mind. Somehow, this questioning has to lead to consideration of the major themes presented in the last three chapters. A style of questioning that might get at this is to ask, "What would Marx or Durkheim or Blumer say about this situation?" or "What are some broader themes that emerge in retrospect about what I just went through?" Questions that news reporters learn to ask can be modified for sociological purposes:

1. Who was there? The sociological "who" is different from the reporter's "who." Age, sex, social class, religion, race, ethnicity, group and community contacts are all ways an individual can be defined sociologically.
2. What went on? How does the event relate to the social forms that affect the lives of many?
3. Where did the action take place? What significance did the location have on the action? What social symbols were prominently displayed?
4. Why did the event take place? Why did the activity take the form it did? What did not happen that usually happens in situations such as this?
5. To what extent did change take place? What changed and what remained the same?

This reflective questioning is quite important in relating one's own perspective on what took place to some broader sociological themes. Another way to gain perspective on an event or situation is to ask others. There is an art in asking questions of others that does not quickly cut off information.

In interacting with strangers, the first few minutes of sizing-up are quite important. If you can demonstrate nonjudgmental interest and generate a sense of trust in your manner, frequently people will open up to you. Simmel writes about the special roles strangers play for people (see chapter 7), and there are times when, as a stranger, you can learn a great deal. Each person in any situation has a unique perspective, but only rarely would you question all of them or find that everyone in the

situation is ready to open up. Stephen Richardson, Barbara Dohrenwend, and David Klein have carefully studied the forms, tactics, and
techniques of the interview, which can be viewed as a more formal
questioning situation. They suggest that when the interviewer

> attempts to see himself as respondents will see him and to de-
> termine which aspects of his over-all role and which of his
> personal characteristics respondents are most likely to un-
> derstand and respect, his success in gaining participation is likely
> to increase considerably.
>
> Even in the briefest, most impersonal type of interview, the
> interviewer must present something of himself that the respon-
> dent will find familiar or of interest. To put it another way, he
> must make an effort not to display anything about himself that is
> likely to provoke distaste, anxiety, or hostility in the respon-
> dent. . . . This is not to imply that the interviewer should at-
> tempt to be all things to all respondents. But within the limits of
> his ethics and his behavioral repertoire, he is likely to have
> some freedom of choice in the presentation of himself. To under-
> stand how best to use this freedom, he must make, as carefully and
> as objectively as possible, a thorough assessment of himself as
> an interviewer and a human being.[3]

Many persons hesitate when approaching strangers; others engage in
interactions with strangers without fear. Information-gathering can be
as natural as a conversation or as structured as a formal interview. The
more open-ended the questions, the richer and more natural the
information. The more closed-ended, the easier to compare different
persons' answers.

Ambiguous questions reap ambiguous answers. Recently, a student
wrote a term paper that surveyed inner-city youth on the problem of
delinquency. The student, coming from the area surveyed, recruited
peers of the potential subjects to do the interviewing. With great
enthusiasm, they completed 100 interviews in two city neighborhoods,
but largely to no avail. On his questionnaire, he had included only a
single question to get at delinquency, "Have you had a brush with the
law?" It is difficult to know what a "yes" response to the question
would mean. Does it mean that a policeman told the informant to get off
the street corner, or does it mean that the informant spent five years at a
center for delinquent youth?

Keep in mind also that answers to questions represent the other person's attitude about a behavior and are not necessarily indicators of the behavior itself. It is difficult to ascertain the relationship between one's attitude about a behavior and the behavior itself, especially on tabooed topics. "Have you been on the verge of a nervous breakdown? Are you contemplating suicide? Have you abused a child? Do you cheat on tests?" It is unclear what a "yes" or "no" answer to such questions really means. To increase the likelihood of an accurate response, such threatening questions are usually not asked until some rapport has been established and other less norm-violating questions have been posed. The truthfulness of answers can sometimes be determined by asking the questions at different times in different ways. However, this must be done carefully to keep the respondent from feeling that you don't believe her or him. Try your questions out on friends before you try them on respondents. Their responses can point up hidden ambiguity.

LEARNING TO REPORT

Frequently, people find looking, listening, and questioning relatively easy but get blocked when it comes time to report. Reporting is not only hard work but time consuming. What purposes does it serve for a clinical sociologist?

A report is a record, frequently the only record, of the clinician's perception of an interaction with a client. As time passes, this record becomes part of a collection to be referred to as a gauge of progress. Increasingly in the public sector, such reports are scrutinized by reviewers to ascertain if treatment or action follows plans and standards. At times, because the confidentiality of records in the public sector is suspect (regardless of official guarantees of the rights of privacy for information stored in large computerized data banks), many clinicians are careful in reporting information that could prove damaging to clients.

The major importance of reporting accurately and in detail is to transmit clearly to others what you comprehend about a person or situation. These others may not be present, as is the case with later clinicians or researchers. Such reporting should involve little abstraction; too frequently the novice clinician does not record what took place, but rather his reaction to it, using value-laden words that do not communicate the content of what went on to the reader of the report. For example, it might be recorded that "the room has shabby furniture" or "Ms. B. is hallucinating." More accurate reporting might specifically state, "There was a seven-foot modern sofa opposite the 25-inch television set. The slipcovers on the cushions were torn in many places," and "Ms. B. said, 'A creature about the size of a man with a long pig-like snout came to the door to repair the furnace.' " (In this actual incident, the repairman wore a gas mask in defense against the stench from Ms. B.'s cats, their excrement, and decaying food.) The detailed examples communicate to the reader a more precise sense of what was learned and can be invaluable for analysis.

At times, it becomes necessary to generalize from a number of specific reports about the broader meaning of what took place and to use all available information to aid in formulating a plan for a person, group, or community. The plan could be a clinical summary and a treatment plan, a grant request, an annual report, or a research report. In each of these cases, the audience or audiences for whom the report is intended must be kept in mind. Effective report writing usually has to fit the formula that is expected by the reader. Clear writing for any audience requires careful organization and choice of language level best suited for the audience. The quality of our communication has a great deal to do with the acceptance of the position we offer. Good report writing can be a highway to the power and resources needed to accomplish therapeutic changes for groups and group members.

The best way to increase reporting skills is to write reports and ask others to comment on what you have communicated. In your reports it is important to separate feelings or hunches about meaning from what objectively took place. These hunches can be quite important in coming to understanding, so they should not be eliminated, simply clearly delineated.

CRITICAL THINKING

Sociologists try to perceive the social meanings of situations for what they are, not what they seem to be to any one faction. Underlying sociological looking, listening, questioning, and reporting is the critical thinking that leads to informed judgment.

Critical thinking is the ability to understand the broader implications of data gathered from situational experiences and to extract the salient factors that necessitate further action or reflection. Informed judgment comes when we are able to communicate effectively our understanding of these salient factors in a manner that inspires the confidence of others. When we are successful, we move beyond techniques to the sociological essence of social situations.

Teachers and trainers struggle with the problem of how to move their students into the realm of the gifted practitioner who is able to use his or her best judgment in most situations, learn from mistakes, and continue to grow in the confident application of an increasing range of skills. There appears to be no set way to accomplish this goal. People need a strong background in the basic skills already described in this chapter. There is a need to keep one's thinking fresh. In working, thinking, or writing about human social situations, it is possible to "burn out" and begin to use ritualized thinking or action, seeing the human being as another product of the assembly line or the situation just experienced as a rerun from the past. Critical thinking isolates the unique and explores its relationship to the regular, leading to theoretical understanding, and to action.

Moving beyond techniques, to the use of critical thinking, means taking chances, but if there is a strong grounding in basic skills, the risk is made from a position of strength and flexibility.

FROM TOOLS TO METHODS

The tools of looking, listening, questioning, reporting, and using critical thinking are the basic building blocks for more formal sociological methods. Each emphasizes a different configuration of the tools; each has advantages and disadvantages both for academic researchers and for clinical sociologists. The following techniques make up most of the formal methodology in sociology: participant observation, historical and documentary analysis, interviewing, surveys, and coordinated substudies. The remainder of this chapter will introduce the basics of these techniques and give some idea of how they have been used in academic sociology for the purposes of pure science research (as noted in chapter 1). More importantly, we will suggest some ways in which these techniques can be used for diagnosis of clinical problems. To develop adequately any of these formal skills requires, however, a great deal of study and practice.

PARTICIPANT OBSERVATION

Traditionally, the participant-observer immerses himself in the situation being studied to learn the social meanings from the

regular participants. He notes in detail what takes place including *what happens to him* and reports on the behavior and attitudes that underlie the situation using a conceptual
framework that comes from his immersion in the situation and the
data collected from his immersion.[4]

The key data for participant observation are field notes written just
after the participant-observer leaves the scene of the observation. These
notes report what took place in as much relevant detail as possible, with
potential hunches by the observer about the meaning of the activities
also noted. Field notes look like these from Jonathan Freedman's observation of a juvenile gang in Chicago in 1960:

The cops drove by a couple of times but did not stop. At various
times people from the boys club, mostly Negro kids, stopped
and talked on the opposite corner and then moved on. Two of
them talked briefly with the boys. After a while the game ended
with the last available "ball" hit over the fence. George had
finished changing tires, taking Larry with him. A little while later,
Mike and one of the younger boys took off in the other direction,
but they soon returned. Two guys drove up in a red Thunder-
bird 1956 vintage. One . . . was starting to grow a beatnik beard
on the lower part of his chin. He immediately walked up to
one of the girls and started questioning her about other girls.
"Was Grace going to be there or was she there already?" "No,"
the girl answered, using her hands for protection. "Was
Sharon or Cynthia getting married?" "No, she's going to Texas
with her father," as she tried to push him away. After gaining the
information, the two returned to the T-bird, and drove away.
There was little conversation with the guys on the stoop.
    Jim drove by in a 1954 Chevie with his girl. He parked next to
the boys' club and entered it before coming out to the corner.
Mike or Sammy said, "He still drives like a Puerto Rican." He was
not very relaxed behind the wheel, looking this way and that
way. Jim sat on one corner of the stairs while his girl joined the
others. He was asked a couple of questions and then ignored.
Most of the talking now was bantering with the girls. The
coeducational conversation ceased and the girls talked quietly
among themselves. A car from the group who hung out at Duo's
passed by and one of its members hurled a series of invectives
at the people at the steps. They laughed and tossed some back.

Another game was invented. Little pebbles were thrown at the
sitters. Sammy invented it and soon pebbles were moving at
ten second intervals.

Usually, notes are collected for a lengthy period, three months to two
ears traditionally. For many observers, there comes a time when they
now the field situation so well that they can almost predict what will
appen. This magic moment is one indicator that it is time to conclude
e field study.

Soon after the field data have been collected, the participant-observer
egins to analyze the data through the inductive development of
ategories. In this movement from the data to the themes within the
ata, the participant-observer tries to present to him or herself and
otential readers an understanding of the situation studied from the
erspectives of the participants, and to maintain the flavor so that
thers can participate vicariously in the studied situation.

Barney Glaser and Anselm Strauss describe the nature of the field
ork process:

> The "real life" character of field work knowledge deserves special
> underscoring, especially as many critics think of this and other
> qualitatively oriented methods as merely preliminary to real
> (scientific) knowing. A firsthand immersion in a sphere of life and
> action—a social world—different from one's own yields im-
> portant dividends for the fieldworker. The fieldworker who has
> observed closely in this social world has had, in a profound
> sense, to live there. He has not only been sufficiently immersed
> in the world to know it, but has retained enough detachment to
> think theoretically about what he has seen and lived
> through. His informed detachment has allowed him to benefit
> not only as a sociologist but as a human being who must "make
> out" in that world. This is true despite the fact that the people
> there generally do not expect perfect adherence to their ways from
> the outsider. His detachment has served also to protect him
> against going more than a little native while yet doing more
> than a little passing as a native, then the people whom he is
> studying either have temporarily forgotten his outsider status or
> have never recognized it. Meanwhile his display of under-
> standing and sympathy for their mode of life permits sufficient
> trust in him so that he is not cut off from seeing important events,

hearing important conversations and perhaps seeing important documents. If that trust does not develop, his analysis suffers.[5]

The advantages of participant observation include its potential communicate the rich flavor of the social situation, its ability to uncove unanticipated information, and its capturing of the perspectives of th actors in the situation. The disadvantages are that most accurate fiel studies take a long time to complete, that the conditions in the situatio can change by the time the study is completed, and that the analysis the data even when rigorous is always fairly subjective. It is sometime unclear how conclusions from one situation might relate to conclusior from another situation.

The clinical sociologist can practice participant observation by ac tively observing the situations in which he or she works or goes t school. Make observations in the cafeteria, and of persons in the class room or office setting. Go to a public place, such as a train or bu station, a sporting event, a hospital emergency room, and just observe Simple participant observation is a technique readily available to all. requires no access to esoteric or expensive tools. On the other hand professional participant observation requires rigorous clinical skills tha need to be highly developed before the method provides useful results

INTERVIEWING

Interviewing involves development of a set of questions to asl people, asking the questions, and recording and analyzing the re sponses. There are open-end and closed-end forms. The former typ gives the respondent an opportunity to respond in a richer, more de tailed fashion. However, closed-end interviews are much easier t analyze because the number of potential answers is limited by the de sign of the interview form:

Open end: Tell me what you think of this book?
Closed end: Please rank this book in relation to others you hav
             used. Is it
             a. one of the best?
             b. above average?
             c. average?
             d. poor?
             e. one of the worst?

To analyze answers to the open-end question, the sociologist must develop analytic categories from the responses, much as the participant-observer develops categories from field notes. The closed-end form sets up the universe of responses in advance, makes an assumption that people's use of language within the range of possible answers is fairly consistent, and that the prearranged answers will force the respondent to the best possible category, while eliminating equivocation.

Interviews provide face-to-face contact with a respondent yet limit the nature of the interaction to reasonably predetermined issues. Much information can be gathered and analyzed in a short time, but we have no way of ensuring reliability of the answers. Without the establishment of clearly shared meanings, interviewing can become a game between interviewer and respondent.

In the case of community or other large-scale analysis, closed-end interviews can be turned into *questionnaires* by eliminating the face-to-face contact and using telephone or postal services to reach respondents. The advantage is the ability to reach a larger number of respondents in a short time. The disadvantage is that response rates are frequently low, and it is usually impossible for the researcher to tell whether those who did not respond are different than those who did.

The systematic use of interviews, questionnaires, or a combination of both to discover the thoughts of a large number of persons is called *survey research*. Surveys can be used to predict behavior, as in marketing studies or pre-election polls. Survey researchers usually develop sophisticated ways to construct randomly selected samples of the population, in hopes that the persons chosen will reflect the total population. Such samples can be taken over time (i.e., longitudinally) to provide a sense of change. For instance, work under the sponsorship of Potomac Associates has been examining the hopes and fears of persons in the United States every few years. They use a clever survey device called the "self-anchoring striving scale" to get at the differences between what persons think of the conditions of their own lives and what they think of national conditions.[6]

The key questions on this survey are as follows:

LADDER RATINGS: HOPES AND FEARS

1. All of us want certain things out of life. When you think about what really matters in your own life, what are your wishes and hopes for the future? In other words, if you imagine your future in the *best* possible

light, what would your life look like then if you are to be happy? Take
your time in answering; such things aren't easy to put into words.

2.   Taking the other side of the picture, what are your fears and worries
for the future? In other words, if you imagine your future in the *worst*
possible light, what would your life look like then? Again, take your
time in answering.

3.   Here is a ladder representing the "ladder of life." Let's suppose the
top of the ladder represents the *best* possible life for you; and the bottom, the *worst* possible life for you. On which step of the ladder do you
feel you personally stand at the present time?

4.   On which step would you say you stood *five years ago?*

5.   Just as your best guess, on which step do you think you will stand
in the future, say about *five years from now?*

6.   Now let's consider just the past twelve months. In terms of your
own personal happiness and satisfaction, would you say that today, as
compared with *one year ago,* you are better off, about the same, or worse
off?

7.   Now, what are your wishes and hopes for the future of the United
States? If you picture the future of the U.S. in the *best* possible light,
how would things look, let us say, about ten years from now?

8.   And what about your fears and worries for the future of our country? If you picture the future of the U.S. in the *worst* possible light, how
would things look about ten years from now?

9.   Looking at the ladder again, suppose the top represents the *best*
possible situation for our country; the bottom, the *worst* possible situation. Please show me on which step of the ladder you think the United
States is at the present time.

10.   On which step would you say the United States was about *five
years ago?*

11.   Just as your best guess, if things go pretty much as you now
expect, where do you think the United States will be on the ladder, let
us say, about *five years from now?*

To get a flavor of the survey process, we suggest you try these questions
on acquaintances.

The clinical sociologist can use results from existing surveys such as
this to aid in understanding the beliefs and behavior intentions of
persons or groups of persons. Especially useful are the periodic national
surveys by the National Opinion Research Center at the University of
Chicago which ask questions about dozens of major social issues and

divide their sample by region, age, ethnicity, and so forth. The clinical sociologist can construct interviews or questionnaires, conduct the survey, and learn to do some data analysis. There are computer programs (e.g., SPSS—Statistical Package for the Social Sciences) that can be easily learned and used to transform raw data into useful statistics.

Frequently the results of surveys are presented in statistical form. Many statistics are gathered routinely on people, and some sociologists use these statistics for the development of trends' studies. The advantages of using statistics are that sample size can be very large and information collected can be used for many purposes (e.g., census data are used to study demography, ethnicity, poverty).

It is important to recognize, however, that even the best collected statistics have built-in biases. Statistics reduce the rich ambiguity of social life to numbers and in the process severely limit the meanings behind persons' answers to survey questions. Some, such as the FBI's *Uniform Crime Reports*, have to be used with great care. Over-reporting and under-reporting can vary by type of crime and locale.

The clinical sociologist can use statistics to discover where a client fits in relationship to broader situations. In working with a community as client, careful examination can point up inequalities in resource allocation that could be turned into an issue. Sunshine laws have freed information which could prove quite useful. Most governmental records are now public, as are many formerly closed meetings.

HISTORICAL AND DOCUMENTARY ANALYSIS

Time passes and critical events fade from participants' memories. What is left? Documents—newspapers, memoirs, public records, deeds, minutes of meetings, statistical tables, and, more recently, audio and video tapes. Through the techniques of content analysis and historiography, one tries to piece together themes from the past. For many situations, this method is all that is available, since actual sociological materials are not available about many historical personalities and events. The application of historical and documentary analysis requires rigorous techniques. One has to make assumptions based on fragmentary data in much the same way as an archeologist tries to reconstruct dead cultures from remaining artifacts.

For the clinical sociologist, knowledge of this approach can be important when fragmentary social histories of a person, group, or community have to be expanded to develop hypotheses about broader meanings and diagnoses of current problems. In a study of an urban renewal project, one of this book's authors demonstrates how historical and documentary analysis can provide insights into current activities:

> A neighborhood a few miles from the center of downtown at the periphery of the slum is to be renewed in order to be saved. Jefferson Park was the name chosen by the redevelopment authority in order to overcome the potential stigma of the former name for the area, Stonetown Highlands.[7] Stonetown was an early expansion from Boston itself which was annexed to the central city. Most people in Boston consider Stonetown a Negro slum. Stonetown Highlands had a history of being settled by the wealthy of minority groups—Irish, then Jews and now Negroes. The higher parts of the Highlands still contain quite substantial housing. In recent years before the urban renewal, the houses lower on the hill had deteriorated. The Jefferson Park (Stonetown Highlands) renewal plan attempted to preserve the houses of quality through rehabilitation and out of sheer necessity to remove the deteriorated housing. The housing to the top of the hill consists of mostly single family houses, while multiple flats used to predominate in the lower part. Large apartment houses face Hancock Park, one of Boston's largest parks. There are reminders of Jewish life in the area although most of the Jews have moved out. A large synagogue faces the park. A Yeshiva still operates next to an African Methodist Episcopal Church, and a restaurant exclusively for Jewish catered affairs still thrives. Many of the store owners are Jewish. As the area is developing in a piecemeal fashion, many of the typical establishments of the ghetto still exist at the boundary lines of the renewal area. Most of the whites who work in the area retreat to the suburbs after the working hours. The neighborhood schools are almost exclusively Negro. A major transportation terminal is at one end of the developed area, so it is possible to see both races waiting for subway transportation at all hours that such service is offered.
>
> These, then, are some of the historical and ethnic characteristics of the area. In examining the plan for the area, the plan of the redevelopment authority, which prides itself on citizens' participation, certain facts emerge. There is a four-lane, limited-

access highway built piece-by-piece through the middle of the
community. It separates most of the upper hill housing from the
lower hill renewal, for most of the rehabilitation is taking place
on the upper hill and most of the renewal on the lower hill. In
its current state, this highway goes from nowhere to nowhere and
this condition will remain for some time. Such a highway can
act as a boundary between neighborhoods. It is not as imposing
as the "Chinese Wall" elevated highway that separates Boston's
North End from downtown, but, in time, the effect might be
the same. Why was the highway built? The area planners noted
that considerable through traffic used small side streets as
shortcuts through the area. By building such a highway,
through traffic would be channeled on the superhighway
leaving the residential streets for residential use. It is unclear
whether this will happen since, at the moment, the highway
goes nowhere. It will be some time before the road goes somewhere. What other purposes could this road serve? It has already
been stated that it separates the upper hill housing from the
urban renewal area. By so doing, it separates most of the social
institutions which now exist or are planned for the upper
side of the hill from the few churches and a boys' club as well as
a large shopping center just at the highway on the lower side. For
the most part, like Hyde Park in Chicago, this separation is on
the class basis: the upper and middle classes are on one side of the
highway and the lower middle and working classes are on the
other. Unlike Hyde Park, with the high class Negroes integrated
with similar status whites, Jefferson Park's Highland
residents will be in an overwhelming Negro enclave with
natural and man-made boundaries on three sides. The effect
of urban renewal, therefore, is similar to Hyde Park. It
stabilizes a higher class community by creation of boundaries.

Now citizen participation is designed into the urban renewal
process, and in Jefferson Park, many meetings were held for those
in the community who were interested to plan the neighborhood. Most meetings were held on the Hillside of the renewal
area. Most participants at those meetings lived in that area. Renewal and planning activities center around a community
agency, Democracy House, again located on the Hillside. Physical
as well as social evidence points to the planning of the neighborhood by those on the Hillside, its Negro elite.[8]

This excerpt shows how historical and documentary material when combined with observation can provide a rich understanding of some of the present dynamics in a situation which is potentially amenable to clinical sociological diagnosis and therapy.

COORDINATED SUBSTUDIES

Several methods may be used in conjunction for some diagnoses. In coordinated substudies, each study explores a key element of the overall problem. Each of the methods already discussed can be applied to manageable segments of the total problem. Then the results of each of the substudies are linked to create a *sense* of the entire problem. This approach can save the sociologist time and money. A disadvantage is that by predetermining the key elements of the problem, the sociologist may completely miss a key factor. Clinical sociologists often find a coordinated substudy approach to their liking because decisions frequently have to be made on a time-limited basis and this approach can provide well analyzed information rather quickly.[9]

CLINICAL SOCIOLOGY AS ART

I think, then, that the supreme aim of social science is to perceive the drama of life more adequately than can be done by ordinary observation. If it is to be objected that this is the task of the artist—a Shakespeare, a Goethe, or a Balzac—rather than that of a scientist, I may answer that an undertaking so vast requires the co-operation of various sorts of synthetic minds: artists, scientists, philosophers, and men of action. Or I may say that the constructive part of science is, in truth, a form of art.[10]

In the mid-1970s Robert Nisbet wrote a book titled *Sociology as an Art Form*.[11] In it, Nisbet argues that sociology is as much an art as it is a science, that "there is no conflict between science and art, but that in their psychological roots they are almost identical." Sociological themes such as community, power, conflict, alienation, and disorganization can best be understood not through mathematical description, but by seeing them as landscapes and portraits, Nisbet claims in his book. Although formal methodological prescriptions and mathematical models are essential to the *logic of demonstration*, this is a phase of inquiry appropriate only after the *logic of discovery* is achieved. Discovery is a delicate art.

The techniques we have discussed in this chapter mostly are amenable to use for either discovery or demonstration, but in clinical work the former is much more important than the latter. We have emphasized previously that clinicians usually rely upon basic research of academic sociologists for the specific information they will apply in individual cases. It is in the analysis of these individual, immediate cases that the clinician as clinician employs sociological methods, and the analysis is properly a process of discovery.

The artistic dimension of clinical sociological inquiry begins with the very choice of what to examine, and continues through to the results of the examination. Only the most creative thinking can hope to avoid repetition of inadequate patterns and to develop new ones. Hence, the change-oriented nature of clinical sociology demands that we emphasize the artistic deployment of techniques. Clinicians deal with persons linked to social structures and processes. The clinical sociologist looks at the nature of the linkage and develops an intervention strategy.

Many fine examples of artistic sociological analyses exist, and we have listed these in the Clinician's Library section. One volume stands alone in our estimation, however, as a most sensitive and insightful inquiry into the lives of a group of people suffering serious social problems. James Agee and Walker Evans wrote about and photographed the daily life of tenant farmers in Alabama in 1936. The researchers were a novelist and a photographer, but their report is highly sociological, and regularly clinical. Some passages from *Let Us Now Praise Famous Men* convey the *feeling* of artistic clinical analysis (and the incredible difficulties thereof):

> . . . how, looking thus into your eyes and seeing thus, how each
> of you is a creature which has never in all time existed before
> and which shall never in all time exist again and which is not
> quite like any other and which has the grand stature and natural
> warmth of every other and whose existence is all measured
> upon a still mad and incurable time; how am I to speak of you as
> "tenant" "farmers," as "representatives" of your "class," as
> social integers in a criminal economy, or as individuals, fathers,
> wives, sons, daughters, and as my friends as I "know" you?
> Granted—more, insisted upon—that in all these par-
> ticularities that each of you is that which he is; that par-
> ticularities, and matters ordinary and obvious, are exactly them-
> selves beyond designation of words, are the members of your

sum total most obligatory to human searching or perception:
nevertheless to name these things and fail to yield their stature,
meaning, power of hurt, seems impious, seems criminal, seems
impudent, seems traitorous in the deepest: and to do less
badly seems impossible: yet in withholdings of specification I
could but betray you still worse.

Here I must say, a little anyhow; what I can hardly hope to bear
out in the record: that a house of simple people which stands
empty and silent in the vast Southern country morning sunlight,
and everything which on this morning in eternal space it by
chance contains, all thus left open and defenseless to a reverent
and cold-laboring spy, shines quietly forth such grandeur, such
sorrowful holiness of its exactitudes in existence, as no human
consciousness shall ever rightly perceive, far less import to
another: that there can be more beauty and more deep wonder in
the standings and spacings of mute furnishings on a bare floor
between the squaring bourns of walls than in any music ever
made: that this square home as it stands in unshadowed earth
between the winding years of heaven, is, not to me but of
itself, one among the serene and final, uncapturable beauties of
existence: that this beauty is made between hurt but invincible
nature and the plainest cruelties and needs of human existence
in this uncured time, and is inextricable among these, and is impossible without them as a saint born in paradise.

I am confident of being able to get at a certain form of the truth
about him, only if I am as faithful as possible to Gudger as I
know him, to Gudger as, in his actual flesh and life (but there
again always in my mind's and memory's eye) he is. But of course
it will be only a relative truth. Name me a truth within human
range that is not relative and I will feel a shade more apolo-
getic about that.

If I were going to use these lives of yours for "Art," if I were going
to dab at them here, cut them short here, make some trifling
improvement over here, in order to make you worthy of the
Saturday Review of Literature; I would just now for instance be very
careful of Anticlimax which, you must understand, is just not
quite nice. It happens in life of course, over and over again, in

fact there is no such thing as lack of it, but Art, as all of you would understand if you had had my advantages, has nothing to do with Life, or no more to do with it than is thoroughly convenient at a given time, a sort of fair-weather friendship, or gentleman's agreement, or practical idealism, well understood by both parties and by all readers.[12]

Very few clinicians reach the level of sensitivity found in these passages. On a day-to-day basis it may not even be wise for clinicians to attempt such intimate and grueling appreciation of their clients. But the struggle to appreciate others in their rich fullness is often what makes the difference between a sociologically *reliable* diagnosis and a sociologically *therapeutic* diagnosis. Achieving reliability requires technical skill, and is surely crucial to academic sociological work. Achieving therapeutic potential requires artistic sensibilities, and is essential to clinical sociological work. One's overall goal, of course, should be the accomplishment of both tasks. As John Dewey wrote in another context, "No experience of whatever sort is a unity unless it has aesthetic quality." [13]

NOTES

1. Jurgen Ruesch and Wendell Kees, *Non Verbal Communication* (Berkeley: University of California Press, 1956), pp. 143–54.
2. Herbert Spiegelberg, "Phenomenology through Vicarious Experience," in E. Straus, ed., *Phenomenology: Pure and Applied* (Pittsburgh: Duquesne University Press, 1964).
3. Stephen A. Richardson, Barbara Snell Dohrenwend, and David Klein, *Interviewing: Its Forms and Functions* (New York: Basic Books, 1965), pp. 91–92.
4. Jonathan A. Freedman, *A Sociological Approach to Rapid Change Conditions*, Ph.D. dissertation (Ann Arbor, Mich.: University Microfilms, 1973), p. 24.
5. Barney G. Glaser and Anselm M. Strauss, "Discovery of Substantive Theory: A Basic Strategy Underlying Qualitative Research," *American Behavioral Scientist* 9(1965):8–9.
6. F. P. Kirkpatrick and Hadley Cantril, "Self-Anchoring Striving Scale: A Measure of Individuals' Unique Reality Worlds," *Journal of Individual Psychology* 16(November 1960):161–62.

7. The local Boston names are substitutes for the real names.

8. Freedman, *A Sociological Approach to Rapid Change Conditions*, pp. 195–98.

9. Robert Weiss, "Issues in Holistic Research," in Howard S. Becker et al., eds., *Institutions and the Person* (Chicago: Aldine, 1968), pp. 343–50.

10. Charles Horton Cooley, *Social Process* (Carbondale: Southern Illinois University Press, 1966), pp. 402–4.

11. Robert Nisbet, *Sociology as an Art Form* (New York: Oxford University Press, 1976).

12. James Agee and Walker Evans, *Let Us Now Praise Famous Men* (New York: Ballantine, 1966), pp. 92, 121, 216, 333.

13. John Dewey, *Art as Experience* (New York: Capricorn Books, 1958), p. 40.

THE CLINICIAN'S LIBRARY

LOOKING

Rowland, Kurt. *Learning to See Series*, Books 1–5. New York: Van Nostrand Reinhold, 1968–69.
Ruesch, Jurgen, and Wendell Kees. *Non Verbal Communication*. Berkeley: University of California Press, 1956.
Webb, Eugene J., et al. *Unobtrusive Measures*. Skokie, Ill.: Rand McNally, 1966.

QUESTIONING

Howard, Robert. *Roles and Relationships*. Palo Alto, Cal.: Westinghouse Learning Press, 1973.
Simon, Sidney, et al. *Values Clarification*. New York: Hart, 1972.

REPORTING

Elbow, Peter. *Writing without Teachers*. New York: Oxford University Press, 1973.
Graves, Robert, and Alan Hodge. *The Reader over Your Shoulder*. New York: Macmillan, 1961.
Tichy, H. J. *Effective Writing*. New York: Wiley, 1966.

SOCIOLOGICAL METHODS: OVERVIEWS

Labovitz, Sanford, and Robert Hagedorn. *Introduction to Social Research*, 2nd ed. New York: McGraw-Hill, 1975.
Madge, John. *Tools of Social Science*. London, New York: Longman, 1953.

PARTICIPANT OBSERVATION

Bogdan, Robert, and S. Taylor. *Introduction to Qualitative Research Methods*. New York: Wiley, 1975.
Liebow, Elliot. *Tally's Corner*. Boston: Little, Brown, 1967.
Wax, Rosalie. *Doing Fieldwork*. Chicago: University of Chicago Press, 1971.
Whyte, William Foote. *Street Corner Society*. Chicago: University of Chicago Press, 1970.

INTERVIEWING

Richardson, Stephen A., et al. *Interviewing: Its Forms and Functions*. New York: Basic Books, 1965.

SURVEY RESEARCH

Davis, James A. *Elementary Survey Analysis*. Englewood Cliffs, N.J.: Prentice-Hall, 1971.

SOCIOLOGY AS ART

Agee, James, and Walker Evans. *Let Us Now Praise Famous Men*. New York: Ballantine, 1966.
Coser, Lewis, ed. *Sociology through Literature*. Englewood Cliffs, N.J.: Prentice-Hall, 1972.
Nisbet, Robert. *Sociology as an Art Form*. New York: Oxford University Press, 1976.

Part 3

Vital Features

If we consider the world of groups, group members, and their communities as a social landscape, certain landmarks, or *vital features*, stand out: ethnicity, stratification, age, family and sex roles, change, and everyday metaphysics. Careful examination of these features relative to the clinical situation offers a basis for diagnosis and for developing therapy.

We recognize that others looking at the social landscapes might be able to see other vital features, notably, population density, law and politics, education, and religion, which we will present as processes of one or more of the vital features listed above (e.g., education is discussed relative to stratification, ethnicity, family, and personal metaphysics).

The specific clinical case will determine which features are most vital to the diagnosis, and scrutiny of these features should reveal in which ways they are contributing constructively and destructively to the *gestalt* of the phenomena under consideration. Thus, in considering the effectiveness of a neighborhood association, one's appropriate initial impulse might be to pay special attention to the change, family, and everyday metaphysics features, since these are crucial to the very nature of such organizations. After some scrutiny, however, sex and ethnicity may turn out to be especially significant, say, in light of the predominantly male and black composition of the organization's leadership group.

The chapters in this part are very basic introductions to major compositional and pathological processes for these vital features. Each chapter provides a general overview of the feature, describing its *composition*, and paying special attention to its *constructive and destructive processes*. These primary concerns of the clinical sociologist parallel those of physiology, pathology, and diagnosis in medicine. Obviously, any particular clinical situation will send the clinician to several theoretical and research publications which describe in detail the workings of the feature. A vital feature is to be understood only in relation to the work available within academic sociology which empirically and theoretically discusses the feature. Check the Clinician's Library section at the end of each chapter for leads to useful literature.

The relationships between these features in social structures have yet to be clearly and carefully delineated. The need for such work is especially apparent to those of us working in clinical settings that involve multiple features. Although the compositions and basic processes can be reasonably well identified, the usual or necessary patterns of interaction between various features have yet to be explained in the sociological literature.[1]

In working with clients, clinicians do best to keep in mind the relevant features, their separate constructive and destructive processes, and how these are operating to determine the existence of the client groups, group members, or communities.

1.   Some work concerning the nature of relationships between features is in process by the present authors. Thus, we are investigating the temporal dimension underlying both change and age; the distributive dimension inherent in both stratification and ethnicity; and the development of everyday metaphysics via group and group members' interactions within the processes of these vital features. Consideration of countervailing factors to these features is also under investigation: ethnicity may be opposed by assimilation, change by stability, age by present time, and so forth.

Chapter 7

Ethnicity

Most ethnic groups are termed "minorities," both in everyday usage and in sociological literature. Some ethnics—white Protestants, for instance—are not considered minorities at present, but by and large the terms "ethnic group" and "minority" have become synonymous. What makes a group a minority?

Mathematically, a minority is a number which is smaller than one to which it is being compared. At first glance this may appear to be the social meaning as well; blacks, Jews, Puerto Ricans, and American Indians are minorities in the United States, and all have fewer members than do white Christians. But in Africa and Rhodesia, blacks are the numerical majority yet for decades have been "minority" groups in these nations.

Some sociologists define a minority as a group, of whatever size, that lacks power. This seems to be a distinguishing feature of numerically large groups such as blacks in South Africa. The distinction does not hold up upon closer scrutiny, however. If power were the determining factor, then the entire lower class would be a minority, and this violates our understanding that within the lower class there are a variety of separate minority groups.

Some groups which have been minorities cease to be minorities, such as the Irish, who received prejudicial and discriminatory treatment in the United States in the mid-1800s but are now fully a part of the American majority. Conversely, some majority participants become a minority group over time. Indeed, nearly all minority groups were at some time and place a majority; various Indian tribes were majority groups in parts of the United States until the Europeans arrived and made minorities of them, many black Africans captured for slavery were members of African majority groups.

Being a minority is a social *process*, then. To understand this process is to answer the question, "What is a minority?" Probably the most informative description of the process was offered by Louis Wirth:

> We may define a minority as a group of people who, because of their physical and cultural characteristics, are singled out from others in the society in which they live for differential and unequal treatment and who therefore regard themselves as objects of collective discrimination.[1]

A great deal of information is packed into Wirth's description, and from it we can ascertain the composition of minority, and thereby the composition of the vital feature of ethnicity. Ethnicity is a special type of minority. Not all minority groups are ethnic groups (e.g., homosexuals and women), but all ethnic groups are minorities, either actual or potential. The constant potential for ethnic groups to become minorities can be seen both in Wirth's definition and in the history of ethnic groups. Becoming a minority is the result of being singled out on the basis of difference, and the potential for this is constantly present among ethnic groups. Historical cases include those mentioned above, the Irish, Indians, and blacks. Contemporary nonminority ethnics such as white Protestants only need be successfully singled out to become a minority. There is evidence that this is beginning to occur in some locations, including South Africa and some central-city locations in the United States.

Within the process Wirth described are two components we will consider: *distinctiveness* and *interpretation and treatment* (both by others and by the minorities of themselves). Major destructive processes we will consider—prejudice, discrimination, and inequality—are also built into the process, as a result of "differential and unequal treatment."

DISTINCTIVENESS

Physical distinctions between ethnic groups may seem at first glance to be major. Skin color, hair color and texture, facial features, and other aspects appear to vary predictably between groups. Upon closer examination, however, these distinctions are not consistent indicators of ethnicity.[2] Americans usually consider dark-skinned persons as blacks (or "negroid"), but many Arabs, Pacific Islanders, and some Southern Europeans are as dark as the average black American. Many American blacks have lighter skin than sun-tanned whites and can "pass" for white.

The same can be said for other physical traits. Curly hair is considered distinctive of some ethnic groups, but it is common of blacks, Jews, large percentages of white Anglo-Saxon Protestants, and thousands of persons who use hair curling devices and chemicals. On the other hand, straight black hair is common among American Indians, Latin Americans, most persons from India, large percentages of white Anglo-Saxon Protestants, and persons who use hair straighteners.

Neither is using several physical traits in conjunction to determine ethnicity objectively adequate, since only a small percentage of the ethnic group will fully exhibit all of the traits. *Everyday* use of physical distinctions is frequent and is generally considered appropriate by both ethnic group members and outsiders. As a result, physical distinctions come to be very important subjectively, as evidenced, for instance, by groups of blacks who proclaim their ethnicity with "Afro" hairstyles while others avoid their ethnicity with hair straighteners and light-toned makeup.

Cultural distinctions are the truly consequential ones for ethnic groups, because they include both objective and subjective distinctions. Indeed, even the choice and interpretations of physical distinctions are the consequence of processes of culture. Four major dimensions of culture indicate ethnic distinctiveness: history, symbols, values, and beliefs.

The *history* of an ethnic group is the major key to understanding the distinctiveness of that group. Most fundamentally, the clinician requires historical knowledge to determine in which ways ethnic group members in a particular time and place are affected by their ethnicity.

One major determinant of current ethnic group activity and consciousness is the manner in which the group came to locate at its present residence. To understand black inner-city schoolchildren in the U.S. and Chinese inner-city schoolchildren in the U.S., one needs to know at least the following: (1) male and female blacks arrived involuntarily as slaves 300 years ago, but male Chinese arrived voluntarily and in search of gold 100 years ago and with plans to return to China; (2) blacks were separated from fellow tribesmen, and the new slave families which developed were also destroyed in many cases, but the Chinese were forced to stay together as a result of their language and segregated housing in the western U.S.; and (3) relatively small percentages of blacks have found the freedom and prosperity they desired in the urban North and West, but the median income for Chinese-American families is slightly above that for whites, although major Chinese urban ghettos still exist.

With this knowledge in hand a clinician can start to understand what may otherwise be a mystery—the relatively high academic achievement levels and lack of "disciplinary problems" for Chinese children compared to black children. Chinese Americans have a history of traditional and strict home environments that stresses self-discipline and achievement, and that evidences that hard work in school brings rewards in later life. The history of black Americans is quite different. As a consequence, the behavior of Chinese-American schoolchildren is quite different from that of black American schoolchildren.

Similarly, research suggests that the social support generated by ready accessibility of ethnically similar people plays an important role in influencing vulnerability to stress and psychiatric disorder.[3] Studying psychiatric admission rates in Canada, Murphy found that the Chinese have the lowest rate of all ethnic groups in British Columbia, where they constitute a large minority. In Ontario, where they are few and scattered, they have among the highest rates.[4] The objective historical events—and resulting structures and interpretations by ethnic group members—in turn develop the symbols, values, and beliefs of the present.

Symbols are objects or gestures that designate something other than themselves. A swastika is nothing but crossed lines with four equal arms. But for Nazis it represents Aryan superiority and political mission, and for Jews it represents a terrifying and disgusting threat. Symbols are collective creations which provide a common shorthand for a group. They range from words to types of cars, and in each case they set a group off from neighboring groups. The French Canadian dialect helps to distinguish French ethnics in Canada from both English and

American Canadians, and from persons from France. In the St. Louis neighborhood where one of the authors lived, the large and polished cars were symbols owned by black working-class residents, and the beat up VW "bugs" were symbols owned by the white, middle-class student residents. In each case, the symbols are products of unique group experiences and needs, and at the same time they shape the group experiences and needs of the future. Symbols are powerful forms of distinctiveness because they result from objective conditions as interpreted by the group and by those with whom its members interact.

Values and *beliefs* are the spiritual creations of groups. Values are the standards which identify for people what is right and wrong. In traditional Chinese and Japanese culture, for instance, walls in homes are literally paper thin, and window shades or drapes are seldom used, so that persons see and hear a lot more of each other than in some other cultures. Most European ethnic groups traditionally consider it improper to be heard or seen in one's house, except by friends and family, and heavy walls and drapes are prevalent. In both cases, however, there are private acts and spaces. The values of ethnic groups guide members in the selection of courses of action and in the designation of desirable or possible ends.

The importance of values also stands out in cases of differential ethnic group behavior in schools. American Indian children have been known to sit totally silent in classrooms when called upon by their teachers. Some investigators have assumed that this behavior results from a psychological fear of being proven wrong by the teacher or by other students. Others have assumed that silence is simply a peer group norm. But the persistence of this type of behavior over time and in various locations has led some researchers to recognize that a significant value underlies the behavior. An ancient Indian value is group achievement. Individual performance conflicts with this value.[5]

Beliefs are conceptions of the world and may be religious, scientific, or ideological. As W. I. Thomas said, "What men believe to be true will be true in its consequences." Thus, members of ethnic groups who believe in religious forms of healing are likely to show signs of recovery as a result of such practices.

Constructive processes of ethnic distinctiveness include the sense of self-worth they provide to ethnic group members and the variety of ways of thinking and acting that they bring via interethnic coalitions. A person draws upon both individual experiences and group experiences in order to form an identity. Otto Feinstein notes this when he defines ethnicity as:

> peoplehood, a sense of commonality or community derived from networks of family relations which have over a number of generations been the carriers of common experiences. Ethnicity, in short, means the culture of people and is thus critical for values, attitudes, perceptions, needs, modes of expression, behavior and identity.[6]

Sigmund Freud in his preface to the Hebrew translation of *Totem and Taboo* clarifies the importance of his own ethnic feelings.

> No reader of [the Hebrew version of] this book will find it easy to put himself in the emotional position of an author who is ignorant of the language of holy writ, who is completely estranged from the religion of his fathers—as well as from every other religion—and who cannot take a share in nationalist ideas, but who has yet never repudiated his people, who feels that he is in his essential nature a Jew, and who has no desire to alter that nature. If the question were put to him: "Since you have abandoned all these common characteristics of your countrymen, what is there left to you that is Jewish?" he would reply: "A very great deal, and probably its very essence." He could not now express that essence clearly in words; but some day, no doubt, it will become accessible to the scientific mind.[7]

The recent American enthusiasm among a variety of ethnic groups to find one's "roots" through research into ancestry is indicative of the constructive potential.

Ethnic financial and civil rights organizations also constitute constructive processes. Organizations such as the Japanese-American Citizens League and Sons of Italy have been based upon ethnic distinctiveness and have provided survival and pride for many ethnic group members. Ethnic organizations and a sense of ethnic roots can enhance support and self-esteem, allowing the person to view her or his actions as part of a common destiny.

Destructive processes of ethnic distinctiveness are primarily those in which apparent or real distinctive features come to be considered immutable, either by members of the ethnic group or by outsiders. All aspects of ethnic groups are changeable, as our discussion above has suggested, and pathology occurs when this changeability is destroyed in some way.

A most notable example of such destructive processes has been the assumption of necessary differences in intelligence among ethnic groups. Citing an average difference of 15 percentage points between blacks and whites on IQ test scores, Arthur Jensen proposed that different types of education be made available to blacks and whites. He recommended in the early 1970s that blacks should be trained for manual trades and whites for professions.[8]

A major problem in evaluating native intelligence for groups by using standard IQ tests is that these tests have tended to use questions relating to the world of the white middle-class family. For example, some of the leading IQ tests reward children for knowing the meanings of words such as "Shetland," "foolish," "stucco," and "brunette." Among the persons one should be able to identify are Genghis Khan, Leif Ericson, and the man who wrote *Romeo and Juliet*. Obviously, these questions will be more familiar to children from certain ethnic and class backgrounds than to others, and are therefore unable to measure native intelligence.

In light of this difficulty, Jensen [9] and others have attempted to create "culture-free" tests of intelligence. These tests are typically nonverbal. That a true "culture-free" IQ test can be developed is improbable, however, because testing itself is a cultural product. Some cultures do not test, and any type of testing must involve cultural elements of interaction, values, and methods of manipulation.

Another way in which the thesis of genetic determination of intelligence has been argued is by comparing large groups. Such a case is made by Jensen, who points to the high IQ scores of American-born Jews as evidence that an ethnic group can be genetically superior.[10] But equally true is that the parents of these Jews, who were foreign born and consequently not as "Americanized," scored below average on IQ tests.[11]

Correlations between test scores and ethnicity or class will probably not explain very much about the importance of native intelligence or educational ability. A look at the genes themselves is more informative.

Geneticists speak of genotypes (a given genetic makeup) which may express a vast assortment of phenotypes (observable characteristics). The genotype produces a host of characteristics in response to environments. Consequently, the genetic makeup does not specify a strict educational ability, as geneticist Gordon Allen explained:

> If a genotype determines an intelligence quotient around 120 in the commonest environments, some rare environments may restrict that individual's achievement to a score of 100 or lower, and others may raise it to 130 or 160.[12]

The vast majority of persons are in the broad middle range of native intelligence, for whom educational ability appears to depend upon interactions within social environments, notably those of the home and the school. A famous case study by Kingsley Davis illustrated this point during the 1940s. Davis studied a child named Isabelle, whose grandparents had concealed her and her deaf-mute mother in an attic for the first six and a half years of Isabelle's life, at which point the police released them. Isabelle was given a test of maturity, which ranked her at a social age of two and a half years, and an IQ test which revealed a mental age of about one and a half years, or an IQ of about 25. After three years of intensive educational therapy in stimulating environments Isabelle achieved the average range on maturity tests and on IQ tests.[13] Recently, long-term severely retarded individuals (IQs under 40) have been taught to assemble complex parts such as bicycle brakes and IBM computer components with fewer errors than persons getting paid for such assembly in factories. IQ tests obviously do not measure such performance potential.[14]

The difficulty with predicting educational abilities on the basis of testing has not prevented such tests from affecting the biographies of many people, especially members of ethnic minorities. A major function of the schools is to serve as distribution centers for the society by sorting and classifying people. Children are often placed in educational tracks according to IQ scores, and such labels as "slow," "average," or "superior" are difficult for a child to remove. Teachers expect "slow kids" to fail and often instill this expectation in the students, thereby creating a self-fulfilling prophecy through grading and teaching practices.

Neither is the idea of the utility of classifying people according to native ability likely to die an easy death. This thinking has been a dominant trend in the Western world since Plato, the Greek philosopher who held that the most intelligent individuals should be trained in "cultural subjects," the second most intelligent in military subjects, and the least intelligent should be given minimum education to enable them to be merchants and tradesmen.

INTERPRETATION AND TREATMENT

The Center on Group Identity and Mental Health of the American Jewish Committee recently examined the linkage between ethnicity and mental health. Four themes from their extensive research are worth noting:

1.   Ethnicity and group identity have a significant influence on mental health.
2.   There are marked differences in how various groups perceive and use mental health services, and in the viability of their family and ethnic systems.
3.   Widespread inequality is visible among services rendered to various social class and ethnic groups.
4.   Mental health practitioners are largely unaware of the differences in how ethnicity affects emotional language, family symbolism, and the variation of family roles.[15]

We have seen that distinctiveness is obviously quite important, but the above study illustrates that ethnicity depends also upon interpretations and treatment of the ethnic group by outside persons and by in-group members.

We will concentrate in this section upon the actions of outsiders, because minority group members' interpretations and treatments of themselves are often replies to or distortions of the interpretations and treatments they perceive from outsiders. These intragroup replies and distortions range from pride and a sense of ethnic identity to denial and shame, and from creation of culture-maintaining organizations (e.g., Sons of Italy and Black Arts Councils) and civil rights groups to joining majority organizations and neighborhoods which admit only token members of one's own ethnic group.

Major dimensions of the interpretation and treatment of ethnics by outside groups and group members are contact and strangeness. *Contact* is the condition of exposure of ethnic group members and outsiders to one another, and is thereby the situation through which interpretations and treatments occur. Contacts can be between equals, between superior and inferior, or between ambiguously related individuals. Internalizing oppression frequently causes the minority ethnic member to view him or herself as the inferior in interactions with persons outside the ethnic minority. These contacts happen in a variety of settings, in media depictions, in schooling, at work, and in the neighborhoods. The setting for the contact influences interpretations and treatment through the selectivity which each setting entails.

The media almost necessarily present stereotypic portraits of ethnic groups. Fictional writing and films attempt to create in the viewer's mind a ready image of the characters, and consequently they present familiar images. A few decades ago, these efficient character-creating images included subservient and inferior blacks who said "dis" and "dat," and lazy Mexicans who said "theenk" rather than "think." Indians in American "westerns" were frequently "bad guys" devoid of all verbal ability except for "ugh" or "kemo sabe." [16] Television situation comedies, notably those produced by Norman Lear (sometimes borrowed from British programs), have created a new ethnic stereotypic role. These programs use leading characters as ethnic foils, complete with sharp ethnic repartee. The humor comes about when these characters are placed in situations that require them to work at maintaining ethnic stereotypes. In response to this effort the Archie Bunkers may mellow a little in their stereotyping, but by the beginning of the next episode they have regained their prejudices.

Schooling contacts are quite varied. Students unwillingly bused to integrated schools can be expected to experience other ethnic groups quite differently than those for whom interethnic schooling seems "just natural." The schooling contact also varies according to treatment of ethnic groups by teachers. In schools where teachers expect minority students to perform poorly, students (both minority and otherwise) often come to the same conclusion.

Work contacts also vary. Majority group members who perceive themselves in competition with minorities for scarce jobs or pay raises have reason to establish more distant or formal contact situations than do those not in competition. Similarly, various neighborhoods are structurally different, have different uses, and fulfill different needs for people. For some persons, a neighborhood is simply a place to eat and sleep, for others it is a place to do business, for others, a home for one's ethnicity. These differences will affect contacts between ethnic groups in predictable ways.

The interpretation and treatment of ethnic groups varies markedly as these settings vary. This has been indicated by numerous studies showing that persons who welcome members of other ethnic groups as union members and officers at work consider these same persons as unwelcome in their neighborhoods, or that children who consider members of other ethnic groups as "best friends" during neighborhood play in some cases will have nothing to do with these same persons at school.

Setting is only one of the major social environmental factors which affect contact. Other significant factors are *status* and *activity*. Whatever the setting, when members of a majority group have higher status than do members of minority groups, the contacts tend to be distant or antagonistic. On the other hand, contacts tend to be more congenial and holistic between groups and group members of equal status. The contacts can become especially rich in those situations where the persons are on equal footing and also are working together for the same goals (e.g., business partnerships and collective living units).[17]

Strangeness characterizes nearly all initial interpretations of outsiders toward ethnic groups and their members. Understanding these primary interpretations of ethnic groups requires appreciation of the phenomenon of strangeness itself.

Simmel has elegantly captured the essence of "the stranger":

> The unity of nearness and remoteness involved in every human relation is organized, in the phenomenon of the stranger, in a way which may be most briefly formulated by saying that in the relationship to him, distance means that he, who is close by, is far, and strangeness means that he, who also is far, is actually near. For, to be a stranger is naturally a very positive relation: it is a specific form of interaction. The inhabitants of Sirius are not really strangers to us, at least not in any sociologically relevant sense: they do not exist for us at all; they are beyond far and near. The stranger, like the poor and like sundry "inner enemies," is an element of the group itself. His position as a full-fledged member involves both being outside it and confronting it. . . .
>
> As a group member, rather, he is near and far *at the same time*, as is characteristic of relations founded only on generally human consciousness. But between nearness and distance, there arises a specific tension when the consciousness that only the quite general is common stresses that which is not common. In the case of the person who is a stranger to the country, the city, the race, etc., however, this noncommon element is once more nothing individual, but merely the strangeness of origin which is or could be common to many strangers. For this reason, strangers are not really conceived as individuals, but as strangers of a par-

ticular type: the element of distance is no less general in
regard to them than the element of nearness.[18]

When outsiders encounter ethnic groups they find them strange because they are different, and difference can elicit fear. Although we
share many common features as a result of similarities between all types
of human beings, the common features seem less significant than do
differences in the case of strangers. As Wirth's definition noted, in the
case of ethnics the physical or cultural differences are singled out.

Constructive ethnic processes of interpretation and treatment include
the enrichments of majority and minority ethnic groups which can
evolve from contact. Ethnic and majority groups tend to fall into
habitual or monotonous ways of living, and a primary source of innovation and change is interaction with other ethnic groups.

An example is the creation of jazz, one of the few truly American
musical forms. Blacks in the United States at the turn of the century had
developed several types of music: spirituals, field hollers, blues, and
ragtime, and many black musicians also played European music for
white audiences. During this period in New Orleans a variety of ethnic
groups, including Creoles, blacks, and Indians, lived in the same city
and suffered similar discrimination by the white majority. Blacks developed a need for their own leisure organizations and gatherings, but
this was difficult owing to the different traditions among them (as
exemplified by the various forms of musical entertainment).

During the first black gatherings in New Orleans the various musical
groups performed one after another; for example, the spiritualists, then
the blues singers, then the ragtimers. Before long, this separation dissolved, and the various musicians would "jam" together. The synthesis
of these forms, plus the wind and string techniques from European
music, was the genesis of jazz. Even in highly abstract contemporary
jazz compositions, most of the original elements are present.[19]

Destructive ethnic processes of interpretation and treatment are unfortunately so numerous that space permits us only to describe some of
them and offer a few examples. Among the processes most frequently
encountered in clinical settings are distributive and ritualized
inequality and prejudice.

Wirth's definition at the beginning of this chapter identified one
characteristic of being a minority as unequal treatment. This may seem
to suggest that inequality is a normal part of minority and ethnic existence, and, in fact, Wirth may have intended to suggest this. By consid-

ering inequality as pathological, we are differing with this view, but only to the extent that we wish to distinguish between *types* of inequality. Some sorts of inequality seem constructive and desirable, others seem destructive and undesirable.

Philosophical and social scientific debates are never ending on the topic of equality, but we can distinguish with some confidence several types of equality. *Close similarity* is central to most notions of equality, but tremendous disagreements exist regarding which areas must be similar for persons or groups to be equal. These areas include number of persons, amount of power, status, interests, and abilities.

Several sorts of equality emerge, and they are quite different. Equal status, for instance, is quite unlike equal numbers. Quite clearly, minority groups are not going to become equal in numbers anytime in the foreseeable future, given the tremendous differences which currently exist. Neither are they likely to become equal in interests, given the varied cultural backgrounds. But neither of these inequalities is pathological. Diversity of size and interest can be constructive processes of distinctiveness.

The inequalities in power, value, status, and abilities are the truly destructive processes, both to the minority ethnic groups which suffer from the effects and for the larger groups, organizations, and societies which house this malady and its side effects (including crime, race riots, and guilt syndromes):

> Telling poor people who live within whistling distance of the richest people in this country to accept the principle that because they have dark skin there are other things they cannot have is to structure an equation that cannot pass for common sense in the modern world.[20]

These destructive processes are manifested in a couple of forms. First, *distributive inequality* is the unequal distribution of valuable material and spiritual products, including money, comfort, security, education, prestige, and love. A few recent statistics illustrate the extent of this type of inequality:

1.   Black families have experienced less increase in income during the past quarter of a century than have whites. The gap between median incomes for black and white families has actually increased by roughly $3000 since 1967.[21] Puerto Rican families experienced a median income

of $6779 in 1973, only 56 percent of the median for all American families.[22]

2.   The unemployment rate for whites was 6.4 percent in the fourth quarter of 1974, but 12.5 percent for blacks, and since 1971 the unemployment rate for black teenagers has averaged more than 30 percent (250 percent the rate of white teenagers).[23]

3.   Causes of death among Indians are: heart disease, 20 percent; accidents, 20 percent; influenza, pneumonia, and tuberculosis, about 10 percent; and cirrhosis of the liver, 7 percent. Contrast this with rates for non-Indians: heart disease, 37 percent; accidents, 6 percent; influenza, pneumonia, and tuberculosis, 4 percent; and cirrhosis of the liver, 2 percent.[24]

4.   San Francisco's Chinatown has one of the highest population densities in the world and suicide rates three times the national average.[25]

Second, forms of *ritualized inequality* are the demeaning styles of personal response and intergroup contact with ethnic minorities. Examples include the following:

1.   *Paternalistic contact* is that in which the majority group considers itself the keepers or teachers of the minority group. This is seen most dramatically in colonial rule. A great distance is maintained between the majority and minority, including rigid etiquette for interaction situations and extensive status inequality:

> Paternalistic attitudes and stereotypes are well integrated in the value system of the society. Elaborate sets of rationalizations come to the defense of the racial status quo and are subjectively, if not logically, consistent with the basic religious and ethical premises of the society. Examples of such rationalizations are the "white man's burden" theory, the "civilizing mission of the West," the "Christianizing of the heathen," among others. In short, there is no ideological conflict between the existing norms of prejudice and the basic value system of the society.[26]

2.   *Competitive contact* occurs when ethnic groups compete with one another and with majority groups. There is frequent aggression and much segregation, as the groups struggle with one another.[27] The pathetic irony in many cases is that the groups have been led to fight one another by a nearly invisible third group which otherwise might be the opponent of both sides.

Similarly, the ethnic group may be manipulated into the position of middleman, as illustrated in incidents from the modern history of the Japanese and the Jews. Anti-Japanese activities on the West Coast at the beginning of this century were prompted by owners of large California farms. The major *visible* participants were white small landowners, however, who blamed Japanese immigrants for their rough times. Through this diversion the large estate owners diverted antagonism of small landowners away from themselves.[28]

Jews became middlemen in medieval Europe by being thrust in the position of moneylenders, an occupation considered sinful by the Church. Jews were made moneylenders because they were damned anyhow.[29]

3. *Acculturational contact* is the pressure by a more powerful ethnic group, or by a majority group, for an ethnic minority to assimilate its values, interests, and customs in line with those of the dominant group. This is seen constantly in the United States in demands made upon ethnic groups to conform to Anglo standards of dress, speech, artistic taste, ambitions, and so forth.

4. *Internal colonization* is a type of contact in which the traditional colonizer-native dichotomy prevalent in previous generations between nations exists within a single nation, between majority and ethnic groups. The major internal colonies at present are ghettos. These areas supply the "mother country" with raw materials in the form of cheap labor, and they buy back the finished products at inflated prices. For instance, consumer goods which wholesale for $100 sell for an average of $165 in stores throughout the United States but $250 in ghetto stores.[30]

These forms of contact all produce ritualized inequality for ethnic minorities, and more than one form may operate at a particular time and place. In smaller-scale clinical situations they may be present in alternating and diluted forms, such as when a majority group member of an organization instructs a minority group member in "good taste" or "the right way to do things."

Prejudice is the destructive *attitudinal* process which accompanies behavioral processes such as those we have just noted. Prejudicing is accomplished through stereotyping, social distancing, and affective simplifications.[31]

Stereotypes are cognitive simplifications, usually in the form of inductive statements (all *A* are *B*), such as "All Mexicans are lazy." Culturally supported ethnic prejudices provide instant definitions of ethnic group members based upon alleged characteristics of the groups to which they belong. This permits the prejudiced person to limit his or her cognitive interactions with these groups to a relatively small number of items. Cases include employers who use stereotypes of ethnic minorities to form a conclusion regarding job applicants' abilities, rather than using a variety of life- and work-histories, interviews, skills tests, and so forth. Although all prospective employers must make their choices on the basis of limited information, this can be accomplished in a variety of constructive ways. A prejudiced strategy occurs when cognitive responses are limited to stereotypes of "this sort of person."

The phenomenon of *social distance* was noted by Richard LaPiere in the 1930s. LaPiere traveled across the United States with a Chinese couple, and in the 10,000 miles of motor travel only once did the trio meet with rejection from hotels, restaurants, or camping establishments:

> We were received at 66 hotels, auto camps, and "Tourist Homes." . . . we were served at 184 restaurants and cafes . . . and treated with . . . more than ordinary consideration in 72 of them.[32]

When LaPiere returned home he sent out questionnaires to all of the establishments, asking, "Will you accept members of the Chinese race as guests in your establishment?" Replies came from 81 restaurants and 47 hotels. Of these, 92 percent checked "no," and the remainder checked "uncertain, depend upon circumstances." These proprietors apparently kept their attitudinal distance from Chinese persons, although in actual situations they did not discriminate.

A variety of researchers have developed measures of social distance since the time of LaPiere's study. The social distances which persons in the United States and Europe wish to keep from ethnic groups against whom they are prejudiced seem to be as follows (from closest to most distant): (1) would marry into group, (2) would have as close friend, (3) would have as next door neighbor, (4) would work in the same office, (5) would have as speaking acquaintance only, (6) would have as visitors to one's nation, and (7) would debar from one's nation.

Simplified affective responses are the third manner of prejudicing. One's interactions with others may be simplified not only by stereotyping and social distancing, but also by simplifying how one feels about the other persons. Affective simplification is the reduction of one's feelings to a few regular and simple feelings, such as repulsion or anger. This destructiveness often occurs within economic competition between ethnic groups, and in interethnic contacts where sexual confusions exist. Lillian Smith pointed this out in her novel, *Strange Fruit*, which depicts the emotional sterility of a small southern town several decades ago. The affective simplification between the races accomplished not only sterility, however, but also pathologies such as racial conflicts and religious orgies, which were also regular features of the town.

To a greater extent than is true with the destructive processes of most other vital features, pathologies noted in this chapter affect the normal and constructive processes of the feature in serious ways. Processes such as immutability, prejudice, and discrimination help determine the structure and distinctive cultures of ethnic groups, and thereby the interpretations and treatment of them. Prejudice and discrimination against Jews, for example, thrust many American Jews into distinctively valuing possession of their own neighborhood businesses. As these neighborhoods changed and Jews were unable to move out along with their white majority fellow residents, they came to be detested by the blacks who moved into these neighborhoods. Many blacks have resented the ownership of neighborhood businesses by members of other ethnic groups.

If there is one thing which both these destructive and constructive processes of ethnicity show us, it is that Confucius was right. "The nature of men is identical; what divides them is their customs."

NOTES

1.   Louis Wirth, "The Problem of Minority Groups," in R. Linton, ed., *The Science of Man in the World Crisis* (New York: Columbia University Press, 1945), p. 347.

2.   Leonard Liebman, "The Debate over Race," in Ashley Montagu, ed., *Race and I.Q.* (New York: Oxford, 1975), pp. 19–41.

3.   Judith Rabkin and Elmer Struening, "Ethnicity, Social Class and Mental Illness," *Working Paper Series* 17, Institute on Pluralism and Group Identity, New York, November 1975.

4.   H. B. Murphy, "Migration and the Major Mental Disorders," in M. B. Kantor, ed., *Mobility and Mental Health* (Springfield, Ill.: Charles C Thomas, 1965).

5.   Rosalie Wax, *Doing Fieldwork* (Chicago: University of Chicago Press, 1975).

6.   Otto Feinstein, "Why Ethnicity?" in David Hartman, ed., *Immigrants and Migrants* (Detroit: Center for Urban Studies, Wayne State University, 1974).

7.   Sigmund Freud, *Totem and Taboo* (1913). The standard edition of the complete psychological works translated and edited by James Strachey (London: Hogarth, 1953), p. xv.

8.   Arthur Jensen, "How Much Can We Boost IQ and Scholastic Achievement?" *Harvard Educational Review* 39(Winter 1969):1–23.

9.   Arthur Jensen, "Another Look at Culture-Fair Tests," in *Measurement for Educational Planning* (Berkeley, Cal.: Educational Testing Service, 1968), pp. 50–104.

10.   Ibid.

11.   N. D. M. Hirsch, "A Study of Natio-racial Mental Differences," *Genetic Psychology Monographs* 1(1926):231–406.

12.   Gordon Allen, "Reports," *Science* 133(February 1961):378–80.

13.   Kingsley Davis, "Final Note on a Case of Extreme Isolation," *American Journal of Sociology* 57(1947):432–57.

14.   Marc W. Gold, "Stimulus Factors in Skill Training of Retarded Adolescents on a Complex Assembly Task: Acquisition, Transfer, and Retention," *American Journal of Mental Deficiency* 76, no. 5 (1972):517–26; Marc W. Gold, "Task Analysis of a Complex Assembly Task by the Retarded Blind," *Exceptional Children* 43(1976):78–84.

15.   Joseph Giordano and M. Levine, "Mental Health and Middle America," *Working Paper Series* 14 (New York: Center on Pluralism and Group Identity, 1975), pp. 5–6.

16.   Jack Levin, *The Functions of Prejudice* (New York: Harper & Row, 1975), pp. 56–57.

17.   Barry Collins, *Social Psychology* (Reading, Mass.: Addison-Wesley, 1970), chap. 10.

18.   K. H. Wolff, trans. and ed., *The Sociology of Georg Simmel* (New York: Free Press, 1950).

19.   Ortiz Walton, *Music: Black, White and Blue* (New York: Morrow, 1972).

20.   Clayton Riley, "Time Is No Longer Running Out; It's Gone," *New York Times,* 17 July 1977.

21.   Bureau of the Census, "Money Income and Poverty Status of Families and Persons in the U.S. 1974," *Current Population Reports,* series P–60, no. 99, July 1975.

22.   Bureau of the Census, "Persons of Spanish Origin in the United

States: March 1974," *Current Population Reports,* series P–20, no. 280, April 1975.

23. U.S. Department of Labor, *Manpower Report of the President,* Washington, D.C.: Department of Labor, 1975, p. 243 n. 26.

24. Joseph Jorgensen, "Poverty and Work among American Indians," in H. Kaplan, ed., *American Minorities and Economic Opportunity* (Itasca, Ill.: Peacock, 1977), p. 178.

25. Harry Kitano, *Race Relations* (Englewood Cliffs, N.J.: Prentice-Hall, 1974), chap. 9.

26. Pierre van den Berghe, *Race and Ethnicity: Essays in Comparative Sociology* (New York: Basic Books, 1970), chap. 1.

27. Ibid.

28. George Simpson and J. M. Yinger, *Racial and Cultural Minorities* (New York: Harper & Row, 1972), p. 118.

29. Max Dimont, *Jews, God and History* (New York: Signet, 1962).

30. Robert Blauner, "Internal Colonialism and Ghetto Revolt," *Social Problems* 16(Spring 1969):393–408; and Arnold Schucter, *White Power/Black Freedom* (Boston: Beacon Press, 1968).

31. Howard Ehrlich, *The Social Psychology of Prejudice* (New York: Wiley, 1973); and Barry Glassner, *Essential Interactionism* (forthcoming).

32. Richard LaPiere, "Attitudes vs. Actions," *Social Forces* 13 (1934):232.

THE CLINICIAN'S LIBRARY

By far the most comprehensive and influential work currently available on ethnic groups is a text:

Simpson, George, and J. M. Yinger. *Racial and Cultural Minorities.* New York: Harper & Row, 1972.

Three excellent collections of sociological writings about ethnicity are the following:

Mindel, Charles, and R. Habenstein, eds. *Ethnic Families in America.* New York: Elsevier, 1976.

Stone, John, ed. *Race, Ethnicity, and Social Change.* Belmont, Cal.: Duxbury Press, 1977.

Van den Berghe, Pierre. *Intergroup Relations.* New York: Basic Books, 1972.

DISTINCTIVENESS

Look to cultural anthropologists as well as sociologists for books on culture:

Dundas, Alan, ed. *Every Man His Way*. Englewood Cliffs, N.J.: Prentice-Hall, 1968.
Hall, Edward. *The Silent Language*. Garden City, N.Y.: Doubleday, 1959.
Henry, Jules. *Culture against Man*. New York: Vintage, 1965.
Linton, Ralph. *The Study of Man*. New York: Appleton, 1947.

New and useful works about specific ethnic groups emerge constantly. A few tentative suggestions for some of the groups:

BLACKS

Lyman, Stanford. *The Black American in Sociological Thought*. New York: Capricorn, 1972.
Malcolm X. *The Autobiography of Malcolm X*. New York: Grove, 1966.
Staples, Robert. *Introduction to Black Sociology*. New York: McGraw-Hill, 1976.

INDIANS OF AMERICA

Linton, Ralph, ed. *Acculturation in Seven American Indian Tribes*. New York: Appleton, 1940.
National Geographic Society. *The World of the American Indian*. Washington, D.C.: The National Geographic Society, 1974.
Wax, Murray. *Indian Americans*. Englewood Cliffs, N.J.: Prentice-Hall, 1971.

JAPANESE

Kitano, Harry. *Japanese Americans*. Englewood Cliffs, N.J.: Prentice-Hall, 1969.
Nakane, Chie. *Japanese Society*. Berkeley: University of California Press, 1972.
Petersen, William. *Japanese Americans*. New York: Random House, 1971.

JEWS

Fine, Morris, and Milton Himmelfarb, eds. *American Jewish Yearbook.* Philadelphia: Jewish Publication Society, annually.
Grayzel, Solomon. *A History of the Jews.* Philadelphia: Jewish Publication Society of America, 1969.
Jewish Journal of Sociology and *Contemporary Jewry.*

PUERTO RICANS

Cordasco, Francesco, and E. Bucchioni, eds. *The Puerto Rican Experience.* Totowa, N.J.: Littlefield Adams, 1973.
Fitzpatrick, Joseph. *Puerto Rican Americans.* Englewood Cliffs, N.J.: Prentice-Hall, 1971.
Padilla, Elena. *Up from Puerto Rico.* New York: Columbia University Press, 1958.

IMMUTABILITY

Gossett, Thomas. *Race: The History of an Idea in America.* New York: Schocken, 1965.
Montagu, Ashley. *Man's Most Dangerous Myth.* New York: Oxford, 1974.

INEQUALITIES

Kaplan, H. Roy, ed. *American Minorities and Economic Opportunity.* Itasca, Ill.: Peacock, 1977.

PREJUDICE

Four comprehensive summaries of the vast literature on prejudice are the following:

Allport, Gordon. *The Nature of Prejudice.* Reading, Mass.: Addison-Wesley, 1958.
Ehrlich, Howard. *The Social Psychology of Prejudice.* New York: Wiley, 1973.
Glassner, Barry. *Essential Interactionism* (forthcoming).
Levin, Jack. *The Functions of Prejudice.* New York: Harper & Row, 1975.

Chapter 8

Stratification

Each group and group member in a society is situated somewhere on a status hierarchy. This hierarchy is the social stratification system, and can be appropriately conceived as a ladder. Each rung of the stratification ladder contains its own level of material wealth, its own rights and duties, and generally its own lifestyle. According to the stratification ladder the "goodies" of society are distributed to people in a systematically unequal manner so that each group has differential access.

Three major components make up the stratification ladder and maintain it. First, the ordering of persons and groups entails *differentiation and differential coping* among them. Second, there is movement along the ladder, or *social mobility*, as persons change their positions. Finally, members of a society must accept the system in order for it to continue, and this is achieved through *ideology*. By understanding these components of stratification, and by ascertaining the position and mobility of his or her clients, a clinician can often acquire insight into their actions and difficulties; an insight almost impossible for a client to obtain alone.

DIFFERENTIATION AND DIFFERENTIAL COPING

A group or group member's location on the stratification ladder distinguishes the person or group from many others in the community and society. This is true both for differences in objective conditions and in ways of coping with these conditions.

The major differences between rungs on the stratification ladder involve access to wealth, power, prestige, and leisure. Several American statistics provide a vivid portrait:

1. *Wealth:* The bottom fifth of families receive 5.4 percent of the income, compared with 41.0 percent which goes to the highest fifth.[1]
2. *Power:* Persons with political power in the United States tend to be wealthy. On the local level power tends to be almost entirely in the hands of powerful interest groups.[2]
3. *Prestige:* The major determinant of prestige is the occupation a person holds. Not only the income, but the type of work is significant for prestige ranking. For instance, a Mafia boss who makes several times the income of a prominent heart surgeon is likely to be lower in prestige.

The most fundamental differentiation among jobs is between blue-collar workers and white-collar workers. The proportion of persons in white-collar occupations is steadily rising, with a projection that they will constitute nearly two-thirds of working Americans in 1980.
4. *Leisure:* The amount of time available for relaxing or doing what one wants has always differed among social classes. Much as a feudal lord could go on an elegant hunt while the serfs worked, so can a contemporary business executive or successful physician arrange for a golf game in the middle of the week while line workers and nurses are on "clock-time." A recent analysis suggests that leisure time is becoming more scarce for most Americans. In addition to work, overtime, and commuting, one must consider the work necessary to maintain a home and the work required by our increasing possession of consumer goods which must be shopped for, used, repaired, and replaced.[3]

The amount of wealth, power, prestige, and leisure one controls both determines and maintains one's position on the social stratification ladder. These determinants also affect how persons are differentially evaluated by others within their social class. This was illustrated in the 1940s by a chart representing a community in the southern United States.[4] Most of the categories are still appropriate (see chart on following page).

We will note in the next section that changes in position are possible, but at any particular time a group of persons will occupy a specific

Upper-upper class

"Old aristocracy"	UU
"Aristocracy" but not "old"	LU
"Nice, respectable people"	UM
"Good people, but 'nobody' "	LM
"Po' whites"	UL / LL

Lower-upper class

"Old aristocracy"
"Aristocracy" but not "old"
"Nice, respectable people"
"Good people, but 'nobody' "
"Po' whites"

Upper-middle class

"Society" { "Old families"	UU
"Society" but not "old families"	LU
"People who should be upper class"	UM
"People who don't have much money"	LM
"No 'count lot"	UL / LL

Lower-middle class

"Old aristocracy" (older) "Broken-down aristocracy" (younger)
"People who think they are somebody"
"We poor folk"
"People poorer than us"
"No 'count lot"

Upper-lower class

"Society" or the "folks with money"	UU / LU / UM
"People who are up because they have a little money"	LM
"Poor but honest folk"	UL
"Shiftless people"	LL

Lower-lower class

"Society" or the "folks with money"
"Way-high-ups," but not "society"
"Snobs trying to push up"
"People just as good as anybody"

position, and their life-coping techniques will depend upon which position they occupy.

Differential coping among the social classes is especially significant in the areas of family, politics, and education. Differences in the *family* begin with the various child-rearing values employed. Middle-class parents tend to teach their children to be responsible and ambitious, while working-class parents teach their children to be conforming and obedient. These teachings parallel the occupational requirements of middle-class occupations, which require independent initiative and interpersonal skills, and those of working-class occupations, which require the ability to follow orders and few interpersonal skills.[5] Distinct from both of these are the socialization values of upper-class parents, which emphasize family pride and traditions, both of which will be required for the offspring to successfully manage and maintain the family wealth and estate.[6]

The size of families varies among the classes, with working-class families tending to be larger, for several reasons. Information, availability, and trust concerning contraception is less within the lower class than within other classes. Children are more often considered assets in working-class families than in others, because they are expected to leave school early and earn money for the family; also because they provide favored companionship. In a report for a course taught by one of the authors, the value of children was vividly displayed. The paper concerned a lower-class family of twelve living in a two-bedroom, inner-city apartment. Asked why they continued to produce children when they often did not have the money to feed or clothe them, the women explained that they love children and prefer to have children to having cars, better housing, or even adequate food.

Types of marriages vary among the classes as well. A variety of studies indicate that three types of marriage exist in American society: (1) the companion marriage—largely an upper-class phenomenon; (2) the partner marriage—largely a middle-class phenomenon; and (3) the "husband-wife" marriage—largely a working- and lower-class phenomenon.[7] Each of these fits the marital role required by the occupational and leisure possibilities open to the various classes.

Differential *politics* also reflects the values of occupations. The lower class tends to be more conservative concerning civil rights and law-and-order issues (i.e., obedience) than do other classes, but more liberal about economic issues. More generally, the lower class is less likely to vote or participate in political activities than are members of other classes, mostly because they are not welcome in such activities or have seen that political organizations are not responsive to their needs. As one sociologist put it, "It is not lack of class consciousness, apathy, disinterest, lack of faith, nor status inconsistency that keep the poor from voting. It is that those in power create sociological barriers that restrain the poor from exercising the franchise." [8]

We have already seen one way in which differential *education* results, namely from the emphasis within the lower class for children to leave school and go to work. Liberal educators have hoped that increased opportunities for education will bring about increased equality generally in society. But this "equality through education" dream ignores objective conditions of the stratification system. Even if a lower-class person makes it through college, he or she must still attend a job interview, where attire, demeanor, hobbies, parents, or religion may become deciding factors of whether or not the person is hired. This is especially true when the person seeks managerial or executive jobs. Several studies indicate that when educational attainment is demanded of candidates for a given job, the actual reason for the requirement is often that the employer wishes to hire someone like him or herself, someone with similar values, politics, hobbies, and tastes—someone of his or her class background. The requirement of a college degree is often to increase the probability that applicants will meet the desired background characteristics. [9]

American statistics indicate that educational attainment does not tend to enable the lower-class person to overcome a low social origin. High school graduations for the sons of manual workers result in only slightly higher incomes on the average than the incomes of sons of nonmanual workers who have not even completed high school. [10] Such tendencies are well known to working-class adults, who may communicate the information to their children. Thus, 63 percent of one sample of persons in professional and managerial positions felt that "the years ahead hold good chances for advancement," while only 48 percent of a sample of factory workers gave this response. Furthermore, the factory workers were more likely to think that "getting along with the boss" or being "a friend or relative of the boss" were important determinants of success on the job. [11] Predictably, the value systems of lower-class persons have not tended to include high esteem for educational achievement, which further contributes to their comparatively low academic achievement.

In short, the life-coping techniques of members of social classes reflect the values which result in reaction to their objective conditions. These conditions vary according to placement on the stratification ladder.

Constructive differentiation processes that result from stratification are similar to those for *distinctiveness* within ethnicity patterns. Classes provide a variety of creative lifestyles, and organizational, cognitive, and coping techniques. This variety would not be likely to evolve in a uniclass society.

Some persons (e.g., some Marxists) would argue that stratification is inherently destructive, and that the potential innovation we find within differentiation is not really innovation at all, but simply adjustment to inequality. Certainly some processes are not subject to such a critique, however, including the rich street culture of many ghetto areas, and the everyday life philosophies and organizational techniques of lower-class heroes such as Saul Alinsky, Danilo Dolci, Cesar Chavez, and Paulo Freire.

The idea that stratification is inherently destructive has a great deal of support, however. Our description of stratification above mentioned several items that might be more appropriately discussed below under "destructive processes," for example, educational inequality and access to power. We include them in the descriptive section because in some cases they may be constructive, as when persons fight the prevalent dictum that "everyone should go to college," or when communities ignore a political machine rather than dignify it with their attention.

Destructive differentiation processes obviously far outweigh the possible constructive processes, and they parallel the destructive processes of ethnic treatment. Several of the *distributive inequalities* are emphatically destructive, most notably poverty and ill health.

Poverty exists among those groups and persons who do not have adequate access even to the basic necessities of life, such as nourishment, housing, security, and clothing. Poverty is sometimes defined as income below a certain level (recently the U.S. level was $5500). Depending upon where one lives, and how much control one has over nonmonetary resources, these dollar figures may be meaningless. In general, persons suffer from poverty who are ill, hungry, or dying at a comparatively high rate in a community, primarily because they are deprived of minimal material necessities.

Contemporary poverty is *not* inevitable, but rather a deliberate part of the stratification system. Herbert Gans has noted that poverty is beneficial to certain persons in other strata. Poverty creates jobs for persons such as police, welfare workers, pawnbrokers, and poverty agency executives. The poor also serve as underpaid maids and gardeners, who in turn recycle old automobiles and toasters and hire the less successful physicians and lawyers. Perhaps most destructively, the poor have many times been made into negative role models for middle-class persons, who argue that persons are poor because they lack middle-class values such as enjoyment of work, monogamy, and thrift.[12]

That poverty is a deliberate pathology of the stratification system is indicated most clearly by a U.S. Bureau of the Census calculation that poverty could be eliminated in the United States by spending $12 billion per year on the impoverished families. This amount equals less than a fifth our annual expenditure on defense, and little more than Americans spend on tobacco. This statistic is especially disturbing in light of another one: nearly 35 percent of the poor are children under age 14, who could neither have placed themselves in poverty nor brought themselves out of its grasp.[13] In all, an estimated one-fifth of the U.S. population is constantly poor, and nearly one-third is poor at least ten percent of the time.[14]

When a clinician encounters members of the poverty class and wants to understand and assist them, an appropriate initial inquiry might be into their relationship to the stratification system, rather than into their own actions and value systems. What purpose are these people serving? Can this purpose be served in other ways, through community, neighborhood, or group restructuring? Can these persons do anything themselves to eliminate this pathology of the stratification system, for example, through civil rights organizing? Or should the clinician's therapy plan concentrate on other persons whose actions can change things?

Similar questions apply to the pathological health care system of the poverty and lower-class strata. Mental retardation due to injury or ill health of the mother occurs in the United States almost exclusively in poor and lower-class families. Many poor persons who are considered mentally retarded are not organically so, however, but simply labeled as such by middle-class processors who disdain or misunderstand their behavior.

The health and life expectancies of poor and lower-class persons are considerably worse than for members of other strata. Reasons range from crowded living conditions to dangerous work conditions to lack of information about health care practices. A central problem is that poor and lower-class persons have had, or have heard about, terrifying experiences in public health clinics. Many stay away from such places, and those who frequent them often do so with feelings of docile resignation and disrespect. A result is that even when they meet with medical personnel they may be unable to understand or take the advice being offered, and the medical personnel may not spend the resources necessary to build up mutual respect and confidence for future visits.[15]

Utilization of dentists reflects the lack of access, trust, and understanding by poor persons regarding health facilities. Less than one-fifth of the poor visit dentists during a year, compared with more than half of the middle class. This is further compounded by the *type* of dentist who sees various strata. Dentists who practice preventive dentistry are more likely to have patients from higher strata.[16]

In some ways, the lower class is actually in a worse relationship with the health care system in America than are the poor, because nearly 24 million lower-class persons are not covered by health insurance of any kind. Their incomes are slightly too high and they are too young for welfare insurance, yet they cannot afford the expensive premiums of private insurance. As a result, lower-class persons often avoid health care facilities except in extreme emergencies, and may receive inadequate care when they do ask for help.

In general, rich people are much healthier than poor or lower-class people. The incidence of major diseases, such as diabetes, heart disease, and cancer, is significantly higher in the lower strata.[17] This situation is true generally throughout much of the world, but the situation is more severe in countries such as the United States, where access to health care is a privilege rather than a right. There is less disparity between classes in the several European countries in which health care is socialized.

MOBILITY

People do change their positions on the social stratification ladder, and such change is called *mobility*. Even in restrictive stratification systems, such as the caste system in India, some persons are able to move from one social stratum to another. The amount of mobility which is possible in a society depends upon the number of strata in the society (i.e., the number of "rungs on the ladder"); the more strata, the more movement. In a feudal society consisting of landowners and serfs, the likelihood of mobility is slim. To become a landowner requires inheritance, and serfs are unlikely to be in a position to inherit land from their masters. In contrast, contemporary industrial societies contain many businesses, each with several layers of workers and owners. A line worker may become a higher paid line worker, or a foreman's assistant, or a foreman, or a union leader, and so forth.

This relatively high amount of movement in contemporary industrial societies is the source of many clinical problems, however, and thereby deserves some close scrutiny. Our popular mythology has it that people can "raise themselves up by their bootstraps," that is, change strata through hard work. To be able to assist persons and groups suffering from this mythology, clinicians need to know under which conditions it is true and how mobility actually tends to operate.

The high amount of movement which occurs in the stratification system is a facade in many ways, hiding or disguising the *types* of movements which occur. A professional's son, for instance, more easily becomes a professional than does a blue-collar worker's son, as Kingsley Davis described:

> Accomplishments, however, are already partial products of
> statuses ascribed at birth. . . . Ascribed statuses, coming first
> in life, lay the framework within which the transmission of
> the cultural heritage is to take place. They determine the general
> goals (e.g., the adult statuses) toward which training shall aim
> and the initial persons who shall carry it out. When, accordingly,
> we know the child's sex, age, age relations, and the class, reli-
> gion, region, community, and nation of his parents, we know
> fairly well what his socialization—indeed, his life—will be.[18]

A detailed study of 20,000 men revealed that class of origin is quite predictive of the class one will achieve as an adult. Other important factors in determining a person or group's adult status include willingness to defer immediate gratification in favor of long-term goals, willingness to postpone marriage, urban rather than rural residence, level of education, ethnic background, childhood nutrition, and physical appearance. Several of these cannot be changed by hard work.[19]

This is not to deny that social mobility occurs frequently, but rather that most mobility is *short-distance* movement. To put movement in its proper perspective, we need to recognize that movement is of three varieties. First, there is *upward mobility*, as when a salesperson becomes a sales manager or an assistant foreman becomes foreman. Upward mobility is the type concentrated upon in our folklore and leads to the bootstrap mythology. *Downward mobility* is at least as prevalent, however, as when a person becomes unemployed, or an assistant foreman moves back onto the line, or the son of a professional becomes a teacher. Third, *horizontal mobility* is perhaps more frequent than either of the other varieties and refers to movement within the same stratum, as when a line worker in a large automobile plant becomes a line worker in a small shoe company. The new work may be preferred by the worker, but no change in status has occurred.

Even in the case of upward mobility, a change in stratification position is not inevitable. As we noted at the beginning of this chapter, there are several determinants of stratification position. A rise in occupational level, without a rise in other areas, is not likely to change one's position on the stratification ladder. This was illustrated by a study of a small eastern city. In this city occupational achievement did not permit persons to enter the highest status groups. The only two ways to enter the highest circles in this town were to be born into them or to be a wealthy newcomer.[20]

Persons need not actually change strata to feel that they are doing well, however, and this is a major reason that the stratification system can be maintained and perpetuated. Persons feel deprivation only when they are aware that they are lacking something which they ought to have. We determine what we ought to have only in comparison to others, however, and hence suffer primarily from *relative deprivation*. Whether or not blue-collar workers, whose comfort and status are dramatically inferior to professional workers, feel deprived depends upon whether they compare themselves to these professional workers. More often, they compare themselves with persons of similar status. A British study reveals this pattern in replies to the question, "Do you think there are any other sorts of people doing noticeably better at the moment than you and your family?"

> "People with no children," said a woman with four of them. "Where there is a man working in the family," said an unmarried woman. "People who get extra money by letting off part of the house," said an 82-year-old widow. . . . "People on night work," said a 63-year-old brazier in the engineering industry. "I have now had to do day work—I'm getting old." [21]

Sometimes the most useful but potentially volatile service a clinician can perform for a group is to point out some other groups to which it might want to compare itself.

Constructive mobility processes are of course those which permit groups and group members to change their positions on the stratification ladder to ones which are more beneficial to the groups and members themselves, and to their communities. Such processes are somewhat rare in capitalistic societies and have been rare in socialistic societies as well. Such processes are most likely in communal organizations in which the goals pursued arise from high consensus among the participants and representatives from the larger community. Instances include collectively owned and operated businesses in which the participants decide upon common goals that fulfill their own needs and those of their customers, then hand out positions and raises according to how well the members contribute to such goals.

Destructive mobility processes can be seen in anxious group members. Most persons feel some degree of pressure to achieve mobility during their lifetimes, and this results in tensions both at work (between workers) and at home. A variety of studies has found that movement from one class to another results in political conservatism and family problems. The disruption of family life due to less interaction by a mobile member is especially marked in the case of downward mobility.

A major difficulty for many mobile persons is adjustment to and acceptance by the new groups that they enter. Persons who desire mobility often think of the mobility entirely in terms of increased income and status, ignoring that they may have to leave behind friends and acquaintances who remain in the other stratum. Often mobility brings with it a change of position in a business, or a change of job, and a change of residence.

Some persons choose to maintain neighborhood ties despite increased affluence. A friend of one of the authors, while doing field work in Chicago, discovered a house which looked on the outside like all of the other poor houses on the block, but which had been completely remodeled and made affluent inside. The occupants did not want to leave their neighborhood, although their economic success would have permitted them to do so.

Destructive results of these adjustment problems can be seen in the relatively high levels of anxiety and psychosomatic illness among upwardly mobile persons, and the higher rates at which downwardly mobile persons come to be treated by mental health officials.[22] A more latent destructive feature of mobility occurs when the illusion of mobility provides persons with a psychological sense that they are progressing faster than others, when actually their progress is at the same rate.

Persons get salary increases that make it appear they have made it to the next level, but with inflation and similar salary increases for others, the change becomes minimal. This pseudomobility creates a sense that things always improve, when actually there may be very little change.

IDEOLOGY

Most of us unthinkingly accept the stratification system as it is; we regard it as "just natural." This everyday acceptance results from ongoing processes of *ideology,* or systematic distortion of reality in order to rationalize some vested interests. David Riesman has described this widespread situation as people "habitually believing their own propaganda."

Constructive ideologies are those which give a group of people the spiritual energy to consider their actions as vitally important and right. The physical scientist who believes that science is the right and natural road to knowledge is more likely to conduct his research devotedly than a scientist who does not hold this ideology. Similarly, a community organization which believes that its humanitarian goals will save a neighborhood will be more likely to work long hours to make the prediction come true.

Destructive ideologies result from three sources: inadequate analysis of how to meet needs; inflexibility in the face of later disconfirmation; and interpreting others in terms of one's own ideology. These conditions exist in several notable contemporary ideological processes:

1. *The stratification system reproduces itself* largely because persons do not consider whether it is adequate. The belief that people have equal opportunity for mobility, for instance, is widespread but not supported by facts; likewise for the belief that welfare or public programs "spoil" people and encourage them not to work. Only about three percent of the people receiving welfare *could* hold a job if they wanted to do so; most are young children, mothers caring for these children, or people with severe health problems. Most of the few remaining welfare recipients have tried seriously to find a job but were unable.[23]

2. *Blaming the victim* also supports the existing pathologies of the stratification system:

The generic process of Blaming the Victim is applied to almost every American problem. The miserable health care of the poor is explained away on the grounds that the victim has poor motivation and lacks health information. The problems of slum housing are traced to the characteristics of tenants who are labeled as "Southern rural migrants" not yet "acculturated" to life in the big city. The "multiproblem" poor, it is claimed, suffer the psychological effects of impoverishment, the "culture of poverty," and the deviant value system of the lower classes; consequently though unwittingly, they cause their own troubles. From such a viewpoint, the obvious fact that poverty is primarily an absence of money is easily overlooked or set aside. . . .

The old-fashioned conservative could hold firmly to the belief that the oppressed and victimized were born that way—"that way" being defective or inadequate in character or ability. The new ideology attributes defect and inadequacy to the malignant nature of poverty, injustice, and racial difficulties. . . . But the stigma, the defect, the fatal difference—though derived in the past from environmental forces—is still located *within* the victim inside his skin. . . . It is brilliant ideology for justifying a perverse form of social action designed to change, not society, as one might expect, but rather society's victim.[24]

3. *Confusing one's own position* occurs when persons interpret their objective status as different than it is. We noted in the discussion of mobility that persons locate themselves on the stratification ladder through comparisons with selected others. Persons also consider themselves to be in groups which they are not, such as when members of a lower-class family consider themselves middle class because they have bought a large automobile. A national survey indicates that technicians, teachers, civil servants, writers, and others whose incomes force them to struggle to maintain a middle-class lifestyle tend to identify themselves as middle class. They likewise share middle- rather than lower-class values and preferred lifestyles.[25] Through such interpretations of one's place on the stratification ladder, persons and groups come to feel that they are doing well enough and that the stratification system is acceptable.

Such destructive ideological processes obfuscate not only the immediate pathologies of stratification systems, but a deeper issue of humanity beautifully expressed by labor organizer Eugene Debs:

While there is a lower class I am in it, while there is a criminal element I am of it; while there is a soul in prison, I am not free.

NOTES

1. U.S. Bureau of the Census, "Money Income in 1973 of Families and Persons in the U.S." *Current Population Reports,* series P–60, no. 97, January 1975.

2. Charles Anderson, *The Political Economy of Social Class* (Englewood Cliffs, N.J.: Prentice-Hall, 1974); and J. Walton, "Discipline, Method and Community Power," *American Sociological Review* 31(1966):684–89.

3. Staffan Linder, *The Harried Leisure Class* (New York: Columbia University Press, 1970).

4. Allison Davis and B. B. Gardner, *Deep South: A Social-Anthropological Study of Caste and Class* (Chicago: University of Chicago Press, 1941), p. 65.

5. M. L. Kohn, "Social Class and Parent-Child Relationships," *American Journal of Sociology* 68(1963):471–80.

6. Ruth Cavan, *The American Family* (New York: Crowell, 1969), p. 96.

7. Daniel Rossides, *The American Class System* (Boston: Houghton Mifflin, 1976), p. 178.

8. Lucile Duberman, *Social Inequality* (Philadelphia: Lippincott, 1976), p. 186.

9. Randall Collins, "Function and Conflict Theories of Educational Stratification," *American Sociological Review* 36(December 1971)1002–18.

10. Seymour M. Lipset and R. Bendix, *Social Mobility in Industrial Society* (Berkeley: University of California Press, 1959), p. 99.

11. Herbert Hyman, "The Value Systems of Different Classes," in R. Bendix and S. Lipset, eds., *Class, Status and Power* (Glencoe, Ill.: Free Press, 1966), p. 492.

12. Herbert Gans, *More Equality* (New York: Pantheon, 1973).

13. Roger Hurley, ed., *Poverty and Mental Retardation* (Trenton, N.J.: New Jersey Department of Institutions and Agencies, 1968).

14. Robert Reinhold, "Poverty Is Found Less Persistent but Wider Spread than Thought," *New York Times,* 17 July 1977, p. 1.

15. Lee Rainwater, "The Lower Class: Health, Illness and Medical

Institutions," in L. Rainwater, ed., *Social Problems and Public Policy* (Chicago: Aldine, 1974), pp. 179–87.

16.   Louis Kriesberg, "The Relationship between Socio-Economic Rank and Behavior," in G. Thielbar and S. Feldman, eds., *Issues in Social Inequality* (Boston: Little, Brown, 1972), pp. 458–82; and L. Kriesberg and B. Treiman, "Preventive Utilization of Dentists' Services among Teenagers," *Journal of American College of Dentists* 29(1962):28–45.

17.   Oscar Ornati, *Poverty amid Affluence* (New York: Twentieth Century Fund, 1966).

18.   Kingsley Davis, *Human Society* (New York: Macmillan, 1948), p. 116.

19.   Peter Blau and O. Duncan, *The American Occupational Structure* (New York: Wiley, 1967); and John Porter, "The Future of Upward Mobility," *American Sociological Review* 33, no. 1 (1968):5–19.

20.   Leila Deasy, "Social Mobility in Northtown," Ph.D. dissertation, Cornell University, 1953.

21.   W. G. Runciman, *Relative Deprivation and Social Justice* (London: Routledge, 1966), p. 194.

22.   Kenneth Kessin, "Social and Psychological Consequences of Intergenerational Occupational Mobility," *American Journal of Sociology* 77, no. 1 (1971):1–18; and Melvin Tumin, *Social Stratification* (Englewood Cliffs, N.J.: Prentice-Hall, 1967).

23.   Lloyd Shearer, "Welfare Facts and Myths," *Parade*, 6 March 1977, p. 4.

24.   William Ryan, *Blaming the Victim* (New York: Pantheon, 1971), chap. 1.

25.   James Wright, "In Search of a New Working Class," *Qualitative Sociology* 1, no. 1 (1978):33–57.

THE CLINICIAN'S LIBRARY

Comprehensive overviews of stratification include the following:

Duberman, Lucile. *Social Inequality: Class and Caste in America.* Philadelphia: Lippincott, 1976.

Rossides, Daniel. *The American Class System.* Boston: Houghton Mifflin, 1976.

Tumin, Melvin. *Social Stratification.* Englewood Cliffs, N.J.: Prentice-Hall, 1967.

DIFFERENTIATION AND DIFFERENTIAL COPING

Bottomore, T. B. *Classes in Modern Society*. New York: Vintage Books, 1966.
Kerckhoff, Alan. *Socialization and Class Structure*. Englewood Cliffs, N.J.: Prentice-Hall, 1972.
Kohn, Melvin. *Class and Conformity: A Study in Values*. Homewood, Ill.: Dorsey Press, 1969.
Shostak, Arthur. *Blue-Collar Life*. New York: Random House, 1969.

POVERTY

Gans, Herbert. *More Equality*. New York: Pantheon, 1973.
Ornati, Oscar. *Poverty amid Affluence*. New York: Twentieth Century Fund, 1966.

MOBILITY

Heller, Celia, ed. *Structured Social Inequality*. New York: Macmillan, 1969.
Sorokin, Pitrim. *Social Mobility*. New York: Harper & Row, 1927.

IDEOLOGY

Marx, Karl. *A Contribution to the Critique of Political Economy*. Chicago: Charles Kerr, 1859.
Merton, Robert. *Social Theory and Social Structure*. New York: Free Press, 1968, chap. 14.
Ryan, William. *Blaming the Victim*. New York: Pantheon, 1971.

Chapter 9

Age

Despréaux commented in 1674, "Every age has its pleasures, its style of wit, and its own ways." His comment is true for ages of individuals, groups, organizations, and entire societies. Age has constructive and destructive features, both resulting from change and continuity processes from birth to death, and the social meanings derived from the passage from one to the other. We will consider this process by looking at its constituent parts: time, cohorts, career, and death.[1]

TIME

Our commonsense notion that the passage of time causes aging is not accurate. If there is any causation between these entities, it is that aging causes time. More specifically, human mortality and the aging process which accompanies it permit our conceptions of time. If we lived forever, how could we even conceive of finite units of time? We might devise time markers in order to coordinate social life and allow for appointments and work schedules with one another, but the frame of reference would be quite different than it is for us mortal beings.

We naturally measure time in ways that relate to our personal and social lives. Pitrim Sorokin [2] notes that it is not the same to experience "the time necessary to cook rice," as a nontechnological tribe might, and our experience of "fifteen minutes on my watch." Time is experienced through events in our lives, and thereby takes on the feel of these events. Most everyone can experience a simple case of this by comparing the passage of time in a boring situation as opposed to an interesting experience. A clock-hour in a boring class is much longer than a clock-hour in an interesting class.

Various groups develop various conceptions of time, according to their needs and values. Five years is a long time for members of groups with short life expectancies, such as terminal cancer patients; but conversely, five years is a long time for young people, to whom it represents a large proportion of all their experiences thus far. On the other hand, five years is a short time for persons in young adulthood or middle age, especially if they have long-term career plans.

Time and age are inseparable. To understand the vital feature of age, clinicians need to understand the prominent types of time and death. Schopenhauer said that "time is the possibility of opposite states in one and the same thing." This is evidenced by the fundamental distinctions among *types of time,* namely cyclical versus linear time, and absolute versus relative time.[3] Cyclical conceptions of time hold that time repeats itself perpetually; linear that time is unidirectional. The East has traditionally been characterized as cyclical in its views, the West as linear. These views are reflected in the ideas of perpetual rebirth in Eastern religions and of progression toward heaven or hell in Western religions.

Persons and groups are seldom conscious of their assumptions about cyclical and linear time. One frequently hears in clinical settings, for instance, that a group or organization is evolving, quite clearly a linear assumption which the clinician might want to question in light of prominent recurring patterns within the group. Perhaps the most widespread linear notion in the West is the political and evolutionary conception of time as *progress;* we assume that things are developing and will get better. Another prevalent linear notion is that older persons generally think and behave differently than do younger persons, an assumption which social-psychological research indicates is false. The activities and ways of thinking which one exhibits late in life usually were present in younger years as well. Styles of adaptation to old age, for example, can be predicted on the basis of adaptation styles in middle age, obviously a cyclical phenomenon.[4]

The absolute versus relative conceptions of time can be traced to Newton and Einstein. Newton held that time flows at a uniform rate independent of anything else occurring in the universe. Einstein found time to be relative to the relationship between the universe and the observer.

Persons who operate from absolute conceptions of social time have been known to create rigid social structures. Instances include health workers who decide that the average recovery time for an illness is the only one permitted of patients at a facility, or educators who contend that a white child is more intelligent because he or she responds more rapidly in class than does a black child.

Of major importance in understanding age and its relation to time is to see that persons build into groups and social structures the four types of time. Thus, the new and repeating changes in a group over weeks or years reflect the concrete presence of both linear and cyclical changes: the coordination of workers in a factory relies upon absolute time, while the varied rhythm of their different types of work denotes the presence of relative time.

Constructive age processes can be found within all four types of time. In cyclical time we find the possibility of learning from the past, that is, knowing what patterns to expect when we see them beginning again. Linear time provides the possibility for groups and their members to go through stages and accomplish end products and a sense of progress. Without the linear aspect of time we could neither leave childhood nor emerge from unorganized to organized groups, nor even complete a project.

Absolute time provides the possibility for coordination and continuity, for different persons to be at the same place at the same time, or for persons to be the same chronological age. Meanwhile, relative time allows for change in groups and structures. John Dewey noted:

> The genuine implications of natural ends may be brought out by considering beginnings instead of endings. To insist that nature is an affair of beginnings is to assert that there is no single and all-at-once beginning of everything. It is but another way of saying that nature is an affair of affairs, wherein each one, no matter how linked up it may be with others, has its own quality. It does not imply that every beginning marks an advance or improvement; as we sadly know accidents, diseases, wars, lies and errors begin. Clearly the fact and idea of beginning is neutral, not eulogistic; temporal, not absolute.[5]

Relative time offers groups the possibility to restructure their relationships with time in order to better accomplish their needs. Groups who want to accomplish changes, for instance, often come to divide time into relatively small intervals which are interchangeable for a variety of purposes.

Destructive age processes also occur within all four varieties of time. Cyclical time delimits the possibility for a better future through the reemergence of old patterns. Linear time not only creates the general problem of past events becoming "lost forever," but it also creates difficulties for persons and groups who are ill equipped to move through stages, or whose needs require that they remain in their current stage longer than is permitted. An example is "growing pains":

> Many people can be adolescents quite successfully, but they have difficulty *becoming* adults. . . . At a turn in life, the resistance to taking a new task can lead to *intertemporal* crises; crises that occur in the interstices between the major times of life. It's hard to become an old person; it's hard to become a middle aged person; it's hard to become a young adult; it's hard to become an adolescent and give up childhood. Always involved is the "giving up" and the adjustment to the new, the uncomfortable, the unknown.[6]

Sometimes rituals or "rites of passage" can help alleviate such difficulties, and similar notes apply to most groups and organizations as they move through stages of formation, formalization, and leadership changes.

Pathologies within absolute time are the habits, routines, and expectations which develop out of coordination and predictability. Our means for getting things accomplished are destructive when they become ends. For example, several communities have developed "task forces on poverty," which spend much of their time and energy on their own public relations and internal operations.

Also destructive is placing human aging in an absolute time perspective, whereby many people uncritically adopt the roles expected of persons their age. Among the most vicious is the "sick role" which old people are often expected to play. This consists of four parts: the individuals are exempted from normal responsibilities and rights such as self-care; their condition requires behavioral and physical change, not "merely attitudinal"; they want to recover; and they are willing to seek the help of competent others and obey these persons' orders.[7]

Relative time becomes destructive when groups or group members use it to avoid holistic or long-run concerns. The many variations and uses of time which are possible by shifting one's position relative to it can lead one to manners of operation which deal primarily with one or a few positions. Instances include organizations that request redistribution of members' time without considering the long-run changes this may produce within other vital features; as when an activist organization decides that "time spent on the revolution *is* time spent for our families."

COHORTS

If we pause and consider a list of our friends and close acquaintances, most of us find that the ages of these people are near to our own age. There are good reasons for this. Persons born at approximately the same time often come to have experiences in common, and as a result of these common experiences, to develop common ways of thinking and behaving. Sociologists call persons with such common characteristics *cohorts*. Thus, Americans born in the late 1940s and early 1950s have thus far shared common experiences such as the Cuban Missile Crisis, the assassination of President Kennedy, black civil rights activities, crowded and expanding public schools, competitive admissions to colleges, the women's movement, the "counter-culture," the Vietnam War and antiwar protests, and tightening job markets. Each generation comes to share *significant events* such as these, though they affect various cohort members in disparate ways, according to differences among other vital features. Sharing these experiences does produce similarities among persons of similar age, however, and thereby binds them as a *cohort*. Among the more important derivatives of cohort similarity are certain norms, statuses, and minority designations.

Norms, the rules of procedure and conduct in social life, emerge from the needs which groups develop from their experiences. They are behavioral demands which reflect values. Some cohort norms which have proven important in clinical practices include marriage age (e.g., early 20s for contemporary cohorts, early teens for Shakespeare's cohort), child support (e.g., cohorts who lived through slavery or the economic depression emphasize material support for offspring, cohorts who lived through Vietnam and Watergate emphasize spiritual support for offspring), and political practices (e.g., "In general, older people are more conservative than younger people in their political ideology" [8]).

Status is usually conceived as derivative of one's economic position, but a more complete view recognizes that persons acquire status in terms of the variety of vital features. Persons of equal wealth and occupation aged 25 and 65 are not equal in status if the former is considered by family and employer as "an increasing asset," and the latter as "a burden to us all."

Age groups carry with them certain statuses. This is most easily seen in cross-cultural comparisons. In traditional China the status of elderly persons was so high that the Chinese social order has been termed a "gerontocracy." [9] In the United States, the elderly tend to have a lower status than do middle-aged persons. This results from cohorts' relationships to other vital features such as technology, sex, and the family. Compare the common conceptions of the elderly in the West and the reasons for these conceptions, with those of the Siriono in Bolivia:

> Since status is determined by immediate utility to the group, the inability of the aged to compete with the younger members of the society places them somewhat in the category of excess baggage. Having outlived their usefulness they are relegated to a position of obscurity. Actually the aged are quite a burden. They eat but are unable to hunt, fish, or collect food; they sometimes hoard a young spouse, but are unable to beget children; they move at a snail's pace and hinder the mobility of the group. [10]

Status of the elderly is low in both cultures, as a result of similar negative relations to different vital features. On the other hand, the relationship of the Chinese elderly to these vital features made them valuable teachers.

Within any culture, persons and cohorts experience status passage throughout their lifetimes. This is not merely movement between positions, but is a change in the prestige and honor accorded to a person or group on the basis of position. [11]

Cohorts often receive minority designation by default. In numbers, power, and in the sharing of ways of thinking and behaving, most cohorts are minorities. The cohort dimension of age is thereby comparable, in part, to dimensions of another vital feature, ethnicity. Of special clinical relevance is the prejudice toward and between cohorts. For instance, prevalent contemporary stereotypes of the elderly include the following: valuing companionship more than sex; being old-fashioned; not caring much about their appearance; being neglected; being in only "fair" health; and being narrow-minded.[12] The elderly in turn direct stereotypes at other age groups, most notably adolescents.

Patterns of social and physical distancing among cohorts are also readily apparent. Most cities contain entire housing units composed of the elderly, and apartment complexes have been built in recent years expressly for young adults, and others expressly for senior citizens. Several studies of hospitals have noted that medical personnel segregate elderly or dying patients, and that staff maintain greater distance from these patients than from others.[13]

Not all cohorts are minorities, however. As we noted in chapter 7, being distinct and numerically a minority does not make a group a social minority. Access to power, and definitions of the group by others, determine whether or not persons constitute a minority group. Middle-aged cohorts in most of Europe and America are not at present minority groups. Most social power (including political and economic) is in the hands of middle-aged persons, and very little prejudice is directed on the basis of age or cohort affiliation.

Constructive age processes made possible by cohorts are primarily the communities which cohorts offer. The adage "misery loves company" is verified at many points throughout our lives. Entry into neither grade school nor college would be easy without groups of peers who suffer through the same processes of adaptation and reorientation of values. Cohort membership provides us with significant others and reference groups who go through similar experiences and are considered our equals. Together we are able to define, and deal with, emerging situations. A passage from a ten-year-old's diary illustrates:

> The President quit. Mother and father watched him on TV. They talked on and on about the bad state of America and how nobody is honest except Teddy Roosevelt was [sic]. I went outside to play with J. and L. and *they* were talking about the Watergate too. We all got scared that another country would attack America. J. said his teacher told their class that it is *our* job to make everybody honest again, by not cheating in school and electing honest kids as class officers. J. and L. and I told each other secrets of when we had cheated in school, and we swore we would keep it a secret. . . .

Cohorts also offer predictability. Some gerontologists have compared the *flow* of a cohort through life to a ride on an escalator. How many and which types of people get on (are born) at any two points are never identical, but in all cases those arriving at the other end at the same time move along collectively. Their experiences en route are similar in some respects and different in other respects. The predictability comes from looking at others in one's cohort who are slightly further along. Thus, a high school freshman looks to sophomores and juniors for information as to what freshman year in high school is like.

From a societal point of view, the cohort flow through educational, employment, retirement, and other stages provides "new blood" in institutions; the new cohorts bring new ideas and techniques. In our terms, the cohort flow serves to revitalize the other vital features. This is most apparent perhaps in changes brought about in technology and the family by recent cohorts. One's notions of time will dictate, of course, how one views this revitalization. Linear concepts suggest that new cohorts bring evolutionary improvement (e.g., better technology), while cyclical notions suggest that cohorts bring new varieties and emphases to long existing ways.

Destructive age processes related to cohorts include the obvious ramifications of prejudice between cohorts, such as discrimination against the elderly, plus the latent result of self-fulfilling prophecies, whereby members of cohorts come to act in stereotypic ways. Teenagers who are expected to be irresponsible drivers or drinkers often become such; the physiologically healthy elderly may come to exaggerate minor illnesses.

The cohort flow has built-in pathologies as well. Older cohorts are employed to teach younger cohorts, on the assumption that older persons have more experience and maturity than do younger persons. This arrangement is quite appropriate in many instances, where the teaching involves established bodies of knowledge (e.g., algebra), but inappropriate in emerging situations (e.g., marital and child-rearing practices). Older-to-younger cohort instruction can also interfere with important intracohort teaching and counseling. Older cohorts have had important experiences which younger ones have not, but this alone does not qualify older cohorts to be the primary instructors. No two experiences are the same, and time separation among experiences increases the dissimilarity. These points are illustrated by the numerous studies indicating that students learn as much or more from their peers than they do from their teachers, even in traditional schooling situations.[14] In examining formal and informal teaching situations, it is important to recognize the important formative experiences of the teacher cohort and how these might affect the knowledge, attitudes, and skills being transmitted to the student cohort.

The revitalization which cohort flow offers to the other vital features has a destructive side as well; it may affect the well-being of the age feature itself. A current example is the forced retirement of elderly workers. Cohort flow contributes to the flow of labor and thereby to technology as well, but thus far without reciprocation from these other features. We now have a situation in which many persons are forced to retire before they need or desire to do so, helping to create clinical problems ranging from cohort members' depressions to generalized cohort poverty (60 percent of older Americans are poor; 96 percent of older black females are poor).[15]

CAREER

While each of us has similar formative experiences to those of our cohorts, each cohort contains within it persons with a range of talent which gets mobilized within the existing occupational structure. How this happens can be understood through the concept of career. A career is a pathway taken by a person that has both social, time, and space elements. Usually, a career is viewed as one's occupational pattern, but there can be leisure careers also. As Everett C. Hughes writes:

> A man's work is one of the most important parts of his social identity, of his self; indeed, of his fate in the one life he has to live, for man there is something almost as irrevocable about choice of occupation as there is about choice of a mate and since the language about work is so loaded with value and prestige judgments and with defensive choice of symbols, we should not be astonished that the concepts of social scientists who study work should carry a similar load.[16]

There are two major foci in the study of careers. One can analyze a single person and how he or she takes certain pathways, or one can analyze a particular occupation and try to delineate how it shapes individual careers to its needs. Both approaches yield rich information concerning a variety of clinical problems.

Persons face a series of options in determining a career direction. This can range from whether to show up on a particular morning at the street corner where garbage truck owners recruit garbage haulers, to the decision to leave a well-paying job to undertake one which pays better but has little security. For the individual, a single choice can be based

on several factors related to family, health, interpersonal relations, location of work, or other factors. Or an otherwise unimportant item can
make the difference; one of the authors remembers being drawn to
investigate the college he subsequently attended because its catalog
(red lettering on black) stood out from all the others.

Within any stop along the course of a career, an individual has to
develop a mode of operation within the organization or profession,
locating one's self in social space and time:

> To the newcomer in an organization, time is problematic. One
> must discover when to take a break; have lunch; or quit work;
> when to read the paper; how long one must stay at a certain
> pay grade; when to press for a promotion, and so on. The
> individual must develop certain short-range timetables
> (which assist him in dividing up the days and weeks into manage-
> able components); as well as certain long-range timetables
> (which provide volumes of how his career will unfold). Only in
> constructing such timetables can the past be linked to the future
> making the present meaningful.[17]

In the last decade, there has been an apparent switch from persons
seeing advancement in the work career as the most important goal in
life to persons trying to create a balance between work, leisure, and
personal growth. There are times when persons question the meaning
of their work. Alienation resulting from such questioning can be
viewed when the person takes work options as a signal that change is
possible. "Thus, through occurrences which create states of anomie or
alienation, the person is literally forced to reconsider his or her situated
identity or self-concept vis-à-vis the organization." [18]

The other focus in the study of careers is from the occupational or
professional perspective. Sociologists, especially students of Everett C.
Hughes, have examined specific occupations and professions, usually
along the following dimensions: who gets recruited and how the re-
cruitment takes place; how persons already recruited orient and train
newcomers; how norms of work and interpersonal behavior are transmitted; and what mechanisms are used to enhance attachment, sever-
ance, and replacement, how timing in status passage is handled:

> Even when paths in a career are regular and smooth, there always
> are problems of pacing and timing. While, ideally, successors

and predecessors should move in and out of offices at equal
speeds, they do not and cannot. Those asked to move on or along
or upward may be willing but must make actual and symbolic
preparations; meanwhile, the successors wait impatiently. Transition periods are a necessity, for a man often invests heavily of
himself in a position, comes to possess it as it possesses him,
and suffers in leaving it. If the full ritual of leave taking is not
allowed, the man may not pass fully into his new status. On
the other hand, the institution has devices to make him forget,
to plunge him into the new office, to woo and win him with the
new qualifications, and, at the same time, to force him to
abandon the old.[19]

Constructive and destructive career processes can be uncovered by the
clinician through charting the career histories of persons and organizations, via methods such as interviewing and observation. Individuals
and organizations offer "cover stories" which tell just enough truth to
satisfy the casual questioner, but that must be dug into by the clinician.

Constructively, careers provide persons with predictable and com-
prehendible futures. Destructively, if these career patterns become unfulfilling they can harm not only the individual but his community:

> In short, to the extent that men are exposed to disciplined work
> routines yielding little gratification and have "careers" which
> are in no way predictable, then retreat from work will be
> accompanied by a withdrawal from the larger communal life—and
> thus will apply to the middle class as well as the working
> class.[20]

If this is correct, a clinical examination of apathy in a community or
organization might look to the frustrations of work in that community
or organization, or the unpredictability of local careers.

To understand fully the centrality of the career concept in linking an
individual to society, choose a person and chart his or her career. (Older
persons make better subjects for charting.) Begin by asking what the
person believes are the major events in his or her life thus far and how
these events were connected to work at that time. Begin with the ear-
liest event: What were the tasks and the roles that the person undertook
in the work setting? What role conflicts were involved? Then expand the
questioning to other factors that could have been influential in the

person's orientation toward work activities at that time—health, family, community, education, mobility, productivity, and personal or societal concerns. After charting the information noted about the first event, move forward along the person's time line (age), filling in the factors that were important as the person made other changes along the career course.

DEATH

Only recently has death been explicitly studied as a *normal* and social process. It is one of the few social phenomena that meets the varied definitions of normality noted in chapter 1: *all* people die, and the conventions of every community expect it. Furthermore, death is usually a constructive phenomenon, at least for societies. We have already noted that the cohort flow is helpful in revitalizing other vital features. Without death, the cohort flow would become top heavy, and eventually, due to overpopulation, the flow would slow down and probably cease. For individuals, too, immortality would create difficulties. Who would want to be a college student for 300 years, or be unable to advance in an organization because those higher up never disappear?

Some of the world's most brilliant art and philosophy has resulted from contemplation on the apparent irony that living is a constant process of dying. Social scientists have considered this process as well, especially the later stages. Elizabeth Kubler-Ross noted five stages in the dying process: denial and isolation; anger and resentment; bargaining and postponing; depression and loss; and acceptance.[21] These stages are actually present throughout our lives, though they are most noticeable toward the end. Middle-aged persons, and even some young adults, occupy themselves with athletic and cosmetic enterprises designed to deny or bargain with death by slowing down the age process. The depression of a person upon recognition that he or she is "no longer a kid," has "become middle aged," or is "an old man or woman," all indicate depression with the prospect of death.

Not only group members, but also groups and organizations often pass through Kubler-Ross's stages of death. Clinicians regularly find that groups that are threatened internally or externally with extinction will deny their difficulties and isolate themselves, then lash out at their antagonists before begging for survival. If all of these steps fail to save the group, widespread depression often ensues prior to a kind of sentimental acceptance that the group will dissipate.[22]

These stages can be seen within groups in another situation as well, that of the loss of a leader. These stages appeared, for instance, in the case of a recent American President who was forced out of office after denying his impending troubles, then becoming isolated, angry, bargaining, depressed, and finally accepting.

The *constructive age processes* of death are, then, the revitalization of features and the circulation of cohorts, plus the psychological preparation which the *stages* of death provide. These are as true within particular groups and leaders of these groups as they are for societies and individuals in general. Groups and their leadership are revitalized through processes of death and replacement.

Destructive age processes result mostly from avoidance or continual denial of death, as well as lack of compassion and preparation for the dying. We see these processes in individual cases frequently among elderly persons who dress and act like their grandchildren, largely in response to a widespread societal fear of death. This fear is also manifest in the clumsy or absent compassion afforded the dying persons. Repulsion at the process of dying prevents many of us from intersubjectively encountering death along with the dying person, thereby increasing the objective isolation of the process of dying.

The actions of groups and group leaders are not destructive when they fight death in its early stages. Such battles are simple self-preservation. But if death becomes apparent, the process can become destructive if denial, anger, or escape takes over. More appropriate activities include preparations for groups or leaders who will follow, or preserving one's contributions to the future. Again, there is need for compassion, both within the group and from other groups. In the case of changes in leadership, the new leader and his or her followers will most likely be destructive if they concentrate solely upon their own concerns rather than sincere comradeship with those who are departing. It is to avoid such destructive self-centeredness that many groups institutionalize various rites of passage for outgoing leaders, such as testimonial ceremonies.

In healthy situations, the incoming group or leader experiences true compassion and sharing (not just ritual emotion) with those who are outgoing. The fact of the matter is that each "birth" of a group or group member is simultaneously the beginning of a death, and hence the incoming and outgoing have a great deal in common and quite a lot worth sharing with one another. This is no less true if the parties have been enemies.

NOTES

1. Research for much of this chapter was supported by the Syracuse University Maxwell Policy Center on Aging (Ephraim Mizruchi, Director), under a grant from the Department of Health, Education and Welfare, Administration on Aging. The grant is Title IV-C, Multidisciplinary Centers on Gerontology (90-A-1054/01).

2. Pitrim Sorokin, *Sociocultural Causality, Space, Time* (Durham, N.C.: Duke University Press, 1943).

3. G. J. Whitrow, *The Nature of Time* (Middlesex, England: Penguin, 1975).

4. Bernice Neugarten, "Personality and the Aging Process," *Gerontologist* 12(Spring 1972):12.

5. John Dewey, *Experience and Nature* (New York: Dover, 1958), pp. 97–98.

6. Edwin Schneidman, "Crisis Intervention: Some Thoughts and Perspectives," in G. Spector and W. Claiborn, eds., *Crisis Intervention* (New York: Behavioral Publications, 1973), p. 12.

7. Talcott Parsons, *The Social System* (New York: Free Press, 1951).

8. M. Riley and A. Foner, *Aging and Society*, vol. 1 (New York: Russell Sage Foundation, 1968), p. 5.

9. P. Welty, *The Asians* (Philadelphia: Lippincott, 1970).

10. A. Holmberg, *Nomads of the Long Bow* (Garden City, N.Y.: Natural History Press, 1969), p. 224.

11. Barney Glaser and Anselm Strauss, *Time for Dying* (Chicago: Aldine, 1968), p. 244.

12. Robert Atchley, *The Social Forces in Later Life* (Belmont, Cal.: Wadsworth, 1977), p. 72.

13. David Sudnow, *Passing On* (Englewood Cliffs, N.J.: Prentice-Hall, 1967); and W. Watson and R. Maxwell, *Human Aging and Dying* (New York: St. Martin's, 1977).

14. Everett Hughes, Howard Becker, and Blanche Geer, "How Colleges Differ," in *Planning College Policy for the Critical Decade Ahead* (New York: College Entrance Examination Board, 1958), pp. 16–22; and Barry Glassner, "Kid Society," *Urban Education* 11(April 1976):5–22.

15. *U.S. Bureau of the Census, 1975*, pp. 114–15.

16. Everett C. Hughes, *Men and Their Work* (Glencoe, Ill.: Free Press, 1958), p. 43.

17. John Van Maanen, "Experiencing Organizations: Notes on the Meaning of Careers and Socialization," in John Van Maanen, ed., *Or-*

ganizational Careers: Some New Perspectives (New York: Wiley, 1977), pp. 19–20.

18.   Ibid., p. 41.

19.   Howard S. Becker and Anselm L. Strauss, "Careers, Personality, and Adult Socialization," *American Journal of Sociology* 62, no. 3 (November 1956):259.

20.   Harold L. Wilensky, "Orderly Careers and Social Participation: The Impact of Work History on Social Integrations in the Middle Class," *American Sociological Review* 26(1961):522–23.

21.   Elizabeth Kubler-Ross, *On Death and Dying* (New York: Macmillan, 1969).

22.   See, for example, Ezra Stotland and Arthur Kobler, *The Life and Death of a Mental Hospital* (Seattle: University of Washington Press, 1965).

THE CLINICIAN'S LIBRARY

Most sociological works which deal with aging concentrate on the last third of the life span. Among the most comprehensive:

Atchley, Robert. *The Social Forces in Later Life.* Belmont, Cal.: Wadsworth, 1977.
Gubrium, Jaber, and David Buckholdt. *Toward Maturity.* San Francisco: Jossey-Bass, 1977.
Hendricks, Jon, and C. Hendricks. *Aging in Mass Society.* Cambridge, Mass.: Winthrop Publishers, 1977.

An excellent book by deGrazia deals with a variety of subjects but pays special attention to age:

deGrazia, Sebastian. *Of Time, Work and Leisure.* New York: Doubleday Anchor, 1964.

COHORT

Among the better works which discuss cohorts are the following:

Gubrium, J. *The Myth of the Golden Years: A Socio-Environmental Theory of Aging.* Springfield, Ill.: Charles C Thomas Publishers, 1973.

Riley, M., M. Johnson, and A. Foner. *Aging and Society*. New York: Russell Sage Foundation, 1972.

CAREER

Major works which discuss the various aspects of the concept of career are these three:

Hughes, Everett C. *Men and Their Work*. Glencoe, Ill.: Free Press, 1958.
Van Maanen, John. *Organizational Careers, Some New Perspectives*. New York: Wiley, 1977.
Wilensky, H. L. "Orderly Careers and Social Participation," *American Sociological Review* 4(1961):521–39.

TIME

Summary statements and collections on the interesting and complex topic of time include the following:

Fraser, J. T., ed. *The Voices of Time*. New York: Braziller, 1966.
Sherover, Charles. *The Human Experience of Time*. New York: New York University Press, 1975.
Whitrow, G. J. *The Nature of Time*. Baltimore: Penguin, 1975.

DEATH

The available sociological discussions concerning death deal primarily with the last few months or years of the life cycle. Among the best of this variety:

Kubler-Ross, Elizabeth. *On Death and Dying*. New York: Macmillan, 1969.
Sudnow, David. *Passing On*. Englewood Cliffs, N.J.: Prentice-Hall, 1967.
Watson, Wilbur, and R. Maxwell. *Human Aging and Dying*. New York: St. Martin's, 1977.

Chapter 10

The Family

Sociologist Lillian Rubin observed the relatively recent phenomena of the pill, the sexual revolution, the counter-culture, the rising divorce rate, the women's movement, and so forth, then concluded as do most researchers of the family:

> Many experienced observers of American life have been proclaiming the death of the nuclear family and preparing its burial. For most people, however, the issue is not *whether* the family has a future, but *what* that future will look like. For after all the questions are asked and the speculations are done, the unshakable reality remains: most Americans of all classes still live in families and will continue to do so for the foreseeable future at least. And it is there—in those families—that the stresses and strains of everyday life are played out—that children are born and brought to adulthood; that women and men love and hate; that major interpersonal and intrapersonal conflicts are generated and stilled; and that men, women and children struggle with the demands from the changing world outside their doors.[1]

Social and medical scientists have traditionally held that families are units consisting of related men and women who care for their own or

adopted children.[2] So many exceptions now exist that this sort of definition will not do: some families are purposely childless, some cohabitate
without legal, or even less formal, marriage contracts, some do not
cohabitate (e.g., because of jobs in different locations or the placement
of children in boarding schools), some are neither biologically nor
tribally related, some consist solely of persons of one sex (e.g., when
one spouse deserts and all the children are of the same sex as the remaining spouse, or in homosexual marriages), and the list continues.
Because of this variety, it is difficult even to define the family, much less
to determine its component parts. But essentially the family is a set of
"socially patterned ideals and practices concerned with biological and
cultural survival of the species." [3]

We can see, then, that the family is an agent for social control, ensuring that persons grow up in socially approved ways, much as is the
justice system or the education system. What does the family control?

1. *Control of sex* is a regular activity (some would say "function") of
the institution of the family. Claude Lévi-Strauss has argued that the
very possibility of human culture and social organization depends upon
the *incest taboo* which prohibits persons from engaging in sex with
those of their own immediate family:

> Exactly in the same way that the principle of sexual division of
> labor establishes mutual dependency between the sexes, com-
> pelling them thereby to perpetuate themselves and to found
> a family, the prohibition of incest establishes a mutual depen-
> dency between families, compelling them, in order to per-
> petuate themselves, to give rise to new families.[4]

The widespread existence of the incest taboo cross-culturally and historically has led some persons to contend that it is a universal proscription
among human societies.[5]

The incest taboo is only the beginning of the family's control of sexual
and other intimate relations, however. The institution of the family
proscribes for most people not only who to avoid as a sexual partner,
but who to engage. This is achieved through methods ranging from
parents selecting sex and marriage partners for their children to the
subtle values instilled by liberal contemporary Westerners in their children concerning the proper ethnicity, social class, attire, education
level, and so forth of their "dates."

Even the frequency and time of sexual intercourse is managed to a great extent by the family. Children pick up cues from their parents and siblings concerning the optimal qualitative and quantitative conditions for intercourse. Thus, children in some families learn that premarital sex is "wrong," while in others a child is considered "queer" who has not engaged in intercourse prior to marriage. In some societies, family members contend that the "proper" amount of sexual activity is once a week, while others accept intercourse as appropriate only every few years, for the sake of reproduction. The contrasts become clear in cross-cultural comparisons. Contemporary Western societies are overflowing with sexual advice books advocating the neo-Freudian position that persons are sexually frustrated and should have sexual intercourse more often each week or month, and in more fulfilling styles. Meanwhile, the Dani of Indonesia regularly abstain from sexual relations for four or five years at a time, without any apparent frustrations, regrets, or special processes of social control.[6]

These differences probably result from different needs of the larger society or community, needs that are facilitated through the family's control of sexual relations. In communities where a population increase is desired (e.g., to facilitate military strength or to increase available farm workers) sexual relations will likely be encouraged. In communities where population increases are not desired but additional *recreational* activities are wanted, sexual relations may become widespread as a result of other factors:

> The rational basis for a society's prohibition of heterosexual intercourse outside marriage has to do with the consequences of such intercourse because many societies—probably most societies—do not have suitable provisions for raising children born out of wedlock. . . . The first consequence of the development of an efficient contraceptive and widespread access to it, then, would seem to be a disappearance of moral and legal sanctions against extramarital sex.[7]

In most contemporary Western communities, sexual relations have come to take on the meaning—and fulfill the needs—of social recreation, rather than of procreation. They are nonetheless controlled largely by the family, as evidenced by the difficulties usually created within a marriage when one partner has an affair or by the continuing expectation among most young people who experiment with many sex partners that eventually they will locate one person with whom they will spend the rest of their lives in monogamous marital bliss.

2. The phenomenon of *love* is also controlled by the family. In most societies this has been accomplished through direct parental control of their children's potential love partners, either through arranging or supervising interactions and marriages or through child marriages, whereby parents actually have their children married before they reach adolescence. In current societies less direct methods are used, but the control, as of sex, is still present:

> Since considerable energy and resources may be required to push youngsters who are in love into proper role behavior, love must be controlled *before* it appears. Love relationships must either be kept to a small number or they must be so directed that they do not run counter to the approved kinship linkages. . . . In our society, parents threaten, cajole, wheedle, bribe, and persuade their children to "go with the right people," during both the early love play and later courtship phases. Primarily, they seek to control love relationships by influencing the informal social contacts of their children: moving to appropriate neighborhoods and schools, giving parties and helping to make out invitation lists, by making their children aware that certain children have ineligibility traits. . . . Since youngsters fall in love with those with whom they associate, control over informal relationships also controls substantially the focus of affection.[8]

Such control is not entirely unwarranted. Research repeatedly finds that persons from different types of backgrounds more often have love and marital difficulties than do persons from similar backgrounds. For instance, spouses from different social status origins are more likely to experience stressful marriages than are persons from similar origins, perhaps owing to feelings of loss on the part of the higher status person.[9] Clinicians are frequently asked by clients experiencing sexual or romantic difficulties, "Why do I end up with these lovers anyhow?" As the above suggests, the wise clinician will likely answer with questions, statements, or other procedures that indicate ways in which the clients' families wrote the romantic scripts years ago.

3. *Connecting love and marriage* in most contemporary minds, "like a horse and carriage," brings love into the domain of the family. For most of us, the movies, novels, and peer culture all have reinforced our parents' instruction that marriage is the union of two people who are very

much in love. Few of us have stopped to think about the point made by psychoanalyst Ernest van den Haag that love and marriage are in many ways incompatible. For one thing, love is a carefree, unruly emotion, while successful marriage requires careful, regular feelings and patterns of living together. The Greeks long ago emphasized that love is a kind of intoxication and longing that is never completely fulfilled in real life. Thus, a precondition of romantic love is a distance between the lovers, and this is antithetical to the shared coping necessary in an ongoing marriage. "One thing is certain," van den Haag reminds us, "if the relationship is stabilized, love is replaced by other emotions." [10] Or as a journalist recently summed up:

> The happiest married couples I know, the ones for whom the burdens of marriage are more than matched by its comforts and delights, are each other's best friend; and the recognition of that friendship underlies any other reasons they might have had for getting married.[11]

The family achieves these various controls, and many others, via its major components: marriage, child-rearing, divorce, and sex roles.

MARRIAGE

As the above suggests, marriage is not an easy social arrangement. Even for couples who are not experiencing marital problems (sexual problems, differential values, fights, etc.), there are the necessary burdens of coordinating schedules to one another, of household chores, of in-laws, and of maintaining social ties to other couples.

Persons have devised a variety of *types of marriage* to meet the needs arising from their position in social structures. Working-class persons get married largely because they are unhappy living with their parents or because marriage will convert them from the status of child to that of adult. On the other hand, middle-class persons often leave home before marriage and tend to marry in order to acquire companionship and intimacy.

These differences are reflected in the styles of marriage in these social classes. Working-class persons usually neither seek nor expect close communication and understanding from their spouses; rather, these attributes are desired in same-sex friends—wives look to other women for their confidants and husbands confide in other men. This is further reflected in the tendency for men and women to separate into two groups at lower-class parties. Middle-class persons tend to seek high levels of communication and understanding from their spouses, and men and women stick together at parties.[12]

Such patterns perpetuate themselves because "like marries like." Most marriages are between persons of similar social classes who live near one another during adolescence and who are similar in age and education.[13] This results both from the pressures of parental norms upon children and from norms worked out among the children themselves in their own peer groups. As Margaret Mead first noted, dating and marrying is oriented primarily toward gaining prestige among peers of one's own gender.[14]

In one major structural way marriages do not differ substantially between groups, however. A popular myth is that in previous eras or in other cultures nuclear families (husband, wife, and children) were not nearly as prevalent as were extended families (several marriage units living together, or tribal or communal units consisting of many persons). Most all family units for hundreds of years have consisted of one or two generations, and no more than five or six members.[15] This is in part a truism, because only in recent decades has the life expectancy rate been high enough that grandparents would be alive to live amid their grandchildren.

Probably the major change in living arrangements lately is that many people go through regular periods of living outside of marriage units. The regularity of divorce and consequent periods between marriages contributes to this, and the other major periods are those of pre- and postmarital independence:

> While more than two-thirds of males 18–24 were living with their families in 1940, fewer than half in that age-group were still home in 1970. Of those 18–24 year olds who had left home in 1940, roughly half had established new families, and half lived as unrelated individuals. As the pool of early leavers grew after 1940 it at first gained family heads, most of whom were married, more rapidly than unrelated individuals. More recently, however, the gain has been of unrelated individuals, so that in 1970, 26.5 percent of 18 to 24 year old males were living apart from any family, up from 16 percent in 1940, and a much higher percentage had passed through such a stage before marriage.[16]

The statistics are equally striking at the other end of marital life, the last third of the life cycle. While 58 percent of women 65 and over who were not themselves family heads lived with relatives in 1940, only 29 percent lived with relatives in 1970. The percentage of males living with relatives dropped from 43 percent to 24 percent. In short, higher percentages of young and old persons are living outside of marriage.[17]

More generally, this increasing autonomy has lead to a decrease in the family's role as the source of intimate relationships, or what Deena and Michael Weinstein call "appreciation," the need which persons have for others to value what they do and create:

> Although the contemporary family is the setting for much appreciative activity, the extent of such appreciation has been decreasing. Playing on fears of the disintegrating family, bowling alleys advertise: "The family that plays together stays together." Nonetheless, most bowling is not done in family groups, nor do families participate in most sports together. Viewing television is a popular family activity, but because many time slots have shows geared exclusively to one or another family member (Saturday morning cartoons for children . . .) only a small portion of the time (prime time) can be shared by the family as a whole. The trend toward personal-size television receivers for different members of the family and the general passivity of television viewing raise questions about whether watching television is a family or personal form of entertainment. Sex is an entertainment for the married pair, but is absolutely taboo among others in the family. Even church attendance is no longer a family affair, since different programs are frequently developed for different family members.[18]

Constructive marriage processes obviously vary according to the societal, group, and personal needs being dealt with in marriage. In general, marriage processes are constructive which help persons and groups facilitate their life encounters with other vital features. Thus, a marital union should assist persons in their life cycle changes, relations to their ethnic communities, social mobility, and so forth. Such assistance can come in a variety of forms, including (1) mutual support practices between the spouses, (2) social interactions facilitated through being married (e.g., making friends with other married persons), and (3) creating a lifestyle separate and more useful than that available when living alone, in collective groups, or with parents.

Destructive marriage processes occur when the relationship between marriage and other features becomes distorted. A couple of distortions are common at present:

1. Marriage frequently becomes a *market commodity*. In some societies this was extended so far that brides and grooms were actually assigned price tags according to the money, power, or prestige they would bring. The process is usually less formal at present, but the continuing "like marries like" phenomenon exemplifies the subservience of marriage and family to the stratification feature, which is reproduced by such processes.

The market connection extends to the age feature as well. Older men tend to be worth more as marriage partners than do older women, in part due to their usual control of greater financial resources, but also owing to stereotypes that hold that older men continue to be sexually or romantically appealing, but that older women do not.

2. Interpersonal relationships derived largely from nonfamily contacts may be disrupted:

> Mary loves to play bridge, but Jerry dislikes card games. Mary and Jerry get married. Mary gives up bridge, Jerry, on the other hand, gives up camping because Mary is not interested in outdoor things. If you are married, stop and think for a minute of the things you either gave up, modified, or failed to pursue because the couple-front demanded of the married couple did not allow you to do otherwise. While you are at it, think about the people you gave up—and the ones who give you up. We do not invite people unless we find both husband and wife acceptable to both of us. That means that we do not see many people that we *both* like, let alone those that only one of us likes, because we do not both like their mates. . . .[19]

Indeed, the "living-together" and group-living families of recent decades are a response to much of the exclusiveness that may result from traditional marital arrangements.

CHILD-REARING

A major activity of family members is child-rearing. As in their marriages, the social classes differ in the ways they perceive and structure their parenting. Working-class parents raise their children to follow the orders of authorities (parents, school officials, bosses), while middle-class parents encourage their children to develop internalized standards of conduct.[20] Again, we find that the family is thereby serving the needs of the larger society, in this case the stratification system. As noted in our earlier discussion of stratification, success in working-class jobs requires the ability to follow orders, while success in middle-class jobs requires individual initiative and the ability to interpret which orders to follow and in which ways. The difference in child-rearing practices is in some ways simply preparation for different adult careers.

These child-rearing differences also serve shorter run expectations which differ among the classes. Working-class children and adolescents are more likely than middle-class children to be considered unruly or delinquent by school and police personnel. As Lillian Rubin notes:

> [Working class parents'] own histories remind them about how easily children can get into trouble, how easily they stray from parental values and injunctions. Thus, like their parents, they believe that children need to be carefully and constantly watched. It matters little that they resented such parental authority, even that they often subverted it. Instead, retrospectively they tend to argue that it was good for them; that without it they might have gotten into still more trouble; that it was a sign of parental love and concern; and that had their parents been less strict, they might not now be living a settled, stable life.[21]

Groups' child-rearing practices vary in another regard as well. Some groups are more likely than others to have both mother and father present in the child-rearing. Approximately 8.3 million American children are being reared only by their mothers, and mother-rearing is more frequent among black than among white families, among poor more than among nonpoor families.[22] But although the frequency is greater, only a minority of families have a single parent.

A variety of clinicians, academic sociologists, and psychologists have assumed—largely on the basis of psychoanalytic assumptions and work by anthropologist Malinowski—that fatherless children will experience problems as adults. A summary of several hundred studies shows that they yield inconsistent and inconclusive evidence on the effect of growing up without a father.[23] One thing is certain, however, the problems of fatherless children are not a *direct* result of not having a father. The intervening processes are those which truly hurt the child—processes such as peer rejection, poverty, or limited access to males.

There are fashions in child-rearing as well. Some popular authority will come up with a definitive approach that gets transmitted to parents. "Everything must be done on a strict schedule," one authority will proclaim. "Do not give in to your child even if he seems miserable. It will teach him self-control in the long run." In another generation, another expert in reaction to the first will stress permissiveness, that denial of the child's basic needs will cause later difficulty. A very current debate is over the importance of the birth process. Some experts believe that the birth process must treat the emerging fetus as a sensate human with warmth and care. Other experts believe that this makes no difference and even attach fetal heart monitors to the baby's head while still in utero.[24]

These fashions often get diffused throughout a culture and can exist alongside each other. The process of diffusion is discussed in chapter 11.

The *constructive processes* of parenting have long been recognized. In rural, agricultural communities children were valued as future farm workers who would eventually take care of their parents and other relatives during old age. In addition, a man gained status not only on the basis of the amount of land controlled, but also according to the size of the family group for which he was responsible. This was compounded by the fact that prestige was accorded to persons who demonstrated generosity, and persons with the greatest number of close dependents were often seen as most generous.[25]

More recently, children have been valued more for the short-run companionship they provide their parents, although the achievements of children can bring prestige to a family, and there are continuing hopes that children will care for their parents in their old age. Especially within the middle class, however, persons are questioning whether the benefits of parenting offset the tremendous costs and obligations. Estimates are that each child costs a family at least $60,000 in shelter, food, education, medical services, and parents' lost working hours.

Destructive processes relate directly to the state of the contemporary family within society. Consider a few of the more prominent problems:

1. Child-beating is often conceived as a psychological, individual problem, but it seems to be found in predictable social settings: among parents who are isolated in the home and find that children do not provide the peer companionship adults need to be happy; among parents who have little real power at work or in political and other social controls of their community and end up with power only over their children; and among parents who had children because it was the ex-

pectation of their own parents and friends, though neither group taught them *how* to be parents.

2. Parents often insist that their children be similar to a person or type of person worth admiring. "Your grandfather was a great man who did such-and-such," children are told, or "Be big and strong like Muhammad Ali." Many societies in the past have offered direct religious processes by which persons were reincarnated, but in our psychoscientific society the only way in which valued persons are reincarnated is through expectations made of children. Needless to say, these expectations may be burdensome for children and parents alike.

Sometimes this process can work negatively in another fashion. A child can look or act in certain ways like a devalued member of the family. The expectations of parents can be that the child will end up just like the devalued person. The child can sometimes come to believe this self-fulfilling prophecy.

3. As much of the above discussion suggests, persons simply are not trained to be parents. Courses on parenting are seldom available in schools or colleges, and most persons learn child-rearing from their own parents. New parents, although they have stated that they would *never* do *that* to their children, are often shocked to see themselves acting just as their own parents did and unable to find alternatives.

DIVORCE

Driving on the New Jersey Turnpike on a sunny summer day, one of the authors did a double-take as he suddenly realized that he had at first misread the sign on the car in front of him. Beer cans hung from the rear bumper of the car, and the big sign in the rear window read, "Just Divorced!" Some readers may do double-takes because this book contains a section on divorce as a regular feature of family life. In a society where 30-year-olds have about one chance in three of being divorced at some time in their lives,[26] divorce is at least a regular statistical phenomenon. But more important than contemporary statistics is the evidence that some type of escape from marriage has existed as a regular feature in nearly all societies. In other eras or locations the escape valve has been desertion, or separation within the home into individual quarters and duties, or uniting with a more extended family of blood relatives or other tribal members to decrease contact between the immediate spouses, or other strategies which do not get labeled "divorce." Among the more dramatic examples from tribal societies is that

of the Iroquois, among whom women for long periods had great power
of divorce:

> No matter how many children, or whatever goods [the husband]
> might have in the house, he might at any time be ordered to
> pick up his blanket and budge; and after such orders it
> would not be healthful for him to disobey; the house would be too
> hot for him; and unless saved by the intercession of some aunt
> or grandmother, he must retreat to his own clan.[27]

To many persons contemplating divorce, and to many clinicians
working with them, ending a marriage is seen as the end of one's
contact with the institution of marriage itself. This had not been true
cross-culturally and is not true in contemporary Western societies.
Roughly 80 percent of all people who divorce remarry, thereby continuing their affiliation with the institution of marriage.[28] Indeed, the regularity of divorce leads to increasing rates of divorce and marriage. With
more people divorcing, there are more like-aged people available to
choose for remarriage.

How can a clinician determine whether or not other persons' marriages are "good" or are in need of divorce? The only pattern found
regularly by sociological research is that long-lasting marriages tend to
occur between persons who feel the same way about most fundamental
things.[29] This may seem a commonplace statement, but it actually offers
a great deal of insight. It facilitates understanding of the inevitability of
high divorce rates in contemporary communities where spouses have
separate groups of friends (e.g., each at their separate places of work or
schooling) and consequently different sources for feelings and opinions. This is in sharp contrast to agricultural or small-town life, where
husband and wife are more often involved with similar circles of
friends, and where the entire community shares quite similar attitudes.
Thus, in looking at a marriage, we can ask whether the spouses agree on
child-rearing, sex roles, politics, leisure activities, and other regular
activities. Couples among whom such disagreement is rampant are unlikely to benefit from the patching up of their marriage.

Constructive processes of divorce are those which permit the divorcing
persons to change their social interactions to those which are more
fulfilling. This is where clinicians are often quite useful. In many or
most cases, a divorced person will simply repeat the poor patterns of the

previous marriage in future relationships and marriages. Ways of selecting and managing close relationships with other persons often become habitual, and persons find no avenues for learning alternative strategies. Thus, for instance, the man who insists upon being boss in his family needs to be aware of his two basic options—either changing his feelings on this topic or finding a woman who truly believes that men should "wear the pants in the family" and will promote such a situation in the home.

More generally, divorce is a good time for persons to evaluate to which groups they wish to belong. Marriage usually constrains persons to associate primarily with other, similar families: middle-class couples hang out with middle-class couples, blacks with blacks, football fans with football fans, housewives with housewives, professional women with professional women, and so forth. In a marriage a person may desire to change group affiliations but be restrained from doing so by a spouse's needs or demands.

Destructive processes of divorce evolve primarily from the un-availability of social supports in contemporary communities. Persons inevitably lose some of the friends they developed through their marriage, and they often experience social stigma for having "failed at marriage," frequently among their own parents or other family members. At the same time, there are legal settlements and often the upsetting difficulties of care for the children.

The question of child care is especially difficult in most communities at present. Children need good parents, not necessarily mothers or even the original biological parents. Usually courts rule that children are the responsibility of their mother, even in cases where the father would make a better parent or where neither of the partners is particularly capable of (or interested in) parenting. Many divorces are of couples who married in their late teens or early twenties and stuck together just long enough to have a child, hoping that the child would improve their marital relations.

If there are children, the divorce usually does not mean the disappearance of the other spouse. Visiting rights mean regular appearances of the former partner, who frequently tries to buy the short-term affections of the children with new clothes and expensive good times, sometimes making the other partner a cheapskate in the eyes of the children. As women frequently have custody of the children most of the time, this is a "sugar daddy" role.

SEX ROLES

Persons learn sex roles at school, at work, and in numerous other institutions, but sex roles are primarily determined by the family. The structure of the family determines much of how sex roles will be allocated. For instance, initiative, ambition, and strength are all associated with the male sex role, and all are quite useful to the traditional male position within the family, as provider. The home-loving, dependent, and subservient qualities expected of women also fit the needs of the traditional family role of housewife.

People learn their sex roles through processes beginning at birth. Observational studies indicate that proud fathers jostle their infant male children, but pet and cuddle girl children, and that mothers speak to infants more if they are females (explaining, in part, why young girls show greater linguistic skills than do young boys).[30] As most of us remember from our childhoods, male children are told that "boys don't cry" and that "little girls should look pretty." Boys play with war toys, girls with dolls. Boys are expected to become athletic, girls to learn to cook. The list of differences is a long one.

The images are reproduced in children's worlds also in the books they are given. A recent study indicates that the ratio of male to female pictures in prize-winning children's books is eleven to one, and that one-third of the books involved males only. When females did appear in the books, they were nearly always indoors: helping, watching, or loving the book's hero.[31] In school, the values are further perpetuated by teachers who assume that girls "are likely to 'love' reading and to 'hate' mathematics and sciences," and the opposite expectation is held for boys.[32] Home economics courses are designed for females, business and engineering courses for males. Studies suggest that many adolescent and young adult females actually become fearful of success. Similarly, a study of 21,000 college students found major differences between the success orientations of males and females. As many men with C+ averages planned to attend graduate school as women with B+ and A averages.[33] Being self-reliant is not in keeping with the traditional female sex role and is likely to bring displeasure from family and friends at the prospect that such a woman will be unsuccessful in relationships with men.[34]

Male and female role expectations are so widespread that they have become virtual stereotypes: male characteristics include aggression, violence, stifled sensitivity and tenderness, rationality, mechanical ability, athletic prowess, and courage.[35] Female characteristics are often just opposites of those for males, plus some others such as concern with appearances.

Some stereotypes are held with absolutely no support. For instance, a sociological researcher found that many women assert the stereotype of male behavior—and their own justification for opposition to the women's movement—as follows: "I like a man to open the car door and light my cigarettes." Yet when asked to recall the last time their husbands opened a car door for them or lit their cigarettes they cannot recall such an event. One woman replied, "I gotta admit, I don't know why I said that, I don't even smoke." [36]

Some sociologists claim that the destructive processes of sex role differentiation are beginning to be felt more by men and women, and that this has led to the increasing divorce rates. The research results on this assertion are not yet conclusive, but such a relationship between sex roles and divorce would not be surprising, given that marriages have sometimes been based primarily upon sex roles which partners expect of one another.

Of course, contemporary Western sex roles are only one of a theoretically infinite number of arrangements for sexual divisions of labor and meaning, and often it is useful for clinicians to point out alternatives. There have been major societies in which women and men were equal in their responsibilities at home and in other economic and social realms, under a variety of arrangements. Consider the Zuni:

> The house belongs to the woman and she receives her husband in it as a guest. He in turn brings the produce of fields and ranch; as it crosses the threshold it becomes the property of the woman. Any omission of these formalities on the part of the woman would be interpreted by the man as an indication that she no longer regards him as her husband.[37]

Or look at the Wyandot Indians of the Huron, in which the head of the family was a woman, and the family heads in turn chose four women to head up the informal government.[38] Or, for a dramatic contrast, consider the Tchambuli tribe of New Guinea in which the women are more powerful, are preoccupied with practical matters, shave their heads, and go off to work each morning, while the men stay at home awaiting gifts and approval from the women. Women take the initiative in courtship, and men do most of the crying.

Constructive and destructive processes of sex role divisions are, respectively, those which provide options for members of a sex and those which restrict options. In their contemporary Western forms we can note several options provided, and several eliminated, for both sexes by sex roles: [39]

Options encouraged for males include:

1.   Males are encouraged to form friendships with other males and to work with other males for mutual goals.
2.   Greater job opportunities and, concurrently, greater financial, legal, and educational opportunities.
3.   Greater sexual freedom is provided males, and they need worry less about pregnancy from such activities.
4.   Less or no domestic (household) work is demanded of males.
5.   Males may be aggressive both in courting and in working.
6.   More escapism (drinking, athletics) is acceptable among males.

These lead nearly inevitably to the *destructive restrictions for males,* which include:

1.   The display of emotions is discouraged among males. Males are not expected to cry when they are sad or to hug one another.
2.   Major activities other than those of provider for the family are seldom permitted, and males are regularly pressured to succeed and be competitive.
3.   Males must demonstrate their sexual prowess and enjoy (or pretend to enjoy) frequent sex.
4.   Certain "domestic" career options are limited, such as that of housekeeper, or house cleaner.
5.   Males who are not aggressive become accused of "sissy" behavior, homosexuality, and so forth. Crime and delinquency rates are higher for males, many of whom commit such acts to demonstrate their masculinity.
6.   Alcoholism rates seem to be higher for males, as do incidences of physical injury from athletics and others forms of escapist recreation.
7.   Expected lifespan for males is shorter.

Female options are somewhat predictable once we know the male list:

1.   Freedom to express emotions is encouraged among females.
2.   Financial obligations and the pressure to succeed are less.

3.   Females are often placed "on a pedestal" as persons to be admired and treated with courtesy.

The constructive list is obviously quite short for females, though their list of *destructive restrictions* is not so brief and derives largely from the male list:

1.   Females' primary work is often restricted to that involving the emotions, rather than reason. Nondomestic job opportunities and education are limited, and there is legal and financial discrimination.
2.   Sexual freedom is limited for females, and they must be concerned about pregnancy.
3.   Females are expected to maintain a good appearance and make themselves attractive to males.
4.   Females often must give in to male wishes.
5.   Aggression in dating, athletics, work, and elsewhere is proscribed for females.

These options and restrictions often combine to provide a kind of destructive *milieu* within particular areas of social life. Within the medical profession, for instance, the restrictions list for women in the West has resulted in comparably low percentages of women. Only 6 percent of American physicians are women, and the highest percentage in Western nations is Great Britain's, at only 25 percent. These compare with the Soviet Union, where 76 percent of medical professionals are women.[40] Another instance of destructiveness is the increasing prevalence of the "empty nest" phenomenon among women:

> Earlier ages at marriage, fewer children per couple and closer spacing of children, means: the girl who marries at twenty will have all her children by age 26, have all her children in school by her early thirties, have the first child leave home for jobs, schooling or marriage in her late thirties, and have all her children out of the home by her early forties. . . . The empty nest thus not only occurs earlier today but it lasts longer, affecting not this or that unfortunate individual woman but many if not most women. Hence what may in the past have been an individual misfortune has turned into a social emergency of major proportions.[41]

Sometimes the restrictions and stereotypes get so muddled that they become absurd, as in the following dialog recorded by Rose Laub Coser between two of her faculty colleagues:

Professor X: I think that Joan [who is now only giving an introductory course] should be given a position in the department. She is a good teacher and does good work.

Professor Y: I don't think so. The other day after classes I said to her: "We should have a conference about our next year's program. Can we talk about it now?" And she said, "No, it's too late. I have to go home because the children are home from school." She is just not committed as a professional.

Professor X to Professor Y (two days later):   We should have a meeting because the deadline for the next year's curriculum is drawing close. How about meeting this afternoon, since there are no classes?

Professor Y: I can't today, I have to go home to babysit.

Professor X: That's good for you. Perhaps we can meet tomorrow.[42]

Needless to say, a clinical sociologist working in such a setting should pick up on these destructive absurdities and be able to point them out to the participants in such ways as to facilitate reform.

NOTES

1.   Lillian Rubin, Worlds of Pain (New York: Basic Books, 1976), p. 5.

2.   For example, see George Murdock, Social Structure (New York: Macmillan, 1949).

3.   Suzanne Keller, "Does the Family Have a Future?" in Rose Laub Coser, ed., The Family: Its Structures and Functions (New York: St. Martin's, 1974), p. 580.

4.   Claude Lévi-Strauss, "The Family," in Harry Shapiro, ed., Man, Culture and Society (New York: Oxford, 1956), p. 276.

5.   That this is something of an exaggeration can be seen in the presence of incest among some Appalachian mountain families in the United States, for instance. Reported or suspected incest relationships occur also with some frequency in clinical settings.

6.   Karl Heider, The Dani of West Iran (Andover, Md.: Warner Modular Publications, 1972).

7.   Robert Winch and Graham Spanier, eds., Selected Studies in Marriage and the Family (New York: Holt, Rinehart and Winston, 1974), p. 485.

8.   William Goode, "The Theoretical Importance of Love," in Rose

Laub Coser, ed., *The Family: Its Structures and Functions* (New York: St. Martin's, 1974), pp. 150–54.

9. Leonard Pearlin. "Status Inequality and Stress in Marriage," *American Sociological Review* 40(June 1975):344–57.

10. Ernest van den Haag, "Love or Marriage," in Coser, ed., *The Family: Its Structures and Functions*, pp. 134–42.

11. Laura Shapiro, "Marriage Menders," *Mother Jones* 2 (August 1977):3.

12. Mirra Komarovsky, *Blue Collar Marriage* (New York: Vintage, 1967).

13. F. Ivan Nye and Felix Berardo, *The Family* (New York: Macmillan, 1973).

14. Margaret Mead, *Male and Female* (New York: Dell, 1970), chap. 14.

15. William Goode, *World Revolution and Family Patterns* (New York: Free Press, 1963).

16. Frances Kobrin, "The Primary Individual and the Family," *Journal of Marriage and the Family* 38, no. 2 (May 1976):233–39.

17. Ibid.

18. Deena and Michael Weinstein, *Living Sociology: A Critical Introduction* (New York: McKay, 1974), p. 360.

19. James Ramey, "Multi-Adult Household: Living Group of the Future?" *The Futurist* (April 1976):79.

20. Melvin Kohn, "Social Class and the Exercise of Parental Authority," *American Sociological Review* 24(June 1959):352–66.

21. Rubin, *Worlds of Pain*, p. 86.

22. An important book on these issues is William Yancey, *The Moynihan Report and the Politics of Controversy* (Cambridge, Mass.: MIT Press, 1967).

23. F. Ivan Nye and Felix Berardo, *The Family* (New York: Macmillan, 1973), pp. 397–401

24. LeBoyer, "A Delivery Room Intervention and Its Possible Consequences," *Behavior Today* 8, no. 32 (22 August 1977).

25. Barbara Harrell-Bond, "The Influence of the Family Caseworker on the Structure of the Family," *Social Research* 44, no. 2 (Summer 1977):193–215.

26. Bureau of the Census, "Some Recent Changes in American Families," *Current Population Reports*, Special Studies Series P–23, no. 52 (1975):1–17.

27. Lewis Morgan, *Houses and House-Life of the American Aborigines* (Chicago: University of Chicago Press, 1965), pp. 65–66.

28. Bureau of the Census, *Current Population Reports*, P-23, no. 52.

29. T. M. Newcomb, *The Acquaintance Process* (New York: Holt, Rinehart and Winston, 1961).

30. Michael Lewis, "Culture and Gender Roles," *Psychology Today* 6(May 1972):54.

31. Lenore Weitzman and Deborah Eifler, "Sex Role Socialization in Picture Books for Preschool Children," *American Journal of Sociology 77*, no. 8 (May 1972):1125–44.

32. Florence Howe, "Sexual Stereotypes Start Early," *Saturday Review* 54(16 October 1971):81.

33. "The Graduates," Educational Testing Service Publication (March 1973).

34. Matina Horner, "Fail: Bright Women," *Psychology Today* 3(November 1969):36.

35. Myron Brenton, *The American Male* (Greenwich, Conn.: Fawcett, 1966), chap. 2.

36. Rubin, *Worlds of Pain*, pp. 131–32.

37. Ruth Bunzel, "The Economic Organization of Primitive People," in Franz Boas, ed., *General Anthropology* (New York: Heath, 1938), p. 370.

38. Eleanor Leacock, "The Changing Family and Lévi-Strauss, or Whatever Happened to Fathers," *Social Research 44*, no. 2 (1977):253.

39. Except where otherwise noted, these "costs and benefits" are derived from the excellent review of this research in Janet Saltzman Chafetz, *Masculine/Feminine or Human?* (Itasca, Ill.: Peacock, 1974), especially pp. 57–58.

40. Evelyn Sullerot, *Women, Society and Change* (New York: McGraw-Hill, 1971), p. 151.

41. Suzanne Keller, "Does the Family Have a Future?" in Coser, ed., *The Family*, pp. 584–85.

42. Rose Laub Coser and Gerald Rokoff, "Women in the Occupational World," in Coser, ed., *The Family*, pp. 508–9.

THE CLINICIAN'S LIBRARY

By far the best collection of sociological works we have seen concerning the family is by Rose Coser:

Coser, Rose Laub, ed. *The Family: Its Structures and Functions.* New
York: St. Martin's, 1974.

The leading sociological journal concerning these topics is *Journal of
Marriage and the Family.*

MARRIAGE

O'Neill, Nena, and George O'Neill. *Open Marriage.* New York: Evans,
1972.
Udry, J. Richard. *The Social Context of Marriage.* Philadelphia: Lippincott, 1971.

The above are fine general discussions, and the following is an
insightful study of working-class marriages:

Rubin, Lillian. *Worlds of Pain.* New York: Basic Books, 1976.

SEX ROLES

The following are good overviews of sex roles:

Chafetz, Janet Saltzman. *Masculine/Feminine or Human?* Itasca, Ill.:
Peacock, 1974.
Epstein, Cynthia Fuchs. *Women's Place.* Berkeley, Cal.: University of
California Press, 1970.
Firestone, Shulamith. *The Dialectic of Sex.* New York: Bantam, 1970.

Chapter 11

Change

Now, for perhaps the first time in his life on earth, man is obliged
to adjust, not simply to changed conditions, but to change itself. In the past he had to give up the old and adapt to the
new; now he must adapt, also, to the certain knowledge that the
new, with unprecedented rapidity, is being replaced by that
which is to follow.[1]

We are in the midst of a society undergoing great changes. This chapter
examines our change-oriented society in order to delineate the effects of
change upon persons, groups, communities, and organizations.

In what ways are rapidly changing societies different from slowly
changing ones?

1. There is a difference in the effectiveness of socialization.

The rapid social changes occurring during a lifetime render
inadequate much childhood learning: technological obsolescence in one's occupation, shifts in sexual folkways, opportunities for equality in employment for minority group members,
are but a few of a myriad of examples that might be set forth.

Discontinuities between what is expected in successive roles are greater; the inabilities of the socializing agents to do an effective job rise as the rate of change increases; subgroups with deviant values emerge which do not prepare the child for roles expected of him by the larger society.[2]

2. There is a difference in people's ability to understand the range of technology. Many writers have noted this technological explosion. Peter Drucker believes new industries with their new technologies represent a qualitative shift.

They are different in their structure, in their knowledge foundations, and in their sociology. They represent, therefore, not just a stepping up of the rate of change. They represent a discontinuity fully as great as the industries that came into being between the 1860's and 1914.[3]

3. Accompanying this significant technological shift is an informational one. People in the industrial societies of the "global village" can be overwhelmed with information, especially about that which is new or different. Drucker states:

What has shortened, and appreciably, is the time lag between the introduction of a new product or process into the market and its general adoption. Fifty or seventy-five years ago there was a good deal of time to adapt to the appearance of a new product or a new process. Today the period of diffusion is a few weeks or a few months.[4]

This rapid rate of diffusion is not limited to information about products or processes, but to information generally. The effect of such an information explosion upon social processes has to be significantly different than under conditions where information about new practices could be assimilated by people routinely. Marshall McLuhan sees man living "in an electric environment of information" in which "we now have new perceptions that destroy the monopoly and priority of visual space. New environments inflict considerable pain on the perceiver."[5]

4. There is a difference in the relationship between past, present, and future under slowly changing and rapidly changing conditions. Under slowly changing conditions the ways of the past clearly influence the

ways of the present, and, for many, the future is viewed as an extension of the present. Under rapid change conditions, there is a discontinuity. While the past forms a dimension of the present, new processes—that obviously have roots in the past, but are much less evident to many in the society—are of increasing importance in understanding the present.

This in part explains the famous contemporary conflicts between parents and their children. In rapidly changing societies the time between the generations becomes significant. Youth is reared in a society and community which has changed considerably since that of their parents. As a result, the parents seem old-fashioned and the youth seem rebellious.[6] Under rapidly changing conditions, it is difficult to predict how the future will relate to the past and present.

5. Institutions and organizations that under slowly changing conditions channel a person's behaviors into those that are rewarded, those ignored, and those punished appear quite different under rapidly changing conditions. Many organizations and institutions are undergoing crises of relevance (e.g., religious and educational institutions); others (e.g., governments) have to face issues of priorities and regulation around issues brought on by new technologies (e.g., pollution, noise abatement, and space exploration).

6. This organizational and institutional crisis is closely related to a crisis in uses of power and social control. Rapidly changing conditions seem to involve charismatic uses of power with ascribed and achieved power deemphasized. Responses by individuals to rapidly changing conditions must take into account those new developments which demand different skills than those brought about through patterns of gaining ascribed or achieved leadership. The creative response to conditions becomes more valued than the routinized, bureaucratic response. Orville Brim suggests an alternative form of socialization to meet such needs.

> Faced with these challenges, complex and changing societies might try to lay the groundwork for the necessary learning in later life when the child will be confronted with adult roles as yet only dimly seen, by providing the individual with initiative, creativity, the power of self-determination, insight, flexibility, and intelligent response to new conditions; to move away from indoctrination and habit formation toward development of broadly useful traits and skills enabling him to meet a variety of social demands.[7]

7. The large-scale event becomes a symbolic socialization process, creating myth-like meanings with a major theme being confrontation of a mass-defined good with evil, a contemporaneous morality play with mass heroes and villains. Collective behavior becomes central in determination of attitudes, values, and personal behaviors. The outpouring of the public upon the death of Elvis Presley, quickly channeled into record and T-shirt sales, still resulted in memorial services throughout the country. Who is Elvis Presley? What social meanings does a popular singer communicate that his death results in such collective behavior?

Rapid change also affects the *sociologist* in several important ways:

1. Under rapidly changing conditions, any situation studied has the potential of being quite different from another even when the superficial dimensions of the situations appear similar. Limitations upon generalizing from situation to situation require an approach in which diagnosis and therapy are situationally grounded.

2. In a slowly changing industrial society, when a researcher or clinician tries to place a person in a social context, information about the person's family, social class, occupation, and organizational and institutional ties are usually enough to type a person. When the researcher concentrates on institutional manifestations used to type a person, he or she concentrates upon trying to discover the actual rules of institutional operation. The concentration is upon similarities of people and their institutions, the uniformities of life in society. In such a society, these tasks have utility since generalization from these findings is possible.

It is possible to have the same research focus today, but in a society undergoing rapid change the results must be interpreted differently. Since people and their institutions react differently to manifestations of change, the meaning of an institution or its rules must be different. Such knowledge reveals more about the person and institution studied than their manifestations of change-oriented behavior (if any).

In a change-oriented society, the sociologist must be sensitive to change-oriented potentials even if the participants are not. This statement opposes a sociological viewpoint that insists that participants' definition of the situation is the most important perspective, such as those of some symbolic interactionists and ethnomethodologists (discussed in chapter 5). Under rapidly changing conditions, such definitions would be insufficient for complete situational understanding. Change elements in the situation—present or soon to be added—will become important parts of a full sociological understanding.

3. In a society undergoing rapid change, sociological findings and theoretical and clinical analyses have validity of an uncertain duration. Key societal elements are subject to change without notice. If change becomes so rapid that usual sociological findings become outmoded almost as soon as they are formulated, usual theory, analysis, and model-building is of minimal importance. A most useful aspect of understanding society becomes understanding change itself.

The critical skill in this orientation is the determination of what is relevant. In a rapidly changing society, social institutions are not necessarily structural bulwarks of social control, but possibly more like mirrors into which groups with an evolving lifestyle see themselves as they wish to be viewed. Many social institutions no longer meet the needs of individuals and groups since rapid social change is not a condition provided for within our institutional ideologies. As Everett C. Hughes points out:

> Institutions, so long as they can meet the crises of the individual are not themselves in a critical state. When, however, some new type of situation, not provided for by the existing institutions becomes chronic and widespread, the institutions themselves are in a perilous state.[8]

If contemporary conditions are indicative of social change occurring more rapidly than ever before, then it is possible that only the contemporary social scientist sensitively dealing with the effects of such rapid change can provide necessary guidelines for social research under such conditions. Boguslaw suggests:

> The authentic squares of our times are to be found among social scientists who insist upon a preoccupation with after-the-fact facts of life; intellectuals who concern themselves with rationalizations about society rather than the realities of social issues; engineers and "hard" scientists who blithely deal with system data presented to them for analysis without wishing to ask questions about the broader context that lends more complete meaning to these data; and the beatniks who withdraw from all meaningful involvement in the affairs of their times from motives of indolence, ineptitude or fear. The world, in a very real sense, belongs to those who know how to harness the dominant ethos of their times while escaping personal entrapment by that ethos.[9]

The attribute of flexibility in method and interpretation is a necessity under conditions of change, both for those who live in changing times and those who wish to study such times. Lack of flexibility by actors and clinicians alike creates a societal developmental crisis. It is unclear whether behavioral guidelines of the past are nothing but mere vestiges from fondly remembered experiences. The actor in the society either develops new strategies in order to survive or leaves the social mainstream. The sociologist has the same choice.

THREE HEURISTICS

In a time of rapid social change, principles that can identify for investigators aspects of the society most likely to be affected by change and provide a rough indication of the effect of such change are necessities for the social science-social practice person. Such principles have been termed heuristics, defined as a method or argument "serving to indicate or point out; stimulating interest as a means of furthering investigation," or (of a teaching method) "encouraging a student to discover for himself." [10] Also, it is "valuable for stimulating or conducting empirical research but unproved or incapable of proof—often used of arguments, methods or constructs that assume or postulate what remains to be proven or leads a person to find out for himself." [11]

The authors' clinical and research experiences have led to identification of three major general heuristics about changing situations. These shall be termed the technological heuristic, the bomb heuristic, and the communication heuristic. Because of the complexities of change-oriented situations, these heuristics often overlap. Indeed, all three involve technological changes.

These heuristics are not the only possible ones. Indeed, they vary in relevance situationally. In a society undergoing rapid change, it is difficult if not impossible to state that these factors are the key ones. So much depends on the position of the observer of change and the indicators he or she discovers. It is possible that the impact of some other heuristic, known or unknown, could influence social change more directly. However, it seems unlikely that such an unknown factor could remain undetected by a sensitive observer if these three heuristics are used in a situational context. They would probably lead the observer to other heuristics.

There are two elements that are key to each heuristic. In each case, the heuristic relates to social institutions: instead of viewing such institutions as structures of stability within the society, institutions are viewed also as processes very much in flux. It no longer seems possible to agree with psychoanalyst Allen Wheelis that institutions act primarily to preserve the status quo. Each social institution in a society undergoing rapid change presents so many alternative structures and functions to society members that social control elements which are institutionally based appear to be contradictory to the person.

The other essential element is the viewing of the heuristic from a gestalt framework. In trying to grasp the whole picture, it is assumed that one will understand more than by examining a series of parts. Past vestigial structures and processes exist alongside those that are emerging. Only by viewing the range of manifestations within each heuristic can this interplay be noted. To use an example of Everett Hughes, one gains a broader insight into the processes of education in contemporary society by examining the total mobilization of persons toward education at various chronological ages, whether or not they are undergoing formal schooling, than one would gain by just examining those pupils who were enrolled in regular educational institutions.[12] Now let us turn to an examination of the constructive and destructive dimensions of the three identified heuristics.

The Technological Heuristic

People are becoming somewhat accustomed to rapid changes in physical environments. New technological innovations, whether these be fads, fashions, or more deeply rooted basic technological changes, seem to make appearance with increased frequency. Within the gestaltist (holistic) framework, it becomes necessary to examine not only that which is new, but also that which is old. One of the characteristics of contemporary society is that the obsolete can exist alongside the newest innovation. Even within a single product category such as the automobile, the latest model with up-to-date accessories and safety features exists in a total automotive population that includes old classic cars and custom car designs. In order to understand the complete technological mobilization around automobiles, it is also necessary to examine the population which gets along without the product, and those who use bicycles, motorcycles, and so forth. The anachronism and the special adaptation into unique form exist along with the latest technological Detroit marvel. All these adaptations are of a device designed to perform approximately the same general purpose—to transport.

It becomes necessary to relate any technological condition to the social institutional pattern in a contemporary society. There have been a series of diffusion studies which show the spread of an innovation through a population. These studies reveal how the social structure in a community determines the movement of a new product as time passes. In general, communities with highly centralized bureaucracies are most likely to facilitate rapid social change, especially if these communities are located at national or international crossroads of commerce. Such communities are most likely to be set up to deal with changes and most likely to come into contact with innovations.[13]

Under conditions of stability, such diffusion of innovations through the fabric of society would be of only marginal importance to the understanding of the broad aspects of the society. On the other hand, in a society undergoing rapid social and technological change, such diffusion becomes quite important. When technology has become central, the introduction, diffusion, and adoption of new products, ideas, and fashions flow through the social structure and identify those who adopt innovations early and others who lag behind. In current societies, the concomitants of technological change have simultaneous positive and negative implications. Even the average citizen is conscious of the scarcity of resources and the negative consequences and side effects of what superficially appear to be positive advances. For such persons a detailed sociological understanding of technological impact on persons, groups, or communities can frequently be of critical importance.

In a society undergoing technological change, the social institutional frameworks are undergoing bombardments by that which is new, and a change in a single condition relating to a technological advance can have widespread impact. Thus, energy shortages have caused changes in the sizes of automobiles, in the efficiency of engines, in the price of gasoline and heating oil, and in public service messages urging conservation. Thus far, in spite of these changes, most people act as if there is no crisis. Automobile sales of the largest, least efficient automobiles have risen, while sales of subcompact cars have decreased. Yet simultaneously, other persons act as if there is a crisis. The President of the United States has issued proposals which would bring greater restrictions. Energy-saving innovators have insulated their homes, experimented with solar energy or windmills, turned to public transportation, car pools, mopeds, or bicycles. The diffusion of adaptation to this technological problem is uneven.

When one examines a community unit such as a neighborhood, it becomes important to understand how the technology has created a series of different adaptations to life in the community by its residents.

We can see a continuum ranging from groups in which the new technology has not yet penetrated, to those in which the new technology has created extensive changes, and finally to groups (or even cities) *created* by the new technology. Under each of these situations the effects of technological development or its lack affect the lifestyles and beliefs of persons. A famous example is the invention of the cotton gin, which not only simplified the process of growing cotton and made the cotton business more profitable. The invention also (1) encouraged the planting of more cotton which (2) required more slaves in the southern U.S. and (3) increased the South's dependency upon cotton export. These results in turn (4) provoked a civil war and (5) stimulated the growth of industrial monopolies controlled by relatively few persons.[14]

Contemporary persons get caught between the two prevailing technological ideologies which Bernard Gendron has called the utopian and dystopian. The utopian believes that "we are presently undergoing a postindustrial revolution in technology. In the postindustrial age, technological growth will be sustained. Continual technological growth will lead to the elimination of technological scarcity and its elimination will lead to the elimination of every social evil."[15] The dystopian believes "that continued technological growth is bringing about, and will continue to bring about, more harm than good. They place the blame for most of our major social problems on the needs and impact of modern technology."[16] There is a third position, socialism, that generally believes technology could be a good thing if it is controlled by the workers. When controlled by the capitalistic class, technology is considered bad. At the time of this writing, the dystopian position seems the most fashionable of the three positions.[17]

Constructive Processes   Correctly used, technology has the ability to improve the lot of every person on the planet. Technological advances in the twentieth century have affected everyone. There have been major breakthroughs in the prevention and treatment of disease; the processing, analysis, and duplication of information; the linking of a person to the wider world through mass communication and speedy transportation; and the development of new jobs that are comparably labor saving—just to name a few advances. Furthermore, once a strong technological base has been established, new advances are easy to build upon this base. As architect and inventor Buckminster Fuller believes:

It is physically practical this minute for the first time in history for men to set themselves methodically to the task of unlimited production for all without invoking a further day of negative reckoning.[18]

For the person, group, or community reaping the benefits of the technology of today, there results an increasing average lifespan, increases in available and easily processed data, almost instantaneous knowledge about events on the planet, ongoing entertainment in the home, the ability to get to most physical locations quickly, new employment opportunities, and a sense that the future will be better than the past or present. That sense keeps alive the hope of progress and makes it possible for persons to handle difficulties believing that, in time, things will be better. Of course, even technological optimists see many problems, but these are viewed as only short term. Herman Kahn, an optimistic futurist planner, states:

> During subsequent years increasing time and attention worldwide
> will be given to these problems; this should result in an even
> greater likelihood that they will be successfully resolved. All
> in all, we remain optimistic about the potential of man's future.
> We can only hope that he does not throw away this potential
> through foolish political behavior or misplaced concern about
> non-existent or badly formulated growth issues.[19]

An advisor with knowledge of technology can aid persons to explore new options in emerging technological fields.

Think of your world without antibiotics, computers, copying machines, telephones, television, jet airplanes, air conditioning, electric lights. There are people alive in our country today who were born before the advent of any of these inventions and who had to adjust to the social effects of their arrival. What new discoveries will each of us have to adjust to during our lifetimes?

Destructive Processes   Many persons have written about the destructive processes of technology. Toffler calls the effect of the accelerating rate of change on persons "future shock":

> Future shock is a time phenomenon, a product of the greatly accel-
> erated rate of change in *society*. It arises from the superimposi-
> tion of a new culture on an old one. It is culture shock in

one's own society. But its impact is far worse. For most Peace
Corps men, in fact most travelers, have the comforting knowledge that the culture they left behind will be there to return to. The
victim of future shock does not.

Take an individual out of his own culture and set him down
suddenly in an environment sharply different from his own,
with a different set of cues to react to—different conceptions of
time, space, work, love, religion, sex, and everything else—then
cut him off from any hope of retreat to a more familiar social
landscape, and the dislocation he suffers is doubly severe.
Moreover, if this new culture is itself in constant turmoil, and
if—worse yet—its values are incessantly changing, the sense of
disorientation will be still further intensified. Given few
clues as to what kind of behavior is rational under the radically
new circumstances, the victim may well become a hazard to
himself and others.

Now imagine not merely an individual but an entire society,
an entire generation—including its weakest, least intelligent,
and most irrational members—suddenly transported into this
new world. The result is mass disorientation, future shock on a
grand scale. This is the prospect that man now faces. Change is
avalanching upon our heads and most people are grotesquely
unprepared to cope with it.[20]

Lewis Yablonsky sees the effect of increasing technology as the
changing of the human being into a machine-like creature, a
"robopath":

This dehumanized level of existence places people in roles where
they are actors mouthing irrelevant platitudes, experiencing
programmed emotions with little or no compassion or sym-
pathy for other people. People with this condition suffer from the
existential disease of robopathology. In a society of robopaths,
violence reaches monstrous proportions, wars are standard accepted practice, and conflict abounds.

Robots are machine-made simulations of people. I would
coin the term *robopath* to describe people whose pathology entails
robot-like behavior and existence. Robopaths have what Kier-
kegaard called "the sickness unto death." A robopath is a human

who has become socially dead. Robopaths are people who
function in terms of a pseudo-image. They are automatons who
may appear to be turned on to other people but are in fact egocen-
tric, and without true compassion.[21]

Herbert Marcuse discusses the relationship between the technological society and social control:

The prevailing forms of social control are technological in a new
sense. To be sure, the technical structure and efficacy of the
productive and destructive apparatus has been a major
instrumentality for subjecting the population to the established
social division of labor throughout the modern period.
Moreover, such integration has always been accompanied by more
obvious forms of compulsion: loss of livelihood, the administration of justice, the police, the armed forces. It still is. But in the
contemporary period, the technological controls appear to be the
very embodiment of Reason for the benefit of all social
groups and interests—to such an extent that all contradiction
seems irrational and all counteraction impossible.
    No wonder then that, in the most advanced areas of this
civilization, the social controls have been introjected to the point
where even individual protest is affected at its roots. The
intellectual and emotional refusal "to go along" appears neurotic and impotent. This is the socio-psychological aspect of the
political event that marks the contemporary period: the passing of
the historical forces which, at the preceding stage of industrial
society, seemed to represent the possibility of new forms of existence.[22]

Sociologist Philip Slater sees two trends happening concurrently:

Technological growth will sag drastically when the motivational
pathology that drives it dries up and there are signs that this
has already begun to happen. On the other hand, if it does
not happen soon, the current impetus of technology is sufficient to
destroy the planet in thirty years and this also has begun to
happen. Which will happen first is a matter of guesswork, but the
drying up of the technological impulse depends in part upon the

diffusion of uncharacteristic thought patterns, a largely spontaneous phenomenon of which this book is a slightly self-
conscious example.[23]

There are persons who become psychiatric casualties through what
psychiatrist-philosopher Robert Daly calls the "Specters of Technicism." Daly views the pathological effects of technology as something
that can either be internalized or externalized by the individual. The
case of Colonel Z contains both internal and external factors:

Colonel Z was in charge of training all the men in the command
who processed, stored, maintained, and repaired nuclear
weapons. His ultimate concern was for the techniques which
permitted this work to go forward. He did not want the world to
blow up by accident. If it were decided that it was necessary to
blow up the world—a determination which he left to the supreme
experts at headquarters—his attitude would be, "That's the way
the cookie crumbles." His ultimate fulfillment was found in
reviewing the documents which objectively and factually showed
the bombs and missiles to be safe and in good working order. The maintenance of their working order was the ultimate
demand which he placed upon himself.
    Colonel Z's inferiors in the ranks found him insufferable as
a person but admired his dedication to duty. His peers and
superiors were scarcely prepared to question his integrity, good
intentions, or technical adequacy. They shared in the work of
the mission but with less passion. His wife and family lived
within the society of the military reservation. Though Colonel Z
and his son were terrified of the civilian world, his troubled
wife found some respite from her husband's urgent and ultimate
concerns in the life "beyond the gates." Colonel Z laughed and
danced, played golf, and told dirty stories at the Officers' Club.
He enjoyed sexual intercourse when it did not interfere with his
work. Families, he knew, were functionally desirable. Colonel Z's brothers in faith were largely abstractions. They were
the officers of the nuclear establishments of the other great nations. According to Colonel Z, the lives of such men were
devoted to saving all the nations. They were the most misun-
derstood elite in the world.

Colonel Z's faith survived disputations with his wife, rejection by his son, a severe episode of anxiety, psychotherapy, and the threat of death. He never expressed a wish to be anything other than a competent "human factor." He knew his place in the new Alpha and Omega of things and stayed there. It was clear that his feelings of well-being and self-esteem were predicated upon a feeling of union with omnipotent forces in the external world, impersonal forces which had issued originally from the minds, hearts, and hands of other men. The names of these forces could not be spoken. No one could question their awful power.[24]

Colonel Z internalized into his personality his desire to be just "a competent human factor" doing his job as defined by others. His reference group, "his brothers in faith," were the officers of the nuclear establishments of all the other great nations. All were devoted to saving the world. With this technological role deeply internalized and externalized, Colonel Z survived critical incidents in his personal and family life. He drew from his belief in the omnipotence of technology to create his own well-being and self-esteem. The clinician can often be useful in helping persons and groups to recognize ways in which they have internalized and externalized technology.

The Bomb Heuristic

The existence of nuclear bombs is the overhanging crisis of our times, but it is hard to state its exact effect upon persons, groups, communities, and societies. Gunther Anders has presented "theses for the atomic age" which suggest basic transformations in the social psychology of individuals as they behave under these conditions. He believes distances have been abolished because of this threat. History of the past, present, and future has been compressed into the moment, so that time no longer has its traditional conceptualization.[25] Destruction can be instantaneous and complete, and the threat of such destruction is omnipresent. Most residents of the world—including many of its social scientist population—have not scrutinized the potential impact of such devastating weaponry even though the bomb, the most lethal weapon of the new technology, has turned the world into a megalopolis. There are no constructive features.

Destructive Features   Because of the lack of investigation, which at times approaches avoidance on the part of most people, it is impossible to judge the effect of the development of nuclear weapons upon actors within most social situations. However, behavior toward the bomb seems similar thus far to behavior in other crises. One notes an intensification of differences such as symbols of class, status, and power. There seems to be a fallback to the old technology and an unwillingness to face what is new. Or alternatively, many emphasize the positive aspects of the new technology, such as labor-saving devices and nuclear energy, while passing off the advancements in weaponry. There is an absurd quality to the existence of such destructive force alongside potential technological advances.

In communication parlance, the bomb is also a medium. The bomb is the ultimate in form-content synthesis. Its form destroys content, while its content destroys form. Ultimately, such eventual nondeterrence makes the rest of the contemporary social system and its future a meaningless analytic endeavor. The bomb places contemporary man in a total institution not of his own making. He has created the tool to which he becomes institutionally subject. The world has become one on this issue, and behaviors should be affected in time by its existence.

The bomb as a factor in the examination of contemporary life is difficult to assess. Perhaps as a major crisis it intensifies the meaning of more limited crises, whether these occur in political, social, or technological realms. This crisis atmosphere could act as a catalyst for more simple institutional responses. Its existence might lead to a greater reliance on extant escapist fare. To most, the changes wrought by the existence of the bomb are like skeletons buried in a closet.

It is difficult to pinpoint the effect of the bomb heuristic on specific situations. The monetary cost of weaponry preparedness limits the funding available for many social projects. The availability of enough destructive force to end life on the planet could tend to color long-term planning with a pessimistic pallor.

The Communication Heuristic

The change in mass communication has considerably influenced the social realities of contemporary culture. Marshall McLuhan has ably examined many of the effects of this new media "implosion" and has suggested that the media be viewed as extensions of man's senses.[26] It is important to place in a different sociological context some of McLuhan's formulations, namely, communication media appear to be having a great effect upon social institutions. Futhermore, Simmel's theorizing about the stranger, sociability, form and content can be used to develop a media theory.[27] In order to show the effect of new media upon social realities, we shall try to combine aspects of both approaches.

Sociologists have long held that social behaviors are usually determined by the structure of the conglomeration of institutions to which persons belong. But such an approach has been transcended by new communication developments. Just as the automobile revolutionized the mobility patterns of an earlier generation, so does the development of the mass media, especially television, influence the institutional structures of those growing up today. In many homes, one notes the television set in the place of honor once accorded to the stranger. Media analysts have noted in certain situations that the set remains on whether it is being watched or not. The stranger for Simmel represents the entrance of one who held a different set of values into the kin or small town grouping. It was necessary to make contact, as one could tell the stranger things that might be considered too intimate for fellow residents of a small community. One gets the impression from Simmel that the stranger's response to this information was not too important. The act of confessing intimate or semi-intimate details made the stranger more like the hearer of confessions.

If the television set is seen as a stranger, one can note the ability of this medium to penetrate attitudes and values of those viewing. The attitudes and values expressed on television apply most usually to the pseudo-mores of the middle-class American majority. In many situations, such expressions would differ from the attitudes and values actually held by those watching the screen. Although short-term studies of this interface of majority and minority attitudes and values do not clearly demonstrate an effect upon socialization, perhaps the impact of this medium upon social institutions is too subtle for short-term examination. Long-term studies of the effect of violence upon viewers point this out. At the very least, we can be confident that the television is a one-way medium—a stranger who talks but does not listen.

Perhaps social change brought about through mass media is more of a wearing away process of social structure than a sudden change in attitude. Process-oriented images replace structurally oriented pseudo-morality plays. The pervasive effect of the media is only minimally that the forces who desire to preserve the status quo have an excellent reinforcement tool. However, these messages of stability conflict with other messages from the same media or from people's lives. As Boorstin points out, image creation has become a basic characteristic of the American way of life. Image creation transcends social structures by violating the normative rules of the game.[28]

The totality of content leads to a form. Culturally, the individual messages of program and product information might not be the important element within the total mass media of communication. The nonverbal or semiverbal aspects might be more important. The quick glimpse, for example, of a white handball player with his arm on the shoulders of his black opponent seen in a beer commercial might be more revealing an indicator than the rest of the message. Here the connection is made between beer, sport, and friendship. Such brief images create a relational form which the sponsor or advertising director ties in with product or program. Such subtle brief images might bear an important relationship to social institutions.

In a society undergoing rapid social change, could it be that the social institutions of the society act as if they have become instant communications media? As McLuhan suggests, their medium has become their message. The institution's form has become its content. What a member of the society learns as he or she interplays between sometimes complementary and sometimes contradictory presentations on mass media with social institutional overtones is not the deeply rooted message of institutional compliance that is internalized when change in the society moved slowly; it is rather a social institutional relativism that is necessary because as a society undergoes rapid social change, social controls that lead to stigmatization have less potency. If, as Goffman suggests, we are all stigmatized,[29] institutional alternatives to those accepted by the majority are less restricted. Therefore, what is communicated is the form of the institution to which its content has been subjugated. It is not what you do within the social fabric; it is the way that you do it. Style, image, and salesmanship replace the substance of the message.

If this has validity, then interpersonal verbal and nonverbal communication take on new importance. One's ability to learn and communicate within the immediate situation to strangers who do not share meanings takes on new importance. The give and take in the search for meaningful communication with others with different and not situationally known attitudes and behaviors becomes a key indicator in learning the increased range of the acceptable.

Again, as in the technological heuristic, this change does not happen all at once, but gets diffused within the society. If much of the social institutional aspects of life in contemporary society are being transformed into media-oriented processes, then an important focus for sociological understanding becomes media competition for social actors' time and devotion. At this stage of social development, the diffusion of the transformation of structure into media is not complete. Institutional structures still exist alongside media, but seem to be in the process of being supplanted with increasing regularity.

Constructive Processes   Mass communication can be a powerful tool for communicating information, knowledge, attitudes, skills, and for entertainment. This tool when used effectively can positively influence the skills of a generation, provide information about events nearly simultaneously almost anywhere in the world through satellite transmissions, influence fads, fashions, and social movements, provide access to a wide variety of local opinions (e.g., through public access channels on cable television, or specialized magazines or newspapers), to name but a few applications. Media are very powerful:

> If the student of media will but meditate on the power of this medium of electric light to transform every structure of time and space and work and society that it penetrates or contacts, he will have the key to the form of the power that is in all media to reshape any lives that they touch.[30]

Destructive Processes   Philip Slater states:

> We are born with energy, matter, and information going in and out of us, and we will continue in this way until we die. Too great a deviation from the normal degree of inflow and outflow is disturbing to our sense of our own boundaries, which means that *too little influence, stimulation, control, or whatever, from outside is just as likely to be experienced as an invasion of our being as too much, even though we have been trained not to perceive it.*[31]

Most of us suffer from informational overload. There is no way to keep up with the knowledge explosion in most fields and with the effect of innovative potentials on our own lives. Each of our activities appear

insignificant in comparison with the range of what takes place throughout the world.

Making the actions of individual persons, groups, and communities
appear relatively unimportant is a recent phenomenon within the mass
media and further illustrates its tremendous power. Just one decade ago
the actions of antiwar, civil rights, and other kinds of demonstrators
were highlighted regularly in the media and considered important new
social forces. At the same time the media concentrated often upon
'great men," building up single persons as "world changers" (e.g.,
President John F. Kennedy, student activist Eva Jefferson, community
organizer Saul Alinsky, environmentalist Barry Commoner, and civil
rights leaders Dick Gregory, Martin Luther King, Jr., and Malcolm X).
Plenty of social movements continue to exist—ranging from thousands
of demonstrators against nuclear energy to hundreds of local community and ethnic rights groups—but they receive far less dramatic exposure in the media. Charismatic, effective leaders are still easy to find in
most every community throughout the world. The difference at present
is that social movements and leaders are no longer *news*, these
phenomena no longer sell books or increase television and film ratings
the way they did when they were first "discovered" in the media.

Movements and leaders have been replaced in media attention by the
1970s phenomenon of "personal growth." In this decade, society has
moved from broad-scale attempts to better the lot of many to small-scale
exercises that enhance the person. *How to Be Your Own Best Friend* and
Looking Out for Number One are popular books illustrative of this theme.
Mass communication has badly frayed the social fabric.

ADAPTATIONS TO SOCIAL CHANGE

It is possible to pinpoint a number of adaptations that persons have
made in order to facilitate their survival in a world of change. It is
difficult to determine whether these adaptations are constructive or destructive, except in specific situational contexts. Each of these responses
at different times might be appropriate for a person. However, if one of
these responses becomes the major one available, this could prove destructive to the person. The authors have noted the following actions
related to the effects of contemporary change upon the person:

1. *Nostalgia* for another period, either in the past or in the distant
future, sometimes replaces the feeling of unsettledness brought on by

rapid societal change, while the awareness of change is deadened by a variety of *narcotizing* immersions that take up almost total experience. This deadening might be induced by drugs, media, routine, or fads, to name a few ways.

2. *"Future shock,"* as defined by Toffler, is "the adaptive breakdown that even the strongest and most stable individual suffers when demands for change overwhelm his bodily defenses and mental capacities." [32]

3. Several aspects of *dehumanization* are "increased emotional distance from other human beings, diminished sense of personal responsibility for the consequences of one's actions, increasing involvement with human problems to the detriment of human needs, inability to oppose dominant group attitudes or pressures, and feelings of personal helplessness or estrangement." [33]

4. *True believers* in intensified social movements frequently deal with one area: pollution, pacifism, minority rights, and so forth, with varying recognition of the interrelationship among problems or causes.

5. *Change agents* manipulate organizations or institutions from a variety of orientations, preaching change within the system or revolution.

6. *"Crazies"* dedicate themselves to exposing the ridiculousness of being serious at a time like this. Some specialize in disruptive tactics. R. D. Laing sees "craziness" as a potential response from persons who cannot feel secure in the world:

> The individual in the ordinary circumstances of living may feel more unreal than real; in a literal sense, more dead than alive; precariously differentiated from the rest of the world, so that his identity and autonomy are always in question. He may lack the experience of his own temporal continuity. He may not possess an over-riding sense of personal consistency or cohesiveness. He may feel more insubstantial than substantial, and unable to assume that the stuff he is made of is genuine, good, valuable. And he may feel his self as partially divorced from his body. . . .
>
> If the individual cannot take the realness, aliveness, autonomy, and identity of himself and others for granted, then he has to become absorbed in contriving ways of trying to be real, of keeping himself or others alive, of preserving his identity, in efforts, as he will often put it, to prevent himself losing his self. What are to most people everyday happenings, which are hardly noticed because they have no special significance,

may become deeply significant in so far as they either contribute
to the sustenance of the individual's being or threaten him
with non-being. Such an individual, for whom the elements of the
world are coming to have, or have come to have a different
hierarchy of significance from that of the ordinary person, is
beginning, as we say, to "live in a world of his own," or has
already come to do so. It is not true to say, however, without
careful qualification, that he is losing "contact with" reality,
and withdrawing into himself. External events no longer affect
him in the same way as they do others: it is not that they affect
him less; on the contrary, frequently they affect him more. It is
frequently not the case that he is becoming "indifferent" and
"withdrawn." It may, however, be that the world of his experience comes to be one he can no longer share with other
people.[34]

He calls this "craziness" schizoid or schizophrenia depending on
whether the person exhibiting the behaviors is viewed as sane or
psychotic.

Out of stances such as these, lifestyles emerge. In many cases,
individual personalities reflect either an overlapping of these stances or
a changing of stance from situation to situation depending upon an
individual's interpretation of events. Sustained happiness combined
with a realistic appraisal of contemporary social conditions becomes
difficult to attain.

What seems a unifying factor among all these heuristics is the replacement of the examination of structure with an examination of process. Such a replacement converges with emerging or reemerging
trends of analysis in other fields. For example, transactional analysis,
psychodrama, participant observation, the responsive-environment
approach of Moore, the dramaturgical approach of Goffman, McLuhan's
approach to media; all seem to emphasize the process inherent in social
situations. It could be that these theoretical or applied approaches cen-
tering around process are responses to the potential structural devasta-
tion of the H-bomb, or simply to widespread and rapidly changing
social structures in contemporary societies.

NOTES

1.   Allen Wheelis, *The Quest for Identity* (New York: Norton, 1958), p. 137.

2.   Orville G. Brim, Jr., "Socialization through the Life Cycle," in Orville G. Brim and Stanton Wheeler, eds., *Socialization after Childhood* (New York: Wiley, 1966), p. 19.

3.   Peter F. Drucker, *The Age of Discontinuity* (New York: Harper & Row, 1968), p. 41.

4.   Ibid., p. 46.

5.   Marshall McLuhan and Quentin Fiore, *War and Peace in the Global Village* (New York: Bantam, 1968), p. 7.

6.   Kingsley Davis, "The Sociology of Parent-Youth Conflict," *The American Sociological Review* 5(August 1940):523–35.

7.   Brim, "Socialization," pp. 19–20.

8.   Everett Hughes, "Institutions," in Alfred McClung Lee, ed., *Principles of Sociology*, 2nd ed. (New York: Barnes & Noble, 1946), pp. 236–37.

9.   Robert Boguslaw, *The New Utopians* (Englewood Cliffs, N.J.: Prentice-Hall, 1965), p. 178.

10.   *Random House Dictionary of the English Language* (New York: Random House, 1966), p. 667.

11.   *Webster's Third International Dictionary of the English Language* (Springfield, Mass.: A & C Merriam Co., 1961), p. 1064.

12.   From a lecture in Social Institutions at Brandeis University.

13.   For some interesting case studies of these phenomena, see Edwin Dowdy, "Aspects of Tokugawa Bureaucracy and Modernization," *Australian Journal of Politics and History* 16(December 1970):375–89; and Davydd Greenwood, "Tourism as an Agent of Change," *Ethnology* 11(January 1972):81–91.

14.   William Ogburn, "The Influence of Invention and Discovery," in President's Research Committee on Social Trends, *Recent Social Trends* (New York: McGraw-Hill, 1933), pp. 122–66.

15.   Bernard Gendron, *Technology and the Human Condition* (New York: St. Martin's, 1977), p. 13.

16.   Ibid., p. 89.

17.   For a controversial and insightful discussion of these issues see Robert Pirsig, *Zen and the Art of Motorcycle Maintenance* (New York: Morrow, 1974).

18.   R. Buckminster Fuller, *Earth, Inc.* (Garden City, N.Y.: Doubleday, 1973), p. 18.

19.   Herman Kahn and William Brown, "A World Turning Point—
And a Better Prospect for the Future," *The Futurist* 9, no. 6 (December
1975):334.

20.   Alvin Toffler, *Future Shock* (New York: Bantam, 1971), pp. 11–12.

21.   Lewis Yablonsky, *Robopaths* (Baltimore: Penguin, 1972), pp.
6–7.

22.   Herbert Marcuse, *One Dimensional Man* (Boston: Beacon Press,
1964), pp. 9–10.

23.   Philip Slater, *Earthwalk* (New York: Doubleday, 1974), p. 37.

24.   Robert W. Daly, "The Specters of Technicism," *Psychiatry* 33,
no. 4 (November 1970):429.

25.   Gunther Anders, "Theses for the Atomic Age," *The Mas-
sachusetts Review*, 3(1962):493–505.

26.   Marshall McLuhan, *Understanding Media: The Extensions of Man*
(New York: McGraw-Hill, 1964).

27.   Georg Simmel, *The Sociology of Georg Simmel*, Kurt H. Wolff, ed.
(Glencoe, Ill.: Free Press, 1950). See our discussions of Simmel in chapter 3.

28.   Daniel J. Boorstin, *The Image: Or What Happened to the American
Dream* (New York: Atheneum, 1962).

29.   Erving Goffman, *Stigma* (Englewood Cliffs, N.J.: Prentice-Hall,
1963).

30.   McLuhan, *Understanding Media*, p. 52.

31.   Slater, *Earthwalk*, p. 55.

32.   Alvin Toffler, "Coping with Future Shock," *Playboy* 17, no. 3
(March 1970):89.

33.   Viola W. Bernard, Perry Ottenberg, and Fritz Redl, "Dehumani-
zation: A Composite Psychological Defense in Relation to Modern
War," in Robert Perrucci and Marc Pilisuk, eds., *The Triple Revolution:
Social Problems in Depth* (Boston: Little, Brown, 1968), pp. 25–29.

34.   R. D. Laing, *The Divided Self* (Baltimore: Penguin, 1965), pp.
42–43.

THE CLINICIAN'S LIBRARY

GENERAL BOOKS ON CHANGE

Cornish, Edward. *The Study of the Future.* Washington: The World Future Society, 1977.

Dunstand, Mary Jane, and Patricia W. Garlan. *Worlds in the Making.* Englewood Cliffs, N.J.: Prentice-Hall, 1970.

Fabun, Don. *The Dynamics of Change.* Englewood Cliffs, N.J.: Prentice-Hall, 1967.

Spekke, Andrew A., ed. *The Next Twenty-Five Years: Crisis and Opportunity.* Washington: The World Future Society, 1975.

The World Future Society through its monthly *The Futurist,* its newsletter, book services, specialized publications and local groups is an excellent way to keep up with this field.

TECHNOLOGY

Ellul, Jacques. *The Technological Society.* New York: Knopf, 1964.

Fuller, R. Buckminster. *Earth, Inc.* Garden City, N.Y.: Doubleday, 1973.

Gendron, Bernard. *Technology and the Human Condition.* New York: St. Martin's, 1977.

Slater, Philip. *Earthwalk.* New York: Doubleday, 1974.

Toffler, Alvin. *Future Shock.* New York: Bantam, 1971.

Yablonski, Lewis. *Robopaths.* Baltimore: Penguin, 1972.

MASS COMMUNICATION

McLuhan, Marshall. *Understanding Media.* New York: McGraw-Hill, 1964.

Tuchman, Gaye. *The TV Establishment: Programming for Power and Profit.* Englewood Cliffs, N.J.: Prentice-Hall, 1974.

Winn, Maria. *The Plug-in Drug.* New York: Viking Press, 1977.

THE BOMB

Anders, Gunter. "Theses for the Atomic Age," in B. Rosenberg et al., eds., *Mass Society in Crisis*. New York: Macmillan, 1971.

Faulkner, Peter, ed. *The Silent Bomb*. New York: Vintage Books, 1977.

Perrucci, Robert, and Marc Pilisuk. *The Triple Revolution Emerging: Social Problems in Depth*. Boston: Little, Brown, 1971, section on weaponry.

Chapter 12

Everyday Metaphysics

Underlying much that comes about in social worlds are the thought patterns of those who decide to work collectively to bring about social realities. When people try to make sense of their lives, certain regularities appear and reappear. In spite of individual differences many commonalities arise from the mutual contact of persons with various vital features. Philosophers, when they move beyond their own cases and consider these commonalities, call the abstracting process metaphysics.

At least since the time of Aristotle, a major branch of philosophy has been metaphysics. Its aim is to study several of the more abstract components of human life, notably, existence, causation, and the nature of reality. Such components may seem "imaginary" or "foolish intellectualizing" to some persons, especially the more empirical social scientists. But, in fact, metaphysical assumptions underlie all scientific and social scientific thinking, even if these assumptions go unrecognized by the scientists and social scientists who employ them. (Metaphysics, literally translated, means "beyond physics.") Let's briefly consider some major social scientific assumptions in light of some major arguments among metaphysicians:

1. *Laws of human behavior* assume that social life is predictable, or basically unchanging. A major goal of pure science sociologists is to

derive formulae which explain and predict how social life operates.[1] In contrast, the goal of the early Greek philosopher Heraclitus was to demonstrate that everything constantly changes, that the only law of nature is the law of change. One can never step into the same river twice, since it will have changed between the steps. A disciple named Cratylus even went further: one cannot step into the same river, he said, since it has changed during (and from) the stepping process. Indeed, one cannot even discuss anything, since the speaker, meanings, and listener are changing even while one is in the process of discussion. Cratylus used to wiggle his finger when he was addressed, to indicate that he had heard but that the universe would not stand still long enough for him to respond.

Soon enough there emerged the metaphysicians who tried to demonstrate that everything is permanent—such as Parmenides and Zeno. The paradoxes of Zeno are designed to show that the notion of change is but an illusion full of contradictions. One of the paradoxes holds, for instance, that for an object to move from one place to another, it first must move half of the distance involved. But to do so it must move half of the half distance, and so forth. This eventually requires the object to move infinitely small distances, and an infinite number of them, thereby requiring also an infinite number of time intervals in which to do so. Hence, to move any distance takes forever.

Other philosophers, from Democritus and Aristotle through William James and contemporaries, have developed elaborate schemes to account for the presence of both change and permanence in nature.

2. *"Sticking to what can be seen"* is an often stated goal of empirical social scientists. In contrast, Plato distinguished between "things seen" and "things unseen," and argued that only the unseen are proper objects of scholarship. Empirical social scientists are, in fact, frequently concerned with "things unseen." A major goal of many social scientists is to explain the causes of events and processes, although causation itself can never be seen.

3. The *"mind-body problem,"* among the most central concerns of metaphysicians since Descartes, is often uncritically assumed solved in one way or another by social scientists. The problem is that of determining whether mental and physical events are separate, and, if so, how and when they are related. Some social scientists (e.g., symbolic interactionists) speak of consciousness, desires, meanings, interpretations, and so on. They see these as affecting or determining the physical world, as when persons decide to burn down a village

during warfare. Most of these social scientists do recognize, however, that physical worlds also affect mental worlds, as when lightning strikes a generator and parts of a city, without electricity, decide to riot.

Other social scientists (notably behaviorists) contend that mental events do not exist, but are solely material processes of the brain. What we call thoughts are the material occurrences in the brain. Our desires, perceptions, interpretations, and so forth are particular responses of our nervous system and brain to the stimuli of the outside world.

FROM PHILOSOPHER TO EVERYPERSON

Metaphysics to philosophers consists of attempts to resolve conceptual conflicts by finding ways of speaking which enable the philosopher to communicate the true nature of things. Numerous other classical metaphysical debates are relevant to contemporary social science debates—including free will versus determinism, teleology, fundamental ontology, and determinacy versus indeterminacy—but our goal here is not to discuss the role of philosophical debates in clinical sociology. Such a role is in desperate need of delineation and must come primarily from academic philosophers of social science. Rather, our aim in this chapter is to consider the *metaphysics of the clients,* or the metaphysical assumptions which persons make in their everyday lives. Assumptions about the nature of reality and existence constitute a vital feature of any social situation. Some of the most consequential of these assumptions concern causation—and "is" versus "ought."

CAUSATION

Perhaps everyday life's most omnipresent entity is also invisible. No one has ever seen a *cause,* yet we talk about them constantly. "What causes his mood swings?" the psychiatric nurse asks. "His lithium level," answers the psychiatrist. "His crazy job," answers the social worker. Or the sociologist talks of how school integration causes "white flight" (white families moving from city to suburb). Or the community organizer claims that apathy caused her neighborhood association to fail.

Philosophers of science have been arguing for many decades about causation, trying to figure out what place the idea has in science, and seldom agreeing. Some refuse to use the term at all; others prefer to speak solely of statistical correlations rather than causations. For most, the idea of "natural law" (à la Carl Hempel) has replaced any need to speak of causes. In this manner, explanation of an event consists of showing that general laws of nature occurred, and that the event was part of their occurrence. Thus, a rock thrown through a window during a riot would be explained in terms of general behavioral laws governing crowd behavior and general laws of physics governing the flight of moving objects.

Scott Greer put the causation and natural law of such cases in a cross-cultural perspective:

> Evans-Pritchard tells of a Nuer whose son drowned when his canoe was charged by an angry rhinoceros. The man immediately began to speculate as to which person had used the poison that caused his son's death. When questioned about the "poison," in the light of the simple sequence of events (the boy crossed the river, the rhinoceros was especially touchy, their paths met, and the rhino behaved predictably) he simply asked: "Why should that rhino appear at that time and place? It was poison." Thus causality is a way of reducing the uncertainties of life to manageable proportion: our own explanation, random variation and natural law, is hardly more attractive than the Nuer assumption of magic. Both are ways of imputing human meaning, order and purpose, to an inhuman world. They are probably projections onto outer reality of our own sense of purpose.[2]

Indeed, the everyday examples noted above are good illustrations of Greer's point. The psychiatrist chooses a cause (or law) that fits his or her projections of what mental illness is all about, and the social worker selects in the same manner. Both could muster good evidence for their selection. That is the difficulty with causal explanations in everyday life; no one really expects to be shown the cause itself, and so all sorts of tangential evidence become applicable. The Greek Skeptic Sextus Empiricus noted the problem in the second century A.D.:

> To say that the Cause is brought into existence after the appearance of its effect would seem ridiculous. But neither can it subsist before the effect; for it is said to be conceived in relation thereto, and they affirm that relatives, in so far as they are relative, co-exist with each other and are conceived together. Nor, again, can it subsist along with its effect; for if it is productive of

the effect, and what comes into existence must so come by the agency of what exists already, the Cause must have become causal first, and this done, then produces its effect.[3]

Empiricus's comment gets right to the heart of the clinical problem illustrated by our examples. Who could ever demonstrate the social worker's position over the psychiatrist's, or vice versa, or the community organization leader's claim over counter-claims? The lithium levels of the mood swinging person changes only *within* social contexts (family, jobs, etc.), so how can primacy be demonstrated for either the lithium level or the job? And the neighborhood association is part of the apathetic community, specifically, a part which is designed to alleviate apathy. These processes are all bound up in the same *webs*.

The *destructive processes* of everyday causal assertions arise in the many cases where such assertions provide a "cover story" for ignoring those factors which we feel are convenient to ignore. The psychiatrist ignores the social context and the social worker ignores the biological context. Probably both do so because they do not understand one another's disciplines, or because they seek to establish political or economic security for themselves and their peers.

Constructive processes of everyday causal assertions are those which permit us to place current conditions in perspective relative to their antecedent conditions. Every current situation is brought into existence in part by previous situations. Empiricus noted this:

That Cause exists is plausible; for how could there come about increase, decrease, generation, corruption, motion in general, each of the physical and mental effects, the ordering of the whole universe, and everything else, except by reason of some causes? For even if none of these things has real existence, we shall affirm that it is due to some cause that they appear to us other than they really are. Moreover, if cause were non-existent everything would have been produced by everything at random. Horses, for instance, might be born, perchance, of flies, and elephants of ants. . . [4]

Determining which social processes lead to which outcomes is crucial to social scientific understanding and, thereby, to the possibility for clinical intervention. Such interventions may take the form of therapeutic techniques described in part 4. Or the intervention may be of the instructional variety, assisting communities and societies in the recognition of positive and negative uses of antecedent conditions. The same conditions which lead to group solidarity, for instance, can be used to create a successful athletic team, but also to create a successful national dictatorship.

"OUGHT" AS "IS"

If clinicians had a dollar for every time their clients uttered statements such as the following, they could retire early: "This place is messy"; "My husband is a rotten man"; "The system made me do it"; "My childhood made me do it."

Each of these statements is so common that it may be difficult for us even to see them as inaccurate. They are all inaccurate, however, and in the same regard. All of these statements confuse moral judgments for objective reality. They confound the unseen (morality) with the seen (certain social events). The first two statements consider "ought" as "is" in different ways than do the last two, however.

The first two statements attribute a moral quality as if it were an objective quality. No husband *is* rotten, and no place *is* messy. Perhaps the husband *ought to be considered* rotten, and the place *ought to be considered* messy, but neither are objectively or "naturally" rotten or messy. Being rotten or messy (or stupid, deviant, bad, organized, intelligent, good, etc.) is not inherent in a person, group, or situation. Such qualities are actually *processes* which depend upon attributes of the person as these are morally interpreted by others. Our considerations of social worlds as they are actually come down, in many cases, to descriptions of how we think they ought to be.

The latter statements are slightly different varieties of this confounding. The system cannot force anyone to do anything except, in some special cases, to die for refusing to do certain things. What we really mean is that certain particular persons or their machines are making us realize that we will suffer certain punishments if we do not do something. And one's childhood cannot force a person to do anything, though it may prevent a person from doing some things (as when a childhood accident creates a lifetime disability).

As Henri Bergson noted, memory itself is an act of interpretation. We reconstruct the past in accordance with our present needs. Persons who truly need something other than what their past would most often encourage in the present are often able to fulfill that need. The basis of psychoanalysis is this reinterpretation of the past. Any situation (including those concerning "the system") provides nearly infinite numbers of items to be dealt with or ignored, and we select from among these. Much of the power that childhood and systems have over us derives from our acceptance that they ought to have such power, or even more strongly, that their power is *real* rather than simply potential. Thus, the man who decides he must be a physician because his father "raised" him to be one may also believe that he "therefore" does not have the experiences (childhood, educational, acquaintanceship, etc.) to be a journalist, which is his ambition. In certain regards he may be correct; perhaps he does *not* have the contact which the son of a writer would have, nor the best educational background. But it does not follow that he must become a physician as a result, simply that it will be more difficult for him to become a journalist. He may, for instance, need to move far away from his parents and their influence.

Constructive processes of converting "ought" to "is" concern the efficiency they provide in everyday life. After we have determined our standards for what constitutes a messy room or a childhood influence, it is simply more convenient to think of them in certain terms rather than qualified terms. Even the most cautious clinician must recognize the constructive nature of such conversions in cases where the operation of social life needs to proceed without constant questioning. In this way, we can see that red lights *are* a reason to stop, rather than that they are suggestions that one *ought* to stop. In short, when such confounding of "is" and "ought" becomes useful for a community, it may be constructive.

Destructive processes result in those cases in which this sort of conversion creates linguistic or structural barriers to useful change. To stick to our simplistic example above, where stop lights are not needed to improve the safety and efficiency of driving in a community, they *should* be considered as "oughts." Likewise, when blaming "the system" prevents a group from making beneficial changes in that system, a destructive process is occurring.

Usually we do better to consider what we are really saying before deciding to abbreviate or otherwise alter it. The "oughtness" of "is" statements should at least be examined, even if such examination reveals that we are better off sticking with our "is" conceptions.

SOURCES OF BELIEFS

There is an alternative approach to personal metaphysics that attempts to locate the source of persons' metaphysical beliefs in the major socializing forces in a society. We have already presented some of the sources of belief systems during the earlier chapters of this section: beliefs can originate through dealings with the vital features of ethnicity, stratification, age, family, and change. In addition, persons derive their beliefs from religion and education.

Religion

Religion provides a way of explaining the unknown. Basic to most religions is belief in a god, usually viewed as greater and more powerful than a person, frequently as the force that creates order out of chaos. Religion creates rituals that allow persons to contemplate the above, and provides recurring events to mark the natural passages of a lifetime: birth ceremonies, adulthood through confirmation, marriage, death, and funeral services. There are many organized religions: Catholicism (Roman and Eastern Orthodox); Protestantism from Episcopal to Pentecostal; Judaism from Orthodox to Reform; Moslem and Black Muslim; Hindu; American Indian, and so on. The clinical sociologist has to be aware of the subtle differences in belief and how these affect personal metaphysics. Also persons grow disenchanted with organized religion and turn to atheism, mysticism, occultism, and so forth. A person's religious history can reveal a great deal.

Constructive Processes   Religion provides a way for persons to discover interpretations about what is happening to them and act on those meanings within a socially acceptable context. Religious groups can provide support during natural crises and unusual circumstances. Identity is gained through location within the group, and group beliefs get enhanced through individual participation. Religious groups channel persons toward conformity with their values.

Destructive Processes   Persons can make the "ought" of religion become their "is" by letting an overpowering moral imagery totally affect their ability to act. By believing that the ordering force in the universe is not under societal control, powerlessness is enhanced. By believing that one slip from moral righteousness brings an eternity in hell, self-esteem can be destroyed. By giving total obedience to tradition, the present becomes the past. In extreme cases, a person quickly senses the aura of every passerby as angelic or devilish and behaves toward the person just on the basis of these instant assessments. Persons desiring to end the ambiguity in their personal metaphysics may embrace a religious sect, thereby exchanging the ambiguity for a total approach to life demanding uncritical commitment.

Education

Education provides a mechanism that generates a person's beliefs. Teachers in schools teach more than facts and concepts, they model as well as teach attitudes, values, and world-views. Schools provide strong socializing experiences with intergenerational continuity. Teachers were earlier students, taught by other teachers, who were earlier students of other teachers. Teachers come from a different age cohort than their students and tend to model different views of social existence. The classroom provides a setting in which intergenerational value acceptance and conflict gets played out. Schools, usually accountable to adult taxpayers or boards, tend to try to preserve traditional values. Students frequently do not yet know whether (or how) to subscribe to these values and have to learn to balance the traditional moral teachings of the school with their own perceptions and desires.

Constructive Processes   Education moves a person beyond the belief systems of family and peers to encounters with teachers, books, classes, and classmates, which can aid a person in developing a culturally applicable belief system, along with the enhanced understanding that other persons believe differently from oneself. Education can expose persons to other personal metaphysical systems that were responses to other social situations throughout history. Concurrently, education can develop personal skills and create a lifetime educational need to provoke continual questioning and readjustment of beliefs.

Destructive Processes   Many educators now believe that the constructive processes enumerated above seldom happen. The educational system has become a glorified baby-sitting service that keeps young persons off the street and out of the unemployment statistics. Many teachers lack the creative spark that motivates students to learn or to accept them as models. Competitiveness as exemplified through grades and the push to get into outstanding colleges, professional and graduate schools deeply affect the learning environment. Frequently students get tracked early in their educational career, and such tracking is often based on the existing stratification system of society or upon ethnic prejudices, not upon ability.

Through several processes, education often enhances a loss of self-esteem and feelings of oppression and powerlessness:

1. Competition has more losers than winners, and losing affects self-esteem.
2. Students are placed in a subordinate role in which they frequently are treated as nonpersons, leading to feelings of oppression.
3. The student role also is generally a powerless one. Despite student revolts around the world in the 1960s, situations enhancing powerless-ness have been restored from elementary schools through graduate and professional schools since that time.

These destructive processes affect personal metaphysics by destroy-ing learning and questioning as an option for persons who are frus-trated by their current situation. The sense of hopelessness engendered by this destruction is difficult to overcome. To see the contrast involved, think for a moment of the best teacher you have ever had and how you were influenced by him or her. How would your life be different if all your teachers were of this caliber?

CONCERNING SELF-ESTEEM, OPPRESSION, AND POWER-LESSNESS

Similar processes to those noted for education occur via several of the features we have discussed in this part. For instance, child-rearing prac-tices may damage the self-esteem and power relations of siblings who are forced to compete with one another for parental attention and affec-tion. Damaged self-esteem, oppression, and powerlessness are regu-larly encountered in clinical sociological practice. They are the forces which prevent persons and groups from developing viable personal metaphysical systems or acting on those already devised. Let us con-sider each of these further.

Self-esteem is the ability to feel good about oneself, to be able to fully appreciate one's abilities and recognize that we each are heroes, making the best choices at every moment given the information and awareness available to us. Our ability to feel self-esteem is hampered by the put-downs we receive from others, the times we are treated like a number rather than a person, and our inability to believe praise when it is directed toward us. We learn to internalize the negativity and believe that we are incapable because others have told us so. Self-esteem is quite important sociologically; unless I feel good about myself, it is difficult for me to feel good about others and treat them in the very human manner in which I want them to treat me. I alternately oppress and feel powerless.

In addition, oppressing others has roots in lack of personal self-esteem. Harvey Jackins notes:

> One of the principal means used by capitalistic societies to maintain their exploitation and oppression of people has been to secure the cooperations of different groups of people in oppressing each other. This has been done by installing and maintaining attitudes of racism, prejudice, sexism, and adultism between the different sections of the oppressed population. Under capitalism (and to some extent under previous oppressive societies) the oppressed have to oppose each other. The oppressors aren't numerous enough, aren't powerful enough. They have to deceive the people they victimize into doing it to each other.[5]

Persons tend to personalize the process, to internalize the oppression at first into a personal hurt and then accept being oppressed as part of their way of life. Persons who recognize for the first time the oppressive elements in being young, old, black, Chicano, Jewish, American Indian, and so forth, often have a greater sensitivity to the ways persons get oppressed than those who have been faced with the oppression all their lives.

Being oppressed affects your personal metaphysics by creating the feeling of being pigeonholed in a category that does not allow others to deal with you as a full person. At times oppressed persons accept the down-graded role and act the imposed stereotype. Another option is to take on an oppressor role oneself in relation to other persons. In either case, being oppressed adds to lack of self-esteem and feelings of powerlessness.

We begin life practically powerless, and any feelings of power come from our ability to overcome our beginnings. Our early socialization, our education, our work, and leisure experiences all mix moments of power with hours of powerlessness. To stick to the educational situation, for instance, a man has some freedom when he gets to college to choose a career—albeit influenced by family, ethnicity, economics—but once that choice is made the curriculum is rigid and he is supposed to attend classes and pass tests in order to demonstrate that he is competent to be awarded a degree that could be a necessity to enter his chosen field. While pursuing the degree, it is likely that he will give up the power to do what he thinks best, in order to demonstrate competence or gain acceptability.

Sometimes the process entails many layers of bureaucracy. While students are giving up power, simultaneously the faculty member may be giving up some of his or her power in order to gain approval of more powerful members of the department who rule on tenure. The more powerful members of the department might be operating on the basis of an order from a still more powerful dean concerning how to treat untenured faculty. Each person along this chain feels powerlessness, at the same time assuming that the next person up the ladder is quite powerful. Feeling powerless keeps one from acting to reach one's goals and allows the outcome to be based on luck or the flexing of another's power.

The clinical sociologist is frequently called upon to overcome personal, organizational, or community apathy. The source of such apathy is often powerlessness, and a needed remedy is to show persons how to get in touch with their feelings of powerfulness. Knowing that we can act to change our condition can bring about positive changes for everyone.

In this chapter, we have shown how the sources of personal beliefs come from features of the social landscape. These beliefs are played out in social contexts. The manner in which many are socialized brings to the foe destructive processes that affect each person's and group's ability to grow, develop, and better the conditions of the society. Part 4 presents some action-oriented approaches that can help persons, groups, communities, and organizations change these negatives to positives.

NOTES

1. See chapter 1.
2. Scott Greer, *The Logic of Social Inquiry* (Chicago: Aldine, 1969), p. 52.

3. R. G. Bury, trans., *Sextus Empiricus I* (London: Heinemann, 1933), p. 343.

4. Ibid., p. 337.

5. Harvey Jackins, "The Theory of Liberation," in *Rough Notes from Liberation I & II* (Seattle: Rational Island Publishers, 1976), p. 46.

THE CLINICIAN'S LIBRARY

Many excellent overviews of philosophical discussions of metaphysics are available, and interested readers should begin with the more general volumes, which will refer them to the technical discussions of specific issues. Discussions of self-esteem, oppression, and powerlessness are considered clinically in books by Harvey Jackins (Rational Island Press, Seattle, Washington). Some Marxist writings noted in chapter 5 also consider these issues.

Part 4

Techniques of Sociological Therapy

Therapy consists of learning which alternative choices are more beneficial than a current state and acting to bring one or more of these choices to reality. This is what the clinical psychologist does when she or he helps a patient reinterpret childhood; it is what the physician does when he prescribes antibiotics; and it is what the clinical sociologist does when she creates a peer self-help group. In each case, the clinician uses the expertise from his or her discipline, along with the client's own knowledge, to decide which choice(s) to pursue. Then the client must perform the acts necessary to pursue the new processes chosen.

Ability to perform therapeutic techniques in any field derives from cognitive understanding and actual practice. No reader will be able to practice any of the techniques from the following chapters simply by reading about them. Our goal is to offer basic descriptions of available techniques, their uses, and the benefits and dangers they provide. The "postscripts" at the end of each chapter offer specific uses and dangers uncovered in the authors' own work.

The major unit of attention in all clinical sociology is groups, although the cinician may work with individual members. *The two major varieties of clinical sociological work are* (1) *therapy for groups and* (2) *therapy for members of groups.* In (1) the clinician works with social groups to develop more adequate structural or interactional patterns. The possible groups range from a married couple to a farm bureau to the entire world. Their problems range from mental illness to disagreements over leadership practices to nuclear war. In each case it is the group itself which must be changed.

In (2) the clinician works with individuals to develop effective strategies for group living. Problems which appear to be psychological are often the result of difficulties a person has within groups. A man who is suicidal may be attempting to escape his marriage, or his inability to perform well in the new job role to which he has been promoted, or his general state of *anomie* in a world which makes conflicting and confusing demands upon him. Therapy for members of groups attempts to provide the members with a better understanding of the structure and interactions within their groups and the consequent possibilities for individual members to fit into or change these groups.

The sociological therapies in this part are divided according to (1) those designed for the therapy of groups and (2) those designed for the therapy of group members. *Peer self-help* and *sociodrama are the major therapies for group members, although some varieties of sociological questioning can also be directed toward specific group members. Sociometry, Simulation, Organization Work,* and *Community Work are all therapies for groups.*

THERAPY FOR GROUP MEMBERS

The process of diagnosis by sociological clinicians employs the same basic logic as used in medical diagnoses, although the specific techniques are obviously quite different.

Diagnosis always begins with listening to and observing the apparent difficulties. Techniques for listening and observing are described in chapter 6. The results of these observations and inquiries are then considered with reference to the *social location* of the person. Determination of social location is achieved by ascertaining the relationship of the group or group member to the various vital features presented in part 3, keeping in mind there might be additional social factors to consider. The same set of complaints from a 60-year-old, upper-class white male and a 16-year-old, lower-class Puerto Rican female will quite likely indicate very different problems and consequently different therapy plans. Both may offer the *presenting problem* of marital difficulties, but this problem can begin to be interpreted by the clinician only when she or he understands the role of marriage in these specific locations. Questions such as the following must be answered initially: What are the *expectations* and *norms* for marriage and divorce in upper-class, white Anglo-Saxon Protestant communities and in Puerto Rican Roman Catholic communities? How long (and how many times) has each been married? In what ways and to what degree are the marriages entrenched in other aspects of the client's world? How do their religious beliefs and customs affect marriage?

These questions will usually be asked not only of the client, but will be researched through the sociological and anthropological literature on the *vital features*. For each aspect of the *social location*, there are likely to be many detailed reports explaining the usual lifestyles of persons at such locations. Much as a medical doctor would keep in mind the expected differences between the physiological structures of a 60-year-old patient and that of a 16-year-old patient, a clinical sociologist would keep in mind expected differences between social structures of 60-year-olds and 16-year-olds. Both would also look for anomalies.

Only after reaching thorough understanding of the vital features relative to the client does the clinician begin to consider the possible sources of difficulties. This process usually begins with consideration of the most common sources. To stick to our marital example, the clinician would do well to consider such sources as desires for experimentation or need to leave parents in the case of the 16-year-old, and differences in future time orientation or general feelings of uselessness among the 60-year-old. These are social conditions which frequently arise among these *age cohorts* and can affect marriages.

The reason for seeking the most common sources of problems is perhaps obvious; the clinician is likely to save himself or herself and the clients considerable time and energy in this way. However, there are a couple of dangers in proceeding to look for the usual sources, and clinicians should guard against these. First, one is tempted to force novel situations into their expected places even when they do not fit. Repetition breeds habit among some clinicians and can result in inappropriate diagnoses. This is especially likely when one is hurried by a tight schedule and is thereby encouraged to make rapid diagnoses.

The other danger is that the clinician may lose rapport with a client through a line of questioning which follows the most predictable expectations. If the questioning is inappropriate to the specific case the client may be insulted, embarrassed, or disillusioned that the clinician would bring up such topics. On the other hand, if the questioning *is* appropriate to the case the client may be forced to confront too early in the relationship some topics which are very painful or revealing.

Sociology is usually presented as a series of regularities which apply to all within a defined category. The clinical sociologist must remember that these regularities disguise the range of behavior within that category. Group members with difficulty might be choosing an action which even deviates from the socially understood deviations of the group. Yet this action might fit into a different cultural context or usage pattern for the client. For example, Karl, an Indian professional, finds himself spending considerable time in state mental hospitals because he acts on complicated hallucinations and is unable to care for himself. His hallucinations have American content, but Indian structure. American popular female figures—Jackie Onassis, Susan Ford—arrive at his apartment to be part of arranged marriages for him. He has chosen an American professor to be his God, but the God functions in an Eastern fashion. The clinical sociologist working with Karl has had to recognize this in order to develop an effective way to help him.

THERAPY FOR THE GROUP

When the unit for sociological therapy is the group, whether that be a family, an institution, or an international social system, to whom should the clinical sociologist turn to identify the sources of pain or loss of ability? No single individual or subunit within a group is likely to have access or interest in the overall workings of the group. Not only do leaders often separate themselves from their followers, for example, but also a well-informed leader will see situations from the leadership position (i.e., in terms of goals for the group, effects on leadership of the group, etc.). Any follower will necessarily be in a different position within the group, and therefore view situations in different ways. Sometimes the members of a group will be in general agreement about a problem and present a unified vision to the clinical sociologist (e.g., a community damaged by floods). Even in such extreme cases there are likely to be segments of the group who disagree with one another about specific details of the problem. More often, there are many notions of which problems exist within a group. It is frequently necessary to go beyond even the various perspectives within the group itself, since other groups may also affect and be affected by the group needing therapy, and, as suggested in chapter 11, the change perspective might be lacking in the particular group. Furthermore, the view from outside the group may point out ways that the group's problems can be prevented in the future.

Preventive therapy is not widely practiced in contemporary societies. Therapy is instead reserved for situations in which persons perceive pain or loss of abilities and seek the help of a clinician. There are at least two reasons for this: (1) therapy is expensive, and most persons or groups afford it only when it is clearly needed; and (2) the everyday notion of illness processing is of a problem detected by a patient and defined by a clinician. Expensiveness is perhaps less of a problem in sociological therapy than in others (sociologists are relatively inexpensive to train and hire). The everyday notion of illness processing does create serious problems for clinical sociological practice, however.

MOVING IN

The variety of relevant perspectives within groups, and the need for preventive therapy in many groups, suggest that sociological therapy for groups is best accomplished through ongoing interactions of the clinician within the group.

Ongoing presence of the clinician is also important for etiological concerns. Most all present problems have developed from structures and conditions in the past; no social situation is born fully developed. Much as embryology is necessary to understand adult physiology, history of a social group is necessary to understand current social situations. Seldom will a clinician have been present in a group since its birth (which perhaps preceded the birth of the clinician), and it will be necessary to acquire much of the historical understanding from reports by long-time members and documents concerning the group. But this sort of material is better acquired and assimilated during periods when the group is not suffering immediate difficulties. Crises provoke especially selective memories of the past as well as feelings that the clinician should concern him or herself with assisting the existing difficulties rather than discussing past situations.

Being a regular participant in the client group also decreases the probability that the clinician will waste time solving problems that have already passed or changed. Too often a client group is aware of a difficulty only too late, or they conceive current problems as variations of old problems. Hegel's note in the preface to the *Philosophy of Right*— that philosophy comes on the scene when "actuality is already there cut and dried, after its process of formation has been completed," and is therefore too late to "give instruction as to what the world ought to be"—is a warning to the clinician.

Yet being a regular participant creates other issues of involvement. Sociologist John Seeley in reflecting on his experience doing a community study of Crestwood Heights states:

> We too wished to be of them and not of them, to redefine ourselves now as in, now as out, to accept and to reject the counterposed definitions offered. We oscillated, as they did, between the detachment or pseudo-detachment in which we had been trained, the stance or substance of lofty leadership, and the kind of encounter that, shattering in its intimacy, sweeps away conventional pretense in its preconditions and its consequences.[1]

The clinical sociologist can participate, but must maintain a healthy detachment to keep from becoming just another group member.

The techniques that follow vary in the type and amount of group involvement appropriate from the clinician. Sociometry and sociodrama, simulation, and asking embarrassing sociological questions represent one extreme in which the clinician acts as an expert advisor or director. This is also the clinician's role in some forms of organizational, community, and self-help work, although more often the clinician is a full group member in such strategies.

Three cross-cutting concerns run throughout the following chapters—the nature of the client (group versus group member, community or organizational setting, etc.), the most effective therapeutic strategies for specified types of situations, and the relationship of the clinician to the group member, group, organization, or community.

1. John R. Seeley, "Crestwood Heights: Intellectual and Libidinal Dimensions of Research," in Arthur J. Vidich, Joseph Bensman, and Maurice R. Stein, eds., *Reflections on Community Studies* (New York: Wiley, 1964), pp. 169–70.

Chapter 13

Self-Help

I think we AA's all carry umbrellas that we put up over each other when the rain seems to be falling a little harder on our neighbor.—Alcoholics Anonymous pamphlet

Self-help groups, broadly defined, include all formal and informal organizations in which persons band together to improve the conditions under which they live or work. Political parties, labor unions, and governments all fit this definition. However, these days, many such groups have become the objects which other groups consider too big, or unresponsive to the needs of their constituents. Today, the self-help group is usually viewed as an antibureaucratic citizen-participation organization. It tries to move the formal power structure to a position that provides better benefits for the members of the self-help group (and those in similar circumstances) or goes about providing those benefits through voluntarism, thereby having no use for the formal power structure. This chapter concentrates upon self-help groups with a particular emphasis on helping persons with problems of everyday life. Peer self-help groups where people join together to gain greater understanding or change behaviors have had exceptional impact on improving lives of persons who choose to affiliate. Clinical sociologists should be aware of the existence of such groups, the range of groups available, how to link with such groups, and how to set up a group should none be available.

Self-help groups clearly are a sociological therapeutic technique, concentrating on groups and members of groups. The goal is increased effectiveness, although the peer self-help approach usually keeps community and societal concerns in the foreground. The emphasis is on the way the group member links with the group and the natural interpersonal relationships that she or he has established. The group is a support and a reference point designed to indicate that successful change is possible for those who adopt the group's approach. This linking of the group member to group, community, and society is a natural feature of most peer self-help groups.

Many persons have shifted from working on changing societal conditions, a fashionable theme in the 1960s, to looking inward at oneself, overcoming one's problems and trying to expand one's personal horizons in the 1970s. Tom Wolfe calls this "the me decade." Peer self-help groups frequently provide a group experience that enhances such inward looking. At the same time, many self-help groups do have social change programs ranging from elimination of stigmas through education of the nonstigmatized, to comprehensive systematic programs reaching into many areas of society. Peer self-help groups can provide an integrative experience in a disintegrating society. Examine what one can frequently get in a peer self-help group—individual counseling, a feeling of self-worth from counseling others, strong support from a group of self-proclaimed peers, an internally consistent ideology, a sense of belonging, working toward a better world, a positive identity, an activity that can fill one's leisure time, a sense that you can do something about the world—all this for minimal monetary cost.

What are peer self-help groups? How can they be typed?

Leon H. Levy, a clinical psychologist, has provided a working definition of self-help groups:

1. *Purpose*. Its express primary purpose is to provide help and support for its members in dealing with their problems and in improving their psychological functioning and effectiveness.
2. *Origin and sanction*. Its origin and sanction for existence rest with the members of the group themselves rather than with some external agency or authority.
3. *Source of help*. It relies upon its own members' efforts, skills, knowl-

edge, and concern as its primary source of help, with the structure of the relationship being one of peers, so far as help giving or support are concerned. Where professionals do participate in the group's meetings, they do so at the pleasure of the group and are cast in an ancillary role.
4. *Composition*. It is generally composed of members who share a common core of life experiences and problems.
5. *Control*. Its structure and mode of operation are under the control of members, although they may, in turn, draw upon professional guidance and various theoretical and philosophical frameworks.[1]

Levy distinguishes four types of groups: I—those working to reorganize or control behaviors, such as Alcoholics Anonymous, Synanon, Tops, and other drug-related groups; II—groups composed of persons who share a common predicament which entails stress. These groups ameliorate stress through mutual support and sharing of coping strategies. The status of the participants is considered fixed and no attempt is made to change it. Both Parents without Partners and Recovery Inc. are type II groups; III—survival-oriented groups, composed of persons the society has labeled deviant or discriminated against. These groups try to maintain or raise their members' self-esteem through mutual support or consciousness raising techniques and political activities designed to change societal treatment. Examples include gay groups, women's groups, race or ethnic pride or power groups; and IV—groups made up of members "who share a common goal of personal growth, self-actualization and enhanced effectiveness in living and loving." In these groups there is a shared belief that the members can help each other to a better life, such as in Integrity Groups, New Environments Association, and informal peer-based experiential groups.[2]

Peer-counseling is of special value to persons who would feel stigmatized if they sought professional help. For many persons, specialized professional treatment for problems in living is a last resort after family, friends, clergy, and the family doctor have been consulted. Others frequently called upon in this role include beauticians, barbers, bartenders, policemen, teachers, work supervisors, and foremen.[3]

There is some evidence of a disparity between persons having emotional difficulty and those who use professional services. The 1960 national sample study of the Joint Commission on Mental Illness and Health indicated that among those persons, 18 percent of the total sample, who had stated that they had feelings of impending nervous breakdown, slightly more than half did not refer the problem to any professional health resource, and only 2.8 percent used psychiatric or social service help.[4] The work of the Joint Commission contributed to the establishment of the Community Mental Health Centers program. With the extensive development of community-based services and the opening up of careers in mental health to a great number of persons trained on a variety of levels, one might assume that help has become more accessible. However, a national health screening in 1972 found that 16 percent of our citizens had psychological disabilities, but only 2 percent of the population went to medical or psychological care resources for the treatment of these disabilities.[5]

Dr. Bertram Brown, former head of the National Institute of Mental Health, states that "throughout the remainder of the decade, three million individuals will seek the assistance of a mental health professional each year if the current patient episode rate remains the same." [6] This is approximately 1.4 percent of the population. Peer self-help groups are an important link in the help-seeking network reaching persons who never would seek professional help, as well as maintaining persons who have been or are involved with professional help.

Furthermore, it is not a link small in size. While statistics on self-help groups tend not to be kept with the same detail as statistics on professional services, Alcoholics Anonymous has more than 28,000 groups, with probable membership of more than a million world-wide. Recovery Inc. had 1045 groups in 1975 and about 18,000 members. The specialized groups have proliferated so that in middle-sized cities in the United States one can find specific self-help groups for alcoholism, relatives of alcoholics, elderly persons, children, parents of the retarded, homosexuals, people with ostomies, single parent families, rape victims, gamblers, mental health patients, veterans, victims of Huntington's disease, widows and widowers, women who want to nurse, the deaf, public interest groups, Indians, general self-improvement, Spanish, losing weight, parents of children with learning disabilities, paraplegics, the blind, inner-city teens, community or block associations, crisis counseling, women, and volunteer fire departments.

HOW ARE PEER SELF-HELP GROUPS DIFFERENT FROM CONVENTIONAL PSYCHOTHERAPY?

Nathan Hurwitz has presented 88 differences between conventional psychotherapy (using the ideal type of neopsychoanalytic interpretation and insight approach with the interpersonal attitude of the non-directive school) and peer self-help psychotherapy groups (his term) for which his ideal type is AA, Recovery Inc. or Synanon—Levy's type I groups.

Structural and Procedural Differences

Peers maintain authority and control, accept free will offerings, do not keep records, and meetings frequently are open and follow a predetermined order of business in a setting not specifically designed for psychotherapy. Peers are not required to have completed a program of professional education or be licensed or certified, although usually they undergo special training. Peers determine therapy procedures and goals and read the literature about their approach.

Reciprocity

Peers reveal themselves to each other, are role models for each other, frequently (in type I organizations especially) have acknowledged their failures in handling the problem, and have experienced trying to overcome the problem. Therefore, they identify with each other and communicate on a "gut" level and take responsibility for a person working through a problem.

Moral Attitudes

Peers profess a moral position and are judgmental, and can make each other feel guilty, ashamed, and so forth. Peers may consider each other sick, but expect "well" behavior of each other. Spiritual and inspirational activities are frequently part of the fellowship.

Social and Psychological Systems

Every aspect of the peer's functioning in the real world is subject to group review and evaluation. The past is reviewed to discover the cause of present behavior. Psychological regression or transference neurosis is not fostered. Peers hold each other responsible for their behavior; they urge responsibility for each other. They support each other's efforts and effective functioning. Peers are active in their relationship with each other, and they confront each other and provoke hostile feelings, but these are viewed as expressions of concern and care. Peers give and receive support and try to move the experience in the group into everyday life. Peers disclose their secrets to one another, and in that process make other members of the group their significant others. All peers consider themselves therapists and can undertake various positions within the organization including publicizing and politicizing. Those who have had an unsuccessful experience drop out while those who have had success maintain a place in the movement.

Group Therapy

All therapy occurs in groups, but individuals may form shifting therapeutic twosomes within the structure of the fellowship. Group leadership develops and is assumed by varying members at varying times. Group membership can be quite varied as to age, sex, social class, race, and so forth. Peers have real-life meaning for each other, assist each other to change real-life behavior and attitudes, and can be called upon for assistance at any time. Peers achieve status in the movement by indicating the contrast between their former and present behavior, by helping others, and by undertaking greater responsibility in the movement.

Peers' Fellowship Identification

Members participate in the fellowship voluntarily and accept the helping activities of their peers only as long as they want. Peer relationships have no economic grounding, and peers are not vulnerable to manipulation on this basis. Different members are regarded as a source of wisdom as they function characteristically in various situations to help their peers achieve goals. A member may become dependent upon the movement, just like being dependent upon an addiction. Peers have faith in each other because of the success of their movement in aiding others with problems like their own. Community attitudes to the movement range from hostility to active support. In general, they are skeptical and resistant.[7]

PEERS AND PROFESSIONALS

None of these groups seek out professionals and frequently discourage their involvement. A major reason is that professionals find it difficult to be peers, rather than "experts," unless they fit into the focus of the group (as when an alcoholic physician joins AA). Another reason professionals have difficulty with self-help groups is that professional training puts emphasis on eclecticism—taking the best from a variety of approaches and putting one's personal stamp on it. Many self-help groups have an accepted orthodoxy that does not allow for much heresy.

However, as Norris Hansell points out, relationships between mutual help groups and professionals are undergoing changes.

> Mutual-help groups, whether of the predicament, bridging or pro-
> fessionally assisted type, are a topic of increasing professional
> interest. The product of their efforts looks good to profes-
> sionals. Clearly it is attractive to the people who make use of such
> groups. Professionals are lately less apt to "look down their
> noses" at the groups. Members of the groups are less apt to look
> down their noses at the professionals. In an interval of only sev-
> eral decades, the relationship between professionals and self-
> help groups has evolved dramatically. Starting with a long phase
> of ignoring one another, they moved to knowing of one
> another, but disapproving. Then came a period marked by at-
> tempts by professionals to dominate the groups. At present,
> many mutual-help groups and many professionals appear to
> be moving into a phase of respectful commerce.[8]

Hansell sees the importance of the groups as

> a temporary kind of social regulation for individuals who are tem-
> porarily bereft of regulation by virtue of the magnitude of their
> distress signalling, by virtue of social isolation, or by virtue
> of a condition of life with minimal affiliations. Mutual-help groups
> can provide a regulatory context for that interval in the middle
> part of adaptation which is *after* the old way, but *before* the new
> way.[9]

Self-help groups reach persons that psychotherapists find difficult to help—alcoholics, drug addicts, chronic schizophrenics—persons quite different from the population most easily reached by psychotherapy and given the acronym YAVIS; Youthful, Attractive, Verbal, Intelligent, Successful.[10]

Another factor that makes peer self-help groups of interest to professionals is their implications for the planning of mental health care, anticipated manpower needs, and the funding of human services. Thomas Scheff has suggested that

> an ideal approach to "mental health" problems would be (1) effective, (2) cheap, (3) quick, (4) free of harmful side effects, (5) applicable to a broad range of problems in terms of social class, race and ethnicity, age, education, etc., (6) have preventive as well as therapeutic potential, (7) . . . and implications for social, cultural and political change as well as for individual change, so that it did not merely help individuals adjust to the status quo.[11]

Similarly, Leo Hollister has suggested five principles of care that form the basis of service parsimony, an end that is followed frequently in self-help groups:

1. The least disruptive intervention is the first treatment of choice.
2. The least separation from family and job will be sought.
3. The least expensive treatment will be used first.
4. The least extensive intervention will be used first.
5. The least trained interveners will be used first.[12]

DO SELF-HELP GROUPS WORK? WHY?

There is little research on self-help groups. As Marie Killilea points out, "Because of its unfashionable nature, much of the work by professionals in this field has to be done with few resources of time, staff, and funds. Most work has been impressionistic and there are few systematic studies; many more are needed." [13]

Many self-help groups are growing. Can we assume from this growth that something works? To a degree we can, but what works might be quite different from the overall goals of the group. Only those persons who are getting something from the self-help group (or who believe they will get something) remain involved. Each group develops a rationale for drop-outs, but it is usually against a group's philosophy to follow up persons who do not want to be involved.

Sociologists Kurt Back and Rebecca Taylor see self-help groups as social movements where it is the "added value" of "belonging to and participating in a movement whether this participation leads to a desired goal or not" [14] that is the basis for effectiveness. The perceptive critic de Tocqueville noted that we are "a nation of joiners," and this has clearly increased since he wrote in the eighteenth century. Think of the range of organizations we join: professional societies, clubs, churches or synagogues, sports leagues, and so forth, and the amount of time many people spend on voluntary organizations. Self-help groups are just another part of the joining phenomenon, frequently allowing persons who are denied in-group membership in more fashionable settings a small group of their own—a group providing clarification of values and support in the midst of a confusing and nonsupportive society.

Paul Antze suggests that the successful internalization of ideology is what makes peer self-help groups work.

Peer therapy groups are social forms well adapted to inducing standardized changes of outlook at a deep level among their membership, the changes in each case being defined by the group's ideology. Let us assume for present purposes that such changes occur. Do they have any therapeutic importance? There are reasons for supposing they might. Jerome Frank's highly influential discussion of psychotherapeutic processes (1961) offers a sustained argument for the view that every effective therapy achieves its ends on changing the client's "assumptive world." The methods used may vary widely, but according to Frank, the crux of the therapeutic process is always some modification of "values, expectations, and images," in short a cognitive change. [15]

In a detailed look at the ideologies of AA, Synanon, and Recovery Inc., Antze generalizes that each organization

achieves its effects by counteracting certain key attitudes that typify its client group. Thus AA counters the assertiveness of alcoholics by teaching surrender. Recovery, Inc., blocks the habitual surrender of ex-mental patients by promoting willpower; and Synanon reverses the addict's social and emotional detachment through a process that expresses feelings and strengthens social engagement. This pattern suggests that there may be identifiable logic that governs all therapy organizations;

every affliction has its typical attitude or style of action, every therapy group has its countervailing ideology.[16]

Another psychiatrist with strong positive regard for peer self-help groups is Gerald Caplan. He views these groups as being able to provide effective support systems for individuals. He ties the importance of psychosocial support to the work of epidemiologist John Cassel. Cassel has postulated that psychosocial processes can be envisaged as affecting susceptibility to disease:

> A remarkable similar set of social circumstances characterizes people who develop tuberculosis and schizophrenia, alcoholics, victims of multiple accidents, and suicides. Common to all these people is a marginal status in society. They are individuals who for a variety of reasons (e.g., ethnic minorities rejected by the dominant majority in their neighborhood; high sustained rates of residential and occupational mobility; broken homes or isolated living circumstances) have been deprived of meaningful social contact. It is perhaps surprising that this wide variety of disease outcomes associated with similar circumstances has generally escaped comment.[17]

Cassel further states that in addition to processes that are detrimental to health, there are processes which might be envisioned as the protective factors buffering or

> cushioning the individual from the physiologic or psychologic consequences of exposure to the stressor situation. It is suggested that the property common to these processes is the strength of the social supports provided by the primary groups of most importance to the individual.[18]

Caplan takes off from this postulation and recognizes while there are many natural support systems in many people's lives, "in an unorganized or disorganized society such spontaneous support systems may be inadequate, especially for marginal people." He suggests that mental health professionals "learn how to stimulate and foster supports in the population without distorting and inhibiting their development by forcing them into our professional patterns." The goal would be the "augmenting of a person's strengths to facilitate the mastering of the environment." [19]

Caplan describes the relationship between such support groups and disease:

> The characteristic attribute of those social aggregates that act as a buffer against disease is that in such relationships, the person is dealt with as a unique individual. The other people are interested in him in a personalized way. They speak his language. They tell him what is expected of him and guide him in what to do. They watch what he has done. They reward him for success and punish or support and comfort him if he fails. Above all, they are sensitive to his personal needs, which they deem worthy of respect and satisfaction.[20]

Peer self-help groups resemble organizations of a far simpler time, when people banded together for mutual aid to overcome various adverse conditions. After generations of "stiff upper lip" individual entrepreneurship and competitive independency, does the recent rediscovery of the self-help group portend a return to interdependency brought on, in part, by the diminishing of a positive view of the future? A lessening of available resources? Or is it merely a return to a nostalgic pining for a simpler time never again to be recaptured, a group delusion turned into collective behavior that bears little relationship to reality?

The evidence is not yet available. At this point, only two partial replies can be offered:

1. In many cases self-help groups have been quite effective, and often in the face of unavailable alternatives. Perhaps the most notable example is alcoholism. No known professional program has been as effective in keeping alcoholics from drinking as has Alcoholics Anonymous. Many of the most effective professional programs include AA as part of their therapy recommendations for clients.[21]

2. A peer self-help group can provide sensitive interpersonal feedback of persons' presentations of self, within the ideology of the self-help group. To the degree we can believe this feedback, we will then emphasize our perceptions that fit this ideology and deemphasize those perceptions that don't fit and, in the process, alter our sense of reality. Group support helps in making this happen. The degree to which we act on the basis of this new perception of reality will, in and of itself, bring change to some extent. When a group of people band together and overcome their feeling of powerlessness, strengthened with a shared activity, a shared ideology, and perceived changes in themselves

and their environment, social change usually takes place, thus changing their objective reality.

CAUTIONS

There are three major cautions to keep in mind: (1) You will not be in the same place in a few months as you were when you began. Sometimes an increase in self-awareness makes the situation harder, not easier. (2) As you change, it is likely that new pressures will be placed on your close relationships. Frequently such relationships have partially or completely hardened into frozen systems of handling each other's needs. As you change, what you need from those close to you also changes, throwing these relationships out of their traditional balance. (3) A peer self-help group presents a powerful, optimistic, deeply reinforced view of reality. It provides you with powerful tools in working with other people and for working on self-development. There is a tendency for those who get deeply involved to subjugate their own good thinking to the thinking of the movement. One's personality can be turned into a client-counselor at all times. Sometimes, to those not involved, it appears that you have become addicted to the movement or substituted one addiction for another. These three cautions might appear to some readers as advantages for peer self-help groups. By describing these general cautions more specifically they become less ambiguous:

1. There are some problems for which self-help groups find it difficult to be helpful: (a) the person does not want to be helped (e.g., the alcoholic who wants to keep drinking); (b) the situation where the prospective member is in need of major medical attention. Some self-help groups have been able to cut down the use of physicians by members, but in some cases, the professional has medical equipment and knowledge at his or her disposal that the self-help group does not have. Self-help groups at times have been effective mediators between professional and group members; and (c) the situation where distance is needed on the problem. Some self-help groups argue that it takes a person who has been through the experience to be able to be an effective counselor, and indeed sometimes this is true. At other times, however, greater objectivity is needed, especially about alternatives that don't fit the belief systems of the peer group regulars.

2. Sometimes the definitions of the problem by the self-help group might be wrong for the particular person. Some prospective self-help

members get repelled by "confessions" that are so extreme and weird that the person cannot identify him- or herself with that level of the problem and refuses to accept the group's definition of his or her problem.

3. Sometimes self-help groups have no peerness, but are vehicles for the leader to increase her or his gratification, whether this be in dollars, power, or private information.

4. A greater extreme of point 3 is when a group has some of the trappings of peer self-help, but is phony. The leadership gets quite rich through an elaborate pyramid club scheme. There would be a great difference between ideology and actual functioning in such groups.

5. In real self-help groups, as well as in the phonies, be quite conscious of the extent of confrontative tactics used to make people believe. We mentioned earlier that confrontation can be an effective therapeutic technique. However, when used to tear down a person's belief system to replace it with that of the group, or used to put down the person, one is treading in dangerous territory. Confrontation is an important ingredient in some very effective self-help groups such as Synanon and Delancey Street. However, it must be used with care and caring.

6. Be wary of groups that demand total commitment spiritually, socially, and monetarily. When that happens, one is dealing with a cult in the garb of self-help.

USES

Keeping these cautions in mind, there are many appropriate uses for peer self-help groups by the clinical sociologist. Clinical sociologists should compile a listing of available self-help groups in their community. When a person comes with a problem that fits within the purview of the self-help group, the clinical sociologist could suggest that the person contact the group. Be sure to follow up with the person; just as it is true with professional services that some are effective and some are worthless, the same is true about self-help. Your listing should be updated according to which groups appear effective for which problems based on the experience reported to you by the persons you referred. Setting up a self-help group can be suggested when the clinical sociologist meets with a group that discovers that they have goals in common. The clinical sociologist can be the catalyst that gets the group started and makes sure the group continues once she or he departs. (Locating groups, and starting new groups, are discussed below.) Some com-

munities have discovered ways to link peer self-help groups with professional services, providing a continuity of support for persons in
need.

Finally, peer self-help can be quite beneficial for the clinical
sociologist. The clinician's role can be a lonely one, and support from a
group given in exchange for your support of group members can be
useful. Discover whether there are groups that fit your needs in the
community in which you live or work, or set up your own. If you do it
yourself, be aware that self-help groups have built up considerable
experience in what works and fails. Find ways to utilize this expertise
in your own activities.

HOW TO FIND A SELF-HELP GROUP

Some self-help groups are easy to find. If your community has a
community services directory, a number of self-help groups will be
listed, though this list probably is not exhaustive. Next stop should be
the Yellow Pages. These headings could be useful: associations, clubs,
fraternal organizations, political organizations, social service organizations, and veterans and military organizations. Alcoholics Anonymous
will have a service center which should have information on AA and
AA spinoffs, including Alanon (for spouses), Alateen, Gamblers Anonymous, Overeaters Anonymous, and Parents Anonymous. Specific
self-help groups might have telephone numbers listed. There is now a
National Self-Help Clearinghouse at 184 Fifth Avenue, New York, N.Y.
10010, that publishes *Self-Help Reporter*, which contains a very comprehensive listing of self-help groups.

Another fine way to find out is to ask. Some human service professionals know about self-help groups. Most do not. Pay attention to
people you know who have begun to change things about themselves
for the better. The heavy drinker who stopped, the formerly fat person,
the aware and alive formerly depressed person, the single parent with
new strength to cope. Sometimes you will find that a self-help group
has made the difference and that they will be glad to refer you to it.

DO IT YOURSELF SELF-HELP

A good way to begin designing new peer self-help groups, for
yourself and your clients, is to read the literature available concerning existing groups. Alcoholics Anonymous, for instance, publishes a
great deal of material about its operation, most of which is free for

the asking. Many self-help groups are based upon the AA model.

During the very early stages of formation, several general points should be kept in mind. The following steps can be instrumental in beginning a peer self-help group of your own. They are based upon the experiences of persons in a variety of such groups. Let your own thinking modify these steps to your situation.

1.   Think about persons you know. Make a list of those persons with whom you share a common problem or common activity. Or make a list of those persons you believe to be the most flexible, most creative, most on-top-of-the-world persons you know.
2.   Check with the persons on either list (but don't combine the lists). Would they like to meet around the common problem? Would they like to give and receive attention from you and others? Overcome your fear (if any) of asking them. We all turn shy when we make unusual requests.
3.   Bring together those who express interest (at a convenient time for all).
4.   Work out an agenda in advance of issues that need clarification and problems that all are likely to be facing. Allow others present to add to the agenda.
5.   Share time equally among each member present. Go through an agenda.
6.   Give everyone an equal chance to express opinions and ideas. Everyone should speak once before anyone speaks twice.
7.   Do not degrade the ideas of others. Consider what they say to be the best thinking they are capable of at that time.
8.   Do not give advice; do not confront. Do not put down. Paying attention and listening carefully is always therapeutic. Allow persons to feel the support of the entire group for their ideas, their feelings, their attempts at problem solving. Sense and deal with the humanness of the human being. Do not push persons beyond what they are ready to do or reveal.
9.   At the end of the meeting, get feedback, share time to discover what worked for the persons present. Decide whether and when you want to meet again.
10.   If possible, share the leadership of the group.

At the beginning, it will probably be difficult to get people involved. However, the effect of such meetings is cumulative. Persons learn that they are not alone. They sense new allies, new support. They (and you) have to get over the fear of being deserted by the group at moments of need. There are a number of available approaches that can aid in turning individuals into self-help groups. These are usually called team-building or group exercises. Each self-help group has developed a format that accomplishes the same ends. Your own best thinking and that of the other group members can come up with the format that is best for your group.

POSTSCRIPT: THREE INSIDERS' ACCOUNTS

1. *Peer Self-Help. The following is an account of a peer counseling session. The organization is not named because it does not recruit through written publicity.*

It is early and quiet when I leave my home in order to meet my regular peer counselor. (Time of day doesn't really matter—just what is convenient.) We both enjoy the early morning, getting awake with another person's excellent attention. I arrive first at the safe convenient place the peer community rents and makes available on a 24-hour-a-day basis to persons active in the peer counseling community. One of my tasks is to be in charge of the place and I check to see if the plants are watered, the notices are current, and the place is neat. Just then my peer counselor arrives. We embrace warmly. We have learned how to be close, loving and supportive without it turning into a love affair.

I client first. My counselor quickly makes sure I am oriented to the present and then asks what good things have happened since we last met. I have three or four things to report: a fine concert, a loving note from my wife, something from work that is going quite well. Then: what little things are upsetting you? Again more reports. My counselor encourages me to get in touch with my feelings about each of the upsets and aids me by thinking of a phrase that gets me more in touch with my feelings. I feel safe to deeply feel. When I'm through with the mildly upsetting topics, I turn to trying to get some leverage on a topic that I need to explore in depth. For example, it could be a troubling relationship, or gorging myself on food, or working on some ethnic material. My counselor encourages me to explore past feelings and aids me to see that there is a difference from the way I acted (unaware) in the past and my present and future abilities to respond differently. My time, half the overall time that we have available, ends. My counselor makes sure I am back in the present and then we switch roles. I become the counselor and she becomes the client. I provide warmth and awareness while she works on what she feels she needs to do. As counselor, I am more than active listener, although I say nothing much of the time. When I sense that she is trying to avoid getting into depth on a feeling, I make suggestions that hopefully lead to the areas in the past where feelings need to be expressed. Today, I suggest towards the end of the time that she praise her own abilities.

Her time ends. We embrace again, then set a time the following week for another meeting. Then each of us, filled with an exhilaration that comes from working hard with the aid of a caring person, begin our day; alert, aware, in-touch and ready to tackle whatever problems the day will bring. One evening later in the week we will attend our regular class, led by a teacher, where we will learn more theory and better practice of this international program, as well as feel the support of a larger group.

2. *Alcoholics Anonymous. The following is from a speech by an AA member.* [22]

Long before the average alcoholic walks through the doors of his first AA meeting, he has sought help from others or help has been offered to him, in some instances even forced upon him. But these helpers are always *superior* beings: spouses, parents, physicians, employers, priests, ministers, rabbis, swamis, judges, policemen, even bartenders. The moral culpability of the alcoholic and the moral superiority of the helper, even though unstated, are always clearly understood. The overtone of parental disapproval and discipline in these authority figures is always present.

I am personally convinced that the basic search of every human being, from the cradle to the grave, is to find at least one other human being before whom he can stand completely naked, stripped of all pretense or defense, and trust that person not to hurt him, because that other person has stripped himself naked, too. This lifelong search can begin to end with the first AA encounter. . . .

It seems to me that what happens to an alcoholic on his first encounter with AA is that he realizes he has been invited to share in the experience of recovery. And the key word in that sentence is the word "share." Whether he responds to it immediately or ever is not at that moment important. What is important is that the invitation has been extended and remains, and that he has been invited to share as an equal and not as a mendicant. No matter what his initial reaction, even the sickest alcoholic is hard put to deny to himself that he has been offered understanding, equality, and an already-proved way out. And he is made to feel that he is, in fact, *entitled* to all this; indeed, he has already earned it, simply because he is an alcoholic. . . .

No newcomer to AA is ever left in any real doubt that recovery can begin only with a decision to "stay away from the first drink." . . . The desire, as well as the ability, to make this decision often results, I believe, from what appears to be AA's third unique quality: The intuitive understanding the alcoholic receives, while compassionate, is not indulgent. The "therapists" in AA already have their doctorates in the four fields where the alcoholic reigns supreme: phoniness, self-deception, evasion, and self-pity. He is not asked what he is thinking. He is told what he is thinking. No one waits to trap him in a lie. He is told what lies he is getting ready to tell. In the end, he begins to achieve honesty by default. There's not much point in trying to fool people who may have invented the game you're playing. . . .

In AA, the reporting is clear and unmistakable. "Here are the steps we took," say those who have gone before. The newcomer finally sees that he, too, must take these Steps before he is entitled to report on them. And in an atmosphere where the constant subject is "What I did" and "What I think," no neurotic can long resist the temptation to get in on the action. In an organization whose members are always secretly convinced that they are unique, no neurotic is long going to be contented with a report of what others are doing. Whether by accident or design or supernatural guidance, the Twelve Steps are so framed and presented that the alcoholic can either ignore them completely, take them cafeteria-style, or embrace them whole-heartedly. In any case, he can report only on what he has done. Till he does, he knows that he is more a guest of AA than a member, and this is a situation that is finally intolerable to the alcoholic. He must take at least some of the Steps, or go away.

But what clinches the result and keeps the recovered alcoholic in AA forever self-determining is, I believe . . . that any
alcoholic on any given day at any given time can find someone
in AA who will in all good faith agree with what he has already
decided to do. Conversely, on any given day at any given time,
the same alcoholic can find someone in AA who in all good faith
will disagree with what he has already decided to do. Thus, sooner
or later, the recovering alcoholic in AA is literally forced to
think for himself. Sooner or later, he finds himself akin to the
turtle, that lowly creature who makes progress only when his
neck is stuck out. The formless flexibility of AA's principles as
interpreted by their different adherents finally pushes our alcoholic into a stance where he must use only himself as a frame of
reference for his actions, and this in turn means he must be
willing to accept the consequences of those actions.

3.   *Delancey Street. The following is an excerpt from an account of a
Dissipation at Delancey Street, a peer self-help organization for ex-
prisoners, ex-addicts, or anyone whose life-fortunes have "hit bottom" and
who sincerely wishes to change his or her entire mode of operating. The
excerpt is recorded well into a 45-hour marathon encounter.*

There is a commotion in the room. They are bringing in a
lighted coffin. It is the symbol of a general catharsis. Soon there
are knots of people around it crying and comforting each
other. While John continues to shout about hard work, Max, who
wrestled his grandmother over a television set he'd stolen and
finally knocked her senseless, is crying over the coffin. "Forgive
me, Grandma, forgive me!" Geordie, who has described a dying
father with cancer in his spine and curses for his addict son is
crying in the candlelight, "I'm clean now, Dad, I'm clean. It's what
you always wanted."

Beth is up by the coffin, too, and three or four people are
wrapped around her in a composite embrace. Suddenly a lone
figure makes his way through the group. It is Dexter.

"Siddown, Dexter!" Stew and James shout. He is led back to his
seat and made to sit down, but moments later he has popped up
and is on the move again. After several attempts he gets
through to Beth. He is repeating the same words over and
over again. "Beth, I'm so sorry! Beth, I'm so sorry! Beth I'm
so. . ."

I continue to marvel at how perfectly Dexter is playing the part intended for him. Accused of being a detail man, he has, under stress, disputed only details. Accused of a machine-like deference to programs imposed upon him, he is now mechanomorphosed before our eyes, walking and talking with the stiffness and repetition of a clockwork soldier. In the surreal atmosphere of flickering lights and hallucinogenic exhaustion, I imagine an enormous key protruding from between his shoulders.

Nearly everyone is around the coffin now. Dugald touches my arm. "Want to go up to the coffin?"

By now I am so suggestible that I'd stick my head up the chimney. He leads me forward and I put my hands on the casket. But it is Beth I am thinking of—her and her dead children. (The first drowned in the bath while Beth fixed and lost consciousness.) The picture in my mind's eye has fused with the mandated drowning of my puppy when I was a child. A little creature spread-eagled in water clouded with regurgitated milk, the limbs still waving, slowing, and then still. The tears are running down my cheeks onto my chin. It is at this moment that Dugald has an inspiration.

"All right, Charles, it's your nanny isn't it? Want to talk about it?" In my pliant condition, grief is attachable to any memory.

"They froze her out," I say.

"You froze her out, Charles, you did it!"

Some residual spark of anger and resistance flickers to life within me.[23]

NOTES

1.   Leon H. Levy, "Self-Help Groups: Types and Psychological Processes," *Journal of Applied Behavorial Science* 12, no. 3 (1976):311–12.

2.   Ibid., 312–13.

3.   Charles Kadushin, *Why People Go to Psychiatrists* (New York: Atherton Press, 1969), especially chapters 8 and 9.

4.   Gerald Gurin, Joseph Veroff, and Sheila Feld, *Americans View Their Mental Health*, Joint Commission on Mental Illness and Health (New York: Basic Books, 1960), table 10.5, p. 310.

5.   Harold DuPuy, "Psychological Section," *Health and Nutrition*

Examination Survey, Department of Health, Education and Welfare (1972). See also: Leo Srole, *Mental Health in the Metropolis II* (New York: Harper & Row, 1977).

6. Bertram Brown, "Foreword," in Benjamin Wolman, ed., *The Therapist's Handbook* (New York: Van Nostrand, 1976), p. ix.

7. Nathan Hurwitz, "Peer Self-Help Psychotherapy Groups: Psychotherapy without Psychotherapists," in Paul Roman and Harrison Trice, eds., *The Sociology of Psychotherapy* (New York: Aronson, 1973).

8. Norris Hansell, *The Person-in-Distress* (New York: Human Science Press, 1975), p. 169.

9. Ibid., p. 170.

10. William Schofield, *Psychotherapy: The Purchase of Friendship* (Englewood Cliffs, N.J.: Prentice-Hall, 1964).

11. Thomas Scheff, "Re-evaluation Counseling: Social Implications," *Journal of Humanistic Psychology* 12(1972):59.

12. William G. Hollister and Quentin Rae-Grant, "The Principles of Parsimony in Mental Health Center Operations," *Canada's Mental Health* 20(January/February 1972):22.

13. Marie Killilea, "Mutual Help Organizations: Interpretations in the Literature," in Gerald Caplan and Marie Killilea, eds., *Support Systems and Mutual Help* (New York: Grune and Stratton, 1976), p. 39.

14. Kurt W. Back and Rebecca C. Taylor, "Self-Help Groups: Tool or Symbol?" *Journal of Applied Behavorial Science* 12, no. 3 (1976):295–309.

15. Paul Antze, "The Role of Ideologies in Peer Psychotherapy Organizations," *Journal of Applied Behavorial Science* 12, no. 3 (1976):326.

16. Ibid., p. 344.

17. John Cassel, "Psychosocial Processes and 'Stress': Theoretical Formulation," *International Journal of Health Services* 4, no. 3 (1974):474.

18. Ibid., p. 478.

19. Gerald Caplan, *Support Systems and Community Mental Health* (New York: Behavorial Publications, 1974), pp. 7–8.

20. Ibid., pp. 5–6.

21. Milton Maxwell, "Alcoholics Anonymous: An Interpretation," in David J. Pittman, ed., *Alcoholism* (New York: Harper & Row, 1967), pp. 211–22.

22. Anonymous, "A Member's-Eye View of Alcoholics Anonymous," Alcoholics Anonymous World Services, Inc., 1970.

23. Charles Hampden-Turner, "The Dramas of Delancey Street," *Journal of Humanistic Psychology* 16, no. 1 (1976):41.

THE CLINICIAN'S LIBRARY

There is a large literature on peer self-help, but it is somewhat difficult to find. Each self-help group produces its own literature. In addition, consult the following general works:

Caplan, Gerald. *Support Systems and Community Mental Health.* New York: Behavorial Publications, 1974.

Caplan, Gerald, and Marie Killilea, eds. *Support Systems and Mutual Help.* New York: Grune & Stratton, 1976. See especially Marie Killilea's review of literature, chapter 2.

Collins, Alice H., and Diane L. Pancoast. *Natural Helping Networks: A Strategy for Prevention.* Washington: National Association of Social Workers, 1976.

Claflin, Bill, and Pat Thaler. "Banding Together: The Best Way to Cope, A Resource Guide to Self-Help Groups." *New York Magazine* 5, no. 2 (February 1977).

Hurwitz, Nathan. "Peer Self Help Psychotherapy Groups," in Paul Roman and Harrison Trice, eds., *The Sociology of Psychotherapy.* New York: Aronson, 1973.

Katz, Alfred, and E. I. Bender. *The Strength in Us.* New York: Franklin Watts, 1977.

"Special Issue: Self-Help Groups." *The Journal of Applied Behavorial Science* 12, no. 3 (1976).

"Special Self-Help Issue." *Social Policy* 7, no. 2 (1976).

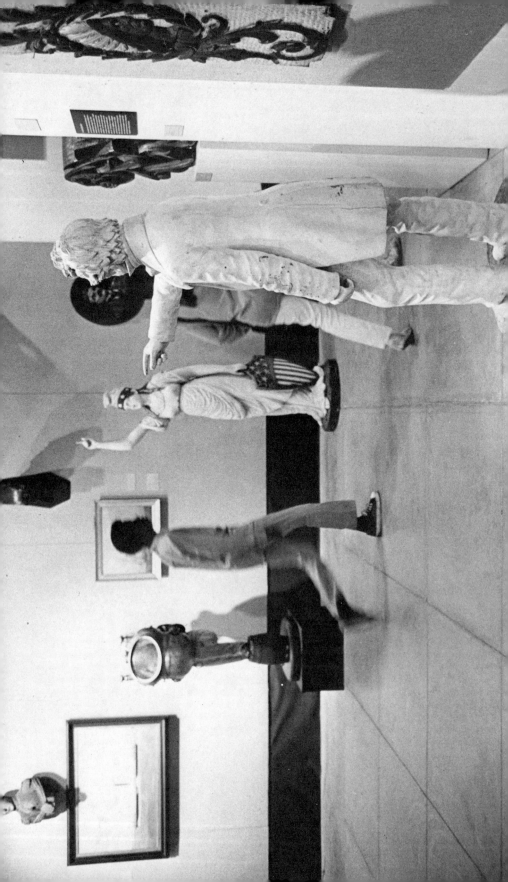

Chapter 14

Sociometry and Sociodrama

Persons who are full and active members of a group or community can seldom derive an overview of the actual structure and activities of that group or community. These persons are too well entrenched in their own roles to place themselves at the necessary angles for understanding others' perspectives or the overall group entity—they "can't see the forest for the trees." The sociometric and sociodramatic techniques developed by J. L. Moreno in the first half of this century aid participants in viewing their own social units from a variety of perspectives, and thereby enable them to see which choices they have for improving these units. This is accomplished by turning up the volume of social structure and process, in sociometry through graphic representations, and in sociodrama through dramatic representations.

SOCIOMETRY

Sociometry is a series of techniques for determining the *emotional structure* of groups and the relationship of group members to one another. Group members are asked their positive, negative, and neutral feelings toward others in the group. The collection of responses are then diagrammed in some manner to reveal the actual meaningful structure of the group. These diagrams provide the individual group members with an understanding of their own position in the group: who are attracted to them and in which ways; who are these persons, in turn, attracted and attractive to; how do their reactions to major figures in the group relate to others' reactions; what is the extent of their connections within the group relative to the minimum and maximum number of connections others have developed; and so forth.

For the group as a whole, the sociometric diagrams provide knowledge of the living structure of the group. Are the formal leaders the true chosen leaders? Are most members generally connected to one another throughout the group, or is the group divided into subgroups of a few persons each? Are many persons generally isolated or alienated from the group?

As therapy, these sorts of questions may be converted by the clinician into ones which allow members to consider changes in the group. Who *should* be the formal leaders? Do we really want to be a single group, or *should* we split up? How can attractions within the group change to bring the isolates back?

The *sociograms* for a group provide its members with more realistic understandings of their own creations. For instance, several types of leaders may be identified by sociograms: the key individual (with a large network of supporting others); the aristocratic leader (with only some supporting key members); the autocrat (with little support but great abilities at manipulation); or the hater (with power deriving from the ability to rally negative feelings within segments of the group).[1] Similarly, the *emotional stratification* within the group may be of a variety of types: top heavy (most attention is directed toward a few leaders); even (most persons receive fairly equal numbers of choices); or unequal (some receive much attraction, some receive a little attraction, and some receive virtually no attraction).

The basic form of a sociometric test to be administered in clinical use may be seen in the following sample. The specific questions will be determined by the diagnosis the clinician has performed, and those above are only the most general. Thus, in cases of goal or value conflicts the clinician may ask questions of the variety, "The persons I would agree with are . . ."

Once the answers have been received, the clinician must tally the results and draw the sociograms. It is usually constructive to draw several sociograms; e.g., a friendship sociogram (based upon answers to the friendship question); a leadership sociogram (based upon answers to the leadership question); a negative sociogram (based on answers to

Your Name _____

Date _____

    Please write out the names of those persons within your group or organization whom you would choose under the circumstances indicated. You may choose a person for more than one relationship, and you should keep in mind all members of the group (including those absent today). Choose as few or as many persons as you desire for each relationship.

The persons I would choose to be close friends are:

The persons I would choose to work with are:

The persons I would choose as leaders are:

The persons I would choose as recreational companions are:

The persons I would choose *not* to have as members of the group are:

the rejection question); and one or more combined sociograms (based on sums of favorable choices, subtracting for negative choices). Comparisons of sociograms then reveal the various and simultaneous structures and processes in the group.

The simplified sociogram that follows is based upon the tally sheet in table 14-1. This sociogram is for a hypothetical community organization made up of five Anglo-Americans and five Puerto Rican-Americans. The sociogram is of their leadership preferences within the group.

The tally sheet divides the group into Anglos and Puertos and computes the number of one-way and mutual choices each member gets within his or her own ethnicity from members of the other ethnicity, and then summed. Other sociograms and other tallies might have been constructed which divide according to sex rather than ethnicity, if that was the relevant concern. Or a more complex sociogram and tally might have been devised which divided into quarters, displaying both ethnic and sex cleavages in the organization.

The tally and sociogram indicate quite a bit about feelings for leadership in the group:

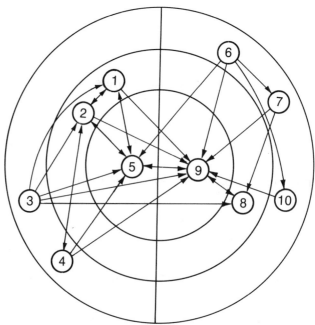

inner circle = 6 through 9 choices
second circle = 2 through 5 choices
outer circle = 0 or 1 choice

Table 14-1

TALLY SHEET FOR LEADERSHIP SOCIOGRAM

PERSONS CHOSEN

Persons Choosing		No.	1	2	3	4	5	6	7	8	9	10
Anglos	Jack	1		X			X				x	
	Claude	2	X			x	X				x	
	Barbara	3	x	x			x			x	x	
	James	4		X			x				x	
	Beth	5	X	X								
Puertos	Jose	6					x		x		x	x
	Mary	7								x	x	
	Juan	8									X	
	Julius	9					x			X		
	Anabel	10									x	
No. of Choices Received	se		3	4	0	1	4	0	1	2	4	1
	de		0	0	0	0	2	0	0	1	4	0
total			3	4	0	1	6	0	1	3	8	1
No. of Mutual Choices	se		2	3	0	1	2	0	0	1	1	0
	de		0	0	0	0	0	0	0	0	0	0
total			2	3	0	1	2	0	0	1	1	0

se = same ethnicity
de = different ethnicity
X = mutual choice

1.   One major Anglo leader (Beth) and one Puerto leader (Julius) clearly emerge. More attraction seems to go toward Julius, but both Beth and Julius see only two others in the group as potential leaders.
2.   Beth is not attracted to Julius as a leader, though Julius is attracted to Beth as a leader.
3.   Julius's strength comes from widespread support throughout both ethnicities, while Beth's is generally limited to support from within her own ethnic group. On the basis of these three comments, then, Julius would seem a more viable leader overall, especially since he apparently respects Beth's leadership within her own ethnicity. Further support for this conclusion would be needed, however, from friendship and work sociograms.
4.   Barbara and Jose are the major leadership isolates, as demonstrated by the fact that they find several people to choose as leaders, but are not attractive to anyone themselves. Their isolation may mean that they feel

a need to rely upon several others in the group but are unable to recip-
rocate. This could well be creating group and group member problems,
since sociometric research has regularly indicated that persons who
choose others are usually chosen in return, and it may well be that
Barbara and Jose have developed a pattern of choosing persons who
demean their leadership potential.
5.   The Anglos turn to one another in relatively high numbers, that is,
leadership is spread throughout them. The Puertos generally turn only
to one or two others within their group for leadership.

Clinical Uses and Dangers

A clinician might turn such analyses into therapy by presenting the
findings to the entire group for discussion, or for development of desired restructuring of the group. Sociometry can be quite useful for
dealing with diagnoses such as inadequate means to desired ends,
alienation within groups, inadequate leadership, communication
breakdown between subgroups, and larger issues of group or community organization. Knowledge of desired choices can often lead to improved actual choices.

Perhaps the best known uses of sociometry are early ones by Moreno
himself in his studies of educational institutions and entire communities. In these works he developed some quite sophisticated
strategies for computing sociometric scores and drawing the sociograms.[2] A danger in therapeutic usage of sociometric tests is that they
may increase tensions. Pointing out attractions may make persons uneasy or upset with one another or further entrench the opinions and
fears that members have. In addition, it may force too much attention
inside the group, when real therapy requires changed processes between the group and those external to it. Sociograms can attend to only
one unit at a time, and sampling limitations may push the clinician to
choose a smaller unit than is appropriate to the needs for therapy. When
sociometry is part of a more elaborated therapy plan, however, these
difficulties may be avoided. Sociometry has often been used therapeuti-
cally as part of the "warm up" process in sociodrama and psychodrama.

SOCIODRAMA

The living space of reality is often narrow and restraining, [the
client] may easily lose his equilibrium. On the stage he may

find it again due to its methodology of freedom—freedom
from unbearable stress and freedom for experience and expression. The stage space is an extension of life beyond the reality
tests of life itself. Reality and fantasy are not in conflict, but both
functions within a wider sphere. . . .[3]

We have seen throughout this book, beginning with discussions in
chapter 3 of dramaturgical theory, that persons and groups take their
everyday reality and roles for real. Through sociodramatic techniques
these realities are reenacted as stage productions, enabling those
involved to determine which parts of reality they wish to keep and
which they can and desire to change. Upon the sociodramatic stage,
experimentation with reality can be safe and creative.

The tools required for a sociodrama are a stage, one or more clients, a
director, a staff of aides ("auxiliary egos"), and the audience. In clinical
work, the only difficult item to obtain might be the stage, which should
be circular and include two or three levels (representing the vertical
dimension of problems and the possibility of mobility). Clinicians who
become trained psychodrama directors and use this therapeutic
technique regularly might build a stage at their offices or at a local
meeting place. Sociodramas can be performed without a stage, however, simply by setting off a large area and having the audience sit
around this space.

The clinician will usually serve as director, along with some group
members or professional assistants who have been trained to play auxiliary roles. In other cases, however, the aides may be nontrained members of the audience, whom the clinician directs in the necessary actions. The audience will be the group itself in those cases where the
clinician's client is a group. When the client is a group member the
clinician will need to find audience members elsewhere, either other
clients or interested members of the community.

The sociodrama begins with a "warm-up" period during which the
director discusses sociodrama and perhaps demonstrates a few of the
techniques via short "scenes." After the audience is fairly comfortable,
a *protagonist* emerges either voluntarily or upon selection by the director or the group. This person, a man say, is asked to be himself in a
certain social role. This may take two forms: either the protagonist
epitomizes a role he plays in everyday life (father, job seeker, etc.) or he
personifies and speaks as an entire group ("the black man in Atlanta,"
"the Irish Republican Army"). Therapy for group members will usually

call for the former, while therapy for groups will usually require the latter.

The action phase of the sociodrama then ensues and always takes place in the here and now, even if the events being enacted are 50 years past and some of the characters are living in other parts of the world. Among many procedures which may be employed in this phase are the following:[4]

Spontaneity Training

In important respects all of the sociodramatic procedures are forms of spontaneity training. A major goal of sociodrama is to bring out in clients their capacities to deal with spontaneously arising situations in spontaneous ways.

"When God created the world He started off by making every being a machine," Moreno remarked. "He made one machine push the other and the whole universe ran like a machine. That seemed to be comfortable, safe and smooth. But then He thought it over. He smiled and put just an ounce of spontaneity into each of the machines and that has made for endless trouble ever since—and for endless enjoyment." [5]

It is important to distinguish the sociodramatist's view of spontaneity from some others, however. Some views equate spontaneity with anarchy, or all people doing whatever their immediate impulses encourage them to do. This is exactly the opposite of what psychodramatists and sociodramatists want when they speak of spontaneity. Our first impulses in reaction to any situation are usually not very spontaneous at all, but rather are the responses which have been programmed into us since childhood. What so many persons have forgotten (or never learned) is how to *create* and *choose* responses according to what would be appropriate and effective in the actual immediate situation.

Sometimes a group will need an entire session devoted to spontaneity training. Other times the sociodrama director will build spontaneity training into sociodramas that center on other issues. A variety of situations are useful for spontaneity training:

Director: "You are alone at home, in bed asleep. Suddenly you smell smoke. Show us immediately, without thinking, what you do." After this is accomplished the director may change the situation as follows: "You are at home in the kitchen. Your infant daughter is upstairs asleep. You smell smoke." Two or three additional scenarios may also be presented in rapid succession.

Another variety of spontaneity training changes the role rather than he environmental conditions: "You are a fireman who smells the smoke," or "You are a paraplegic and you smell the smoke," or "You are furious with the infant and you smell the smoke."

Soliloquy

Persons often find that they talk to themselves. The sociodramatist uses this ability to increase insights by persons about the thoughts that emerge from their social roles. In the course of the drama the therapist-director asks patients to think out loud what they are saying to themselves:

> I hate these kids. I could never tell that to anybody because it sounds so awful, but I really hate them running around bothering me all morning. Why can't I just sit in this chair and watch the football game like my bachelor friends instead of being bothered every few minutes by these kids? The only reason my wife goes shopping on Saturdays is to force me to take care of the kids. . . .

Therapeutic Soliloquy

Soliloquy can also be used with more than one person, to bridge gaps between them. It permits persons to hear the thoughts of one another and to share some of the feelings that accompany these thoughts but usually go unattended:

> The patient and his wife are both present; they portray the scene which, according to him, propelled him to propose to her two years earlier. They are in a boat, he is holding the line while she is baiting the hooks for him. His expression is one of complete bliss, he is quite obviously happy. He cannot see her facial expression, for she is seated at the very end, half turned away from him, looking completely miserable. The patient takes a deep breath, says out loud: "Oh what a beautiful day. Weren't we lucky the weather held out for this trip, Marlene?" Marlene responds non-committally: "Hm, hm." The director instructs each one to soliloquize at this point. The patient: "I'm so glad I thought of taking her fishing. It's a good thing for us to do things together, to share each other's pleasures. I wonder if I will have the courage to ask her to marry me this evening? I do love her

and we get along so well. We have similar goals and interests. I
hope she will say yes. Now's a good time to ask her, after such a
peaceful, blissful day." Marlene: "My God," she blurts out,
"this is a revolting job to give me. I should have refused to do it
when he asked me. It's my first experience at fishing, and it's
going to be my last, too. Imagine his nerve to make me do this!"
At the sound of her words—to which he is not permitted to
respond in the soliloquy situation—the patient looks up as-
tounded and falling out of the role, he states, "Good Lord, if I
had known she felt that way about it, I'd never have dared
to propose to her that evening." [6]

The technique also permits corrections between the parties when one
member perceives inaccuracies. Sometimes the soliloquy will be halted
with the exclamation, "No, it wasn't that way at all!" Different perceptions of the same experience are important in sociodrama; through such
corrections clients come to see that no person's perception of a social
situation is *the* correct perception, but each perception that is honest
and careful is *a* correct perception.

Auxiliary Ego

The most common usage of trained assistants in sociodramas is as
auxiliary egos, persons playing the parts of missing parties in a sociodramatic scene. For instance, a protagonist may be enacting an event
involving herself and her mother, but her mother is not present at the
sociodrama. It is necessary for all relevant persons to be enacted during
the sociodrama. Consequently the patient (or the director) will appoint
a member of the audience or a trained assistant to play the part of the
mother, largely according to the ways in which the protagonist describes the mother having behaved. Persons serving as auxiliary egos
become actors who represent absentee persons as they appear in the
world of the protagonist.

Instead of discussing with the protagonist her subjective experiences,
the auxiliary ego enacts these experiences and thereby permits the protagonist on the stage to see what she previously saw only in her mind.
In general, the protagonist is encouraged to correct the auxiliary ego
when the auxiliary is playing the role in ways different than the protagonist's perception of the role.

The following two procedures are special applications of the use of
auxiliary egos.

Double   The protagonist portrays him or herself, while the auxiliary
go is asked to act like the protagonist and to fill in the gaps of the
protagonist's performance:

> The patient [protagonist] is preparing to get up in the morning; he
> is in bed. The auxiliary ego lies down on the stage alongside of
> him, taking the same bodily posture. The double may start
> speaking: "What is the use of waking up? I have nothing to live
> for." Patient: "Yes, that is true, I have no reason for living."
> Auxiliary ego: "But I am a very talented artist, there have been
> times when life has been very satisfying." Patient: "Yes, but it
> seems a long time ago." Auxiliary ego: "Maybe I can get up and
> start to paint again." Patient: "Well, let's try and get up first,
> anyway, and see what will happen." Both patient and aux-
> iliary ego get up, go through the motions of washing, shaving,
> brushing teeth, all along moving together as if they were one.
> The auxiliary ego becomes the link through which the patient
> may try to reach out into the real world.[7]

The protagonist may correct the double if there is inaccuracy, but pro-
essionally trained auxiliary egos are often so perceptive of pro-
agonist's thoughts and feelings that they need no correcting.

The double technique is sometimes expanded to include several dou-
les, each of whom portrays a part of the protagonist. One auxiliary ego
may act as the protagonist acts now, another as he or she will act in 10
years, and another as he or she will act in 50 years, while the pro-
agonist acts as he or she did as a child. Thus in a sociodrama with a
protagonist representing "white South Africans," we may have past,
present, and future white South Africans portrayed (and compared) on
he stage simultaneously.

Mirror   Another strategy which requires competent auxiliary egos is
used to assist protagonists who have difficulty presenting their group or
role. The auxiliary plays the protagonist and is addressed by others by
the protagonist's name. The auxiliary attempts to reproduce the protagonist's behavior and interactions with others. If necessary, the mirror may purposely distort or exaggerate in order to arouse the protagonist to correct the auxiliary or to represent him or herself. Thus, a
mirror for a group of powerless nurses may exaggerate their frightened

behavior by running and crying each time approached by someon€ playing a physician.

Role Reversal

Probably the most famous technique within sociodrama an(psychodrama is role reversal, whereby persons in interactional situa tions play one another. Persons are often amazed at their own abilitie₃ to take the role of someone with whom they are having misunder standings or other conflicts:

Black Women (playing White Women): The way you black women hav€ to run after your men just to keep them away from other women i₃ disgusting. It's like you all act like whores.

White Women (playing Black Women): It's not nearly so bad as yoυ little prissy honkeys sitting around all day with the soap opera₃ while your man has five different mistresses all over town anc comes home to you only for his supper and to beat you up before h€ falls asleep in front of the TV.

Future Projection

The protagonist looks and feels his or her possible future situation₃ by portraying them on the stage. The protagonist selects the time, place, and people with whom he or she expects to be involved at the tim€ explored. Through this method clients can improve their insights abou† goals and views of the future while experimenting with alternative courses open to them, as when a client plays the role of an entire farm- ing community:

Director: What important change would you like to see in your lives five years from now?

Farming Community: I would like to have decreased the average length of the work week for each of us.

Director: How?

Farming Community: Through government subsidies to buy better equipment.

Director: Let's look at that possibility. It is five years from now. You are on a typical farm. What's going on?

The sociodrama then commences at the location and time specified.

The Magic Shop

The director or an auxiliary ego plays the shopkeeper of a special store where valuable but nonphysical items can be obtained. The items are not for sale, they can be bought only through trade of other valuable nonphysical items. The technique encourages persons to evaluate the sacrifices they are willing to make for the values they want most:

Shopkeeper: Will each of you tell me the changes you desire most in each other?

Husband: I guess some of the important things I want from my wife are faithfulness and respect for me and my abilities.

Wife: I want my husband to be more forceful and assertive.

Shopkeeper: Let us begin with the negotiations. (To the husband:) What are you willing to exchange for this faithfulness and respect? Are you willing to give some assertiveness?

The partners then barter back and forth until they reach some agreement, or realize they cannot reach agreement concerning their needs. Often the outcome of negotiations in *The Magic Shop* is realization that what one wants is not nearly as valuable as what one would have to give up to get the desired item. Other times the parties come to realize that in exchange for some minor changes in values or behavior they can dispel recurring difficulties they have encountered.

USES AND DANGERS

J. L. Moreno's own uses of sociodrama and psychodrama were with groups and problems ranging from race riots to marital difficulties to a man who thought he was Hitler. Sociodrama is effective with the wide variety of sociological maladies that entail inadequate interactional or role patterns. To name a few:

1. Prejudice
2. Inability to deal with change
3. Inadequate leadership or division-of-labor allocations
4. Inappropriate use of types of time
5. Unfulfilling career patterns
6. Marital conflicts

In some cases, sociodrama serves more as immunology than as therapy. By experiencing problems and potential solutions in small safe doses on the sociodramatic stage, group members are encouraged to develop ways to deal with problems when they arise in real life.

The dangers of sociodrama arise from the possibility that attention may be directed toward ways of coping with existing social structures rather than fundamentally changing those which require change. Sociodramas concentrate upon social roles rather than social structures. On the other hand, it is human actors in their social roles who bring about social structural change, as Moreno recognizes in his critique of Freud:

> I did not think that a great healer and therapist would look and act the way . . . Freud did. I visualized the healer as a spontaneous-creative protagonist in the midst of the group.
> My concept of the physician as a healer, and that of theirs were far apart. To my mind persons like Jesus, Buddha, Socrates and Gandhi were doctors and healers; for Freud they were probably patients.[8]

POSTSCRIPT: A SOCIAL PAIN IN THE BACK

Sociodramatic and psychodramatic techniques were used by one of the authors in work with a client a few years ago. The following is an abbreviated case description:

> M. was a female college sophomore at a large university. Several of her friends requested that I "counsel" her because they were quite worried about her condition. I was a teaching assistant, and part of my duties included counseling. When I first met with M. she was in the student infirmary suffering from back pain. Each time she moved in bed or walked to the bathroom she experienced excruciating pain in her middle and lower back. Even when lying still in bed she felt some back pain.
>
> The physicians had conducted two full weeks of tests on M., including inspections by orthopedic and urinary specialists, as well as the medical director of the health center. A few days before I arrived the director had declared that nothing physiological caused M.'s perpetual discomfort, and consultations with a clinical psychologist had begun.

In my first meeting with M., I concentrated upon two goals: (1) development of rapport and friendship and (2) solicitation of a sociological history and current location for M. Accomplishing the first task proved surprisingly easy. M. was a talkative and likable person, and we got along beautifully in talking about some of M.'s friends who had been students in my classes, and joking about the food they had brought her for lunch. After the first few minutes, in fact, I began to wonder if M. was *too* nice and friendly, and perhaps using these ways of interacting in order to avoid being serious with me. But soon enough that fear vanished when she answered my casual questions about her classes. "I hate this place. I'm in the journalism school and have to work myself to death for a bunch of *idiots*," she practically spit at me. "The professors are all has-beens who don't know what they're doing. And the damned dorms are overcrowded. I live in a room the size of a prison cell." She jerked around in bed to point, angrily, out the window to her high-rise dormitory. After M. finished turning she let out a scream that must have carried throughout the corridor. I'd never seen such a physically small person (she was no taller than 5' 4") let out such a noise.

M. stopped screaming after five or six seconds, then lay on her back, whimpering, for a couple of minutes. Finally she turned her head to me and said in her earlier, smiling tone, "I'm sorry. It hurts like crazy whenever I move." For the rest of the hour-long visit, M. stayed in her talkative mood. I found out some sociological items: she's Catholic, from a white middle-class suburb of a large midwestern city, and her father is an upwardly mobile and energetic corporate scientist. She is a member of a variety of groups around the campus, including the student newspaper staff and two or three friendship circles. But the ones which seem to matter to her are her living-together relationship with a man, a friendship with her female roommate, and her membership in the journalism school. Our discussion about these was cordial.

I visited M. three times in the next ten or twelve days, for about an hour each time. Once or twice in each visit I got to hear that incredibly painful scream when she moved. My notes indicate that in each case the scream accompanied a different specific topic, but all of them were subdivisions of two major groups: (1) M.'s cohabitator threesome, and (2) M.'s family.

Below are listed the approximate utterances which directly preceded the pain, along with some details which came out about these during the more peaceful discussions and during my questioning of her significant others:

1. "You can't imagine the pressures in that tiny room." M., her assigned female roommate, and M.'s boyfriend all live in a dorm room the size of a single in most other universities with which I have been familiar. My visit revealed a room just large enough for two single beds, two desks, two chests, and a single-file aisle to walk between these items. In addition, the occupants had placed brick-and-wood bookshelves, a stereo system, and M.'s roommate's cat (complete with litter box).

M.'s boyfriend was a premedical student, also a sophomore, but attempting to finish undergraduate work in three years and gain admission to a prestigious medical college. He had little time to talk with me (and according to others, with anybody), as he spent 14 to 16 hours a day in a corner of the library. Of M.'s current problems he commented, "I hope you can do something about it. You know, doctors can only treat real diseases, so there's not much they can do for her." He seemed to approach the world with the same disdain as M. during her angry phases, but his anger showed more in his posture of *resolve* in his studies than in his words or other actions. His position toward M. seemed multi-sided, the central dimensions of which came out in sentences I made sure to write down after talking with him: "She is the artist type. I feel sorry for her. It's hard being an artist in a world that won't let you. But it's hard doing what I do, too, and the difference between M. and me is that I keep myself under control. She doesn't keep herself together."

The female roommate was somewhat shy and obviously quite concerned about the overall situation. In response to a question about how she liked the living arrangement she said, "It's a little crowded, but I like having a lot of people around. Otherwise I feel lonely." The roommate repeated several times in the conversation that she wanted to be "closer friends with M." She offered stories of her attempts to have close conversations with M. and her inability to do so. (M., too, expressed the desire to become closer with her roommate, but confusion about why they were unable and a feeling that they were both "trying too hard.") The roommate felt uneasy sleeping in the same room with M. and M.'s boyfriend when they were fighting or "acting like they wanted to have sex." Occasionally she stayed with female friends down the hall.

2. "I *detest* talking to my parents," and "To hell with those courses." M. said her father talks to her mostly about money matters, either concerning his own job ambitions or M.'s. M. is the youngest of two girls, and the older is a housewife with two children. M.'s mother has been "deeply depressed" since M. left home. M. and her mother apparently were never especially good friends, their interactions having been limited to her mother helping her with school work, driving lessons and so forth, and M. helping her mother locate community-service and club activities outside the home.

Much of the conversation lately from M.'s father has concerned his worry that jobs in journalism are difficult to find, and M.'s replies that she's not certain she wants a career in journalism in any event.

3. "The whole world's depressing," and "Why am I rotting like this?" In addition to the depression of M.'s mother, M. has experienced several others in the past year including a couple of significant ones: (1) the only journalism professor M. admires has been depressed and confided in M. that at age 45 he has "finally figured out that journalists can't save society and usually only make it worse." He listed a variety of cases in which journalists invaded personal privacy, distorted their reports to suit editors or advertisers, reported government statistics or press releases nearly verbatim, and so forth; and (2) M. had been depressed "at least a couple of hours each day" herself. She claims that her depression does not concern anything specific. "That's what makes it so unbearable, I just sit around being sad about *everything.*"

Diagnosis

M.'s social worlds are putting *real and painful jabs* into her: those of her boyfriend's work and his feelings that M. should "get herself together"; impending adult responsibilities to provide for oneself and concurrent disillusionment with her chosen occupation, coupled with stress from her father to "make it" and implicitly from her mother to avoid a housewife career; from and toward her roommate to develop a closer friendship; the crowded living spaces; and so forth.

People have three choices under such conditions: adapt to them, change them, or avoid them. The question for the clinician in dealing with the immediate problem of back pain is to determine which of these is being taken, and in which forms. Obviously, M. is not avoiding or changing things, but rather is adapting, but in a very particular way. How is the back pain an adaptation? On first glance it seems more like refusing to adapt. But this usually takes the form of avoidance, which M. is not doing, as indicated by her confrontations with the topics in casual discussion and with deep feeling just prior to the terrible back pains. Her only obvious escapes were the depression periods, and it's not even clear that she really avoided anything during *those* times.

It is in that pattern of pain and depression that the diagnosis is to be found. *Pain is a concretization of something that is wrong.* If the physiological diagnoses are correct, then M.'s pain is the concretization of something nonorganic that is wrong. She is exhibiting very little psyche difficulty, but much difficulty in her socius; her social world is throwing jabs at her. The apparent psyche problem—depression—fits into this as well. Here is a bright, self-assured woman who has suddenly been made to believe that she is powerless to fight the various groups and structures which jab at her. Depression is itself concretized powerlessness.

Therapy

The immediate therapy needed to deal with the back pain. The task was to devise a technique whereby she could obtain concretized power to fight off this concretized pain. A long-run strategy was necessary as well, which would begin to restructure her social worlds in ways which would allow M. to regain her power over those worlds.

During a discussion with M., I moved her gradually into a sociodrama/psychodrama. This was accomplished by a warm-up in which M. was led to discuss in more depth than before the actual pain she was experiencing. I asked questions such as: Exactly where does it hurt? Does it feel like any other pain I may have had in the past? Could you press on my back to make me feel what the pain is like?

Once the descriptions of the pain were vivid in both of our minds I asked M. to participate in an "experiment" with me. I then took the chair in her infirmary room, placed it beside the bed, and asked M. to sit up, which she did. The following is a much abbreviated reconstruction of the 70-minute exchange which followed (this could not have been recorded unobtrusively):

Therapist: We're going to make that pain be right here in front of us, sitting in this chair. Can you see it?

M: No. I don't know what you mean.

T: OK. Anything sitting in this chair is your back pain. By putting it out here like that we can work with it. Let's start by having you sit here. (M. moves slowly from bed to chair.) Now what are you?

M: (giggling) I'm the pain.

T: Describe what you look like.

M: Mean . . . and big.

T: Bigger than M.?

M: Yes. Several inches bigger.

T: How are you "mean"?

M: I do disgusting things . . . I hurt M. all the time.

T: What exactly do you do?

M: Well, I make her ache all the time. . . .

T: How?

M: By squeezing her back up and kind of twisting it around.

T: Show with your hand how you do this.

(This continues for several minutes: "the pain" shows in detail her methods of operation.)

T: How did you manage to get inside of M.?

M: She let me in somehow. I'm not sure how.

T: OK, now move back up on the bed and be M. again. (She does so.) On what day did the pain arrive?

M: February 18 was the first day I noticed it.

T: What were you doing?

M: I was sitting in the library, feeling very depressed.

T: Show me what that looked like. (M. sits in a hunched over position, nearly crying.) Now show me what happened when the pain arrived. (M. presses on her back, then gets a pained expression on her face.) OK. Now switch back to the chair, and you are the pain again. (She does so.) Tell me, pain, what do you think of M.?

M: I detest her. . . . She's a pain to me. (M. realizes what she said, and laughs.) . . . She's boring.

T: I didn't know that pains could have feelings like hate?

M: *I* can. . . .

T: Tell us more about yourself. What do you look like?

M: I don't know. I don't look like anything, because I'm not visible.

T: That must be convenient sometimes.

M: Sure. Nobody can mess with me.

T: But if you're not visible, how do you exist?

M: In M.'s back.

T: In what form?

M: Just as a kind of force or something.

T: An invisible force, eh? Who sent you?

M: I sent myself.

T: Let's change back again. (M. returns to the bed.) The pain said it sent itself. Do you believe that?

M: Not really, but I don't know where it came from.

T: When you look at it, sitting in that chair, what does it look like? Look at the chair and try to see it, M.

M: It's hard to see . . . . It's big and has faces.

T: Faces?

M: Yes, it's a big wad of faces . . . and some hands.

T: Can you make out any of them?

M: No. None are distinct. They just look like general human faces and hands. Like anybody's.

T: How do you feel when you look at them?

M: Scared.

T: OK, switch back. (She does.) Pain, M. says you look like a bunch of faces. What do you say about that?

M: She better stop messing around. It's time for me to hurt her again.

T: You don't like being seen, do you?

M: No, I don't.

T: Can you make out any of your own faces? Walk over to this mirror and try. (T. walks M. to the mirror on the other side of the room. M. stares intently for a couple of minutes.)

M: I look like M. . . .

T: But you are made up of several faces, aren't you?

M: Yes, but they are all variations of M.

T: What do these variations look like?

M: (long pause) They don't look like anything really. Sometimes there are parts of other people's faces mixed in.

T: Like whom?

M: Like the president of the United States . . . like M.'s boyfriend . . . like M.'s father when he was a child in his baby pictures on the mantel.

T: How do you like the way you look?

M: I don't know. . . . Not too well.

T: All right. Let's go back to your seat. (They do so.) Pain, is there anything you want to say to M.?

M: M., you are a royal pain. (She giggles again.)

T: You don't say it like you mean it.

M: (without laughing or any affect) I mean it. She's a pain.

T: Then *tell* her.

M: (same monotone) You're a pain.

T: Scream it at her.

M: (a bit louder) You're a pain.

T: Louder.

    (This continues until "the pain" is yelling at M. almost as loudly as she yelled in previous days when pained.)

T: OK, switch roles again. (She does.) Now M., what do you have to say back?

M: (quietly) Just that the pain is a pain too.

T: Louder.

    (The same process ensues, until M. is screaming at the pain. T. has her switch again, but this time to the chair in a different location in the room.)

T: We found out that the pain is made up of features from a bunch of people. Let's have some of these people. The first was the president of the United States. You be the president. Sit in this chair and tell us what the president wants to convey to M.

M: Listen, M., I run this country. . . .

T: Is that all you have to say?

M: I run it and I'm going to make sure that you never get anywhere in it.

T: How will you do this?

M: By keeping you miserable. You will never find a job you like.

T: How can you make sure of that?

M: By keeping you down. You'll see that every job is terrible and stop trying to get one.

T: Is *your* job terrible?

M: No, I'm the president. But M.'s will be.

    (This discussion continues for several minutes.)

T: Now let's move the chair a bit, and you be your boyfriend. (She does so.) What do you think of M.?

M: I care about her a lot. But she's a mess, and I don't want to put up with a mess.

    (T. questions the "boyfriend" at length about the ways in which M. is a mess and how he handles the situation, which is explained to be by encouraging M. to improve. Next the father as a young man is presented. He describes himself in some detail. Then the sociodrama proceeds as follows.)

T: Tell me, father, are you going to have children?

M: Yes, in a few years. Two girls (a slight laugh).

T: What will you do while they are growing up?

M: Same thing I do now, improve myself. I'm from a poor family, and my kids aren't going to be from a poor family.

T: How will you prevent that?

M: By working hard and becoming an executive with my company. (Details of his procedures for accomplishing this then follow.)

T: OK, and after you have accomplished this, how will you feel?

M: Great. I'll feel great. Honestly, I will.

T: And what will you want for your daughter, the one named M.?

M: Happiness . . . I'll love her very much.

T: What kind of happiness?

M: Every kind. I know what you're getting at. But it's not true. I want her to be happy with herself, and with us, *and* to have material things.

T: OK, now we need the pain to be back in the chair. (T. moves chair back to original location.) Now you return to the bed and be M. again. (She does so.) Look at that chair and get a good clear vision of the pain. What can you do about it?

M: I don't know.

T: Who *would* know?

M: I can't say.

T: Perhaps the pain would?

M: Maybe.

T: Switch back then. You be the pain. How can M. get rid of you?

M: Just get tired of me and I'll go away.

T: Switch back. What do you say to the pain's suggestion?

M: I don't believe it.

T: OK, let's test it out.

(T. then simulates the pain as it has been described by M. He sits behind her and hits with both hands at the middle and bottom of her back.)

M: It's not going away.

T: Is it saying anything?   `

M: Yeah, it's laughing at me.

(T. then increases the force of the hitting and begins laughing at M. Several minutes pass.)

M: Now my back is hurting from you *and* from itself. This is torture.

(T. increases both the hitting and the laughter, M. attempts to push him away and gradually begins crying, then screaming with pain.)

T: (still hitting and laughing). You make me sick, M.

M: You're making me *actually* sick. Go away! Go away!

> (M. pushes T. harder and harder, until he falls on the floor beside the bed.)

T: Quickly switch with me. You be on the floor; be the pain. (She does so.) How do you feel?

M: Hurt. M. just hurt me.

T: Now quickly switch back. (She does.) The pain is hurt.

M: But he's still here, damn him. Can I kill him?

T: Ask him that.

M: Can I kill you? (She switches to the floor and responds:) No, you're a big baby. You couldn't kill a flea.

T: Switch back. (She does.) Well, what do you say to that?

M: Go to hell.

T: What?

M: (louder) Go to hell.

T: What?

M: (louder) Go to hell! Go to hell! Go to hell! (M. begins to weep on her pillow, then suddenly picks it up and bangs it 15 or 20 times against the floor at the location of the pain. She stops and weeps. T. holds her in his arms for nearly thirty minutes, after which they discuss the feelings they both experienced during the sociodrama. T. relates his fear that this sociodrama would increase the pain or create other problems. M. talks about how it felt to play each of the parts.)

In the couple of months after this session I checked periodically with M., and the pain never returned. The sociodrama was in many regards only the beginning of the therapy, however.

M. was a very unusual case in two key regards: (1) only one major sociodrama session was required to deal with the immediate difficulty, and (2) she had previously been a quite successful and self-directing person. As a result of the second condition, it turned out that once the pain was gone she literally acted like "a new person" (or more accurately, like her old social self). Within a week her boyfriend and her roommate's cat had moved out (though the relationship with the boyfriend continued under other structural conditions).

The only real needs M. had for the clinician was in restructuring the social worlds of her nuclear family and work. The former case was accomplished in part through additional sociodramas, and in part through accompanying M. and her parents at dinner when they were visiting the university. At that time I discussed with M.'s parents the tremendous drive and skills M. displayed, and the confusing job market for young people in nearly all occupations at present. Some statistics on jobs were helpful in that discussion.

M.'s own difficulties with her chosen profession were not effectively encountered during my period of interactions with M. We lost contact when M. transferred to another university. In retrospect, I see that for both the family and work relationships other techniques also should have been attempted, perhaps of peer counseling or the construction of self-help groups.

Social pain is a topic which warrants far more investigation than currently exists in the literature. In his excellent book on the subject, Thomas Szasz notes the core of the problem among helping services practitioners:

> One wonders if the terminology (and philosophy) of mathematics has not had an influence on medical matters relative to this issue of "real" and "imaginary" pains. In mathematics, of course, we speak of real and imaginary numbers. Today this no longer means to the mathematician that so-called imaginary numbers are any more or less "real" than so-called real numbers. However, when imaginary numbers were first discovered the situation was probably different, in that real numbers were felt to bear some transcendental relationship to "physical reality"; in contrast to this, imaginary numbers must have seemed as man-made, and thus not quite "real." The error of such a distinction, illustrated in this example by the terms "real" vs. "imaginary," is now a part of the history of scientific philosophy.[9]

NOTES

1. J. L. Moreno and Z. Moreno, "A Sociometric View of Recent History," *Group Psychotherapy, Psychodrama and Sociometry* 29(1976):64.

2. J. L. Moreno, *Who Shall Survive?* (Beacon, N.Y.: Beacon House, 1953).

3. J. L. Moreno, *Psychodrama and Group Psychotherapy* (Beacon, N.Y.: Beacon House, undated).

4. These are from Zerka Moreno, *A Survey of Psychodramatic Techniques* (Beacon, N.Y.: Beacon House, 1975), monograph no. 44; Z. Moreno, *Psychodramatic Rules, Techniques and Adjunctive Methods* (Beacon, N.Y.: Beacon House, 1966), monograph no. 41; and J. L. Moreno, *Psychodrama*, vols. I, II, and III (Beacon, N.Y.: Beacon House, 1972 and 1975).

5. J. L. Moreno, *Preludes to My Autobiography* (Beacon, N.Y.: Beacon House, 1955), p. 9.

6. Moreno, monograph no. 44:2.

7. Ibid., monograph no. 41.

8. Moreno, *Preludes*, p. 19.

9. Thomas Szasz, *Pain and Pleasure* (New York: Basic Books, 1975), p. 89.

THE CLINICIAN'S LIBRARY

Most major books on sociometry, sociodrama, and psychodrama are published by the Moreno Institute (Beacon, New York). The most influential are the following:

Moreno, J. L. *Psychodrama*, volumes I, II, and III. Beacon, N.Y.: Beacon House, 1972 and 1975.
Moreno, J. L. *Who Shall Survive?* Beacon, N.Y.: Beacon House, 1953.

Other authors have written books describing these practices. Among the best:

Haskell, Martin. *Socioanalysis*. Long Beach, Cal.: Role Training Associates, 1975.
Yablonsky, Lewis. *Psychodrama*. New York: Basic Books, 1976.

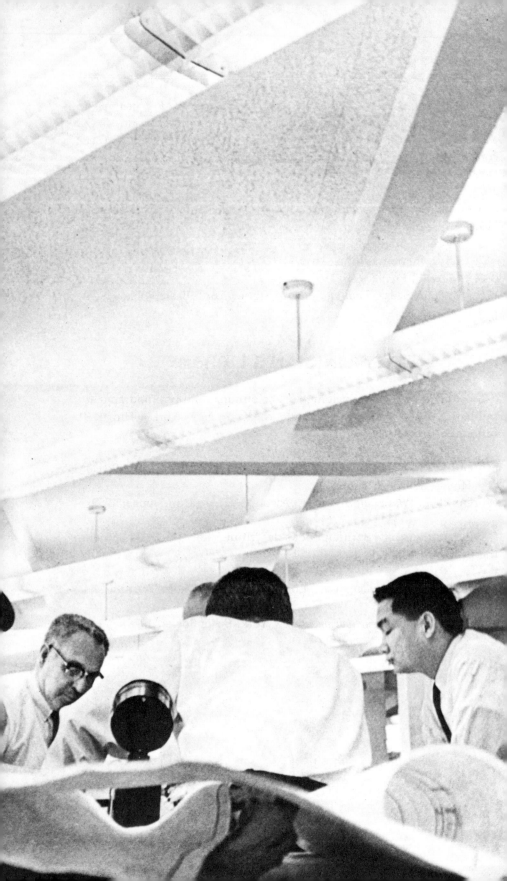

Chapter 15

Working with Organizations

It is likely that the clinical sociologist will be working from an organizational base. She or he could be an organization consultant, hold a position at some level of bureaucracy, or intervene in disputes between organizations. Much has been written about the structure and functions of organizations, and there is considerable sociological organizational theory. This material is listed in the Clinician's Library section. Our major goal in this chapter is that of practical advice for persons working in organizations: how to change them and survive in them.

Organizations are compromises. They meet no individual's needs fully. Even the person at the top usually feels frustration. Organizations can be efficient, but usually cannot maintain a high level of efficiency over a long period. Organizations can be quite understanding of the human condition, but usually they fall far short of reflecting human concerns. Organizations can appear quite rational, yet usually this is a veneer which covers great irrationality.

In chapter 2 we presented a model that placed worker, agency, and client within a community and societal context. One part of that model is relevant now:

Every person in most organizations has a describable job. Sometimes, the job description is written and readily available; at other

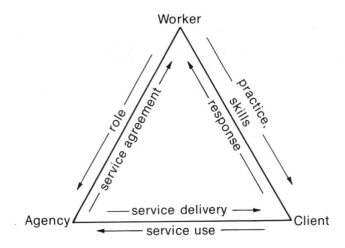

times, it occurs verbally. All too frequently the job description remains in the boss's head and other persons have to try to second-guess what the boss is expecting.

Every person in an organization plays a role in relationship to the job description, whether this is stated or unstated. The role can be integral to the basic operation and success of the organization or it can be window-dressing. For example, sexism still pervades many organizations, and a female window-dressing role might be to look pretty, answer the telephone, type poorly, and be available to sleep with the executives. Visible minority members and pushed-upstairs executives with no work to do are other forms of window-dressing.

Whatever the role and job description, recognize that these take place within a community and societal context. The most important community for the worker is the organizational community. It is here that the range of acceptable organizational behavior is determined. Because of the importance of the organization for survival—paychecks are important—the organization affects other community activities. It is desirable (often mandatory) for executives to live in certain areas (frequently to the east of the work locale so that the sun is at their back when commuting, some hypothesize), shop in certain stores, marry an acceptable spouse, be seen only with certain kinds of people, drive a car of appropriate status, even drink in cocktail lounges frequented by others like him or her. The wage worker settles in different areas, and so forth, so that we see that organizational stratification carries over into formal and informal elements of community life.

Societal standards place emphasis on the need for work and belong-ingness as basic components of identity. When one is unemployed, there are identity problems. Work is valued and organizations are the channels through which work is given its social meaning.

Roles and job descriptions also create a stratified hierarchy within the organization. Formal organizations usually have organizational charts in which each layer of the hierarchy is presented with clear lines of authority. However, more critical to effective organizational function-ing is the informal social organization. How others view you informally is a key factor in organizational effectiveness. Informal structure can be quite different from the organizational chart. Certain persons at fairly low pay levels can be important gatekeepers. Others, because of their popular position with numbers of staff, must be consulted before any action is taken. One learns from practical experience who can be effec-tive in pushing a proposal, who is the kiss of death, who is unimpor-tant.

LEADERSHIP

A study by Alvin Gouldner illustrates that earned, informal power may be more effective than ascribed, formal power.[1] In his study of a gypsum plant, two styles of leadership were studied—democratic and authoritarian. When an authoritarian style was present, resentment and apathy resulted, and workers used rules to excuse their lack of effort, while under more democratic leadership the workers were mostly self-regulating. The right to lead others is usually awarded by those others on the basis of legitimacy, or feelings that the leader is worth following.

Douglas McGregor distinguishes two sets of assumptions that under-line managerial decision-making, theory X and theory Y.

Theory X managers act on the following assumptions:

1. The average human being has an inherent dislike of work and will avoid it if he or she can.
2. Because of the human characteristic of dislike for work, most people must be coerced, controlled, directed, and threatened with punishment to get them to put forth adequate effort toward the achievement of organization objectives.
3. The average human being prefers to be directed, wishes to avoid responsibility, has relatively little ambition, wants security above all.[2]

Theory Y managers operate from a different set of assumptions:

1. The expenditure of physical and mental effort in work is as natural as play or rest.
2. External control and the threat of punishment are not the only means for bringing about effort toward organizational objectives. Humans will exercise self-direction and self-control in the service of objectives to which they are committed.
3. Commitment to objectives is a function of the rewards associated with their achievement.
4. The average human being learns, under proper conditions, not only to accept but to seek responsibility.
5. The capacity to exercise a relatively high degree of imagination, ingenuity, and creativity in the solution of organizational problems is widely, not narrowly, distributed in the population.
6. Under the conditions of modern industrial life, the intellectual potentialities of the average human being are only partially utilized.[3]

Much organizational managerial effort takes place in creating and maintaining a theory Y environment. It is assumed that involving behavior by those in the organization is better than alienated behavior. Management is the key to making a theory Y organization. The good manager must neither be too authoritarian nor too democratic, too task oriented nor too staff oriented, too tight nor too loose.

There is a crisis in many organizations because the management style is either too theory X or is too nonmanagerial. Warren Bennis points out one factor that might be causing this crisis:

> It is the paradox of our times that precisely when the trust and credibility of leaders are at their lowest, when the beleaguered survivors in leadership positions feel unable to summon up the vestiges of power left to them, we most need people who can lead.[4]

This leadership gap turns organization into ritual and limits innovative responses to situations. When ritual overtakes an organization, everyone goes through the motions without being concerned about improving the conditions under which the task is accomplished. Organizations that become totally ritualized can last a long time before they die.

CHANGE FROM WITHIN

Critical to a clinical sociologist's effectiveness in improving an organization is the position in which the clinician operates within or outside the organization. When working within the organization (as a member), the clinician needs to develop a base of power and, concurrently, the respect and freedom that power brings. Some basic suggestions can assist the clinician in the early stages of designing programs for change within organizations. First, it is necessary to determine the *type* of organization in which you are working. Sociologists have effectively classified organizations in two ways, according to why people join and who benefits from the organization. Three basic types can be distinguished on the basis of why people join. First, *voluntary organizations* are those that persons join because they choose to do so and share the organization's goal. Most social clubs, political organizations, and religious groups meet this description. Second are *coercive organizations*, such as prisons and schools, which force people to join. Finally, *utilitarian organizations* attract members for practical reasons, as when persons choose to join a factory in order to earn money. Persons' relationships to the organizations will differ predictably according to the type of organization. Thus, a person will likely obey rules in voluntary associations most energetically if they seem to contribute to the well-being of the entire organization; but they obey coercive organizations primarily if they feel they will suffer punishments for not doing so; and rules in utilitarian organizations are obeyed principally if they seem to benefit the individual member (who, after all, joined specifically for individual rewards).[5]

On the basis of benefits derived, we can distinguish three additional categories of organizations: In *mutual benefit organizations* the goal is to improve all members' situations, as with grass-roots unions and community organizations. Organizations such as hospitals may be *client-centered organizations*, designed primarily for their clients (e.g., the patients). And third, *commonweal organizations* are operated for the general public, as with (ideally) police departments and government agencies.[6] Again, the self-conception of members of an organization will largely determine its operation. For instance, a police department that views itself as a commonweal organization will not be serving any one group in a community more than any other. But a police department which considers itself a client-centered organization may well favor certain groups over others, depending upon which groups it considers its clients (e.g., big business, the poor, a particular neighorhood).

The authors have found that several heuristic guidelines are helpful in actual research and diagnosis within organizations:

1. *Don't be impatient.* Many persons fresh to organizational life make a fatal assumption that the organization has been waiting all these many years for the person to arrive and change it within three months. Nothing could be further from the truth. There are hundreds of reasons and thousands of excuses put forward why organizations are not open to change-oriented hotshots. Staff committed to the long organization marathon (counting the years to retirement) have learned that they can outlast the new arrival, sabotage the new approaches to show that the change cannot possibly work, and revert to the old approach. Set a careful timetable and include a lot of time at the beginning to get to know the interpersonal territory.

2. *Find out how the organization really operates.* After studying the organizational chart, learn the informal organizational structure. Who are the gatekeepers (i.e., controllers of your access)? Who are the roadblocks? Who says all the right phrases and does nothing? Which leaders have earned the personal respect of the persons who work under them? Participant-observation approaches suggest ways of discovering the perspectives of key participants, and questionnaires may also be useful. Do not be surprised, however, when others try to place you in a single location within the organization (spy, coworker, supervisor, etc.), and when the ability to move freely between layers of the organization usually is not open to you. Be aware that sometimes there are persons quite marginal to the operation of the organization who are ready to enlist new organizational members as allies. Sometimes those who put down the welcome mat first are persons who have been so discredited by the powers in the organization that your affiliation with them is the kiss of death.

Sometimes overtures will be made to you because the organization is in the midst of conflict, and each side wants to recruit you to its position. Usually, the first few months in an organization is a honeymoon period, but it is also a probationary period. Be sure to do the tasks that are expected of you. First impressions last for years, and negative ones are difficult to overcome.

3. *Make friends.* Organizations frequently run through interpersonal work (and occasionally extracurricular) relationships. "Will you do me a

favor?" a call can begin. "Jack will do that. He owes me a favor." Sometimes information about what is to happen within the organization is at a premium, and it becomes necessary to use contacts to get inside information. Be careful not to get involved in the "favor" and information network in such a way that you become an object to be used, rather than a person to be respected.

4. *Keep confidences.* Do not tell everyone you know everything you know. For every truth floating through the informal organization there are ten rumors that sound like the truth. Both rumor and truth get distorted as they circulate.

5. *Don't believe it until you see it in your hand.* Promises are made in all good faith (and sometimes without it). Because the person who made the promise is in a position of authority, there is a tendency to believe; better to retain skepticism until the promise is actualized. We have seen persons wait for years for promotions that never materialize, all the time maintaining loyalty to the leader who promised the change.

6. *When you make a promise, follow through.* One of the most important organizational assets you have is your credibility. Your ability to deliver what you say you will deliver will enhance your credibility. When you find you can't deliver, let the people who are counting on you know.

7. *Everyone makes mistakes, admit yours.* No one expects perfect performance. An acknowledged mistake in the long run can prove easier to handle than a cover-up; Richard Nixon, a case in point. However, no one wants a daily confessional of errors. Let your competence on the job be known to all, too.

8. *Do not depend on the organization to feed you forever.* It won't. Your growth and movement must come from your own best thinking, not from an operation that exchanges a paycheck for your total powerlessness. Be prepared to move on.

9. *Anticipate the organizational needs* as they affect your activities within the organization. Have potential, workable solutions ready to bring to others' attention when the time is ripe.

10. *Minimize your griping.* It accomplishes little except to create an image of your own ineffectiveness in the minds of others.

If you keep in mind all of the above guidelines, you can begin to decide what needs to be changed and have a good chance of success. There will be some things that your position within the organization will enable you to change easily because you will have the responsibility for how that task is done. There will be other things that will be difficult to change because someone else has the responsibility but has no desire to change. And there will be other changes that can be achieved cautiously, and about which your best organizational assessment has led you to believe that virtually *no one* cares. Usually, there are cracks in organizational control, where change can be made cautiously. Some general patterns emerge when dealing with change:

1. *People are willing to accept changes that differ only a little bit from what they are used to.* When the proposed change is dramatically different, gaining acceptance of the informal network is difficult.

2. *The most effective way to bring change is by modeling it.* People believe what they see more than what someone tells them. Your own place in the proposed new situation is usually the first you need to specify.

3. *Persons adapt better when they know what is going on.* Managers frequently assume that passing information down the chain of command is all that is necessary to communicate to everyone what is about to take place. Chain of command communication is frequently unreliable because the information is sometimes not transmitted at all or transmitted with a coloring to predetermine the attitude of the persons hearing the information. Make sure everyone understands the change and the reason for the change. If you don't understand the change, ask about it (keeping in mind that sometimes just asking can be considered a black mark—"Either he's stupid or a troublemaker").

4. *When a change is being instituted, it is possible to "piggyback" other changes.* It is possible to institute other changes at the same time because a climate for acceptance of change has been created.

5. *Change is easier to bring about when people agree to it.* The time spent informing persons about the change—working with them to bring understanding of what it will mean to them personally—will pay off in acceptance of the change. Attitude here is quite important. If you appear to be the all-knowing expert and place them in the role of stupid followers, their enthusiasm and effectiveness will be nonexistent. Everyone who works in an organization has some expertise. Involving everyone in the change process can be the difference between success and failure, both of the changes designed and of the probability that they will be instituted.

6. *Appreciate persons' positions within the organization.* A person's objective position within organizational structure is an excellent indicator

of how that person will respond to change. Thus, middle managers are go-betweens in the organization, who carry out the directives of "those above" by enforcing them upon "those below." As a result of this middle location, such persons are trying to get along with both sides and are likely to concentrate much energy on belongingness. The middle manager will likely go along with anything that will create the least strain between the various levels of the organization. On the other hand, top-level persons are likely to be more concerned with establishing themselves as creative and effective leaders, and will usually best adapt to proposed changes if they are allowed to believe that they discovered the changes themselves.[7]

CHANGE FROM WITHOUT

Clinical sociologists often get placed in consultant positions or are hired into positions with planning, training, or evaluation functions. In these cases the sociologist is not a true member of the organization. From such "outsider" positions, the sociologist can develop recommendations for an organization, but seldom is given the authority to carry them out. A range of options are available to the sociologist, the three major forms of which are described by Robert Chin and Kenneth Benne:

The first . . . and probably the most frequently employed by men of knowledge in America and Western Europe, are those we call empirical-rational strategies. One fundamental assumption underlying these strategies is that men are rational. Another assumption is that men will follow their rational self-interest once this is revealed to them. A change is proposed by some person or group which knows of a situation that is desirable, effective, and in line with the self-interest of the person, group, organization, or community which will be affected by the change. Because the person (or group) is assumed to be rational and moved by self-interest, it is assumed that he (or they) will adopt the proposed change if it can be rationally justified and if it can be shown by the proposer(s) that he (or they) will gain by the change.

A second group of strategies we call normative re-educative. These strategies build upon assumptions about human motivation different from those underlying the first. The rationality and intelligence of men are not denied. Patterns of action and practice are supported by sociocultural norms and by commitments on the part of individuals to these norms. Sociocultural norms are supported by the attitude and value systems of individuals—normative outlooks which undergird their commitments. Change in a pattern of practice or action, according to this view, will occur only as the persons involved are brought to change their normative orientations to old patterns and develop commitments to new ones. And changes in normative orientations involve changes in attitudes, values, skills, and significant relationships, not just changes in knowledge, information, or intellectual rationales for action and practice.

The third group of strategies is based on the application of power in some form, political or otherwise. The influence process involved is basically that of compliance of those with less power to the plans, directions, and leadership of those with greater power. Often the power to be applied is legitimate power or authority. Thus the strategy may involve getting the authority of law or administrative policy behind the change to be effected. Some power strategies may appeal less to the use of authoritative power to effect change than to the massing of coercive power, legitimate or not, in support of the change sought.[8]

Empirical-rational strategies include general education, personnel selection and replacement, systems analysis, applied research linked to bringing change, utopian thinking, and changing persons' perceptions and conceptions through the clarification of language. Normative-reeducative strategies of changing include improving the problem-solving capabilities of a system and fostering growth in the persons who make up the system to be changed. Power-coercive approaches include strategies of nonviolence, use of political institutions to achieve change, and changing through the recomposition and manipulation of power elites.[9]

Each of these strategies entails a variety of systematic techniques which are described in books noted in the Clinician's Library at the end of this chapter. Some initial heuristics that could prove useful when you take on the consultant role are as follows:

1. *Be clear about why you were hired.* Organizations usually have reasons when they hire consultants. Frequently, these reasons are not

communicated clearly to the consultant. Sometimes the organization is on a fishing expedition and will be satisfied with whatever catch you bring up. At other times, a decision has already been made and the consultant is there *only* to provide outside support for the decision. In the latter cases you would be serving as a sociological engineer, as described in chapter 1, rather than as a clinician who can facilitate constructive processes.

2. *Get as much information as possible on both the formal and informal organization structure.* Your recommendations, if they are to be adopted, must be viewed as feasible by the organization. Frequently this means that you must have a detailed understanding of how the organization really functions. Given that you are not going to spend much of your working life within the organization, you have to find a quick, effective way of getting such information. Looking, questioning, and reading information the organization publishes about itself are key strategies. Don't forget bulletin boards and informal discussions as sources of information and as indicators of trouble spots.

3. *Interview persons at several levels of organization.* We have already noted that different persons in an organization have different perspectives on its operation. Perspectives are more likely to be shared at each level of an organization than between levels.

4. *Try to identify and then interview leaders of the informal organization.* One way of discovering these leaders is asking your first round of interviewees to name other persons important to the organization, or you may wish to use sociometric tests (see chapter 14). Also be sure to talk to the gatekeepers, whom you should be able to identify by position, for example, the key executive's secretary, the purchasing agent, the personnel officer.

5. *If there is a loyal opposition to current practices, find it.* As stated earlier, organizations do not fulfill everyone's needs. Frequently, there exist one or more persons who are opposed to current practices. Sometimes, visits with such persons cannot be made publicly. Gatekeepers for the opposition have to decide whether you can be trusted before you are informed about the existence of opposition.

6. *Assume one or more persons will be watching your activities.* On many occasions, key persons open up to a consultant only after they see how the consultant has approached the job. Much consultation is viewed by members of an organization as a joke, or as a way for the boss to discover who is loyal. Some persons within an organization can have heavy investments in the outcome of your consultation and will be quite concerned about who you see and what you are trying to find. When one of the authors was engaged in research on a college campus, he met with the editor of the campus newspaper in the evening informally. The editor accurately told him whom he had seen during the day and at what times (although there was no formal schedule). Having discovered the author's thoroughness, the editor then shared much confidential information.

7. *People in organizations have cover stories and cover behaviors.* They have learned how to deal with strangers who come in for short-term visits. However, these cover stories and behaviors break down over time. One of the authors remembers working in a state school for the retarded. When groups of visitors came to look at conditions, a show would be put on by residents and staff that would heighten the abnormal behaviors and increase the staff-resident interaction. This could only be maintained for short periods, but most visitors left quickly.

8. *Do not assume what you observe is the way it is all the time.* One of the authors visited a state prison for women. The tour guide explained the rehabilitative nature of making state flags, then took the visitors in the sewing room where the prisoners were supposed to be busily at work. But no one was. The visitors were quickly asked to tour the chapel. When we returned to the sewing room, everyone was busily at work and the supervisor, still wearing his golf shoes, explained the operation. Which of those working conditions is present most of the time?

9. *Be sure to relate your understanding of the organization, its strengths, and its problems to the purpose of your consultation.* As you get to know an organization in this manner, you will be gathering much more information than is called for in your particular assignment. Think of ways of relating what you know about the organization to your task. The skill with which you are able to do this will determine the effectiveness of your consultation.

10. *Keep in mind the wide range of recommendations you can make. Think through the monetary and social costs of each of them.* Some recommendations are clearly beyond the scope of the organization. Underlying each recommendation is a strategy, and most strategies have both positive and negative characteristics, both of which should be pointed out to the clients. Thus, one widely used strategy is to reeducate the staff to accomplish new skills. When used appropriately, staff development can be quite effective. But too frequently training is recommended to solve problems that are not training problems, but leadership or middle-management problems. Frequently managers underestimate both the

time necessary and the costs of effective training and end up with poor piecemeal approaches with fancy titles and price tags.

DANGERS

Organizational work simply is not for every clinician. It is usually a gradual, tedious way to accomplish sociological therapy. Those who seek more rapid or far-reaching change may do more harm than good, including actions which force themselves or others to lose jobs or mental well-being. Acting effectively in organizations frequently involves considerable compromise. One can lose sight of both personal and organizational goals to keep the paycheck coming or to keep the boss happy. It is easy to become a person who goes through the motions without much satisfaction, believing you have no way to make conditions better.

Nevertheless, persons almost always have power within an organization, even if it is only the power to say a meek "no." Organizations can be oriented to workers' needs, moving toward the theory Y model of McGregor. The degree to which your own personal metaphysics within an organization can build your self-esteem and those of your coworkers; can have persons judged on ability not on sex, age, formal education, race, ethnicity, and so on; and can allow you to exercise well thought through power—will move the organization to greater human effectiveness.

POSTSCRIPT 1: GRANT GETTING

All sociological change costs money, and persons within organizations are especially sensitive to this fact. Clinicians working within organizations can often be useful by acquiring the funds (1) to determine which changes are needed and (2) to experiment with these changes. Clinicians working outside can often use grant money to avoid the problem noted previously, of being coerced into certain actions or conclusions by those who control the organization. By fully or partially funding their own work, they acquire some power and freedom over their work.

There are three important elements in getting a grant: (1) researching the sources, (2) writing the grant, and (3) approaching the funding source.

Research the Sources

The two major sources of grant funds are foundations and governments. For foundations, the best generally available resources are *The Foundation Directory* (currently in its sixth edition) and *Foundation News*. For federal government sources, see the *Catalog of Federal Domestic Assistance, Business and Commerce Daily,* and the *Federal Register* (which is updated twice a year). More and more federal programs are being administered through states, counties, cities, and sometimes even neighborhoods.

Writing for Grants

Foundations and governments also have guidelines for what they will and will not fund, and for the way you are to tell them what you plan to do. Most foundations want short letters of inquiry with a three- or four-page prospectus detailing what you propose. Frequently governments want more elaborate write-ups: preliminary statements followed by long and detailed applications. Perhaps the most useful approach to grant writing is that taught by the nonprofit Grantsmanship Center.[10] *Center News* has more relevant how-to-do-it information than any other source on grants. Their reprint, *Program Planning and Proposal Writing,* will provide the basics of how to write a successful grant.

Briefly, a good grant request contains a summary, a few paragraphs spelling out accurately what is being requested and what it will cost; an introduction that builds the credibility of the applicant in relation to the proposed project; a statement of the problem to be addressed by the grant; objectives, including what will be different when the project is complete; activities and methods; descriptions of what actions will take place; evaluation (how will you know that the project has been successful?); and a budget that spells out in detail what costs are being requested and which will be donated by the applicant.

Approaching the Funding Source

Sometimes it is necessary to research who must be approached and the best way to do so. If you have decided on a particular foundation, it can be beneficial to find out what they have funded in the past and the level of funding. It is fruitless to approach a foundation that does not fund at the level you are requesting. From the sources mentioned already, you can discover who should be approached, how they should be approached, and the likelihood of the foundation funding your project. Keep in mind that approaching a foundation requires that applicants appear at their best at all times. Each telephone, personal, or postal contact should reflect the applicant's integrity and credibility.

Approaching governments requires a mixture of formal and informal contacts. Formally, it is possible to receive technical assistance in the preparation of the grant and a critique from the review committee if it gets turned down. It is also possible to try to anticipate what new program areas are likely to be funded by watching the content of bills in your area of interest and thinking along similar lines. Every few years there are "okay words" which reflect fashionable concepts. Lately, in the field of mental health some okay words are: "community support systems," "rehabilitation in the community for severely disabled," "training in delivering services in the community." Increasingly the government is requesting that groups bid on contracts which cover new approaches. Also, federal funding has been localized through such programs as CETA (Comprehensive Employment Training Act). In such cases, ongoing activities and political power with the organization which gives out the funds can be useful. Recognize that occasional contacts with government officials can be useful, but don't overdo it. In the "good old days," when money for social program grants was growing on trees, it is rumored that more than one grant was given just to get the grantee to stop bugging the personnel of the grant agency.

POSTSCRIPT 2: A CASE EXAMPLE

One of the authors was asked to consult the director of personnel for a large state agency. The problem was to discover the best way of implementing in every institution in the state a court-mandated training program that was much more extensive and much more compulsory than the existing program. The author-consultant suggested the following strategy:

The new training program should be sent out in advance to every person attending the meeting. These training directors and personnel directors of local institutions would also receive a questionnaire with three questions: (1) Name the three things you like most about the program; (2) Name the three things that you dislike most about the program; and (3) Name the three questions that you would like answered about implementing the program at your institution. This was done. The author-consultant was asked to chair the meeting that took place in the state capitol.

After official words of welcome, the author-consultant divided the 150 persons into ten parts, each with a facilitator from the group. They spent the next hour or so sharing what they liked about the program. After a coffee break (good organizers keep the need for such amenities in mind in their planning), the groups gathered for another round on what they disliked about the program and what questions they needed answered.

Before lunch the entire group gathered and a group member reported the problems brought up in the small groups. The facilitators gathered during lunch and developed groups (an intensive, but *ad hoc* group creating process). After lunch, problem groups met to come up with solutions to the problems that were identified. Considerable progress was made that day. Within two months, a detailed memorandum from the state office arrived spelling out potential solutions to some of the qroblems that still remained.

Diagnosis

The author-consultant is a veteran of the usual state meeting in which nothing is done except sitting around and griping. He knew there was a desperate need for action on this program or it would die like so many others. Having dealt with many of the persons involved in other contexts, he knew that most of them were capable of moving the program in their own institution if they wanted to move it. Therefore, he wanted to create a climate during that meeting that would make it clear that the program was to be implemented and a contagion effect so that everyone else in the state would try to make it take place.

Strategy

Griping had to be allowed, but it was severely limited to a particular part of the program. If griping was not checked, the program could never be implemented. The author-consultant devised the questionnaire strategy as one that would limit the griping. He then allowed a limited time for the griping to take place, sandwiching it between segments on what was good about the program and what questions the

articipants needed answered. This placed positive elements on each
de of the griping.

Most statewide meetings consist of a few persons talking at many
ther persons. The author-consultant wanted to emphasize participa-
on, since his goal was active implementation of the program. He rec-
gnized that extensive change meant fear, but felt that the participation
rategy would allow persons to talk through their problems. He wanted
o provide equal time for each participant (as might take place in certain
elf-help groups), but his facilitators, while generally quite effective,
ere not comfortable with the concept.

nalysis

The program has been implemented with surprising success in al-
ost every state institution. The meeting was instrumental in getting
ie program accepted.

NOTES

1.   Alvin Gouldner, *Studies in Leadership* (New York: Harper & Row,
950); see also Peter Blau, *The Dynamics of Bureaucracy* (Chicago: Uni-
ersity of Chicago Press, 1963).

2.   Douglas McGregor, *The Human Side of Enterprise* (New York:
IcGraw-Hill, 1960), pp. 33–34.

3.   Ibid., pp. 47–48.

4.   Warren Bennis, *The Unconscious Conspiracy* (New York: Amacom,
976), p. 157.

5.   Amitai Etzioni, *A Comparative Analysis of Complex Organizations*
New York: Free Press, 1961).

6.   Peter Blau and Richard Scott, *Formal Organizations: A Comparative*
pproach (London: Routledge, 1963).

7.   Deena and Michael Weinstein, *Living Sociology: A Critical*
itroduction (New York: McKay, 1974), p. 24.

8.   Robert Chin and Kenneth D. Benne, "General Strategies for Ef-
cting Changes in Human Systems," in W. G. Bennis, K. D. Benne,
nd R. Chin, eds., *The Planning of Change*, 2nd ed. (New York: Holt,
inehart and Winston, 1961), p. 34.

9.   Ibid., pp. 32–59.

10.   1015 West Olympic Blvd., Los Angeles, California 90015.

THE CLINICIAN'S LIBRARY

A reader that provides a comprehensive overview of organizationa theory with case studies is:

Litterer, Joseph A. *Organizations,* 2nd ed. New York: Wiley, n.d.

The following two books are useful for persons who work with or ganizations as consultants:

Bennis, Warren, Kenneth Benne, and Robert Chin, *The Planning o Change,* 3rd ed. New York: Holt, Rinehart and Winston, 1976.
Levinson, Harry. *Organizational Diagnosis.* Cambridge, Mass.: Harvarc University Press, 1972.

The following two books are useful for persons who work with or ganizations as managers:

Drucker, Peter. *Management: Tasks, Responsibilities, Practices.* Nev York: Harper & Row, 1974.
Townsend, Robert. *Up the Organization.* New York: Knopf, 1970.

The following two books would be useful to persons working fo hourly wages:

Bensman, Joseph. *Dollars and Sense.* New York: Macmillan, 1967.
Terkel, Studs. *Working.* New York: Pantheon, 1974.

These books will be useful for persons involved in training and sta development:

Boshear, Walton C., and Karl G. Albrecht. *Understanding People.* L Jolla, Cal.: University Associates, 1977.
Craig, Robert L., ed. *Training and Development Handbook,* 2nd ed. Nev York: McGraw-Hill, 1977.
Patten, Thomas H., Jr. *Manpower Planning and the Development o Human Resources.* New York: Wiley, 1971.

Chapter 16

Simulation

"Truth," proclaimed Sir Francis Bacon, "is found more often through error than through confusion." Simulations are techniques for searching for truth via relatively structured, safe, and active experimentation. Simulations are special kinds of models. Other models describe verbally, mathematically, or pictorially the components of something, and the relationship of these components. These models—for instance, plastic representations of molecules—display the static structure of whatever they depict. Simulations, on the other hand, display not only structures, but also *processes*. As we saw throughout part 3, the vital sociological features are processes, and to understand or treat them one requires process-oriented techniques.

Uses of simulations have varied from development of space technology to training of business executives. In the social sciences, simulations have been used primarily as research and teaching tools. A classic example is the International Simulation (INS) employed for many years at Northwestern University and elsewhere for both teaching and research in political science. Persons play the roles of decision-makers from various nations. These participants are given information about the military, resources, prestige, and other aspects of the nation they represent. They must then make decisions about how to run their nations, worrying about consumer goods levels, national defense, public opinion, revolutions, democratic values, and so forth. All sorts of military activities from alliances to wars may occur.

As a teaching tool, INS provided students with a chance to experience the processes of international relations, rather than simply to read others' written or mathematized accounts of such processes. As a research tool, INS was employed to examine the effect of spreading nuclear weapons capability and of the impact of nuclear invulnerability.[1]

The INS simulations involved people making decisions, the consequences of which were calculated by a computer in relation to all of the decisions made in the simulation and the state of the simulated world. Simulation techniques vary from those involving only people to those involving only computers.

An all-computer simulation called PLANS researched the interactions of major interest groups in American society, including labor, business, civil rights groups, and the military. The formal documents issued by labor unions, businesses, civil rights groups, and others were used to ascertain the goals of each group, which were programmed into a computer. The computer then proceeded to translate the decision implications of these goals into action. Based upon probability programs, the computer can determine a most efficient way for a group to acquire its formally desired ends.

In an interesting paper, the inventors of PLANS note a difficulty with such computer simulations:

> Unfortunately, people sometimes behave rationally within what are essentially irrational or outdated systems of goals and objectives. They accept and pursue, in a rational manner, goals set for them by others and perhaps even by themselves—goals which are self-defeating and inimical to their own long-range welfare and survival. . . . The capacity to change goals one would like to believe is an indispensable defining quality of human beings. Yet increasingly it is more difficult to do this in a world which is ever more insistent that they remain efficient instruments rather than unpredictable and uncontrolled elements within rigorously controlled social systems.[2]

A readily available sociological simulation called SIMSOC has thus far been used primarily for educational purposes. Group size may vary from 15 to 60 participants, who are divided into three or four "regions."

Each of these regions is roughly equivalent to a social class, with some regions being allocated the industries, courts, and capital, while others are allocated only the ability to sell their labor. Players form alliances or become isolates and work to achieve group, regional, political, personal, and other goals. In the process, a great deal of conflict arises in the forms of protests and negotiations. Most players are forced to confront their social abilities to communicate and work with others.[3]

Both authors have used SIMSOC in several classroom situations and have discovered that it provides a unique opportunity for persons to see society from "the other side of the tracks." Students who live in wealthy suburbs in real society often end up in the ghetto region in SIMSOC, or vice versa. Several commented upon their experiences:

> Watching the evening news on TV will never be the same for me after this simulation. I always thought that protestors were rotten people who should be out earning a living. Boy was I shocked to see myself joining a protest in SIMSOC! But when you try for a long time to get a job and can't get one, you get frustrated and can't figure out anything to do *but* protest.

> I became a *prostitute*. If my prim-and-proper mother ever found out, she'd just die. I'm still not sure how it happened. Somehow our region figured out that it was the best way to raise money since we didn't have any money to invest in other businesses. So we started a "house of ill repute." Thank God the simulation didn't get too detailed!

> There I was, acting just like "the Man." Ripping people off and everything. Seems like no time at all before I knew just how to spend all that money you gave us. I was hiring poor folks to bring me soft drinks while they were starving. Pretty soon we built up a police force, too, to shut them up when they started screaming and yelling at us.

A great value of a simulation is for persons who are usually isolated through divisions of labor within groups or communities to derive an understanding of the entire group process. This is a social parallel to the psychological notion of "pattern matching." If we imagine the task of identifying the "same" dot of ink in two newspaper prints of the same photograph, a distinction becomes clear. The task is impossible if we view one dot at a time. It is feasible only once we have comprehended the whole picture in order to ascertain relative regions.[4] To really understand one's own place in a group, community, society, or world requires knowledge of the totality and of the other locations as well.

SIMULATION AS THERAPY

Simulations offer tremendous potential for the therapy of groups, although this potential has seldom been explored. In diagnoses of the following varieties, simulation may be the therapy of choice:

1. Inadequate group or community role allocations
2. Destructive inequalities
3. Communication breakdown
4. Prejudicing (including assumed immutability of characteristics of groups or group members)
5. Need to model decision-making
6. Overcoming apathy or powerlessness
7. Sex role conflicts

Clinicians may be able on occasion to use existing simulation packages for the immediate therapeutic needs. SIMSOC, for instance, may be practicable for some types of community therapy or for facilitating communication or redistribution of power and resources in an organization consisting of members from different social classes. More often the clinician will work with the clients to develop a simulation which fits pressing therapeutic needs. There is evidence that in instructional use of simulations the effectiveness is enhanced when the participants also help to construct the simulation.[5] In clinical applications, this enhancement is likely to be even more pronounced, since the very act of collectively choosing what to include in the simulation may be therapeutic.

The actual procedure of simulation development is that of abstracting and simplifying the real world situation into a game world. The goal is not to replicate the real world situation, but rather to include the necessary detail for dealing with the problems at hand. A determination must be made on which elements, processes, and relationships should be included and which can be neglected. In a hospital where organization in unpredicted emergencies is the central problem, likely candidates for inclusion would be (1) persons playing patients, orderlies, nurses, and doctors; (2) physical space and facilities like those of the ward; (3) randomizing devices for determining when the simulated emergencies will occur and which sorts they will be (e.g., a random numbers table and lists of possible emergencies); (4) consensual agreement of ways to evaluate the team's overall performance (e.g., "A," "B," "C" grades); (5) concretized units which may be exchanged during the simulation (e.g., paper "money" representing personal favors, pay raises, days off, attitude changes); and (6) time allocations similar to those during actual emergencies.

In a hospital with a quite different problem—inadequate leadership and role allocations among nurses—only the second and fifth items above would likely be major candidates for inclusion. Others might be (1) persons playing nurses and supervisors of nurses; (2) concretized units representing nursing roles; (3) rules for the exchange of these role-units; (4) situations such as those in which conflicts emerge; and (5) a list of outcomes to be achieved during the simulation (e.g., number and type of visits to certain patients, lists of forms to be filled out, or overall satisfaction scores to be achieved by the participants).

Once the simulation is developed the group and the clinician must expect the first few runs to be more developmental than therapeutic:

> If one is forced to design a replica of what one intuitively understands . . . one may be better able to make that knowledge explicit. Furthermore, the replica is to some extent self-correcting. Just as one could not describe a familiar landscape fully, but could recognize the fact that an important feature was missing if shown a sketch, so might the observer of a simulation recognize that some significant aspect of the real world was missing, the importance of which he had not made explicit.[6]

How does one judge whether a simulation is adequate? The final answer to this will be, naturally enough, whether things changed for the better within or between groups. Along the way attention should be paid to questions of *isomorphism* and *richness* of the simulation. We discussed isomorphism in chapter 3, in our critiques of organic, systems, and dramatic analogies in social theory. Our present concern is with determining whether the structures and processes of the simulation conform to those of the relevant real world situations. This can best be determined through adequate observation and note-taking by the clinician prior to the simulation. The clinician should be able to compare the abstracted and simplified events of the simulation to his or her notes from previous real world occurrences. The question to be asked in this comparison is not whether the two look alike, however, but whether they are parallel. Are the major roles being played? Are the central constraints built into the simulation? Are the same types of items available for exchange? Do participants have comparable possibilities and limitations for interacting?

A major indicator of a good simulation is that it provides rich possibilities for actions based upon realistic choices. This is best ascertained for the clinician through observations and discussions with the participants. Adequately isomorphic simulations provide participants with a feeling that they have acted pretty much as they would in a similar real world situation. This is not to say that participants should "lose themselves" in the simulation (as in a psychodrama or sociodrama), or that they should feel comfortable with what occurred. A therapeutic simulation is an experiment with new structures and processes, and such experimentation is by no means necessarily pleasant nor a total immersion.

BENEFITS AND DANGERS

Simulation is frequently a relatively inexpensive therapeutic method. Less expenditure of time, energy, and money is required for building and working with a model than for working in a natural setting. Experimentation on real world social structures and processes can result in costly mistakes, whereas the mistakes made in simulated worlds are less damaging. Thus, the use of a new person as a group leader may permanently destroy a real world group, but in a simulation would at worst only end the current run.

A major benefit of simulation is that the central goal of sociological therapy, *alternative world building*, is inherent in the technique. Sometimes participants will build into the simulation some of the fantasies they have long held for their group, or these may develop from interactions during the simulation or revision of the simulation components for later runs. In appropriately complex and rich simulation environments, participants are almost forced to generate new structures and processes that were not predicted in advance. An important illustration, from the research uses of gaming, is from Herman Kahn, who is famous for his explanations of ways in which accidental nuclear war could occur. Kahn claims that many of his scenarios for nuclear war between the United States and the Soviet Union were suggested to him through gaming exercises.[7]

The dangers in simulation arise from translation problems. First, it is always possible that a simulation which appears to be adequately isomorphic with real world situations is lacking in some crucial regard which will make dangerous the learning acquired from the simulation. Second, the participants themselves may be unable to translate what they learn in the simulation back to real world situations. Conversely, they may be unprepared to leave the real world in order to be creative in the simulation world. Some simulations turn out to be mere depictions of inadequate habits found in the group when it operates in the real world. In therapeutic simulation games, the old aphorism is literally true, "It's not whether you win or lose, it's how you play the game."

Another danger is that roles taken during simulations can affect actions outside the simulation in undesirable ways. For instance, a student took a dictatorial role during a SIMSOC held early in his graduate educational career and had to spend considerable energy in the following years to overcome others' negative image of him.

Cathy Greenblatt points out a final, more encompassing warning—that most simulations miss reality because they present a single statement of the information about that reality to all participants, while in real life, persons have different perspectives on the reality:

> For the sociologist, then, an important step in trying to comprehend a social system is to learn how the actors define their situations and the events that transpire. If, as game designers, we wish to create models that operate like these real systems, we must simulate both the structural elements and the differential perceptions of system participants.[8]

POSTSCRIPT: SIMULATIONS AS FOLK MODELS

We have seen throughout this book that persons and groups manage their everyday lives via their models of what social worlds are "really" like. Much of what the clinical sociologist does is to offer alternative models based upon systematic sociological inquiry. Simulations provide the possibility for the sociologist and clients to work together to build more adequate models. Omar Moore and Alan Anderson distinguish between noninteractional models such as puzzles and interactional models such as games of strategy, noting that "theoretical and technological successes in the physical sciences have 'depended' in some sense, on looking at nature from the point of view of a puzzle model, rather than a social interactional model. . . ." [9] The authors contend that the puzzle model is not appropriate to the social sciences and that the social interactional model is more appropriate because "a decent theory is likely to influence the behavior of those who know it." [10]

The implications of this alternative are then examined in detail. They suggest a potential direction for the activities of the social scientist since if the puzzle model is inappropriate in interactional settings, so is the tool of descriptive mathematics. This direction, the creation of folk models, is deemed necessary to become the usual task of scientists; prediction and control take on "a fairly ominous ring when the object of the endeavor is other people." [11]

The need for the creation of folk models in contemporary society comes about because modern industrial societies—as opposed to stable, static societies or slowly evolving societies—"are in a state of unstable, dynamic disequilibrium." [12] "If we can't tell what kinds of problems are likely to face us, we can even less predict the kinds of solutions they will require. In such a situation it becomes urgent to supply not only new folk-models, but also models which will enable people to cope with situations in which the rules are constantly changing." [13] The creation of a viable folk model requires its creator to understand the dynamic of contemporary society so that the folk model created bears a heuristic relationship to the social dynamic of the society.

If one accepts the "unstable, dynamic, disequilibrium" aspect of contemporary society, the model must allow for the propensity for sudden contradictory changes and the adaptation without hesitation of an alternative folk model.

NOTES

1. John Raser, *Simulation and Society* (Boston: Allyn and Bacon, 1969), p. 57.

2. Robert Boguslaw and R. Davis, "Social Process Modeling: A Comparison of a Live and Computerized Simulation," *Behavioral Science* (May 1969):203.

3. William Gamson, *SIMSOC: Simulated Society* (New York: Free Press, 1972).

4. Donald Campbell, "Pattern Matching as an Essential in Distal-
Knowing," in K. Hammond, ed., *The Psychology of Egon Brunswick*
(New York: Holt, Rinehart and Winston, 1966).
5. Raser, *Simulation and Society*, p. 131. Also, one of the authors had
social work students create games that illustrated how social problems
were played out in society. The students collectively created the games,
and some of the results were remarkably accurate simulations of conditions surrounding the problem.
6. Sidney Verba, "Simulation, Reality, and Theory in International
Relations," *World Politics* 16, no. 3 (1964):499.
7. Herman Kahn, quoted in Raser, *Simulation and Society*, p. 82.
8. Cathy Greenblatt, "Sociological Theory and the Multiple Reality
Game," *Simulation and Games* 5, no. 1 (March 1974):6.
9. Omar K. Moore and Alan R. Anderson, "Some Puzzling Aspects
of Social Interaction," *The Review of Metaphysics* 15(1962):417–20.
10. Ibid., p. 419.
11. Ibid., p. 427.
12. Ibid.
13. Ibid., p. 429.

THE CLINICIAN'S LIBRARY

By far the most useful book we have located is Raser's:

Raser, John R. *Simulation and Society*. Boston: Allyn and Bacon, 1969.

Others are good for describing specific simulations:

Gamson, William. *SIMSOC*. New York: Free Press, 1972.
Guetzkow, Harold, et al. *Simulation in International Relations*. En-
    glewood Cliffs, N.J.: Prentice-Hall, 1963.
Hermann, Charles. *Crises in Foreign Policy: A Simulation Analysis*.
    Indianapolis: Bobbs-Merrill, 1969.

A couple of interesting books on the general topic of social gaming:

Huizinga, Johan. *Homo Ludens*. Boston: Beacon Press, 1950.
Rapoport, Anatol. *Fights, Games and Debates*. Ann Arbor, Mich.: Uni-
    versity of Michigan Press, 1960.

There are a vast number of simulations at all levels of complexity. The following simulations could be considered for use:

Compacts (University of Michigan: School of Social Work).
Group Therapy (Head Box, Parks Plastic Co., 1969).
Propaganda (Wff'n Proof Games).
They Shoot Marbles, Don't They? (Rochester, N.Y.: Urbex).

A good source is the journal *Simulation and Games* (Beverly Hills, Cal.: Sage Publications).

Chapter 17

Community

This chapter presents tactics that can enhance group members' and groups' functioning in the community. Community work is of a higher order of complexity than the tactics already described. Persons, group members, groups, and organizations are all part of a community. Each influences the fabric of community life and each in turn is influenced by this fabric. Community organizer Saul Alinsky points this out:

> An understanding of the role of the individual in terms of his relationship to the general framework in which he lives brings to light the motivation that underlies his behavior. In order to live in any kind of social arrangement or culture, a person must adjust to that culture. The adjustment process involves the acceptance of traditions, taboos, folkways, mores, values, definitions, and all other social elements which regulate our behavior. The process of adjustment is a continuous series of experiences for the individual in which acceptable and taboo thoughts and modes of behavior are impressed upon him. This social conditioning begins in the earliest days of a person's life and goes on from the time his original environment is limited to his family to the time when his sphere of activities and understanding expands through secondary groups, then the community, and then the general culture of which the community is a part.[1]

While the community is complex in character, it is still changeable by the activities of groups and group members. Indeed, the degree to which persons within a community are successful in bringing about desired changes usually corresponds to the degree to which their actions are based upon realistic conceptions of the complexity and distinctiveness of that community.[2]

Robert Park, an important sociologist of the Chicago School of the 1920s and 30s, "cherished a vision of a developed science of the community which could chart patterns of change so that men might finally fashion their social environments to conform more closely with their ideals."[3] Park describes community as follows:

> The simplest possible description of a community is this: a collection of people occupying a more or less clearly defined area. But a community is more than that. A community is not only a collection of people, but it is a collection of institutions. Not people, but institutions, are final and decisive in distinguishing the community from other social constellations.
>
> Among the institutions of the community there will always be homes and something more: churches, schools, playgrounds, a communal hall, a local theater, perhaps, and, of course, business and industrial enterprises of some sort. Communities might well be classified by the number and variety of the institutions—cultural, political, and occupational—which they possess. This would indicate the extent to which they were autonomous or, conversely, the extent to which their communal functions were mediatized, so to speak, and incorporated into the larger community.
>
> There is always a larger community. Every single community is always a part of some larger and more inclusive one. There are no longer any communities wholly detached and isolated: all are interdependent economically and politically upon one another. The ultimate community is the wide world.[4]

At present, a variety of institutions are decentralizing their dealings with members of communities. This can be seen in the expanded tolerance of deviance in our society, including the release of persons from total institutions. The criminal, mentally ill, mentally retarded, elderly, disabled, and others (most of whom are poor) are increasingly being placed "back in the community." As a result, there is an increasing need for persons to work in communities on behalf of such new residents. New roles are currently being developed for community workers to act as advocates for these new residents. Perhaps out of nostalgia for the legendary communities that watched out for all in their midst, the community has become the planner's and therapist's setting of choice for all but the extremely distressed.

Communities will have to be made to tolerate and be helpful to this population. Community advocates will try to marshal resources on behalf of clients, and to move the more typical resident to care. Until now, this task has been only sporadically successful.

The goal was described by James Taylor and Jerry Randolph, whose *Community Worker* is an exceptional guide for approaching this work:

> The person in trouble is imbedded within a network of family processes and community systems. Your help will be most effective when you can use those systems to support your efforts—or at least, not stand in the way of what is needed. Although this way of looking at problems can be applied to all class-levels and groups, in practical fact most of your work will be carried on with the poor, the stigmatized, and the deprived.
>
> Effective community work requires that you work with individuals who are somehow failing to cope adequately with their problems. Any individual problem may require a variety of approaches: individual counseling, life-planning, occupational training, medical care and psychotherapy. Community work often requires work with the total family: family counseling, family planning, and family training. It may require special efforts aimed at managing conflict between the client and outside organizations: such organizations as welfare, schools, and loan companies. In working with individuals and families, you will often take on the responsibility for coordinating and orchestrating all relevant and available resources.
>
> As a community worker, you may also be asked to take on a second kind of role: you may be asked to help community agencies and institutions. Often the request is for help with individual problems, the agency asking for consultation about "especially difficult" cases. This consulting relationship may broaden, so that advice on agency policies, programs and practices is sought.
>
> Eventually you may play a third kind of role as well; you

may be called on to serve as organizer, administrator, manager, and group leader. Rare indeed are the settings in which a community worker acts as a solo agent. Most commonly, community work is coordinated within some kind of community agency. Managing such an agency calls for special skills and perspectives. The community worker may also need to organize groups for special purposes: for civil rights activism, for social activities, for mutual aid, etc. This too calls for special skills. Probably every community worker will be called on for these skills some time in his career.[5]

COMMUNITY WORK AS SOCIOLOGICAL THERAPY

A community focus is necessary when problems of groups and group members can be solved at a community level:

Concern with a decent sewer system, with public transportation, with police protection, or with attracting new industry to town, may actually prove to have a good deal of relevance to the community's mental health. A community is a social and ecological system wherein changes in any part affect the whole.[6]

Planned intervention at the community level "is based on the presumption that the nature of social organization and community life (civilization) significantly affects, if not determines, the focus and extent of individual discontent." [7] A substudy by Dorothea Leighton and Irving Stone points this up. The overall study, the Stirling County study, examines five rural areas for psychiatric disorders and sociocultural patterns. Two of these were relatively affluent, well integrated communities, and three were examples of the most economically depressed, socially disintegrated settlements to be found in the county.[8] The overall study found that "communities at opposite ends of the integration-disintegration continuum stood in strong contrast with regard to the amount and intensity of psychiatric disorder which could be identified in individual residents." [9]

The substudy then tried to see what would happen if the living conditions for one of the socially disintegrated communities was improved; whether this would lessen the psychiatric symptomology of its residents. At the beginning of the study, inhabitants of an area called "The Road" were considered "monkeys" by other residents of the county:

Road inhabitants were found in 1950 to share a widespread reputation for laziness, drunkenness, fighting, thievery, illicit sexual indulgence, and a variety of other traits deemed indicative of amorality and mental inferiority. These characteristics were
attributed, in the popular stereotype, to excessive inbreed-
ing.[10]

Their community was a striking example of the worst rural poverty that
one can imagine.

The intervention in this community took place through an adult
educator who began by showing free films as a way to interest adults in
adult education classes at the school. Using techniques that heightened
involvement of the residents, he was able to get them interested in their
own welfare. His work was followed up by that of another teacher. This
eventually led to the inclusion of the small rural school with a consoli-
dated school district. In addition, a new way was provided for the
residents to work at better paying jobs in a large city part of the year.
The city work greatly influenced the former activity patterns and gave
persons from The Road an ability to deal with outsiders on an equal
footing. Housing was replaced or painted, lawns were kept up. The
standard of living changed. Social involvement was greater, and income
level rose.

The study resurveyed the mental health of Stirling County residents
in 1962. In 1952, The Road was the worst area surveyed. In 1962,
analysis of the psychiatric data from The Road revealed a significant
change in a positive direction so that its mental health rating had
shifted to a position virtually equivalent to the mean for the county as a
whole.[11] The other depressed communities of the 1952 study did not
record such a positive change. One of the highly integrated communities showed a decline in its mental health rating after ten years.
This paralleled social changes that lessened the level of intracommunity
solidarity and organization.

These findings clearly suggest the potential significance of community development programs for improving mental health in
psychiatrically impaired, economically, and socially
depressed local groups. Individuals depend upon the support of
others for carrying out the activities and winning the recognition necessary to satisfy the needs, values, and goals upon which
their psychological well-being and mental health depend. Their

capacity to secure such support can suffer significant impairment where prevailing social patterns deny some persons access to interpersonal bonds of solidarity and trust or when access is denied to collectively organized and performed activities which would provide roles accorded social value and respect. Insofar as programs for community development include successful efforts to alter such social consequences of membership in a socioeconomically depressed local group, benefits in the form of improved mental health for the population are likely to result.[12]

GUIDELINES FOR THE CLINICAL SOCIOLOGIST

The goal of community clinicians, then, is to redistribute or otherwise improve the allocation of social resources and structures in order to improve the life situations of groups within the community. The clinical sociologist is usually not identified as such in her or his community work. The roles are usually ones available to persons trained from a number of fields and include community organizer, client advocate, case manager, social planner, service coordinator, and program administrator. Being a *citizen* is a community role shared by all. The approach that follows concerns all these roles, and once again the suggestions are presented heuristically. As Saul Alinsky points out:

Among the organizers I trained and failed with, there were some who memorized the words and the related experiences and concepts. Listening to them was like listening to a tape playing back my presentation word for word. Clearly there was little understanding; clearly, they could not do more than elementary organization. The problem with so many of them was and is their failure to understand that a statement of a specific situation is significant only in its relationship to and its illumination of a general concept. Instead they see the specific action as a terminal point. They find it difficult to grasp the fact that no situation ever repeats itself, that no tactic can be precisely the same.[13]

The following are some specific guidelines:

1. *See the relationship between a person and a community.* Alinsky states this as a goal for the organizer, but it also applies to persons in the other roles:

The organizer should at all times view individuals or groups in terms of the total social situation of which they are a part. The concept should be so thoroughly understood and accepted and should so completely become a part of the organizer, that he never sees individuals only as individuals or groups only as groups but always sees them as component parts of a total social situation. He knows that individuals and groups must make an adjustment to their social situation because they have to live with it. He knows that the opinions, reactions, and behavior of persons and groups will, to a large extent, be determined by what their own community thinks.[14]

In examining persons and groups within the total social situation, recognize that each can have a different perspective on issues in the community. This perspective frequently is based on key features of their social situation, some of which are detailed in part 3.

2. *Do not assume that your own perspective on the community is more useful than others'*. If you are an outsider, spend time learning the perspectives of various members of the community. Even if you are a community resident, you need allies. The best way to begin to get allies is to find out where they stand on community issues and the community's future. Organizers trained by Alinsky have a six-step approach to gain a community perspective useful as a base for organizing. Through questioning and more formal interviewing they

(1) plot the power pattern, (2) search out and evaluate the local leaders, (3) gather statistics and other data on the community, (4) discover the grievances of the residents, (5) bring people together so they can articulate their frustrations and problems, and (6) solicit suggestions on solutions and methods of achieving solutions.[15]

Doing your homework provides the data base for community action.

3. *Communities have power structures*. If you are working for change in the community, the power structure is quite important. Sometimes, your goals will be similar to those of the power structure. At other times, your goals will be in opposition. Working for change in a community requires power. Sometimes you can coopt others'. Frequently, you will have to establish your own power base, whether this be a personal base or an insurgent organizational base. Don't be scared of

power or politics. There have been ample demonstrations that new forces can become part of the political spectrum on national and local levels; Common Cause, Nader's Raiders, environmental action, and others illustrate this fact.

4. *Delineate goals for yourself, both short term and long term.* Make your community behavior goal-directed behavior. However, keep in mind that communication is the key to community effectiveness and that time spent getting known or visiting, while appearing purposeless, really has its own goal of integrating you into the community.

Sometimes goals can appear superficially simple. For example, on the day of this writing one of the authors is seeking a place to live for someone leaving a total institution. Solving that problem will bring him into contact with landlords, persons who know where a place might be found (postmen, storeowners, bartenders), potential neighbors, policemen, and so forth. The ongoing relationship with these community informants and influentials will not only make the goal easier to achieve, but also aid in providing a support system for the person who will live in the community. "If you vouch for him, then it's okay." "Can I call you if there is any difficulty?"

The following questions could help in clarification of goals:

—If planning is successful, what behaviors will the participants (people planned for or with) exhibit?

—In what surroundings will these behaviors take place? Will this mean a change in what now exists?

—How will the behaviors and surroundings in the segment you planned differ from other segments of the community, city, or society that are unplanned or planned by others? Use the statement of goals that you develop as a way to distinguish between actions that are goal directed and those that have other functions.

It is possible to use techniques of group process to aid a community to come to clearly delineated goals. Warren Ziegler of the Syracuse Research Corporation has developed an elaborate strategy called "futures invention" that brings participants to trying to put their ideal future 25 years from now into goal formulations that are then clarified with other citizens. After clarification, one moves to and fro on a time continuum between present and future and devises tactics that can move the group goals to fruition. Others, including Alvin Toffler (author of *Future Shock*), are working on similar projects.

5. *In consensus there is strength.* If the community residents believe that the most important task to accomplish immediately is to paint the fire hydrants in patriotic hues, and you believe that the most pressing

need is a new sewerage system, be actively involved in the fire hydrant project. Then, given the success in the completion of that task, it could be possible to turn persons' attention to the sewerage problem. Persons will have learned the advantages of working together. In such unified action on a successful project there is strength and enthusiasm to tackle others.

6. *Learn how to be a peer.* When working for change in a community, everyone has an important role to play. Persons who hide behind professional credentials, persons who emphasize their social class differences, or persons who assume that they have little to offer, all need to learn to work better with others. Even if your status in other settings is high or low, in the community context you are an equal citizen with a chance to make an important contribution to the success of the community change. If you are working from an outsider role, those things that you can do that demonstrate you care about the community are important. Show genuine warmth and empathy, but also toughness when it is called for.

7. *Have a community action timetable* that is long enough to accomplish the task and short enough so that if the task is not accomplished within that length of time, you do not suffer from frustration or inability to find another way to reach your goal.

8. *Think through which (if any) elements come from sources outside the community.* Can solutions come from outside? Can you be helpful in bringing the solution to the community?

> It requires nothing more than plain common sense to realize that many of the problems in a local community which seemingly have their roots in the neighborhood in reality stem from sources far removed from the community. To a considerable extent these problems are the result of vast destructive forces which pervade the entire social scene. It is when these forces impinge upon the local community that they give rise to a definite community problem. It should, thus, always be remembered that many apparently local problems are in reality malignant microcosms of vast conflicts, pressures, stresses and strains of the entire social order.[16]

9. *Read community studies.* Use them to get a sense of the many factors that make up a total community. Keep these in mind when you work in your community. Learn how community researchers do their work, and relate their structural understanding and other insights to your own

community. For example, the Lynds in their studies of Middletown organize their findings around the following factors: getting a living, making a home, training the young, using leisure, engaging in religious practices, and engaging in community activities.[17] How does each segment of your community accomplish these tasks? Gerald Suttles in his study of a Chicago slum examines territoriality and ordered segmentation, institutions and patterns of communication, ethnicity, and the meaning of morality.[1W] How are these factors important in your community? (See the Clinician's Library for some suggested community studies.)

10. *You must put yourself on the line.* There is no way to do community work from a detached observer position. Your personal involvement is a necessity. You are a person with feelings, a participant in community activity, a person committed to the outcome. Any other role will in time prove ineffective, because when it comes time to stand up and be counted and you remain seated, you have no further effectiveness.

You must learn to use your commitment and your involvement on behalf of the persons with whom you work. In every community, there are persons who become known for their efforts to make community systems work for people. Sometimes, they exist in the formal social service structure. Frequently, they have no official position, but have learned how to move formal organizations on behalf of persons. Knowing such persons is invaluable, but becoming such a person links you to the community in a more major way. Being such a person means putting yourself on the line.

11. *Cultivate allies.* You will always need allies you can call upon to aid in accomplishing particular tasks. They should also be able to call upon you for aid. This can be done informally or formally. A new human service style is the setting up of networks of persons giving each other mutual aid, expanding the nonmonetary resources of each member of the network. One of the authors has lived in his community for 12 years. Some of the networks, both formal and informal, he belongs to are:

1. A group of human service persons interested in getting information about emotional health noted in the local mass media.
2. Trainers working for governments in the region.
3. Some of the persons who work in the same job position in institutions around the state.
4. Local community change agents.

5. A resource for persons needing career counseling.
6. A resource for persons writing grants.
7. Members of the peer self-help group to which he belongs, both locally and nationally.
8. Neighbors.
9. Persons in the local school district interested in developing a program for gifted talented students.
10. Parents of pupils of the local Hebrew day school.
11. A group of social scientists in local colleges.
12. Persons with whom he works.
13. Certain senior and middle-levels administrators at the place he works.
14. His relatives, and to a lesser extent, his wife's relatives.
15. Students and former students (who link to each other at times).
16. Faculty members and former colleagues.
17. Members of a newly formed consortium writing a grant to obtain funding for community-based staff training.
18. Local members of a national Jewish organization. Certain members of the local Jewish community.
19. His own family.

He probably also belongs to other networks which do not come so quickly to mind. If every one of these networks tried to contact him at once or came through with requests for his involvement, sleep would be out of the question; fortunately, this never happens. The value of so many networks is that the author can frequently bring persons of similar interest together. He can bring one network to bear on the needs of another. He has many sources of information about what is going on in the community, having found that relying on a single informant from one network is a dangerous practice.

12. *Learn to use the mass media to your advantage.* Community issues can be enhanced by excellent media presentation. Ongoing contact with reporters can turn them into your allies. This means that you will have a say in how things are publicized.

13. *Have a wide range of tactics at your disposal.* Saul Alinsky presents thirteen rules for tactics:

1. Power is not only what you have but what the enemy thinks you have.
2. Never go outside the experience of your people.

3. Wherever possible go outside the experience of the enemy.
4. Make the enemy live up to their own book of rules.
5. Ridicule is man's most important weapon.
6. A good tactic is one that your people enjoy.
7. A tactic that drags on too long becomes a drag.
8. Keep the pressure on with different tactics and actions, and utilize all events of the period for your purpose.
9. The threat is usually more terrifying than the thing itself.
10. The major premise for tactics is the development of operations that will maintain a constant pressure upon the opposition.
11. If you push a negative hard and deep enough it will break through into its counterside.
12. The price of a successful attack is a constructive alternative.
13. Pick the target, freeze it, personalize it, and polarize it.[19]

Alinsky's style, while effective in creating "Peoples Organizations," in its early stages is an adversary strategy. Some might prefer less conflict-oriented approaches, in which case tactics that put emphasis on reaching consensus need to be developed.

14. *Find ways to keep yourself fresh.* If you are an outsider, find ways of having a life other than the job. Community organizing, client advocating, and social planning all can require long hours. Each of these roles requires fresh thinking on your part. Take time for your own mental health.

If you are a community resident, you need time away from the fray. One of the authors now limits his organizational commitments in his community and tries not to take on more than he can handle. The most important word in his community vocabulary is "no," as in "No, I can't do that," or "No, thank you for the honor, but I won't be on your board," or "No, I can't do you that favor." When he says "yes," it is because he feels he can make a meaningful contribution with time, ideas, and commitment.

CAUTIONS

The community might be a passé unit of organization. Communities traditionally had boundaries, mores, socialization functions, and some control over their destinies, and there is evidence that these are disappearing. As Arthur Vidich and Joseph Bensman point out in *Small Town in Mass Society*, communities are closely linked to broad factors of the larger society.[20] Is it possible then to create an enclave of improved community life when the state, industries, international trends all have major effects upon community development?

We do know that some communities appear more desirable than others. Quality of life surveys point out places that rank high on desirable qualities.[21] In coming to personal goals, one must consider whether goals at the community level will be achievable in the larger society, or meaningful even if they are achieved. As Taylor and Randolph note, there are some areas in which "urban gangrene" is so strong that the community is in its death throes.[22] It is too late for community work to be effective in such locations.

OPPORTUNITY

Saul Alinsky is eloquent on why working to better communities is a meaningful vocation:

The opportunity is another one of the many chances which have been given to mankind to realize that the hope for the future life is in working with the substance of the world, its people, rather than continued concentration upon its structure. The substance of society is not to be found in a few scattered, rarefied seminars, but in the tremendous masses of struggling, sweating men and women who make up the billions of peoples of the world.

We must devote everything we have to working with our people, not only to find the solution but in order to insure that there will be a solution. The chance to work with the people means the opportunity for the fulfillment of the vision of man. It is the opportunity of a life for mankind of peace, happiness, security, dignity, and purpose. An opportunity to create a world where life will be so precious, worth while, and meaningful that men will not kill other men, will not exploit other men, either economically   politically, or socially; where values will be social and not selfish; where man will not be judged as Christian or non-Christian, as black, yellow, or white, as materially rich or poor, but will be judged as a man. A world in which man's practices will catch up with his ethical teachings and where he will live the full consistent life of practicing what he preaches. A world where man is actually treated and regarded as being created in God's own image, where "all men are created equal." This is the opportunity. Dare we fail? [23]

POSTSCRIPT: VESTIGIAL ORGANIZING

Saul Alinsky is dead. Large-scale publicity for the efforts of community organizers has stopped. While organizing continues, Alinsky's tactic of "rubbing raw the sores of discontent" seems to have ended with recognition of the energy crisis, recession, and consumer power. Demonstrations have continued on campus and in community and there have been riots and looting, but these now seem routine. One of the authors recently talked about the quality of student life to the immediate past president of the student association of a large independent university. The ex-president stated there was a 200-person demonstration in the university chancellor's office during the past year. The author wondered what was the cause of the demonstration. The student replied, "It was National Student Activism Day. All the local issues were trivial, but we demonstrated anyway." More of the dehumanization that we talked about early in this book—a ritual demonstration without a real cause—just to keep the process alive.

In community work, strategies bring counter-strategies. Demonstrations used to work, but police and organizations have been trained in techniques that minimize the disruption. Buildings have even been constructed to allow for demonstrators to sit-in indefinitely without disrupting the work of the organization.

The great threat and challenge to community workers in the coming years is survival—*to* be changing agents of change within the central destructive structures and processes in communities, and *not* to seek survival for its own sake; continuing to devise tactics that will continue to work for positive change, without becoming a ritualized part of the problem.

NOTES

1. Saul D. Alinsky, *Reveille for Radicals* (New York: Vintage Books, 1969), pp. 113–14.

2. Seymour B. Sarason, *The Psychological Sense of Community* (San Francisco: Jossey-Bass, 1974), pp. 131–32.

3. Maurice R. Stein, *The Eclipse of Community* (Princeton, N.J.: Princeton University Press, 1971).

4. Robert E. Park, "Organization and the Romantic Temper," in *Human Communities* (Glencoe, Ill.: Free Press, 1952), p. 66.

5. James B. Taylor and Jerry Randolph, *Community Worker* (New York: Aronson, 1975), pp. 7–8.

6. Louisa Howe, "The Concept of Community," in Leopold Bellak, ed., *Handbook of Community Psychiatry and Community Mental Health* (New York: Grune & Stratton, 1964), p. 384.

7. John H. Marx, Patricia Rieker, and David L. Ellison, "The Sociology of Community Mental Health: Historical and Methodological Perspectives," in Paul M. Roman and Harrison M. Trice, eds., *Sociological Perspectives on Community Mental Health* (Philadelphia: F. A. Davis, 1974), p. 35.

8. Dorothea C. Leighton and Irving T. Stone, "Community Development as a Therapeutic Force: A Case Study with Measurement," in Paul M. Roman and Harrison M. Trice, eds., *Sociological Perspectives on Community Mental Health* (Philadelphia: F. A. Davis, 1974), p. 211.

9. Ibid.

10. Ibid., p. 214.

11. Ibid., p. 223.

12. Ibid., p. 224.

13. Saul D. Alinsky, *Rules for Radicals* (New York: Vintage Books, 1971), p. 67.

14. Alinsky, *Reveille for Radicals,* p. 106.

15. Lyle E. Schaller, *Community Organization: Conflict and Reconciliation* (Nashville: Abingdon, 1966), p. 97.

16. Alinsky, *Reveille for Radicals,* p. 60.

17. Robert S. Lynd and Helen M. Lynd, *Middletown* (New York: Harcourt, 1929); and *Middletown in Transition* (New York: Harcourt, 1937).

18. Gerald D. Suttles, *The Social Order of the Slum* (Chicago: University of Chicago Press, 1968).

19. Alinsky, *Rules for Radicals,* pp. 126–30.

20. Arthur Vidich and Joseph Bensman, *Small Town in Mass Society* (Princeton, N.J.: Princeton University Press, 1968).

21. David Franke and Holly Franke, *Safe Places: East of the Mississippi;* and *Safe Places: West of the Mississippi* (New York: Warner Books, 1973).

22. Taylor and Randolph, *Community Worker,* pp. 15–18.

23. Alinsky, *Reveille for Radicals,* pp. 41–42.

THE CLINICIAN'S LIBRARY

COMMUNITY STUDIES

The best overall review of the field remains:

Stein, Maurice. *The Eclipse of Community*. Princeton, N.J.: Princeton University Press, 1971.

This book can serve as an introduction and lead you into the classic community studies.

ORGANIZING

Alinsky, Saul. *Reveille for Radicals*. New York: Vintage Books, 1969.
Alinsky, Saul. *Rules for Radicals*. New York: Vintage Books, 1971.

These books spell out basic philosophy and practice for this organizing style.

The O-M Collective. *The Organizers' Manual*. New York: Bantam, 1971.

This manual, while based on the social activism of the sixties, still offers considerable practical information.

COMMUNITY WORK: SEVENTIES STYLE

Lewis, Judith A., and Michael D. Lewis. *Community Counseling: A Human Services Approach*. New York: Wiley, 1977.
Taylor, James B., and Jerry Randolph. *Community Worker*. New York: Aronson, 1975.

Practical realistic approaches on how to mobilize communities on the behalf of members.

Sarason, Seymour B. *The Creation of Setting and the Future Societies*. San Francisco: Jossey-Bass, 1972; *The Psychological Sense of Community*.

San Francisco: Jossey-Bass, 1974; and *Human Services and Resource Networks*. San Francisco: Jossey-Bass, 1977.

rason's work is an unusual combination of theory and practice in munity psychology.

Chapter 18

Asking the Embarrassing Sociological Questions

On many occasions the clinical sociologist will not be in a position to conduct the "action-oriented" therapeutic techniques described thus far in this part. Communities, organizations, groups, and individual members are often unwilling to participate in such activities or are unable to schedule such work into their regular daily schedules. Even where some groups or members will participate in self-help groups, sociodramas, simulations, and the like, their neighbors may refuse and thereby undercut the overall effectiveness of the therapy plan.

Sometimes *effective questioning* can become a therapeutic technique. Much as some forms of psychoanalysis and psychotherapy consist of the clinical psychologist or psychiatrist bringing the client to awareness and new courses of action via his or her questioning, so can this be useful in clinical sociological work.

Clinical sociologists are persons who are professional observers of sociological processes and structures. They are in a unique position usually unavailable to other participants in social situations. The clinician is able to view a variety of factions, roles, and other angles in a problematic situation, and to compare what she or he finds with the established theories and research from similar situations in the past.

Through questioning of the participants he or she can often bring them to the self-discovery of broader or "behind the scenes" sociological insights. Exposure to the proper questions can prompt persons to think about their social worlds in new ways and consider the possibilities for changing these worlds.

Questioning is a process, a give-and-take, in interaction with one or more others. For this strategy to work, the major questions must be placed in a rational place in a conversation or interview. That requires the questioner to become sensitive to the conversational and interview process. To be effective, the questioning must occur only when the client is physiologically, psychologically, and sociologically able to use the questions. Clients who are not in a position to do anything constructive about the situations being questioned will only be embarrassed or disturbed by the clinician's questioning. To ask a beginning psychiatric nurse, for instance, why medication is substituted for rehabilitative programs, is unlikely to accomplish anything other than ill feelings by the nurse about the clinician.

This is not to suggest that embarrassment is always bad. Indeed, the marks of effective questioning are threefold: (1) shock, (2) evaluation, and (3) change. Shock may take the form of embarrassment, surprise, fear, or other "ah-hah!" experiences. Through shock, the client expresses recognition that something significant has been understood. For such recognition to matter, however, the learning must be evaluated in terms of possible courses of action, and a reasonable new course of action actually attempted.

The possibilities for therapeutic questioning are nearly as extensive as the whole of sociological literature. Clinicians will need to consult the relevant theoretical and research works for each client situation. The following are some sample questions derived from earlier chapters of this book and from a few choice additional sources.

PERSONAL METAPHYSICS QUESTIONS

Some persons go through life being acted upon without taking the time to think through their beliefs, the origins of these beliefs, and what it might take to bring about changes in their belief systems. These questions place their beliefs within a social as well as a personal context and can increase their (and your) personal and social awareness:

Tell me something special about you.
When were you proud of something you did?

Tell me a time you acted rationally.
What do you like about other persons?
What do they like about you?
What keeps you from having more close friends?
Name some social situations in which you know you have difficulty.
Why is that?
In what ways are you lacking?
In what ways are you a delight?

What caused you to be in this room today? Can you point to this "cause"? What makes you think that it is real? How could you explain being in this room other than with the word "cause"? What is your definition of "cause"?

Name a room that is messy. What makes it messy? Who else considers it messy? Who considers it not messy? How can some people say a room *is* messy, and others that it is not? Are some actually saying it *ought to be considered* messy?

In what religion were you brought up? Do you still practice that religion? If so, why? If not, what caused you to end your religious relationship?
Are you religious now? Do you go to formal worship services? How often? What does this activity mean to you right now? What are your current religious beliefs? Do you believe in God? If so, what does God mean to you?

How many grades of school have you completed? How many do you want to complete?
Think back to the first teacher you liked. What did you learn from him/her? How does that learning affect your present life?
Think back to the first teacher you really disliked. What did you learn from him/her?
In what ways does that learning affect your present life?
What has to happen for you to increase your motivation to learn?
In what ways was your self-esteem enhanced in school? In what ways were you made to feel inadequate?
Given your experience in the world outside of the classrooms, what societal values that were transmitted to you have little factual basis in your everyday life?
You have just become superintendent of schools in the community

where you went to elementary school. Name the three major changes you would make in the first year of your administration.

What is your name? For whom were you named? Where did your family originally come from? Did your family name get changed? For how many generations can you trace your family? Are there holes in the genealogy? Why?
In the present, what special ways do you acknowledge your background? How was it different when you were growing up? Compare and contrast the way you celebrate a family festival today from the way you remember celebrating it when you were growing up.

In what ways do you feel oppressed? Who oppresses you? What groups do you oppress? What groups do you stereotype? Who stereotypes you?

In what ways do you feel powerful? What areas of your own life do you feel are under your total control? Name ways you recently have exercised this power?
In what areas of your life do you believe you have some say in the outcome? What say? In what areas of your life do you believe you are powerless? Why? What do you believe you can do about that? What keeps you from doing that which it takes for you to become powerful in those areas? What can you do about those things?

What justification do you think you have that leads you to believe that you have the ability to help others? Who sanctions that justification? You have just been appointed World Problem Solver with all the power you need to create the ideal world. What would you do? How would you do it? Why?

SOCIAL LOCATION QUESTIONS

Some groups and group members are quite unaware of their position relative to their neighbors. Yet their place in social structures may be the major determinant of their problems.

How old are you? What do people expect of persons your age? What do you have in common with other people your age? What do you think of teenagers? of the elderly? of the middle-aged? What do these groups think of persons your age? Which age groups hold the most money? The highest respect? The most political power? How did this all come about?

How did you come to live in this town? If you had completely free choice, where would you live? Why aren't you living there now? What would it take for you to be able to live there?
What do people call this neighborhood (this part of town)? What kinds of people live here? Which is the best house on the block? (in this area) the worst? Where would you rank your house?
In what areas do the rich people live? the poor? the hourly workers? the professionals? With which group do you identify yourself? Where do people of this group mostly live?

Do you earn money through your own labor, or through the investment of your capital? How does each type of self-support affect your relationship to others in your community (e.g., consumers, bankers, the poor)?

How much money do you make? How does this compare to others in the community?
Has your station in life changed in the past couple of years? If so, did you move up, down, or horizontally? Which people seem to move up most often? Who makes the short-distance moves and who makes the long-distance moves? How come?

On the average, is the income of members of your ethnic group roughly equivalent to that of white Protestant nonforeigners in this country? If not, why not?
What is your ethnicity? Is your ethnicity a minority? If so, why (because of numbers of you in the community, owing to political power, owing to prejudice)?
How did your ethnic group come to this country, and why? How has this affected them since they have been here?
What do you share with other members of your ethnic group? Organizations? Customs? Neighborhoods? How do these items separate or integrate you into the wider community?
Do others in the community hold prejudices against you? If so, which prejudices?
Which aspects of your ethnic culture have disappeared? Why? Has any other group prospered from your ethnic group? What effect has this had on the ethnic group?

Could anyone you know get elected to public office? If so, what would it take for him/her to do so? If not, why not?

Do you and your peers vote? Which groups vote in highest percentages in the community?
Who holds the political power in this community? How much are they worth?
How do the politicians find time to work on their campaigns? Why do they not have to work all day earning money?
If you were going to gain power in this community, how would you go about it?
If you are not currently doing this, what stands in your way?
Who are the people in this community who hold no public office but who seem to control what happens?
List the ten most powerful persons in this community and state why they are powerful.
Which jobs in this community do you have to know someone to get? What is the annual cost to the employee of holding that job? Who gets the "contribution"?
Who else is paying off? To whom? How much?

How many children do you have? How does this compare to community averages for persons in your social class?
Do you live in a nuclear family? If so, why?
Do aunts and uncles or grandparents or nongenetic relatives live with you? If so, why? If not, why not?
When do most people you know first have sexual intercourse? Why at that age? How does this compare with other groups in this country?
At what age do most people you know get married? Why at that age? How does this compare with other groups? Why do people get married?
Which activities do women you know do that men you know do not do?
Which attitudes do women seem to have that men do not seem to have? Why are these differences occurring? What purpose do they serve?
Who keeps your family's money? What do they do with it?

INSTITUTION QUESTIONS

Robert Bogdan [1] has put together a long series of questions for persons evaluating public institutions such as state mental hospitals or schools. These questions may serve therapeutic ends under certain conditions, such as for facilitating changing norms or structural arrangements. Most of the questions below are derived from his list, though we have added a few which reflect discussions elsewhere in this book:

How do people come to enter this institution?

How much time per week is spent on meetings between the institution's clients and its professional staff?

What is the ratio of various staff positions to clients? What determines this ratio?

Which instructional or rehabilitative programs are used? Who determines which will be used and how they are controlled?

To what extent are patients given medication rather than rehabilitative programs? How often are prescriptions reviewed? Do patients complain about untreated physical ailments?

Do some clients receive more attention than others? If so, how does this come about?

What classes, wards, and so forth do staff like and dislike? What are their reaons? What rules do staff members ignore?

Do staff members feel that clients owe something to the institution? Under what conditions do staff members talk to clients? Do staff hide things from residents, or vice versa?

What is the condition of the physical plant? Are any areas locked up? Is the institution crowded compared to others of this variety? How do these situations come about here?

How are clients punished? Who determines that they need punishment? Is there a client bill of rights? Is it followed? Is there a known channel for legal resource?

How are staff punished? and who determines? How is each group rewarded? How did the institution come to exist? Whose needs are being served by it? Are these the needs it was originally built to meet? Are its advertised functions different from its actual functions?

In what ways does civil service interfere in institutional operations? What effect does a union or lack of union have on operations?

Where is the fat in your budget? Which staff members are not earning their salaries? Why?

Who has been placed in this institution who doesn't belong here? Why are they here?

What part of this institution do you seldom show to visitors? May I see it?

If I cannot, why not?

What is the percentage of your discretionary fund to your total budget?

Do you have any contradictory policies?

Who really makes decisions for clients here?

What activities take place for clients on weekends? Which senior staff members work weekends? in the evening?

CHANGE QUESTIONS

Groups, group members, organizations, and communities sometimes get so involved with the static quality of their present that they neither face issues of change nor the future. The questions in this section try to get at change-oriented issues.

What about your world (group, group member, organization, or community) is still the same and is likely to remain the same?
What used to be static and now is in movement?
What used to be moving and is now static?
What was moving then and continues to move?
Which of these changes is due to changes in technology? in mass communication? in advances in weaponry? in the human condition? What new technology have you adopted? In what ways is it an extension of your human abilities? In what ways does it bring pain? short-term? long-term?
What technology did the new technology replace? Why? What difference does this change make?
Who controls the new technology? Do you feel safe about that?

In what ways do you use mass communication? What newspapers do you read? what magazines? How often do you listen to the radio each week?
What do you listen to? How much television do you watch? Which programs?
How often do you go to the movies?
When are you not in touch with mass communication?
When you listen or watch a show that features violence, how do you feel when it is over? More generally, what programs of the mass media move you? Why? If you remain unmoved, why not? If you were out of contact with mass culture for a year, what would you miss? In what ways do the mass media narcotize you? If you could command the ultimate in education and entertainment from mass communication, what would you ask for? Why are you settling for less than that?

Do you think about the fact that there is enough weaponry in the combined nuclear arsenals of the world to destroy each one of us many times? What effect does this knowledge have upon your lifestyle? If not, why not? If your response is, "I have no control over that," why not? How would you get control?

For what are you nostalgic? Why?
In what ways are you narcotized to the present? Why?
Have you suffered future shock? How do you know?
In what ways do you believe you are dehumanized?
Do you believe you are crazy? In what ways?
What are you looking forward to today? Tomorrow? Next week? Next
month? Next year? In five years? In ten years? In twenty-five years?
forever? How will your world be different after each period? What goals
do you have for each period?

POSTSCRIPT: SOME UNEMBARRASSING SOCIOLOGICAL ANSWERS

A decent definition of sociology holds the discipline to be the study of
the structures and interactions within and between human groups and
societies. A decent definition of pathology equates it with destructive
processes. A decent definition of a clinician is a person who treats
pathological conditions. A clinical sociologist, then, is a person who
treats the destructive processes involving structures and interactions of
human groups and societies.

Clinical sociologists are the exodisciplinary correlates of the type of
academic practitioner who C. Wright Mills claimed epitomizes good
sociology. Mills suggested, much as have we, three major types of
sociological questions:

1. What is the structure of this particular society as a whole? What are
its essential components, and how are they related to one another? How
does it differ from other varieties of social order? Within it, what is the
meaning of any particular feature for its continuance and for its change?
2. Where does this society stand in human history? What are the
mechanics by which it is changing? What is its place within and its
meaning for the development of humanity as a whole? How does any
particular feature we are examining affect, and how is it affected by, the
historical period in which it moves? And this period—what are its
essential features? How does it differ from other periods? What are its
characteristic ways of history-making?
3. What varieties of men and women prevail in this society and in this
period? And what varieties are coming to prevail? In what ways are
they selected and formed, liberated and repressed, made sensitive and
blunted? What kinds of "human nature" are revealed in the conduct
and character we observe in this society in this period? And what is the

meaning for "human nature" of each and every feature of the society we are examining? [2]

Answering such questions necessitates Mills's distinction between biography and history, a distinction which is the raison d'être for a clinical sociology. By *biography* Mills indicated those conditions that a person experiences as uniquely her or his own. *History,* on the other hand, consists of the large-scale changes in social structures, changes that affect the personality of entire societies. If clinical sociologists accomplish nothing else, perhaps they can bring a few more persons to understand Mills's distinction.

> Nowadays men often feel that their private lives are a series of traps. . . . Underlying this sense of being trapped are seemingly impersonal changes in the very structure of continent-wide societies. The facts of contemporary history are also facts about the success and failure of individual men and women. When a society is industrialized, a peasant becomes a worker; a feudal lord is liquidated or becomes a businessman. When classes rise or fall, a man is employed or unemployed; when the rate of investment goes up or down, a man takes new heart or goes broke. When wars happen, an insurance salesman becomes a rocket launcher; a store clerk, a radar man; a wife lives alone; a child grows up without a father. Neither the life of an individual nor the history of a society can be understood without understanding both. . . . [The sociological] imagination is the capacity to shift from one perspective to another—from the political to the psychological; from examination of a single family to comparative assessment of the national budgets of the world; from the theological school to the military establishment; from considerations of an oil industry to studies of contemporary poetry. It is the capacity to range from the most impersonal and remote transformations to the most intimate features of the human self—and to see the relations between the two. Back of its use there is always the urge to know the social and historical meaning of the individual in the society and in the period in which he has his quality and his being.[3]

Clinical sociologists are not persons who blame society, the system, or the bad guys for current maladies. True sociological understanding obviates both blame and single-cause reasoning by demanding that the sociologist constantly take on the role or perspective of other persons, groups, or historical periods.

A FOLK TALE

The questions were all asked. The Clinsoc tribe had gathered on the top of a high peak from which they could see sharply the distinct features of the social landscape. They smiled when they noticed the relationship between a feature and a group or group member who had been helped by their insight, helped to become actively involved in a meaningful endeavor that enhanced the socius. A special music was in the air. It reached the top of the high peak faintly at first, then it grew louder as the Clinsocs used their listening skills to pick out the words and tune. Soon every member of the tribe joined in the song. And when they began to sing, the Clinsocs realized that each of them had heard a different song, but that all the songs blended together. They returned to the hills and valleys to join, and to teach, the continuing melody.

NOTES

1. Robert Bogdan, *Observing in Institutions* (Syracuse, N.Y.: Center on Human Policy, 1974).
2. C. Wright Mills, *The Sociological Imagination* (New York: Oxford, 1959), pp. 6–7.
3. Ibid., pp. 3–8.

THE CLINICIAN'S LIBRARY

A general book of useful questions is:

Howard, Robert. *Roles and Relationships.* Sunnyvale, Cal.: Westinghouse Learning Press, 1973.

Specialized questions can be found in:

Bogdan, Robert. *Observing in Institutions.* Syracuse, N.Y.: Human Policy Press, 1974. Provides excellent questions to ask in institutional settings.

Clark, Ramsey. *Crime in America.* New York: Simon & Schuster, 1970, chapter 4. "The Mother of Crime" raises excellent questions about the social conditions in a community.

Index